# Microsoft's
# 80386/80486
## Programming Guide

Microsoft's

# 80386/80486

## Programming Guide

Ross P. Nelson

PUBLISHED BY
Microsoft Press
A Division of Microsoft Corporation
One Microsoft Way
Redmond, Washington 98052-6399

Library of Congress Cataloging-in-Publication Data

Nelson, Ross P., 1957-
    Microsoft's 80386/80486 programming guide / Ross P. Nelson. -- 2nd
ed.
        p.    cm.
    Second ed. of : 8086. c1988.
    Includes bibliographical references and index.
    ISBN 1-55615-343-0
    1. Intel 80386 (Microprocessor)--Programming.      2. Intel 80486
(Microprocessor)--Programming.      3. Assembler language (Computer
program language)      I. Nelson, Ross P., 1957-      80386.      II. Title.
QA76.8.I2684N45      1991
005.265--dc20                                                        90-26294
                                                                          CIP
Printed and bound in the United States of America.

    4 5 6 7 8 9    AGAG    4 3 2

Distributed to the book trade in Canada by Macmillan of Canada,
a division of Canada Publishing Corporation.

Distributed to the book trade outside the United States and Canada by Penguin Books Ltd.

Penguin Books Ltd., Harmondsworth, Middlesex, England
Penguin Books Australia Ltd., Ringwood, Victoria, Australia
Penguin Books N. Z. Ltd., 182-190 Wairau Road, Auckland 10, New Zealand

British Cataloging-in-Publication Data available.

IBM® is a registered trademark of International Business Machines Corporation. All
mnemonics copyright Intel Corporation 1986, 1987. Intel® is a registered trademark of Intel
Corporation. Microsoft® and MS-DOS® are registered trademarks of Microsoft Corporation.
OS/2® is a registered trademark licensed to Microsoft Corporation.

**Acquisitions Editor:** Michael Halvorson
**Project Editor:** Jack Litewka
**Technical Editor:** Jim Johnson

*To Robert and Ardell Nelson*

# CONTENTS

# ACKNOWLEDGMENTS

A number of people deserve credit for helping make this book a reality. Some I have spoken with and worked with directly; others have worked behind the scenes, doing a wonderful job nonetheless. Working with the people at Microsoft Press was a positive experience, and I sincerely thank them all for their support and encouragement. In addition, my thanks to Ray Duncan for getting the ball rolling, to Intel Corporation for its cooperation, to Matt Trask and Jim Johnson for their technical reviews, to my coworkers at Answer Software for their support, and especially to Pam for believing in me.

This is a book about microprocessor technology, so of course it was written with the assistance of microprocessor technology: I completed a large portion of the first-edition manuscript using a Toshiba T1000 portable computer while riding Santa Clara County Transit. I used Word for Windows to create this edition, with great appreciation of its revision-marking features.

*Ross Nelson*

# INTRODUCTION

The Intel 80386 microprocessor was probably the most widely discussed central processing unit (CPU) chip since the introduction of the 8080 in the early days of personal computing. The first edition of this book explored the capabilities of the 80386. Since then, Intel Corporation has introduced three additional processors with the same basic architecture. The 80386 family of processors now includes the original 80386, the 80386SX, the 80376, and the newest and fastest member of the family, the 80486. I have expanded the book to describe the differences among the processors.

Chapter 1 presents a history of the x86 microprocessor family. Each subsequent chapter discusses a portion of the 80386/80486 processor architecture. The organization of the CPU is presented in Chapter 2. The basic memory architecture is discussed in Chapter 3. Chapter 4 introduces the basic instruction set and the floating-point instruction set. Chapter 5 explains protected-mode operation. Chapter 6 tells how paging extends the memory system and how the cache works in the 80486. Compatibility with previous processors via real mode, virtual 8086 mode, and protected mode for the 80286 is covered in Chapter 7. Finally, Chapter 8 provides a full instruction set reference.

This book focuses entirely on programming. It does not discuss the hardware features of the processor unless those features relate to specific instructions. If you are interested in the hardware characteristics of any of these processors, you can obtain the appropriate data sheets and reference manuals from Intel.

To get the most from this book, you should be familiar with computer systems. In particular, an understanding of binary and hexadecimal arithmetic and machine-language programming for some other processor(s) will be helpful.

A large portion of the book is devoted to protected mode. Although you do not need to understand this feature to program applications, it is important to understand protected mode to grasp why system designers made the choices they did in implementing the OS/2, Microsoft Windows, PC-MOS/386, and UNIX operating environments.

The conventions used throughout this book are summarized on the following pages. If you are familiar with other Intel microprocessors, you are probably already familiar with these concepts.

# Number Formats

I use numbers in three bases: binary (base 2), decimal (base 10), and hexadecimal (base 16). You can assume that all numbers are base 10 unless they are followed by the suffix "B" (for binary) or "H" (for hexadecimal). For example:

1AH = 26 = 00011010B

# Data Types

The most commonly used data types are 8-bit, 16-bit, and 32-bit quantities. In this book, an 8-bit quantity is called a byte, a 16-bit quantity is called a word, and a 32-bit quantity is called a doubleword, or dword. This nomenclature is unusual because the standard data item size of a computer is commonly called a word. In the Digital Equipment VAX computers, for example, a 32-bit quantity is a word, and a 16-bit quantity is a halfword. The same is true for the Motorola 68000 family and the IBM 370 and 390 mainframes.

Although the standard 80386/80486 operand size is 32 bits, Intel retained the naming conventions of its earlier processors because the 32-bit processors are descendants of the 8086 and the 80286, which were 16-bit processors. This simplifies running software from the 8086 or the 80286 and lets you use the same assembler to generate code for any of the four processors.

The smallest addressable data item in the x86 family is the byte. All other data items can be broken down into bytes. The processor stores larger data items in memory low-order byte first, as the following diagram shows:

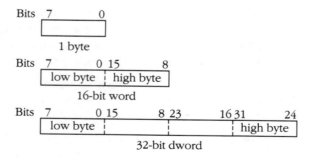

Assume that the 32-bit value 100F755DH is stored in memory, beginning at location 10. The individual memory bytes are:

| *Address* | 10 | 11 | 12 | 13 |
|-----------|-----|-----|-----|-----|
| *Contents* | 5DH | 75H | 0FH | 10H |

It is unnecessarily complex, however, to show words and doublewords broken down in byte order, and illustrations in this book treat the quantity as a unit. For example, the book would present the previous value as:

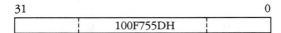

31                                                                  0

| | 100F755DH | |
|---|---|---|

When performing operations on items smaller than a single byte—for example, on a single bit or bit field—the processor always fetches at least 1 byte from memory.

# Assembler Notation

An executable instruction is a binary pattern that is decoded by the logic inside the CPU. An instruction can be from 8 to 128 bits in length. Because coding a program using binary patterns would be tedious, programmers use a type of program called an assembler. The simplest type of assembler takes a set of keywords and symbols and translates them into an instruction. The set of keywords and symbols is called the assembly language. Typically, there is a one-to-one mapping between an instruction in assembly language and an actual machine instruction. The assembler would take an instruction such as:

```
ADD     EBX, 5
```

meaning, "Add 5 to the value in register EBX and store the result in EBX," and would translate it into the bit pattern:

```
10000000110000110000000101B
```

The names of the instructions, called mnemonics, usually occupy the first field in an instruction line. The subsequent fields are the operands of the instruction and can take a number of forms. The simplest is a numeric value, such as the 5 in the example above. A register name is another form of operand. An expression within brackets, such as [EBP+2], signifies an operand that is a memory reference.

Throughout the book, I use standard Intel mnemonics. Notice, however, that a mnemonic does not necessarily specify the exact encoding of an instruction. For example, the "increment" instruction has a general form in which any operand may be encoded, and the instruction INC EAX would be encoded as FFH 00H. A single-byte instruction also exists for incrementing a general register. In this form, the INC EAX instruction is encoded 40H. An assembler will generally choose the most compact form of instruction for any given mnemonic, but the effect of executing either form is the same.

I also use a common convention in discussions about setting bits. I use the term "set" when assigning the value 1 to a bit, and the term "reset" when assigning the value 0 to a bit.

# Syntax

This book uses the following syntax:

| Operator | Meaning | Operator | Meaning |
|----------|---------|----------|---------|
| + | Addition | & | Boolean AND |
| − | Subtraction | > | Greater than |
| × | Multiplication | < | Less than |
| / | Division | >> | Shift right |
| ~ | Not | << | Shift left |
| = | Equal to | ≤ | Less than or equal to |
| != | Not equal to | ≥ | Greater than or equal to |
| ¦ | Or | ← | Assignment |
| ∧ | Exclusive OR | | |

# 32-Bit Instruction Set

The 80386, 80386SX, and 80486 support several modes that are compatible with previous Intel processors (the 16-bit 8086 and 80286). However, this book focuses on new features and does not discuss the 16-bit architectures of the 8086 and the 80286, even though they are a subset of the 80386/80486 processors capabilities. Programmers using either the 80386 or 80486 as a replacement for previous processors can simply continue to use reference materials for the 8086 or the 80286.

# Operating System Services

The 80386 family architecture is quite complex, and it is not reasonable to expect a stand-alone program to take advantage of all the CPU's capabilities. At various times, I make statements such as "The operating system will…" or "At this point, the operating system…." In these cases I am not referring to any particular operating system; instead, I am highlighting a feature that will be implemented by the operating system software and not by an application.

# 1

# EVOLUTION OF THE 80x86-FAMILY ARCHITECTURE

Although I have spent more than a decade working with microcomputers, the phrase "computer system" still brings to mind images of the installation in the basement of the campus library at Montana State University. There, in air-conditioned comfort, behind glass walls, lived Siggie, the university computer system (a Xerox Sigma 7). Housed in several refrigerator-size units, Siggie served the computing needs of the entire university.

By 1986, the 80386 microprocessor, born of a technology that was first realized while Siggie was still considered state-of-the-art, could serve as the heart of a desktop microcomputer that had greater computing power than Siggie. And now the even faster 80486 is merely one more member of a processor family that Intel claims will be continuously improved through the year 2000.

## The First Components

The 80486 is the latest member of a line of microprocessors built by Intel Corporation. Intel claims to have invented the microprocessor in 1971, as a result of having been approached by a (now defunct) Japanese corporation to build a custom circuit to serve as the "brains" for a new calculator. Intel designer Ted Hoff proposed that a programmable, general-purpose computing circuit be built instead, and the 4004 chip became a reality. The 4040 and 8008 chips soon followed; however, these chips lacked many characteristics of microprocessors as we know them today.

# The 8080

The chip that, by most accounts, led to the birth of the microcomputer industry was the 8080, which Intel introduced in 1974. An article in the September 1975 issue of *Popular Electronics* brought the idea of a "personal" computer to the mass market, and, as they say, the rest is history. The 8080 was the CPU (central processing unit) in such pioneering systems as the Altair and the IMSAI. Intel did not enjoy a monopoly on the market for long, however; Motorola Corporation introduced the 6800, MOS Technology responded with the 6502, and two designers of the 8080 left Intel for Zilog Corporation, which soon produced the Z80. Unlike the 6800 and the 6502, whose architectures were completely different from those of Intel processors, the Z80 was compatible with the 8080 but had an expanded instruction set and ran twice as fast. The battle for CPU supremacy was on.

The 8080 was an 8-bit machine—that is, it processed data 8 bits at a time. It had a single accumulator (the A register) and six secondary registers (B, C, D, E, H, and L, shown in Figure 1-1). These six registers could be used in 8-bit arithmetic operations or combined as pairs (BC, HL) to hold 16-bit memory addresses. A 16-bit address allowed the 8080 to access $2^{16}$ bits, or 64 kilobytes (KB), of memory.

Intel also developed a refinement of the 8080 called the 8085, an 8080-compatible processor that featured better performance and a simpler hardware interface.

|    |     | PSW |
|----|-----|-----|
|    |     | A   |
| BC | B   | C   |
| DE | D   | E   |
| HL | H   | L   |

|    |
|----|
| SP |
| PC |

**Figure 1-1.** *The 8080 register set.*

# The 8086

In 1978, under pressure from other manufacturers' faster, more powerful microprocessors, Intel moved to a 16-bit architecture. The 8086 was touted as the successor to the 8080 microprocessor, and, although the instruction set was new, it retained compatibility with the 8080's instruction set. Figure 1-2 shows how the new registers of the 8086 could be mapped into the set of 8080 registers.

Programs that were written for the 8080 could not be run on the 8086; however, almost every 8086 instruction corresponded to an 8080 instruction. At worst, an 8080 instruction could be simulated by two or three 8086 operations. An Intel translator program could convert 8080 assembler programs into 8086 assembler programs, and the first versions of Microsoft Corporation's BASIC and MicroPro International Corporation's WordStar for the 8086 were ported from 8080 systems via the Intel translator. This concern for compatibility has characterized Intel's presence in the microcomputer market. Every new generation of microprocessor has been able to run software written for the previous generation.

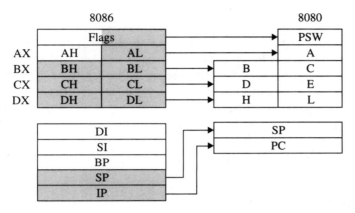

**Figure 1-2.** *The 8080-8086 register set map.*

In addition to providing software compatibility, Intel was interested in supporting high-level languages. At Intel, almost all programming was done in an Algol-like language called PL/M. Intel believed that a language such as PL/M or Pascal would become the dominant microcomputer development language, so Intel dedicated many 8086 registers to specific purposes, as shown in Figure 1-3.

|    | Flags | | |
|----|-------|------|---|
| AX | AH | AL | Accumulator |
| BX | BH | BL | Base pointer |
| CX | CH | CL | Count register |
| DX | DH | DL | Data register |

| | |
|-----|-----|
| DI | Destination index r egister |
| SI | Source index r egister |
| BP | Stack frame base pointer |
| SP | Stack pointer |
| IP | Instruction pointer |

| | |
|-----|-----|
| CS | Code segment |
| DS | Data segment |
| SS | Stack segment |
| ES | Extra segment |

**Figure 1-3.** *The 8086 register set.*

3

The next two examples show dedicated registers in use. Figure 1-4 shows how high-level languages such as Pascal use the stack pointer (SP) and base pointer (BP) registers.

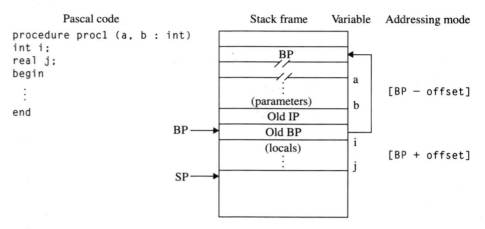

**Figure 1-4.** *Subroutine context.*

In a Pascal program, the context of the currently executing subroutine is maintained on the stack. The values (parameters) provided to the subroutine by the calling routine are first on the stack, the saved IP of the calling routine are second, and the saved BP of the calling routine are third. The context also contains stack space for any temporary or local variables that the subroutine uses. Access to either the parameters or local variables is relative to the current value of BP.

Consider the Pascal assignment statement in Figure 1-5. Because an entire record must be copied, the compiler generates a block move instruction that uses the SI, DI, and CX registers.

The advantage of dedicated registers is that it allowed Intel to encode the instructions in a compact, memory-efficient manner. The opcode specifies exactly what is to take place; for example, in the MOVSB instruction, specifying the three operands (source, destination, and count) is unnecessary. As a result, the MOVSB opcode is only 1 byte. The disadvantage of dedicated registers is that if you are using SI or DI and want to do a MOVSB instruction, you can't use another register.

The 8086 also introduced segmentation to the microprocessor world. A segment is a block of memory beginning at a fixed address that is determined by the value in the appropriate segment register. This concept, probably the most despised feature of the 8086 because of the restrictions it imposes, was incorporated for compatibility with the 8080; each segment was 64 KB, equivalent to one 8080 address space. Using segmentation, software can maintain the 16-bit addressing used in the 8080 while expanding (through the use of multiple segments) the memory that the chip

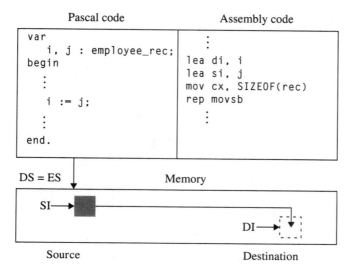

Pascal code          Assembly code

```
var
   i, j : employee_rec;
begin                       lea di, i
   ⋮                        lea si, j
                            mov cx, SIZEOF(rec)
   i := j;                  rep movsb
   ⋮                          ⋮
end.
```

DS = ES            Memory

SI→                DI→

Source            Destination

**Figure 1-5.** *Block move.*

can address. The 8086 provides four segment registers that can point anywhere in the 1-megabyte (MB) address space. They are defined as follows:

***CS—The code segment register:*** All calls and jumps refer to locations within the code segment.

***DS—The data segment register:*** Most memory-reference instructions refer to an offset within the data segment.

***SS—The stack segment register:*** All PUSH and POP instructions access data in the stack segment. Additionally, any memory reference done relative to the BP register is also directed to the stack segment.

***ES—The extra segment register:*** This segment specifies the destination segment in certain string processing instructions.

The way an application manages memory (the memory model) is usually consistent throughout a program. When Intel introduced the 8086, three memory models were postulated, which are shown in Figure 1-6 on the following page.

The tiny model mimicked the 8080 address space. The code segment and data segment were in the same area of memory, and the program was limited to 64 KB. The small model was expected to be prevalent because it allowed programs to double in size. By having separate code and data segments, programs could expand to 128 KB and still retain 16-bit addressing. The large memory model allowed the use of multiple code and data segments. In this model, the entire 1-MB address space of the processor could be used.

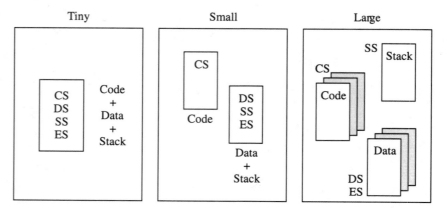

**Figure 1-6.** *Memory models.*

When the 8086 was introduced in 1978, most microcomputers were limited to 64 KB; almost no one realized how quickly the 64-KB segment limitation would become a serious problem. Although the large model allowed programs to fill the entire 1 MB of 8086 address space, using the large model meant using 32-bit pointers. On a 16-bit machine, 32-bit pointers exacted a size and performance penalty that most programmers were unwilling to pay. By the early 1980s, even the 1-MB limitation became confining. Additional memory models with names such as "compact" and "medium" were introduced to optimize performance for special programming needs.

Other processors in the 8086 family were the 8088, the 80186, and the 80188. The 8088, introduced a year after the 8086, had the same 16-bit internal architecture but a restricted 8-bit external bus. The 8088 could run the same programs as the 8086 but typically ran them 30 percent slower. The 8088 became wildly successful when IBM chose it for the PC and the PC/XT. The 80186 and 80188 were announced much later, in 1982. These processors kept the same base architecture but included features such as direct memory access (DMA) controllers, on-chip counter/timers, and a simplified hardware interface. They also operated more quickly than did the 8086/8088 and became popular in controller applications.

## The 8087

An innovative part of the 8086 family of CPUs is the coprocessor. The ESC or coprocessor escape class of instructions generated only a memory address on the 8086. Additional, special-purpose CPUs could be created to monitor the instruction stream and watch for ESC sequences, as shown in Figure 1-7. Whenever an ESC was detected, the coprocessor could decode the escape as an instruction for itself and perform a function that the 8086 was incapable of doing efficiently on its own.

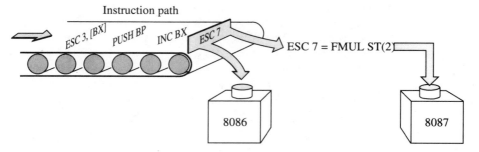

**Figure 1-7.** *8086 coprocessor interface.*

The only coprocessor developed for the 8086 was the 8087. The 8087 implemented a floating-point instruction set, capable of as much as 80 bits of precision. Intel worked closely with the Institute of Electrical and Electronics Engineers (IEEE) and professors at the University of California, Berkeley, to create a floating-point representation that was flexible and accurate. This representation and its numeric properties have since been formalized as Standard IEEE-754.

The 8087 contributed to the popularity of the 8086. A desktop computer that contained both an 8086 and an 8087 could do more substantial scientific work than the 8086 alone. Implementing floating-point functions in hardware improved the performance of mathematical calculations over existing software routines. However, the 8087 exemplified the problems of the 64-KB segment size. As soon as scientists and engineers had the computing power to handle real-world problems, they often needed to deal with large arrays of numbers. The 64-KB segment limit restricted a vector of double-precision floating-point numbers to no more than 1024 elements. Software capable of getting around the restriction was soon available, but the large memory model was difficult to program in and was slow.

# The 80286

The next major introduction from Intel, the 80286, came in 1982. The 80286 is compatible with the 8086 family, but it also provides a significant performance improvement. It boasts two operating modes: real mode and protected mode. Real mode, which emulates the 8086, is the default mode. The new mode is called protected mode. In protected mode, the 80286 supports the 8086 instruction set but places a new interpretation on the contents of the segment registers that control how memory is accessed.

Although operating systems that are implemented under protected mode are different from those that are designed for real mode, applications can be developed that run in either mode. The design of these dual-mode applications requires that the application observe certain memory restrictions.

Unfortunately, MS-DOS, which is the dominant operating system for 8086-based machines, places no restrictions on how an application addresses memory, and protected mode proved incompatible with a majority of MS-DOS applications. As a result, for a number of years the 80286 was generally treated as a fast 8086 because no one knew how to use the beneficial new feature—protected mode. This was unfortunate because protected mode expands the amount of physically addressable memory from 1 MB to 16 MB, allows the implementation of virtual memory, and provides for the separation of tasks in a multitasking or multiuser environment.

Versions of UNIX run in protected mode, but UNIX has not been successful on the 80286 because competitive products usually run on more powerful 32-bit computers. Subsequently, Microsoft introduced OS/2, which uses almost all protected-mode features, and more recently introduced Windows 3, which also runs applications in protected mode.

The 80286 is the first Intel microprocessor designed for "serious" computing. Provisions were made for multitasking, data integrity, and security. The designers examined the architecture of minicomputers and mainframes as they developed the 80286. In addition, two of the main influences on the 80286 designers were the Multics project and a continued belief that Pascal would become the preeminent application-development language.

Reading the conference papers about the Multics project will enlighten anyone who thinks that protected mode is the product of some Intel designer's fevered imagination. Multics began in the mid-1960s as a joint research project among MIT, Bell Laboratories, and General Electric. The project combined hardware and software and was based on the GE 645 mainframe. The following is a partial list of architectural features that the Multics group "pioneered":

- Virtual memory*
- Protection rings
- Segmented addressing*
- Descriptor access rights
- Call gates
- Conforming code segments

Some features of Multics also made their way into existing 80286-based software systems. Microsoft's OS/2, for example, uses dynamic linking, another Multics innovation.

The influence of Pascal on the design of the 80286 is shown by the addition of the ENTER instruction to the 80286 instruction set. The ENTER instruction simplifies

---

* The Multics group did not invent these features, but it made them an integral part of the system.

creating a stack frame such as the one shown in the subroutine context illustration in Figure 1-4. ENTER can also copy the context or stack frame of the previous subroutine. This ability is not necessary in languages such as FORTRAN or C but is useful in languages such as Pascal and Ada that allow nested procedure declarations.

## The 80287

Intel also introduced a new coprocessor for the 80286, but the 80287 was a bit of a disappointment. Although the 80286 executes programs two to three times faster than the 8086, the performance of the 80287 is about the same as that of the 8087. Intel did not really modify the computational engine of the 8087 in creating the 80287, so the new coprocessor does not run any faster. Intel did change the interface between the CPU and the coprocessor, however, eliminating the need for the coprocessor to monitor the instruction stream of the main CPU.

In this new interface method, illustrated in Figure 1-8, the main CPU decodes the ESC instructions and then passes the information to the coprocessor via the I/O channel. Because addressing is treated differently in real mode than it is in protected mode, the coprocessor would have had to operate in different modes as well, using the old interface method. Instead, the new interface requires the 80286 to validate all addresses before signaling the 80287. This interface allows the coprocessor to run at a clock rate different from that of the main CPU, and it also allows the 80287 to be used with CPUs other than the 80286.

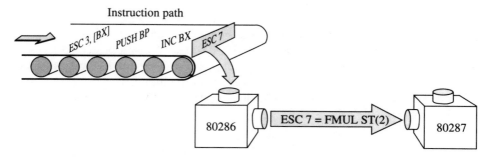

**Figure 1-8.** *80286 coprocessor interface.*

# Competitive Pressures

Between the introduction of the 8086 and the 80286, Motorola developed what became the strongest competition to Intel's dominance of the microprocessor market, the 68000 family. Several features of the Motorola microprocessors were attractive to the development community. The 68000 family incorporates a 32-bit internal register file for data and addressing. This allows a large application address space without the limitation of 64-KB segments. This 32-bit capability also makes it easy to port operating systems (such as UNIX) and minicomputer applications to the 68000-family processors.

Motorola also boasted about the "orthogonality" of the 68000 instruction set. Unlike the 8086 and the 80286, with their special-purpose registers, the 68000 allowed programmers to specify any register for a given instruction. Although all 68000 microprocessors had 32-bit register files, the first two CPUs (68000 and 68010) were limited to 24-bit addresses and a 16-bit memory interface. In 1985, however, Motorola began sampling the 68020, which had a full 32-bit address bus and a 32-bit data bus. Although Intel had most of the business microcomputer market, makers of scientific and engineering workstations almost unanimously chose Motorola CPUs for their products.

# Intel's 32-Bit Microprocessor

Intel's design engineers faced two problems: compatibility and performance. They needed to maintain compatibility with the previous generation of processors to re-tain their share of the PC business market; Intel's marketing force frequently referred to the "billions and billions" of bytes of code (applications) that the 80386 had to be able to run. At the same time, they needed a product that would address the shortcomings of the 8086-family architecture, which gave Motorola an edge in scientific and engineering markets. The resulting product, the 80386, addressed these issues by operating in a number of modes. At boot time, it operates in real mode like the 80286 and is nothing more than a very fast 8086. It uses 16-bit regis-ters and the 8086 segmentation scheme, and it is subject to the 1-MB memory limitation.

But the 80386 can also be switched to protected mode. In protected mode, each segment is marked by a bit that designates whether the segment is a protected-mode segment containing 16-bit 80286 code or a 32-bit protected-mode segment. Programs residing in 32-bit segments can use the extended address space (segments larger than 64 KB) and additional features, including array indexing, orthogonal use of the register set, and special debugging capabilities not found in previous processors.

A protected-mode operating system can also create a task that runs in virtual 8086 mode. An application running in this mode believes that it is running in real mode or on an 8086. However, the operating system can designate certain classes of in-put/output (I/O) operations that it will not allow. If the application attempts to vio-late any operating system rules, an interrupt is generated that transfers control from the application to the operating system. By examining the instruction that the appli-cation was trying to execute, the operating system can choose to block the applica-tion from running, simulate the operation, or ignore it and let the application continue. The operating system also maps the 1-MB 8086 address space that the ap-plication believes it is running under to the actual memory space that the operating system wants the application to use. A protected-mode operating system can estab-lish multiple virtual 8086 tasks.

The 80386 also extends the similarities between the Intel architecture and the Multics system. Like Multics, the 80386 integrates the ability to perform demand paging (a virtual-memory technique used in minicomputers and mainframes) with segmentation.

Intel also continued a tradition it began with the 8088: It offered a low-cost version of the processor. The 80386SX is identical internally to the 80386. However, it has only a 16-bit external data bus and a 24-bit address bus, and it is generally available at slower clock speeds than the full 32-bit version (sometimes called the 80386DX).

Another variant on the 80386 is the 80376. This chip is identical to the 80386SX except that it operates only in 32-bit protected mode and does not support paging. It cannot run real-mode programs and has no virtual 8086 mode capability. It is designed for embedded process control applications.

## The 80387

The 80386 microprocessor line from Intel also boasts new coprocessors, the 80387 and the 80387SX. The interface between the 80386 CPU and the coprocessor is the same as that defined for the 80286 and the 80287. The 80386 can also be coupled with the slower 80287 to provide a lower-cost floating-point environment. If the system board has the appropriate socket, the 80387 provides a significant performance improvement over its predecessor, executing floating-point benchmarks about five times faster.

# The 80486

In 1989, the newest kid on the block was the 80486. Its basic architecture is identical to that of the 80386, but the following advances are part of its design: single-clock execution for the most basic instructions, an 8-KB cache to speed access to frequently referenced memory locations, and an on-board numeric coprocessor. Because all the floating-point logic has been incorporated directly into the 80486, an 80487 will never be needed. Additionally, the chip was redesigned to make it easier to build computers with multiple 80486 CPUs.

Intel has indicated that the 80x86 product line will continue to evolve. The next-generation processor will be called the 80586 and will include capabilities beyond those of the 80486. However, Intel has committed to broadening the microprocessor line as well as lengthening it. The CPUs are also available in a wide range of clock speeds, from 16 through 33 megahertz, with even faster models promised for the future.

# Summary

The first processor of the line to feature 32-bit computing was the 80386, so I will refer to the 80386, 80386SX, 80376, and 80486 as the "80386 family." As you can see from the following table, the technology has advanced significantly beyond that of its predecessors; however, the road to 32-bit computing was not necessarily straight and narrow. Processor design has been shaped by a number of forces: the ideals of the designers, the limits of compatibility (some stemming from the early days of the 8080), threats from the competition (both real and perceived), and other factors such as Pascal, Multics, and UNIX. Now that I've shown the origins of the 80386 family, the remainder of the book will show how it works.

### Relative Performance

|  | 8086/87 | 80286/287 | 80386/387 | 80486 |
|---|---|---|---|---|
| *Integer* | 1.0 | 2.7 | 9.0 | 20.0 |
| *Floating point* | 1.0 | 1.7 | 10.0 | 40.0 |

For example, the 80486 is approximately 20 times faster than the 8086/87 performing integer calculations and approximately 40 times faster performing floating-point calculations. (Measurements refer to the clock rate of the chip when first introduced. Faster versions of all the processors have subsequently been made available.)

# 2

# THE CPU ARCHITECTURE

Back in 1837, when Charles Babbage was musing over the idea of computation automata, he referred to his grandest scheme as an "analytical engine." At that time, especially considering the mechanical aspects of Babbage's idea, an engine was an apt metaphor for a computing device: fuel, combustion, and power became input, computation, and output.

## A Data-Processing Factory

In recent years, the machinelike cycle led to limitations on the amount of work that could be accomplished. A modern microprocessor is more analogous to a factory than to an engine. At the heart of this data-processing factory, the computational engine remains, but it is surrounded by a bevy of supporting departments.

Figure 2-1 on the following page illustrates our imaginary widget factory. It is composed of three departments: Shipping and Receiving, Materials, and Manufacturing. The Shipping and Receiving department deals with the world outside the factory. It orders truckloads of raw materials from suppliers and passes them to the Materials department. The goods are sorted here and warehoused until needed. The Manufacturing department, the "engine" of the factory, forges the finished widgets from the raw materials and routes them to Shipping and Receiving, where they are sent to the outside world.

The efficiency of this model lies in the parallel nature of the different activities. At the same time as the Materials department requests the raw goods necessary to build widgets, Manufacturing builds the current supply of widgets, and Shipping and Receiving deals with the outside world, buys unfinished goods, and ships the newly finished widgets.

Conventional microprocessors, or CPUs, receive two classes of data: instructions and operands. The instructions tell the computer which operations to perform on the operands.

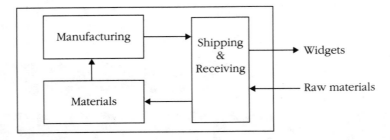

**Figure 2-1.** *Widget factory.*

Like our imaginary factory, the 80386 and 80486 can work on more than one instruction simultaneously. In the jargon of the computer industry, this is called *pipelining*.

In Figure 2-2, I recast the widget factory as a data-processing factory analogous to the operation of a microprocessor. The Shipping and Receiving department pulls in bytes of data from memory. Instructions then move to the Materials department, where they are decoded and stored. When requested, the new instructions and any necessary operands pass to the Manufacturing department, the computational engine. The results of an operation pass back to Shipping and Receiving, which stores the results outside the CPU, in memory.

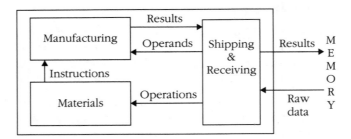

**Figure 2-2.** *Data-processing factory.*

Although simple, this picture of the flow of information through the processor is fairly accurate. The three departments in the example correspond to six logical units in the 80386, as shown in Figure 2-3. The 80486 is somewhat more complex, adding an additional execution unit for floating-point operation and a cache unit that sits between the rest of the processor and main memory. Each unit operates in parallel with the other units. Later sections of this chapter describe the operation of each unit.

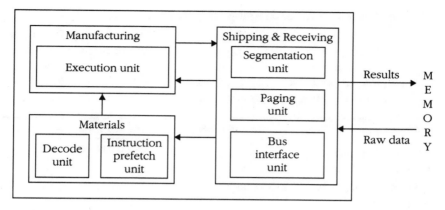

**Figure 2-3.** *80386 factory.*

# Keeping the factory moving

The heartbeat of a microprocessor is the clock signal. This regular electronic pulse keeps all units of the processor synchronized. The clock signal is a square wave oscillating at a specific frequency, as shown in Figure 2-4. Instruction timings, memory access times, and operational delays are measured in terms of clocks, or one complete square-wave cycle. The 80386SX is available in versions that run at either 16 or 20 megahertz (MHz). The DX or standard 80386 is available in models that run at a variety of speeds, from 16 through 33 MHz. The 80486 is available in 25-MHz or 33-MHz versions. The figure below shows a system running with a 25-MHz clock. At 25 MHz, each cycle lasts 40 nanoseconds.

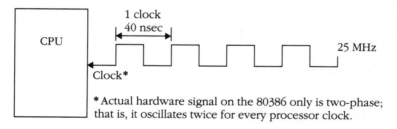

**Figure 2-4.** *A square-wave cycle.*

You can compute the time it takes a single instruction to execute using the tables provided in Appendix D. Figure the time for a single cycle and multiply it by the clock count given for the instruction. You figure the cycle time by dividing the clock speed (in MHz) into 1000. For example, the cycle time for a 16-MHz 80386 is 1000/16, or 62.5 nanoseconds. Notice that in the 80386 (SX and DX), the actual hardware clock device oscillates at twice the chip's clock frequency; this is called a two-phase clock. The 80486, however, does not use a two-phase clock.

## Performance advantages of parallelism

The pipelined operation of the 80386 and the 80486 "hides" portions of instruction execution time. Some operations necessary to execute an instruction occur during the previous instruction. The table that follows illustrates the difference between executing a typical instruction (ADD ECX, [EBP+8]) on the 80386 and executing it on a similar but imaginary processor without pipelining.

| Operation | With Pipelining | Without Pipelining |
| --- | --- | --- |
| Instruction fetch | 0 clocks | 2–4 clocks |
| Instruction decode | 0 clocks | 1 clock |
| Operand address xlate | 0–6 clocks | 2–8 clocks |
| Operand read | 3 clocks | 3 clocks |
| Execute | 2 clocks | 2 clocks |
| Total: | 5–11 clocks | 10–18 clocks |

Pipelining lets the 80386 execute an instruction about twice as quickly as a similar processor that performs each step of the instruction sequentially. Some instructions that have no operands appear to execute in "zero" time because of the parallel nature of 80386 operating units. The 80486 has an even greater advantage. First of all, the basic processor is faster. The execute time for many instructions on the 80486 is a single clock, and the operand read time is only 2 clocks. In addition, the 80486 contains an on-chip cache that holds 8 KB of the most frequently referenced information. If the operand address references a value that is stored in the cache, the operand read time is 0, meaning that the entire instruction could execute in as little as 1 clock cycle.

# CPU Microarchitecture

Figure 2-5 shows a block diagram of the internal operating units of the 80386. Although the programmer sees the 80386 as a single entity, it is instructive to see how the 80386 achieves the division of labor that contributes to its speed.

## Bus interface unit (BIU)

The bus interface unit (BIU) is the 80386's gateway to the external world. Any other unit that needs data from the outside asks the BIU to perform the operation. Similarly, when an instruction needs to write data to memory or to the I/O channel, the BIU is presented with the data and address and is asked to place it on the bus. The BIU deals with physical (hardware) addresses only, so operand addresses must first pass through the segmentation unit and the paging unit, if necessary.

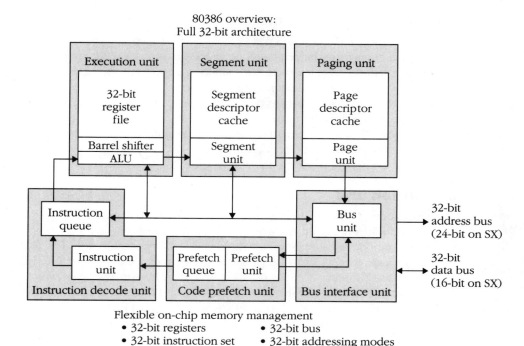

**Figure 2-5.** *80386 microarchitecture. (Reprinted by permission of Intel Corporation, copyright © 1986.)*

## Instruction prefetch unit

The job of the prefetch unit is relatively simple. The instruction decode unit extracts from a 16-byte queue, and the prefetch unit tries to keep the queue full. The prefetch unit continually asks the BIU to fetch the contents of memory at the next instruction address. As soon as the prefetch unit receives the data, it places it in the queue and, if the queue is not full, requests another 32-bit piece of memory. The BIU treats requests from the prefetch unit as slightly less important than requests from other units. In this way, currently executing instructions requesting operands receive the highest priority and are not slowed down, but prefetches still occur as frequently as possible. The prefetch unit is notified whenever the execution unit processes a CALL, a JMP, or an interrupt so that it can begin fetching instructions from the new address. The queue is flushed whenever a CALL, a JMP, or an interrupt occurs, thus preventing the execution unit from receiving out-of-sequence instructions.

## Instruction decode unit

The instruction decode unit has a job similar to that of the prefetch unit. It takes individual bytes from the prefetch queue and determines the number of bytes needed to complete the next instruction. A single instruction in the 80386 can be anywhere from 1 through 16 bytes. After pulling the entire instruction from the prefetch queue, the instruction decode unit reformats the opcode into an internal instruction format and places the decoded instruction into the instruction queue, which is three operations deep. The instruction decode unit also signals the BIU if the instruction just decoded will cause a memory reference. This allows the operands of the instructions to be obtained prior to the execution of the instructions.

## Execution unit

The execution unit is the part of the CPU that does computations. It performs any shifts, additions, multiplications, and so on that are necessary to accomplish an instruction. The register set is contained inside the execution unit. The unit also contains a logic component called a barrel shifter, which can perform multiple-bit shifts in a single clock cycle. The execution unit uses this capability not only in shift instructions but in accelerating multiplications and in generating indexed addresses. The execution unit also tells the BIU when it has data that needs to be sent to the memory or I/O bus.

## Segmentation unit

The segmentation unit translates segmented addresses into linear addresses. Segment translation time is almost entirely hidden by the parallelism of the 80386. At most, 1 clock is required to complete the address translation. The typical case is 0 clocks. The segmentation unit contains a cache that holds descriptor table information for each of the six segment registers. The segmentation unit is described further in Chapter 3.

## Paging unit

The paging unit takes the linear addresses generated by the segmentation unit and converts them to physical addresses. If paging is disabled, the linear addresses of the segmentation unit become the physical addresses. When paging is enabled, the linear address space of the 80386 is divided into 4096-byte blocks called pages. Each page can be mapped to an entirely different physical address. Chapter 6 discusses the paging process in detail.

The 80386 microprocessor uses a page table to translate every linear address to a physical address. The paging unit contains an associative cache called the translation lookaside buffer (TLB), which contains the entries (new addresses) for the 32 most recently used pages. If a page table entry is not found in the TLB, a 32-bit memory read cycle fetches the entry from RAM. Under typical operating conditions, less than 2 percent of all memory references require the 80386 to look outside the TLB for a page table entry.

The time required to perform the translation varies between 0 and 5 clocks. Thanks to the TLB, the typical delay is only ½ clock.

# The 80486 Microarchitecture

Figure 2-6 contains a block diagram of the 80486 microarchitecture. It is quite similar to that of the 80386. The differences include an additional execution unit, which handles floating-point processing, and the cache unit, which is located where the BIU is in the 80386. A BIU is present in the 80486, but it will not be activated if a request for data can be satisfied by the cache.

The floating-point execution unit of the 80486 can operate in parallel with the standard execution unit, with floating-point and standard operations occurring simultaneously. The floating-point capabilities of the 80486 are covered later in this chapter.

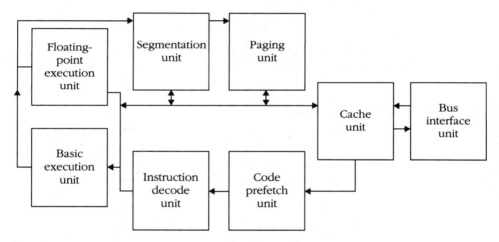

**Figure 2-6.** *80486 microarchitecture.*

## The cache connection

With a cache enabled, the 80486 obtains significant performance advantages over the 80386. This cache provides a general-purpose scratchpad for frequently used memory references. (Other processing units contain special-purpose caches, such as the TLB; these special-purpose caches exist in both the 80386 and the 80486.)

The slowest 80486 has an instruction cycle time of 40 nanoseconds. External RAM that can respond to the requests of a processor that fast is prohibitively expensive. As a result, system designers use slower RAM and induce *wait states*. A wait state gets its name because the CPU must wait for external RAM to read or write the requested information. The cache holds duplicate copies of data in external memory. Reading the cached copy allows the 80486 to eliminate wait states.

The size of the cache is only 8 KB, so the processor tries to use the space intelligently and only cache the most frequently used memory values. By reading the cached copy, the 80486 can get its operands immediately, without memory reference times (at least 2 clocks) or wait states (system dependent).

The cache is described in detail in Chapter 6.

# Instruction Set Architecture

The execution unit presents the programmer with the model for instruction execution. It contains the logic to process instructions, to operate on various data types, and to interpret control information.

Because the 80386, 80386SX, and 80486 are 32-bit processors, the typical size of an operand is a 32-bit quantity. Also, because these chips process data 32 bits at a time, it is customary to say that they have a *word size* of 32 bits. Unfortunately, the term word is ambiguous when referring to Intel processors.

For simplicity, *word* refers to a 16-bit quantity, as it did in the 8086 and 80286 environments. The term *dword,* or *doubleword,* refers to a 32-bit quantity. The term *32-bit word* is also used.

## Bits and bit strings

Although the basic (default) operand size on the 80386 family of processors is 32 bits, these processors can manipulate quantities of various sizes. The most elementary is the bit. A bit is a single binary digit, and the 80386 family implements a number of instructions that test and modify individual bits. Bits are addressed as an offset from a register or memory location. The low-order bit of the operand is designated as bit 0, the high-order bit in the low-order byte is bit 7, and the low-order bit of the next byte is bit 8. Figure 2-7 shows the bits in a register and in memory. If the operand resides in memory, negative bit offsets can also be used. Bit −1 is the high-order bit of the byte immediately preceding the memory address.

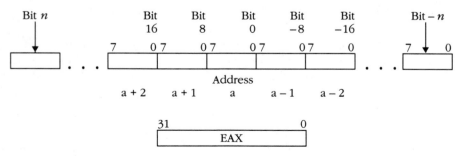

**Figure 2-7.** *Bit strings.*

## Bytes

The byte is the basic unit of addressability in the 80386 family; that is, address 2 refers to the third byte in memory, not the third dword. A byte is an 8-bit quantity that can be interpreted as either a signed or an unsigned value. Figure 2-8 shows the layout of a byte and the range of values that it can specify.

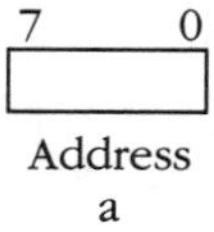

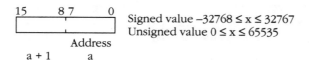

Signed value $-128 \le x \le 127$
Unsigned value $0 \le x \le 255$

**Figure 2-8.** *Byte value range.*

When a byte is interpreted as an unsigned number, it can take on a value ranging from 0 through 255. If a byte is interpreted as a signed number, it is assumed to be in *two's complement* notation. This notation allows a single byte to store values ranging from −128 through +127. To determine the value of a two's complement number, follow these steps:

1. Examine the most significant bit (MSB) of the value. If the MSB is 0, the number is positive and can be read as if it were an unsigned value. If the MSB is 1, the value is negative.

2. You can find the absolute value of the number by taking the *complement* of the number (inverting the value of each bit) and adding 1.

For example, consider the binary value 10111100B. The most significant bit, 1, indicates that the number is negative. To find the absolute value, take the complement (01000011B) and add 1. The result, 01000100B, is 68 decimal, so 10111100B represents the value −68.

## Words

Words, as previously defined, are 16-bit quantities. Figure 2-9 shows the range of values that can be stored in a word. When a word is written to memory, it is stored in two bytes. The low-order byte is written to the specified address, and the high-order byte is written to the next consecutive memory location.

Word values are interpreted as signed or unsigned in the same way as are byte values. The only differences are that bit 15 is the MSB and that there is a greater range of possible values.

Signed value $-32768 \le x \le 32767$
Unsigned value $0 \le x \le 65535$

**Figure 2-9.** *Word value range.*

## Dwords

Dwords are 32-bit quantities. Like bytes and words, they can be signed or unsigned. The extra bits allow representation of integral values greater than 2 billion. Figure 2-10 illustrates the range of values for dwords and the way they are stored in memory. As with words, dwords are stored in memory low-order byte first. If the low-order byte is stored at address $m$, the high-order byte is stored at address $m + 3$.

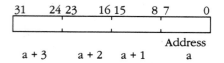

Signed value $-2147483648 \leq x \leq 2147483647$
Unsigned value $0 \leq x \leq 4294967295$

**Figure 2-10.** *Dword value range.*

The computer industry does not agree on the proper method of breaking up large values into bytes for memory storage. Computers like the DEC VAX use the same technique as the 80386. Others, such as the IBM 370 and the Motorola 68020, store the high-order byte first. In homage to Jonathan Swift, the two formats are known as "big-endian" (Motorola) and "little-endian" (Intel). New to the 80486 are two instructions for swapping dwords from one form to the other. Data format must be a consideration when porting programs from one computer to another.

## Quadwords

Quadwords are 64-bit numeric quantities. Only floating-point instructions reference quadword memory operands, with two exceptions: The 32-bit Multiply instruction generates a 64-bit value, with the high-order 32 bits in register EDX and the low-order 32 bits in register EAX, and the 32-bit Divide instruction accepts a 64-bit dividend stored in the same register format.

## ASCII and BCD

In the previous examples, the values discussed represent numbers. For ASCII and BCD, the binary patterns represent encodings of information. (ASCII stands for American Standard Code for Information Interchange.) ASCII values are 7 bits of information stored in a single 8-bit byte. The most significant bit is 0. A particular bit pattern represents a predefined value. For example, the binary pattern 0101011B represents the plus character (+). 1010011B represents the letter S, and 0110101 represents the digit 5. Appendix B contains a table of all ASCII characters.

Similarly, BCD, which stands for binary coded decimal, encodes representations of decimal numbers in binary format. Encoding a decimal digit requires 4 bits. Because using only 4 bits of a byte is inefficient, two BCD digits are often stored in a single byte. This representation is called *packed BCD*. Figure 2-11 shows how values are stored in BCD notation.

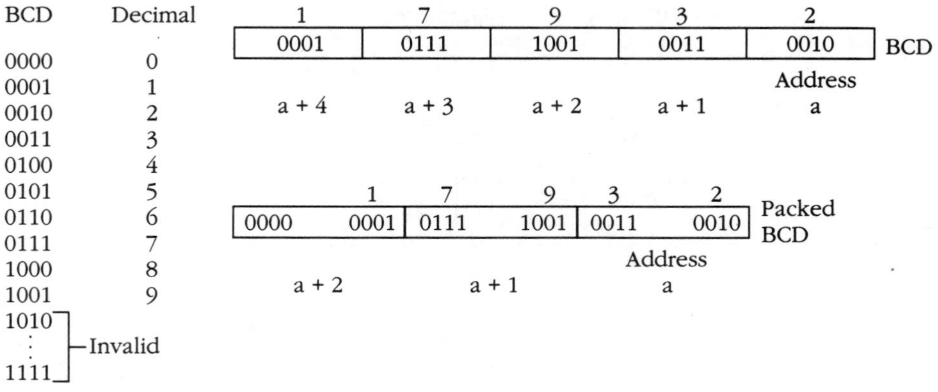

| BCD | Decimal |
|------|---------|
| 0000 | 0 |
| 0001 | 1 |
| 0010 | 2 |
| 0011 | 3 |
| 0100 | 4 |
| 0101 | 5 |
| 0110 | 6 |
| 0111 | 7 |
| 1000 | 8 |
| 1001 | 9 |
| 1010 ⌉ | |
| ⋮ ⎬ Invalid | |
| 1111 ⌋ | |

**Figure 2-11.** *BCD storage.*

Because ASCII and BCD provide ways to encode numeric values and do not have a fixed length for such encoding, they can be used to implement variable-precision numbers. The 80386 and 80486 chips support ASCII and BCD arithmetic via the Decimal Adjust and ASCII Adjust instructions. ASCII and BCD arithmetic are discussed in Chapter 4.

# The Register Set

In addition to implementing the logic to execute instructions, the 80386 and the 80486 have storage locations on the chip, called *registers*. Because they are inside the CPU, registers can be accessed as operands much more rapidly than can external memory. The general registers are used to store frequently accessed operands. Other registers contain special values that control specific aspects of the processor's operation.

The register set is partitioned into five classes: the *general registers*, which applications use for data storage and computation; *segment registers*, which affect memory addressing; *protection registers*, which help support the operating system; *control registers*, which modify the behavior of the processor; and *debug* and *test registers*, which are used as their name implies.

## General registers

The general registers are named EAX, EBX, ECX, EDX, ESI, EDI, EBP, and ESP, as shown in Figure 2-12 on the following page. As a rule, any instruction can use any general register except ESP, either as an operand or as a pointer to an operand in memory. Exceptions are noted in Chapter 4 in the discussion of the instruction set.

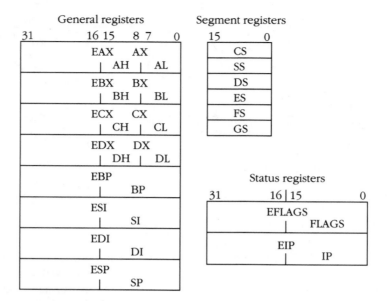

**Figure 2-12.** *Base register set.*

In the 80386 family, you can address selected portions of these registers. The part of the register accessed depends on whether you are performing an 8-bit, a 16-bit, or a 32-bit operation. Each division of a register has a separate name. For example, EAX is the name of one of the 32-bit registers. The lower 16 bits are addressable as AX, and that half of the register is accessible as AL (the low-order 8 bits) or AH (the high-order 8 bits). These names are left over from the previous generation of micro-processors, the 8080 and 8086, as discussed in Chapter 1. The 80386 extended the 80286 register set to 32 bits, similar to the way in which the 8086 and 80286 extended the 8-bit registers of the 8080 to 16 bits. The 80486 did not introduce any changes in the register set. Figure 2-13 shows a map of the register extensions.

Two additional registers hold status information about the current instruction stream. The EIP register contains the address of the currently executing instruction, and the EFLAGS register contains a number of fields relevant to different instructions.

Like the other registers, EIP and EFLAGS have 16-bit components—IP and FLAGS. The 16-bit forms of these registers are used in virtual 8086 mode and in running code written for the 80286.

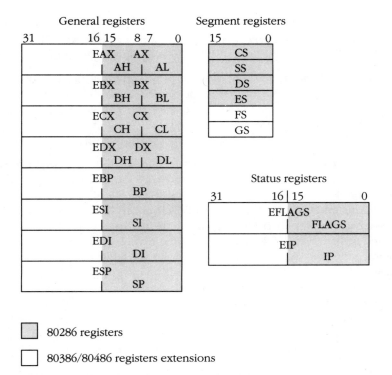

**Figure 2-13.** *80386/80486 vs. 80286 registers.*

## EFLAGS register

A breakdown of the EFLAGS register looks like this:

\* 80486 only

*AC—Alignment check:* This bit exists only in the 80486. When AC is set to 1, the 80486 will expect all memory references to be aligned, so only the minimum possible number of memory accesses are required to reference an operand. Because of the way the hardware memory interface works, a 32-bit operand must begin at a memory address divisible by 4, or it will require two memory cycles to read the operand. When AC=0, the 80486 will simply issue the necessary read cycles, despite the performance penalty. This is the standard behavior for the 80386. When AC=1, however, the 80486 assumes that the software is designed to run in the most efficient way possible and will issue an alignment fault (INT 17H) if it finds this condition to be untrue. Both 16-bit objects and 80286-compatible selector:offset pairs need only be aligned on even-address boundaries. Double and extended precision floating-point numbers must be aligned on memory addresses divisible by 8. (Note: The AC bit applies only to code running at privilege level 3, application programs.)

***VM—Virtual 8086 mode:*** When this bit is set, it indicates that the currently executing instruction stream is 8086 code. The implications of virtual 8086 mode are covered in Chapter 7. Applications cannot change the VM (virtual mode) bit, and instructions that modify EFLAGS leave the VM bit unchanged. Only the task switch operation or an interrupt/interrupt return can alter the VM bit.

***RF—Resume flag:*** This bit controls whether a debug fault can be generated during the execution of an instruction. When an exception occurs during program execution, the processor pushes the current CS, EIP, and EFLAGS registers onto the stack and transfers control to the proper exception handler. The stack image of the EFLAGS register has the RF bit set to 1. When the exception handler returns to the interrupted instruction, the RF bit is on, which prevents a recursive debug fault from being generated. Any other faults (such as page faults or protection faults) occur as usual. The debug exception has the highest priority of all 80386/80486 exceptions; if, therefore, an instruction causes multiple faults, the first one processed is the debug exception. When control returns to the interrupted instruction, the RF bit is set, and the instruction is completed without retriggering the debug fault. The processor clears the RF bit upon completion of the interrupted instruction. Chapter 5 contains a discussion of exceptions and support for debugging.

***NT—Nested task flag:*** Whenever a CALL, an interrupt, a trap, or an exception causes a task switch, this bit gets set. The bit is set in the EFLAGS register of the new task and indicates that a reverse task switch (IRET) is valid. Task switching in the 80386 and 80486 is discussed further in Chapter 5.

***IOPL—I/O privilege level:*** This 2-bit field holds a value of 0–3 that indicates the privilege level required to perform I/O instructions. Although IOPL is in the EFLAGS register, no procedure can modify it unless the procedure is running at privilege level 0, and then only by using the POPF or POPFD instruction.

A procedure's current privilege level (CPL) must be equal to or more privileged than the IOPL to execute any of the following instructions: IN, INS, OUT, OUTS, CLI, or STI. A procedure that can execute these instructions is said to have *I/O privilege.*

***OF—Overflow flag:*** When an arithmetic integer instruction is executed, the OF bit is set if the result is too large or too small to fit in the destination register or memory address. Because the OF flag is set relative to integer instructions, the CPU presumes that the destination register is one bit smaller in size to allow for the sign bit. The following instructions illustrate some examples.

```
MOV AL, 127          ; AL = 7FH, largest 8 -bit
                     ; signed integer OF = 0
ADD AL, 2            ; result, AL == 81H (-127)
                     ; should be AX == 0081 (129), OF = 1

MOV CX, -35000       ; CX = 7748H, OF = 0
SUB CX, 7002         ; result, CX == 5BEEH (42002)
                     ; should be ECX == FFFF5BEEH (- 42002),
                     ; OF = 1
```

Notice that the OF bit is ignored if unsigned arithmetic is intended. For example, adding 127 and 2 in register AL generates the valid unsigned result of 129.

**DF—Direction flag:** The direction flag bit modifies the behavior of the string instructions: MOVS, STOS, LODS, CMPS, SCAS, INS, and OUTS. When DF is 0, the string instructions operate on incrementally higher addresses. When DF is 1, the memory addresses are decremented, and the operand addresses become progressively lower. The STD instruction sets the direction flag bit, and the CLD instruction clears the bit.

**IF—Interrupt enable flag:** When this bit is set, the processor responds to external hardware interrupts. When the bit is reset, interrupts are disabled—that is, hardware interrupts are ignored. Notice that this bit does not affect the NMI interrupt. The processor always responds to faults (exceptions) and software interrupts regardless of the setting of the IF bit. When IF is 0, interrupts are said to be *masked*.

The STI instruction sets IF to 1, and the CLI instruction clears IF to 0. The interrupt enable flag is also modified when an IRET is executed. POPF and POPFD instructions modify the interrupt enable flag only if the procedure executing the instruction has I/O privilege.

**TF—Trap flag:** The trap flag bit assists in application debugging. When the TF bit is set, an interrupt occurs immediately after the next instruction executes. The trap flag is usually set by a debugger; the debugging capabilities of the 80386 family are covered in Chapter 5.

**SF—Sign flag:** The sign flag bit changes when arithmetic or logical instructions are executed. The sign flag bit receives the value of the high-order bit of the result and, when set to 1, indicates that the result of the instruction is negative.

```
MOV EDX, -1          ; sign flag unchanged by MOV
ADD EDX, 3           ; EDX == 2, SF now 0
NEG EDX              ; EDX == -2, SF now 1
```

**ZF—Zero flag:** The zero flag bit is set when arithmetic instructions generate a 0 result.

```
MOV  AL, 0           ; zero flag unchanged by MOV
OR   AL, AL          ; AL unchanged, ZF now 1
```

**AF—Auxiliary carry flag:** The auxiliary carry flag bit indicates that a carry out of the low-order nibble of the AL register occurred in an arithmetic instruction. This bit is used by the ASCII and BCD instructions. It allows implementation of multiple-digit precision decimal arithmetic. The following example assumes an ASCII encoding of the characters 4 and 7.

```
MOV AL, '4'          ; AL = 34H, AF unchanged by MOV
ADD AL, '7'          ; AL == 6BH, AF now 1
AAA                  ; ASCII Adjust, AL = 1, AH = AH + 1
```

**PF—Parity flag:** The parity flag bit is set to 1 when an arithmetic instruction results in a value with an even number of 1 bits. For example, if you issued the following instructions, the resulting parity flag bit would be 0.

```
MOV   AH, 91H        ; AH = 10010001B, PF unchanged by MOV
ADD   AH, 05H        ; AH == 10010110B, PF now 1
```

**CF—Carry flag:** The carry flag bit is set when the result of an arithmetic operation is too large or too small for the destination register or memory address. It is similar in operation to the OF bit but indicates an unsigned overflow of the destination.

```
MOV AL, 127          ; AL = 7FH, CF unchanged by MOV
ADD AL, 2            ; AL == 81H, CF now 0
ADD AL, AL           ; AL == 02H, CF now 1 (the
                       mathematical result is 102H, but no
                       value is "carried" into the AH register)

MOV AL, 3            ; CF unchanged by MOV
SUB AL, 4            ; AL == FFH, CF now 1 (borrow bit)
```

## Segment registers

The segment registers hold the values that affect which portions of memory a program uses. Four segment registers are used under specific conditions, and two are available as pointers to frequently used areas of memory. The CS, DS, SS, and ES registers were inherited from the 80286 and perform the same functions as they did in that CPU. Two additional registers, FS and GS, were introduced in the 80386 and are also found in the 80486.

Associated with the segment registers is a descriptor cache, which holds the starting address of the memory segment and other related information. Chapter 3 details the relationship between segments and memory addresses. The descriptor cache for the segment registers is not accessible to the programmer; only the 16-bit register portion can be accessed directly. Figure 2-14 illustrates the segment registers and the internal descriptor cache.

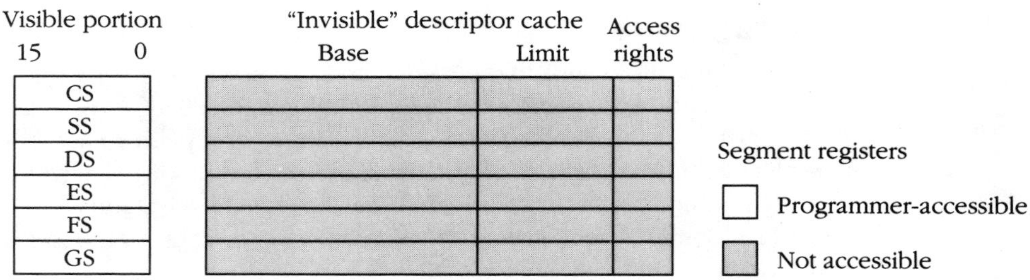

Visible portion | "Invisible" descriptor cache | Access rights

Figure 2-14. *Segment registers.*

## Protection model registers

Four registers support the protection model of the 80386 family. (See Figure 2-15.)

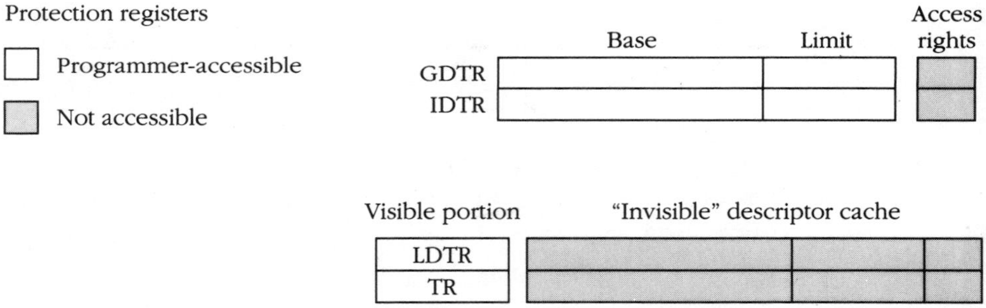

Protection registers

Figure 2-15. *Protection model registers.*

The protection model registers are:

*GDTR*—Global Descriptor Table Register

*IDTR*—Interrupt Descriptor Table Register

*LDTR*—Local Descriptor Table Register

*TR*—Task Register

The GDTR and IDTR contain linear base addresses that point to the start of the GDT and the IDT descriptor tables. They also contain limit fields that describe the size of the GDT and IDT tables.

The LDTR and TR hold 16-bit selector values, similar to the segment registers. As with the segment registers, an inaccessible descriptor cache exists for both the LDTR and TR. The LDTR holds a selector for an LDT descriptor, and the TR holds a selector for the TSS (task state segment) descriptor of the currently executing process. Chapter 5 discusses how these registers work.

## Control registers

The control registers regulate the paging and numeric coprocessor operation of the 80386 and additionally control cache operations in the 80486. A general description of the registers follows; refer to the specific chapters on paging and coprocessors for more detailed information. A programmer can read or modify control registers only by using instructions of the form MOV CR*x*, *reg*, where *reg* stands for one of the general registers. A procedure must be running at privilege level 0 to execute these instructions.

### CR0—Control register 0

The following illustration shows the contents of control register 0. The LMSW and SMSW instructions allow access to the low-order 16 bits of CR0 as the machine status word.

| 31 30 29 | | | 18 | 16 15 | 8 7 | 5 4 3 2 1 0 | |
|---|---|---|---|---|---|---|---|
| P G | C D | N W | A M | W P | Reserved | N E | E T | T S | E M | M P | P E | CR0 |

*PG—Paging:* Paging is enabled by setting the PG bit to 1. Typically, the operating system does this once, at initialization. Chapter 6 discusses the paging mechanism.

*CD—Cache disable:* The cache disable bit is present in the 80486 only. When it is set to 1, cache filling is disabled, and a reference to a memory address outside the cache will not cause new values to be read into the cache. Clearing the CD bit to 0 enables cache fills. Notice that operands will continue to be read from the cache even when CD=1. To completely turn off the cache, you must set CD and NW to 1 and then flush the cache using the INVD instruction.

*NW—No write-through:* The NW bit is also 80486 specific and is normally set to the same value as CD: NW=1 when caching is disabled, and NW=0 for normal cache operation. The state CD=1, NW=0 is useful, however, to temporarily disable cache fills while leaving write-through enabled.

*AM—Alignment mask:* The AM bit is present only in the 80486. When set to 1, it enables the AC (alignment check) bit in the EFLAGS register. When AM=0, the AC bit is ignored.

*WP—Write protect:* The write protect bit is present only in the 80486. It affects the behavior of the paging unit. When WP is cleared to 0, the operation of the 80486 is compatible with that of the 80386. When WP is 1, a supervisor-mode write to a read-only page will cause a page fault. See Chapter 6 for more information on paging.

*NE—Numerics exception:* The NE bit is present only in the 80486. When it is set to 1, unmasked floating-point exceptions vector through interrupt 16H. Clearing NE through 0 puts the 80486 into a DOS compatibility mode, and floating-point exceptions vector through interrupt 13H.

***ET—Extension type:*** In the 80486, this bit is always 1 because the floating-point coprocessor extension is always present in the 80486. The 80386 sets the ET bit to 1 at boot time if the processor determines that an 80387 is present. If this bit is 0, the coprocessor either is an 80287 or is not present at all. When ET is 1, the 80386 uses a 32-bit protocol to communicate with the coprocessor; otherwise, it uses a 16-bit protocol.

***TS—Task switched:*** The CPU sets the TS bit when a task switch operation occurs. When the TS bit is on, the next coprocessor instruction causes a trap to the operating system. This feature lets the operating system implement multitasking without requiring the operating system to save the state of the math coprocessor every time a task switch occurs. The context of the floating-point unit is more than 100 bytes, so saving the coprocessor state at every task switch would waste valuable CPU time.

***EM—Emulate math coprocessor:*** When this bit is set, floating-point instructions that would normally control coprocessor operation trap to the operating system instead. This bit is most useful in the 80386, where the numerics processor might be missing. Proper use of this bit allows programmers to write applications as if a coprocessor were present. If an 80287 or 80387 is present, the operating system initializes the EM bit to 0, and the application's floating-point instructions will be executed by the coprocessor. If an 80287 or 80387 is not present, the operating system sets the EM bit to 1. Then, when an application executes a floating-point instruction, the 80386 will trap back to the operating system, which either emulates the instruction in software or passes the operands to other floating-point hardware in the system.

***MP—Monitor coprocessor:*** The MP bit affects the operation of the WAIT instruction, as described in Chapter 8.

***PE—Protect enable:*** Setting the PE bit places the processor into protected mode. Typically, this is done once, at initialization. In the 80386 and 80486, it is possible to switch the CPU back into real mode after entering protected mode. (This was not possible in the 80286.) Some implementations of the OS/2 operating system use this technique to allow real-mode MS-DOS programs to run concurrently with protected-mode OS/2 applications.

## CR1—Control register 1
Control register 1 is not used in the 80386 or 80486 and is reserved for future Intel processors.

## CR2—Control register 2
When a page fault occurs, CR2 is loaded with the linear address that caused the exception. Refer to Chapter 6 for more details on paging.

### CR3—Control register 3

The paging hardware also uses this register. The CR3 contains the twenty high-order bits of the linear address of the starting point of the page directory. In the 80386, the twelve low-order bits should always be zero; in the 80486, bits 3 and 4 of the twelve low-order bits are used only in the 80486. Bit 3 controls page write-through (PWT), and bit 4 controls page cache disable (PCD). The implementation of paging is covered fully in Chapter 6.

## Debug and test registers

The 80386 contains eight debug registers and two test registers. The 80486 adds three test registers. The test registers TR3–TR5 control testing of the cache; registers TR6 and TR7 allow diagnostic software to test the translation lookaside buffer (TLB).

The debug registers, labeled DR0–DR7, allow the 80386 and 80486 to implement a hardware breakpoint capability that previously required an external in-circuit emula-tor. By setting the address registers (DR0–DR3) and the control register (DR7), the programmer can halt the CPU when a particular memory location is read from, writ-ten to, or executed. The breakpoints are noninvasive (they don't require modification of the program under debug), and they are also real-time (they don't degrade the performance of the program). The debugging techniques using the debug registers are described in Chapter 5.

# Floating-Point Support

Originally, the 8086 family of microprocessors did not support floating-point arith-metic directly. Instead, separate chips, optimized for numeric processing, were offered as options. The 80486 is the first chip to support floating-point arithmetic on the main CPU. Its floating-point instruction set is completely compatible with the 80387 coprocessor that was designed to support the 80386. Actually, the 80386 will work with either the 80387 or the 80287. The 80287 is a slower chip with a 16-bit interface, originally designed for use with the 80286. Floating-point performance of the 80287 is approximately 320,000 whetstones when running at 10 MHz. (A whetstone is a relative performance value that is used to compare the throughput of floating-point processors.) The 32-bit 80387 offers higher performance. This processor is software compatible with the 80287 and can execute about 1,800,000 whetstones when running at 16 MHz. A 80486 operating at 25 MHz can run the same benchmark at approximately 4,000,000 whetstones. Appendix F notes the dif-ferences between the 80287 and the 80387. In the following text, I will use the term NDP (numeric data processor) to refer to the 80287, the 80387, or the floating-point capabilities of the 80486. Exceptions will be noted by an explicit processor reference.

The NDP is another source of parallelism in the system. As soon as the execution unit sees a floating-point instruction, it passes the instruction to the NDP. The execution unit begins executing subsequent instructions regardless of how long the NDP takes to complete its operation. Of course, if the execution unit encounters another floating-point instruction, it must wait for the NDP to complete the current operation before it can begin a new one, and the main processor might be forced to wait.

To use a value computed by the 80387 and written to memory, you must ensure that the 80387 has completed the write operation. The FWAIT instruction ensures synchronization between the 80386 and the 80387. (FWAIT is a synonym for the WAIT instruction. FWAIT is commonly used to indicate waiting for the NDP.) Because the NDP is not a physically separate processor in the 80486, use of FWAIT is not necessary. However, if you are writing code that might be executed on an 80386, you must use the FWAIT instruction.

If a coprocessor is absent, the 80386 allows an operating system to emulate one and remain invisible to the application. For additional details on coprocessor emulation, see the discussion of the EM bit in control register 0 earlier in this chapter.

## Additional data formats

The NDP adds direct hardware support for three floating-point number formats and one BCD integer format. The NDP also supports three integer formats in common with the basic execution unit. These are the 16-bit, 32-bit, and 64-bit two's complement (signed) integers previously mentioned. Figure 2-16 on the following page shows the additional numeric formats.

### Floating-point numbers

The NDP supports three floating-point formats. This allows a programmer to make compromises between the amount of memory required and the precision of the results. The *short real* format lets programmers specify numbers of about seven decimal digits of accuracy. This format is also known as *single-precision* because a short real number fits into a single 32-bit machine word. The *long real* format, also known as *double-precision,* represents a floating-point number of up to 15 decimal digits of accuracy. Holding a long real number requires a double machine word (64 bits). The third format is called *temp* (temporary) *real* or *extended-precision.* Temp real numbers are 80 bits and represent about 19 decimal digits of precision.

Just as scientific notation represents floating-point quantities in decimal notation (for example, $4.74 \times 10^3$), the Intel floating-point format is a type of binary scientific notation. The general format of a floating-point number is $\pm f \times 2^e$, where $f$ represents a binary fraction and $e$ is an exponential power of 2. Three fields are required to make up a floating-point number: the sign, the exponent, and the fraction, or *significand.*

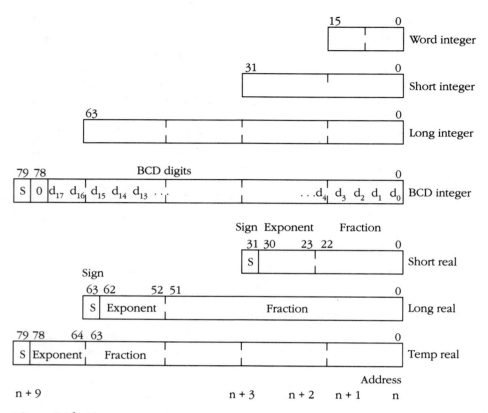

**Figure 2-16.** *Floating-point formats.*

The sign field is a single bit that is set to 1 to indicate a negative number and reset to 0 for a positive value. No value manipulation is necessary to change the number from positive to negative (or vice versa) other than toggling the sign bit. (Such manipulation is necessary when dealing with the two's complement notation of the integers.) This notational format allows the representation of +0.0 and −0.0, which is useful in certain circumstances.

The exponent field represents a multiplier of $2^n$. This field ranges from 8 bits in the short real format to 11 bits in the long real format to 15 bits in the temp real format. To accommodate negative exponents (such as $2^{-6}$), the value in the exponent field is *biased*—that is, the actual exponent is determined by subtracting the appropriate bias value from the value in the exponent field. For example, the bias for short reals is 127. If the value in the exponent field is 130, the exponent represents a value of $2^{130-127}$, or $2^3$. The bias for long reals is 1023, and the bias for temp reals is 16383. The values 0 and all 1's (binary) are reserved for representing special values and cannot be used to represent floating-point numbers.

The significand field contains the fractional part of the floating-point number. The significand occupies 23 bits in short reals, 52 bits in long reals, and 64 bits in temp reals. Figure 2-17 shows how to interpret floating-point fractions. The significand is encoded in two ways. In temp real format, the significand field holds the binary fraction in the form $s_0.s_1s_2\ldots s_{63}$, where $s_n$ is bit $n$ of the significand.

The authors of the IEEE-754 format took advantage of a representational trick to squeeze out an extra bit of precision in short real format and in long real format. A review of scientific notation shows that the values $40.103 \times 10^7$, $4.0103 \times 10^8$, and $0.040103 \times 10^{10}$ all represent the same number. A binary notation has the same property.

Shifting the fraction by one position can be compensated for by incrementing or decrementing the value of the exponent. Because a binary number consists of only 0's and 1's, the designers of the floating-point format decided that the fractional portion of the short and long reals would be shifted left until the most significant bit was 1. Because this bit was now *defined* as 1, there was no point in storing it, and it was assumed to exist. The fraction for a short or long real, therefore, has the value $1.s_0s_1s_2\ldots s_n$, where $n$ is 22 for short reals and 51 for long reals.

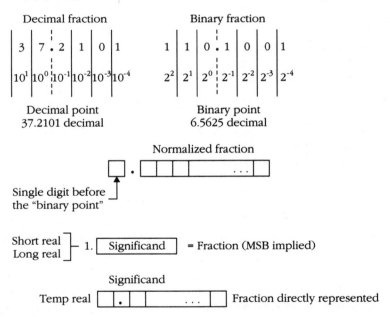

**Figure 2-17.** *Floating-point fractions.*

### *Short real:*

Absolute value = $1.s_0 s_1 \ldots s_{22} \times 2^{(exp\,-127)}$

The bias for the short real exponent is 127. The significand includes the "implied 1" bit and allows a precision of about seven decimal digits. Representative values range from $\pm 1.18 \times 10^{-38}$ through $\pm 3.40 \times 10^{38}$.

### *Long real:*

Absolute value = $1.s_0 s_1 \ldots s_{51} \times 2^{(exp\,-1023)}$

The bias for the long real exponent is 1023. The significand includes the "implied 1" bit and allows a precision of about 15 decimal digits. Representative values range from $\pm 2.23 \times 10^{-308}$ through $\pm 1.79 \times 10^{308}$.

### *Temp real:*

Absolute value = $s_0 .s_1 \ldots s_{63} \times 2^{(exp\,-16383)}$

The bias for the temp real exponent is 16383. The significand represents the fractional portion of the value (with no implied bits) and allows a precision of about 19 decimal digits. Representative values range from $\pm 3.37 \times 10^{-4932}$ through $\pm 1.18 \times 10^{4932}$.

**Special floating-point values:** In addition to intuitive values such as 3.14159 and $6.03 \times 10^{23}$, the NDP represents values that arise under unusual conditions. These values are called *infinities, denormals,* and *NaN's.* (NaN stands for "not a number.")

Infinity, positive or negative, is represented by a value whose exponent field is all 1's and whose fraction is 1.0B. Notice that in short and long real numbers, 1.0B is represented by a significand of all 0's, whereas in temp real numbers, the significand is a binary 10000000...0B.

Denormals are values that are too small to be represented in the standard (or normalized) fashion. Denormals are represented by a value with an exponent field of 0 and any nonzero value in the significand. A floating-point number with both an exponent of 0 and a significand of 0 represents 0.0.

NaN's are invalid representations of floating-point numbers. They are identified by an exponent field of all 1's and a significand other than the one representing infinity. The two kinds of NaN's are the signaling NaN and the quiet NaN. A signaling NaN has a fraction of the form $1.0xxx\ldots xB$, where $x$ represents any bit value. Notice that the binary value represented by the $x$ cannot be zeros, as that value is reserved for infinities. The NDP generates an exception whenever a signaling NaN is used. The NDP never creates a signaling NaN, but a programmer can use one to indicate some error condition such as an uninitialized floating-point variable. The quiet NaN has a fractional format of $1.1xxxxxB$. Recall that the leading 1 is implied in the significand of short and long reals but must be present in temp reals. The 80387 generates a quiet NaN instead of a numeric result whenever a floating-point instruction causes an invalid operation. Any instruction that receives either type of NaN as an operand generates a NaN as a result. The following table lists special values used by the NDP.

| Sign | Exponent | Fraction | Value |
|------|----------|----------|-------|
| x | 11...11B | 1.1xx...xxB | Quiet NaN |
| x | 11...11B | 1.0xx...xxB | Signaling NaN |
| x | 11...11B | 1.00...0B | Infinity |
| x | 00...00B | 0.xxxxxxB | Denormals |
| x | 00...00B | 0.00...0B | Zero |

Except for the signalling NAN (in which at least one of the $x$'s must be a 1), the $x$ indicates that it makes no difference whether the bit is 0 or 1. The 1 before the decimal in the fraction is physically present only in temporary real format. It is implied in the short real and long real formats. Denormals are recognized in the short and long formats by the 0 exponent value.

## BCD integer

The other new data type that the NDP supports is a packed decimal integer of 18 digits stored in 10 consecutive bytes of memory. The high-order bit of the high-order byte is interpreted as a sign bit. A 0 indicates a positive number, and a 1 indicates a negative number. The rest of the high-order byte is unused. The remaining bytes each contain two BCD digits.

| 79 | | 72 71 | 64 63 | 56 55 | 48 47 | 40 39 | 32 31 | 24 23 | 16 15 | 8 7 | 0 |
|----|---|-------|-------|-------|-------|-------|-------|-------|-------|-----|---|
| s | 0 | d d | d d | d d | d d | d d | d d | d d | d d | d d | |

The value range of the BCD integer is 0 through ±999,999,999,999,999,999. Programmers who work with BCD numbers might want to run the NDP with the precision exception unmasked (PM bit and bit 5, in the control word register). Because BCD formats often represent monetary values, it is important to avoid losses due to rounding or truncation.

## NDP register set

The NDP contains a register file of eight 80-bit floating-point registers and a number of status registers. Floating-point instructions refer to these registers rather than to the general registers EAX, ESI, and so on. (See Figure 2-18.)

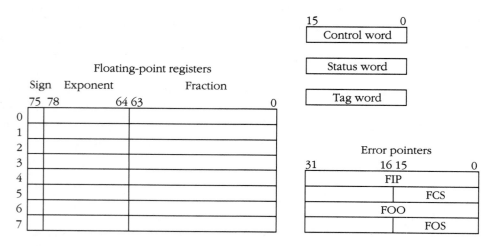

**Figure 2-18.**  *80387 register file.*

Unlike the general registers of the 80386 and 80486, however, the NDP's floating-point registers are addressed as a stack. The current top-of-stack (the value most recently pushed) is indicated by a field in the status word register and is addressed as ST or ST(0). The next register (the previous value pushed) is ST(1), and so on. This is best illustrated by the following example.

Assume that the configuration in Figure 2-19 shows the initial state of the NDP. Register 2 is designated as the current top-of-stack, but nothing is stored in the registers. The TW (tag word) register holds a 2-bit field for each register, marking it as valid, 0, special, or unused. To evaluate the polynomial $y = 3x^2 - 7x + 4$, we will use the following code fragment. (Figure 2-19 shows how the function evaluation progresses on the floating-point stack.)

```
x       DD      ?               ; short real variable "x"
y       DD      ?               ; result of computation
const   DW      ?               ; memory word for integer constants
```

```
FLD      x              ; load x to top of stack
FLD      ST(0)          ; duplicate copy of x
FMUL     ST(0)          ; square copy of x at top of stack
MOV      const, 3       ; integer multiplier
FIMUL    const          ; multiply top of stack by 3
MOV      const, 7       ; integer constant
FILD     const          ; load 7 to top of stack
FMULP    ST(2), ST      ; ST(2) = x * 7, pop ST
FSUBRP   ST(1), ST      ; ST(1) = ST - ST(1), pop ST
MOV      const, 4       ; integer constant
FIADD    const          ; 3x² - 7x + 4
FSTP     y              ; store result and pop, clearing stack
```

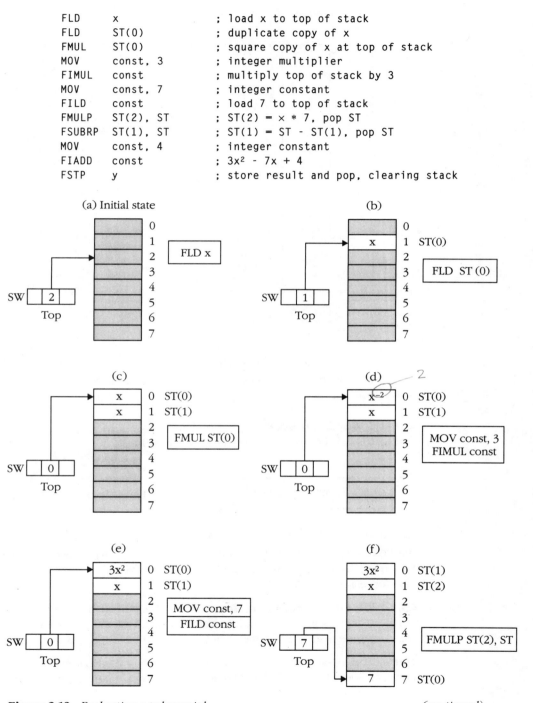

**Figure 2-19.** *Evaluating a polynomial.*                    *(continued)*

**Figure 2-19.** *continued*

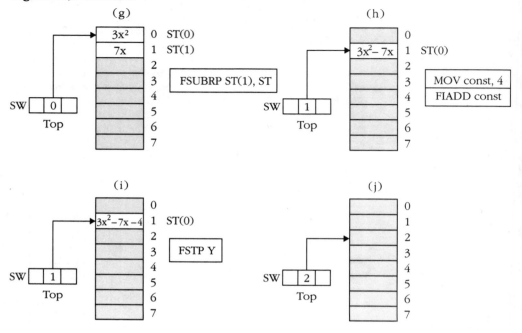

The NDP register addressed by ST($n$) varies according to the value of the TOP field in the status word register. The following section describes the other fields in the status word register.

## Status word register

The status word register can be illustrated as follows:

| 15 | | | 8 | 7 | | | | | | | | 0 |
|---|---|---|---|---|---|---|---|---|---|---|---|---|
| B | C3 | TOP | C2 | C1 | C0 | ES | SF | PE | UE | OE | ZE | DE | IE |

**B—Busy:** This bit is 1 when the NDP is executing an instruction or when an unmasked exception (bits 0–5) is indicated. Execute the instruction FNSTSW AX, which copies the status word register to the AX register, to examine this bit available for testing.

**C3, C2, C1, C0—Condition codes:** The NDP sets these bits when a floating-point compare, test, examine, or math instruction is executed. The various combinations that occur are discussed under the relevant instructions in Chapter 8.

**TOP—Top-of-stack:** This field indicates which of the floating-point registers is currently identified as the top-of-stack. When a new value is pushed onto the register stack, the value of TOP is decremented by 1. When a value is popped from the stack, TOP is incremented by 1. The results of the increment or decrement are truncated to three bits to allow addressing of eight floating-point registers.

***ES—Error summary:*** The NDP sets this bit to 1 whenever a floating-point instruction generates an unmasked exception. Indication of such an exception is found in bits 0–5 of this register. The exception masks themselves are located in the control word register.

***SF—Stack fault:*** The NDP sets this bit to 1 if an instruction causes a stack overflow by pushing too many operands or a stack underflow by popping the stack when there are no more values. This field does not exist in the 80287, so floating-point code that must run on any possible 80386 configuration should not rely on having the bit. A stack fault also results in an invalid operation exception.

Before discussing each field, let's note a couple of things about bits 0–5 of the status word register. These bits correspond to exceptional conditions that can occur while floating-point instructions are being executed.

Whenever a condition represented by an exception bit occurs, the NDP first sets the appropriate bit in the status word register. Next, it checks the corresponding mask bit in the control word register. If the mask bit is 0 (unmasked), the NDP triggers the numeric exception. If the mask bit is 1 (masked), the NDP continues by executing the next instruction.

Additionally, the exception bits are "sticky." Once set, they remain set until the programmer loads the status word register with a new value. This lets the programmer write a series of numeric instructions and place a test for errors at the end of the instruction stream rather than after each instruction.

***PE—Precision exception:*** This exception occurs when the NDP cannot represent the exact result of a floating-point instruction. For example, the fraction $\frac{1}{3}$ cannot be represented exactly as a decimal fraction because it produces an infinitely repeating result. Any finite representation, such as 0.3, 0.333333333, or even 0.333333333333333333333333333333, is only an approximation. Similarly, the NDP cannot represent this fraction exactly in binary format. Dividing 1 by 3 results in the infinite binary fraction 0.01B.

This exception also occurs when a temp real number is converted to a lower precision and bits are lost in the conversion.

The precision exception is almost always masked because a rounded or truncated result will suffice in most cases.

***UE—Underflow exception:*** The underflow exception is triggered when the result of an operand is too small for the NDP to represent. For example, the smallest value that can be represented in the 80-bit extended-precision format is $3.37 \times 10^{-4932}$. Attempting to square a number such as $10^{-3000}$ results in an underflow exception.

***OE—Overflow exception:*** This exception is the converse of the underflow exception. It occurs when the result of a floating-point operation is too large for the NDP to represent. Like the precision exception, UE and OE can be generated when a normally representable number is converted to a format in which it is not representable.

***ZE—Zero divide exception:*** Whenever division by zero is attempted, the ZE exception occurs. This exception can be caused by floating-point operations other than the divide instruction, such as sine, cosine, remainder, and so on.

***DE—Denormal exception:*** This exception occurs whenever an operand of a floating-point instruction is a denormal. Denormal numbers are discussed earlier in this chapter.

***IE—Invalid operation exception:*** This exception traps all error conditions not handled by the previously discussed exceptions. These can include arithmetic faults (such as an attempt to take the square root of a negative number) or programmer faults (such as specifying a register that contains no value as an instruction operand).

### Control word register

A programmer modifies the CW (control word) register of the NDP to alter its behavior. The format of the control word register and the definition of each field follows:

| 15 | | | 12 | | | 8 | 7 | | | | | | 0 |
|---|---|---|---|---|---|---|---|---|---|---|---|---|---|
| X | X | X | 0 | RC | PC | X | X | PM | UM | OM | ZM | DM | IM |

***Bit 12 = 0 (infinity control on 80287):*** Bit 12 is ignored on the 80387 and 80486. On the 80287, this bit selects either affine (bit is on) or projective closure (bit is off). Affine closure allows the use of both positive and negative infinity. In projective closure, very large or very small numbers overflow to a single unsigned infinity. Only affine closure is supported by 80387 and 80486 NDP's.

***RC—Rounding control:*** This field specifies how the NDP handles values that it cannot represent exactly. The RC field can be set to one of the following modes:

00—Round toward nearest (choose even number if equidistant)

01—Round up (toward negative infinity)

10—Round down (toward positive infinity)

11—Round toward zero (truncate)

Node 00 (round nearest) is the default.

To see how the rounding control affects the results of a computation, assume that the NDP can represent only the integers −5 through +5. Figure 2-20 shows the results of rounding the values 2⅓, 1⅔, −1⅓, and −2⅓ in each rounding mode.

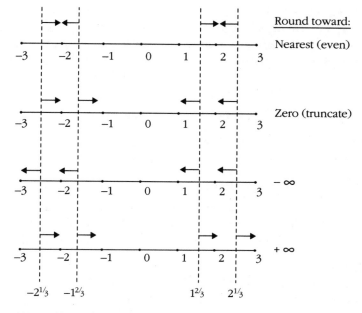

**Figure 2-20.** *Rounding control.*

*PC—Precision control:* The PC field tells the NDP which floating-point format to use when generating the results of add, subtract, multiply, divide, and square-root operations. This field can hold one of the following values:

00—Single-precision (24-bit significand)

01—Reserved for future coprocessors

10—Double-precision (53-bit significand)

11—Extended-precision (64-bit significand)

Node 11 is the default.

Instructions other than those affected by the PC field generate extended-precision results or have a precision specified by the operand.

*PM, UM, OM, ZM, DM, IM—Mask bits:* The remaining bits in the control word register are the mask bits for the exception conditions and correspond to bits 0–5 of the status word register. The mask bits are:

PM—Precision mask

UM—Underflow mask

OM—Overflow mask

ZM—Zero divide mask

DM—Denormal operand mask

IM—Invalid operation mask

## Tag word register

The remaining status register on the NDP is the 16-bit tag word register. This register consists of eight 2-bit fields, each corresponding to a floating-point register. T0 is the field for register 0 (not ST0), T1 is associated with register 1, and so on. Each tag field holds one of the following values, which give additional information about the contents of the corresponding register:

00—The register contains a valid floating-point number.

01—The register contains the value 0.0.

10—The register contains the value infinity, a denormal, or an invalid number.

11—The register is empty (unused).

The tag word register is normally not used by the programmer. A debugger that displays the contents of the floating-point stack must examine the contents of the tag word register to properly interpret the contents of the floating-point registers.

## Error pointer registers

The only other registers on the NDP are the error pointer registers. These registers are updated each time a new floating-point instruction is executed. Whenever a floating-point instruction causes an exception, these registers can be queried to determine which instruction is at fault. Note that no instructions directly address these registers. The store environment operation (FSTENV) copies the contents of all NDP status and error-pointer registers to memory, where the data can be examined.

The error pointer registers are necessary because of the parallel operation of the main execution unit and the NDP. The main execution unit, which is executing simpler, faster instructions, might be executing code in a different segment when the NDP generates an exception. The error pointer registers make it much easier to determine what went wrong when a floating-point exception occurs.

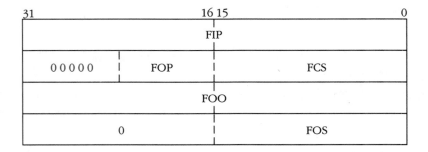

*FIP—Floating-point instruction pointer:* This register is loaded with the contents of EIP when a coprocessor instruction is executed.

*FCS—Floating-point code segment:* This register is loaded with the value of the CS register when a floating-point instruction is executed.

**FOP—*Floating-point opcode:*** This register is loaded with 11 bits of opcode information. A coprocessor instruction always has the following format:

First byte      Second byte

| 7 | | | | | | | 0 |
|---|---|---|---|---|---|---|---|
| 1 | 1 | 0 | 1 | 1 | ? | ? | ? |

| 7 | | | | | | | 0 |
|---|---|---|---|---|---|---|---|
| ? | ? | ? | ? | ? | ? | ? | ? |

(Optional bytes)

The second byte of the instruction is concatenated with the 3 low-order bits of the first byte to form the contents of the FOP register. Early versions of the 80386 did not generate this information for the 80387, nor is it available when the 80386 is used in protected mode. It might be simpler to use the FCS and FIP values to determine the opcode at fault, unless you know your code is running on an 80486.

**FOS—*Floating-point operand segment:*** This register contains the segment register of the memory operand (if any) referred to by the most recent floating-point instruction.

**FOO—*Floating-point operand offset:*** This register holds the offset (within the segment pointed to by FOS) of the memory operand (if any) referred to by the most recent coprocessor instruction.

# MEMORY ARCHITECTURE: SEGMENTATION

A segmented memory architecture is a hallmark of the Intel 8086 family of processors. The 80386 was the first of these processors in which segmentation was not considered an impediment to the programmer.

## Linear vs. Segmented Memory

The hardware interface between the CPU and memory is virtually the same in almost every computer. A set of address lines goes out from the processor to memory. The CPU places an address on the bus, and memory responds by returning the value stored at that location or by accepting a new value. Figure 3-1 shows the hardware relationship between the CPU and memory.

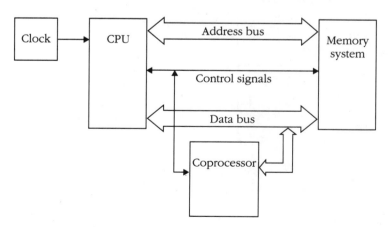

**Figure 3-1.** *CPU–memory interface.*

Because of the binary nature of the digital computer, a system with $n$ address lines allows the system to reference $2^n$ elements of memory. The hardware behaves in a *linear* fashion—that is, for each of the $2^n$ possible combinations of address lines, a separate memory element responds.

Most computers also have a linear *memory model.* They allow programmatic access to memory, beginning with address 0 and continuing through address $2^n - 1$. Theoretically, an application could read the byte at location 0, then read the next byte, and so on until it reads the last byte of memory in the system. This model parallels the hardware interface.

However, the 8086, 80286, 80386, and 80486 have a programmatic memory model different from the hardware memory model. These processors have a *segmented* memory model. To a program, the address space is divided into *segments,* and the program can access only data contained in those segments. Within each segment, addressing is linear, and the program can access byte 0, byte 1, byte 2, and so on. The addressing is relative to the start of the segment, however, and the hardware address associated with software address 0 is hidden from the programmer.

This approach to memory management is natural. Programs are typically divided into segments of code and data. A program can be made up of a single code segment and a single data segment, or of many code and data segments. In a multitasking environment, segmentation also isolates processes from one another. If *my* program can look at only my code and my data, it cannot illicitly modify *your* program's code or data. Figure 3-2 shows a multiprocessing system with many segments coexisting in memory.

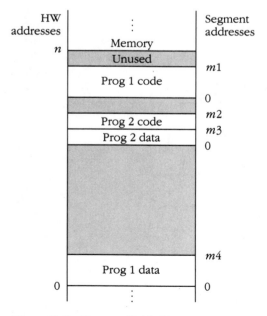

**Figure 3-2.** *Memory divided into segments.*

The 80386 and 80486 have six segment registers. The values in these registers determine the memory segments that a program can access. The CS register points to the segment that contains the program's code. CALL and JMP instructions implicitly refer to the current code segment. The DS register points to the program's main data area. For example, the instruction:

```
MOV     AL, [0]
```

copies the first byte (byte 0) of the data segment into register AL.

The stack segment (pointed to by register SS) is commonly (but not necessarily) the same segment as the data segment. The PUSH and POP instructions store data into or read data from the stack segment.

Three additional registers (ES, FS, and GS) point to auxiliary data that the program needs to access less frequently, such as COMMON variables in a FORTRAN program. You can apply a special prefix to an instruction that accesses the data segment register. The prefix causes the instruction to act on one of the additional segments instead. For example, the previous instruction might be written as:

```
MOV     AL, ES:[0]
```

to fetch the first byte from one of the alternate data segments, or even as:

```
MOV     AL, CS:[0]
```

to fetch the first byte from the code segment.

Previous generations of the 8086 family also dealt with segmented memory; however, these processors limited the size of a segment to 64 KB, which was often much too small. A single segment in the 80386 and in the 80486 can be as large as 4 gigabytes (GB).

An operating system designer can choose to simulate a linear memory model (also called a *flat* model) on the 80386 and 80486 by creating one very large code segment and one very large data segment and having all programs use the same values for CS and DS. This is a common technique when porting systems that have run on linear address machines. The UNIX operating system—with its VAX heritage—is typically implemented on linear memory machines.

# Virtual Addressing

Except when operating in real mode, the 80386 and 80486 are *virtual memory* processors. When an instruction requests the contents of a memory location, the instruction refers to the location not by an actual hardware memory address but by a *virtual address*. The virtual address is really a *name* for a memory location. The processor translates the location name into an appropriate physical location. The operating system must maintain the proper mapping between virtual and physical memory.

This concept is not as convoluted as it might sound. For example, suppose someone says to me, "Put this report on the boss's desk." In my particular department, that might mean, "Put this report on Simon Legree's desk." If, however, I transfer to a new department, I might be placing my report on Ebenezer Scrooge's desk. "The boss's desk" is a virtual location, and I can carry out the instruction to turn in my report even though the desk on which I place the report varies according to the circumstances.

A virtual address on the 80386 family is specified by two numbers, a *selector* and an *offset*. The selector is a 16-bit value that serves as a virtual name for a memory segment. It is the selector that is loaded into the segment registers (CS, DS, and so on). The offset is the distance from the beginning of the segment, and it is a 32-bit value. Examples of virtual addresses include:

| *Virtual Address* | *Interpreted Virtual Address* |
| --- | --- |
| 3F11:00000000 | Offset 0H from selector 3F11H |
| 01A9:0001FF00 | Offset 1FF00H from selector 01A9H |
| EC2C:31887004 | Offset 31887004H from selector EC2CH |

The CPU translates a virtual address to a single 32-bit number called a *linear address*. Figure 3-3 shows an example of address translation. This linear address goes out on the system bus unless the paging feature is enabled. Paging is another level of address translation and is discussed fully in Chapter 6.

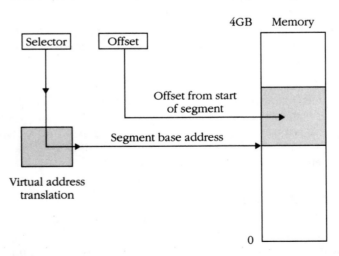

**Figure 3-3.** *Linear address translation.*

## Virtual-to-linear address translation

The CPU uses the selector as an index to a set of system tables called *descriptor tables*. A *descriptor* is a block of memory that describes the characteristics of a given element of the system. In the case of a memory segment, the characteristics include the segment's linear *base address, limit, access rights,* and *privilege level.*

The base address is the starting point in the segment's linear address space. The offset portion of a virtual address is added to the base address to generate the linear address of the desired memory element. Figure 3-4 illustrates an example. The virtual address 13A7:0010F405H is broken down into its segment and offset components. The system uses the selector 13A7H as an index into its descriptor tables. It pulls out a descriptor that says, for example, that the segment has a base address in the linear address space of 0032DD000H. The virtual address offset is combined with the base, and the resulting value, 33EC405H, is the translated linear address.

The linear address is a full 32-bit value in all members of the 80386 family; however, the 80386SX hardware supports only a 24-bit physical address. The 80386DX and 80486 hardware supports the full 32-bit linear address space ($2^{32}$, or 4 GB). The base address of a segment will always fall within this range. In the same way that the base address defines the starting point of a segment, the limit field defines the end point. The limit specifies the segment's last addressable byte. The processor checks every instruction that addresses memory to determine whether the instruction is attempting to read into or to write from memory within the boundaries of

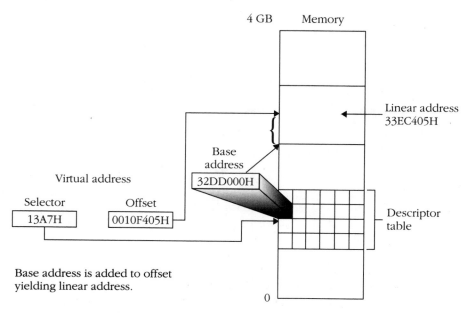

**Figure 3-4.** *Virtual-to-linear address translation.*

the segment's descriptor. An out-of-bounds reference causes an interrupt called a *general protection fault* to occur. Faults are discussed in the section on interrupts and exceptions in Chapter 5. The access rights field defines the type of segment and the privilege level required to access it.

## Segment descriptors

At this point, you probably visualize a descriptor as something like the item in Figure 3-5. Indeed, all the data in this figure is in the descriptor; however, because of space and compatibility constraints, the real thing is not quite so pretty. Figure 3-6 shows the actual format of a segment descriptor.

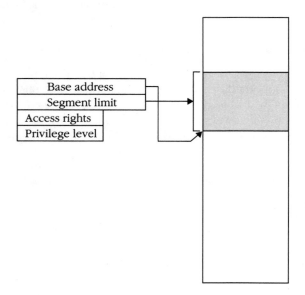

**Figure 3-5.** *Visualized descriptor.*

80386/80486

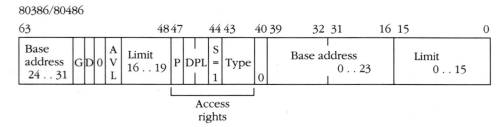

**Figure 3-6.** *Actual 80286/80386/80486 descriptors.* (continued)

**Figure 3-6.** *continued*

80286

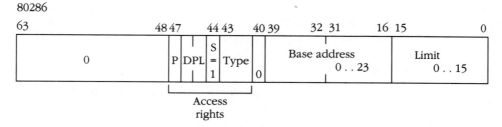

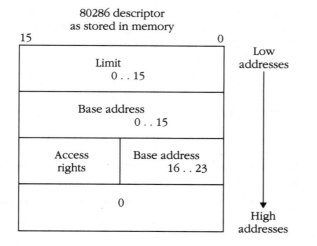

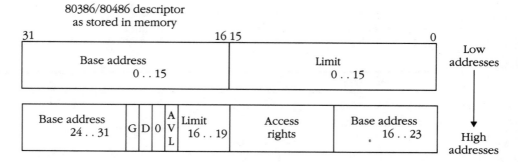

***Base address:*** The base address portion of the descriptor is the address of offset 0 in the segment. This field is 32 bits and is constructed from bytes 2, 3, 4, and 7 of the descriptor. In the 80286, the base address is only 24 contiguous bits. However, Intel specified that bytes 6 and 7 of the 80286 descriptor were to be set to 0 to ensure that 80286 code would run properly on an 80386/80486.

*Limit:* The limit field determines the last addressable unit of the segment. The limit field is 20 bits, comprising bytes 0 and 1 of the descriptor and the low-order four bits of byte 6. Again, the split occurs because of the difference in the limit field sizes between the 80286 and the 80386/80486. Those of you handy with binary arithmetic might note that a 20-bit limit field allows the addressing of only $2^{20}$, or approximately 1 million, items.

At first glance, this seems to mean that an 80386/80486 segment is limited to 1 megabyte. This is not the case, although the segment *is* limited to 1 million *items*. The G bit in byte 6 of the descriptor stands for *granularity,* and 80386/80486 segments come in two forms, *byte* granular (G = 0) and *page* granular (G = 1).

The terms *granularity* and *resolution* are similar in meaning. A high-resolution image is made of very tiny items, and a lower-resolution image is made of larger items. The limit of a byte granular segment is measured in bytes; a page granular segment is measured in larger pieces called pages.

A page is $2^{12}$, or 4096, bytes. This makes the limit on the size of a segment $2^{20}$ pages of $2^{12}$ bytes, for a total of $2^{32}$ bytes (4 GB). Again, a segment of code ported from the 80286 is always a byte granular segment because the seventh and eighth descriptor bytes are required to be 0.

For example, assume that the DS register points to a byte granular segment with a limit of 001FH. The size of the segment is 20H (32 decimal) bytes, and the last addressable byte of that segment is byte 001FH.

| Illegal Instruction | Reason |
| --- | --- |
| MOV EAX, [1234H] | Memory address beyond limit |
| MOV EAX, [001DH] | Size of item read extends beyond limit |
| MOV AL, [0020H] | Memory address beyond limit |
| MOV [001FH], AX | Size of item written beyond limit |

| Legal Instruction | Reason |
| --- | --- |
| MOV EAX, [0000H] | Last byte read is 3H |
| MOV EAX, [001CH] | Last byte read is 1FH |
| MOV AL, [001FH] | Last byte read is 1FH |
| MOV [001EH], AX | Last byte written is 1FH |

Now imagine a page granular segment with a limit of 0000H. The size of the segment is one page, and page 0 is the last addressable page. A page has 1000H (4096 decimal) bytes in it, so the last addressable byte is 0FFFH.

| Illegal Instruction | Reason |
|---|---|
| MOV  EAX, [1234H] | Memory address beyond limit |
| MOV  EAX, [0FFDH] | Size of item read extends beyond limit |
| MOV  AL, [1020H] | Memory address beyond limit |
| MOV  [0FFFH], AX | Size of item written beyond limit |

| Legal Instruction | Reason |
|---|---|
| MOV  EAX, [0000H] | Last byte read is 3H |
| MOV  EAX, [0FFCH] | Last byte read is 0FFFH |
| MOV  AL, [0FFFH] | Last byte read is 0FFFH |
| MOV  [0FFEH], AX | Last byte written is 0FFFH |

***Access rights:*** The access rights portion of the descriptor has the following format:

```
7  6  5  4  3  2  1  0
P | DPL | S | TYPE | A
```

The P bit stands for "present." It is set to 1 when the segment indicated by the selector is present in physical memory. In a virtual memory system, the operating system can move the contents of some segments to disk if physical memory is full. It then marks the descriptor as not present by resetting the P bit to 0. If an application loads a selector into a segment register and the descriptor associated with the selector has P = 0, the not-present interrupt (11 decimal) is generated. The operating system then looks for a free area of physical memory, copies the contents of the segment from disk back into memory, updates the descriptor with the new base address, sets P to 1, and restarts the interrupted instruction.

The DPL field contains the privilege level of the descriptor. The privilege level ranges from 0 (most privileged) through 3 (least privileged). A task can access segments of equal or lesser privilege. A task can only read data from or store data into segments of equal or lesser privilege. A task can call only code segments of the same privilege; however, access to segments of higher privilege can be granted indirectly via the gate, a feature of the protection mechanism. A task can never invoke a code segment of lesser privilege.

The privilege level of a task, called the *current privilege level* (CPL), is the privilege level of the currently executing code segment. Typically, the most secure portions of the operating system run at level 0. Other system software might run at a less privileged level, and applications typically run at level 3. (See Chapter 5 for a description of the protection mechanism.)

The S (segment) bit is always set to 1 for a memory segment. When S is equal to 0, a descriptor describes an object other than a memory segment. These objects are described in Chapter 5.

The TYPE field indicates the types of operations allowed on the segment. Valid values for TYPE are:

| | |
|---|---|
| 0 | Read-only data segment |
| 1 | Read/write data segment |
| 2 | Unused |
| 3 | Read/write expand-down data segment |
| 4 | Execute-only code segment |
| 5 | Execute/readable code segment |
| 6 | Execute-only "conforming" code segment |
| 7 | Execute/readable "conforming" code segment |

The type indicator defines the access rules applied to a segment. The CS register cannot be loaded with a selector of a segment of type data (0–3). No program can modify a segment that cannot be written. Segments that are not readable can be executed but not read as data. An attempt to violate any of these rules results in a protection fault. Conforming segments are discussed in Chapter 5. Expand-down segments are covered later in this chapter.

The processor sets the A (accessed) bit when the selector for the descriptor is loaded into a segment register. The operating system can use this bit to find out which segments are not frequently used and can therefore be swapped to disk if necessary.

***Additional fields:*** Four additional fields in the segment descriptor are located in the high-order nibble of byte 6.

The G bit, described previously, regulates the granularity of the segment.

Bit 6 is referred to as the D bit if the descriptor is for an executable segment or as the B bit if the descriptor type is a data segment. The D bit is set to 1 to indicate the default, or *native mode,* instruction set. When D is equal to 0, the code segment is presumed to be an 80286 code segment, and it runs with 16-bit offsets and the 80286-compatible instruction set.

The B bit is set to 1 in any data segment whose size is greater than 64 KB.

Bit 5 must be set to 0. It is reserved for use in a future Intel microprocessor.

Bit 4 (AVL) is available for use by system programmers. Possible uses include marking segments for garbage collection or indicating segments whose base addresses should not be modified.

Expand-down segments, indicated by TYPE = 2 or TYPE = 3, are a special kind of data segment designed for use with the stack. Figure 3-7 shows a stack that resides in its own segment.

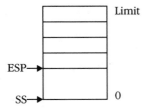

**Figure 3-7.** *Stack residing in its own segment.*

As more data is pushed onto the stack, the stack pointer (ESP) nears 0. If too much data is pushed onto the stack, the program attempts to decrement ESP beyond 0, resulting in a stack fault. At this point, the operating system has no choice but to terminate the program.

Placing the stack in an expand-down segment rather than in a normal data segment, however, will change the way memory is addressed inside the segment.

Although normal segments are addressed beginning at 0 and extending to *limit*, expand-down segments begin at *limit* + 1 and extend to FFFFFFFFH. Figure 3-8 illustrates the difference.

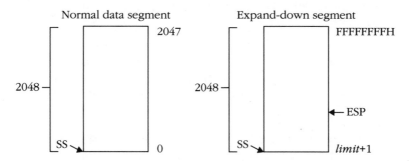

**Figure 3-8.** *Normal data segments and expand-down segments.*

The advantage of this approach is that when the stack pointer is decremented past the limit and triggers a stack fault, the operating system can extend the size of the segment and decrement the limit. The faulting instruction is then restarted, allowing the program to run with a larger stack segment. Figure 3-9 on the following page shows how this is accomplished.

Notice that when a descriptor for an expand-down segment is created, the base address must be set to the linear address of the first byte after the *end* of the segment rather than to the address of the start of the segment. Because addressing arithmetic is limited to 32 bits, large offset values can be viewed as if they were negative numbers. For example:

$$base + FFFFFFFFH \cong base + -1 \cong base -1$$

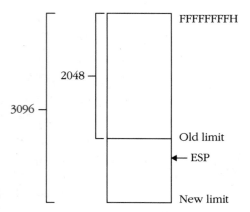

**Figure 3-9.** *Extending the size of the segment.*

## Descriptor tables

All the descriptors are grouped together in descriptor tables. The two system descriptor tables are the Global Descriptor Table (GDT) and the Interrupt Descriptor Table (IDT). The IDT contains no segment descriptors, so it is not discussed here.

A full description of the IDT and other facets of the protection mechanism is given in Chapter 5.

An operating system can also implement various Local Descriptor Tables (LDTs). Segment descriptors are found either in the GDT or in the currently active LDT. The selector used to identify the descriptor determines which table to use. The location of the tables in memory is determined by the GDTR, IDTR, and LDTR registers.

## Selectors

A segment, as we have seen, is *described* by a descriptor that has been *selected* by a selector. A selector is made of three components, as shown in the following illustration:

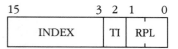

The INDEX and TI (table indicator bit) fields tell the CPU where to find the descriptor. When the TI bit is set to 0, the descriptor is in the GDT. When TI is set to 1, the processor uses the current LDT instead. The INDEX field identifies which entry in the descriptor table to use. Be aware that the RPL (requested privilege level) can differ from the actual descriptor privilege level. The reason for this is discussed in detail in Chapter 5.

As an example of how the selection mechanism works, assume that the value 1A3BH is a valid selector. The selector is divided as follows:

Selector = 1A3BH          INDEX = 0347H (839 decimal)

0001101000111011B         TI = 0        (GDT)

                          RPL = 3       (lowest)

To use a selector, hardware must first break it into three fields: INDEX, TI, and RPL.

Figure 3-10 illustrates how hardware separates a selector into its components.

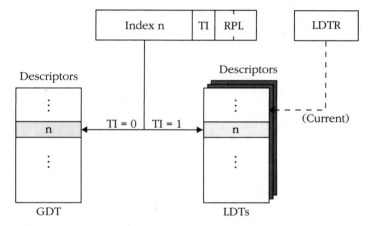

**Figure 3-10.** *Hardware's separation of selector components.*

# Games Segments Play

By making use of the virtual addressing capabilities, an operating system designer can provide a number of interesting features. One such feature is virtual memory. Virtual memory gives the appearance of physical memory where none exists.

To illustrate how this can be accomplished, imagine an environment such as the one pictured in Figure 3-11 on the following page. The figure represents a multitasking system in which four tasks are to be run. One MB of memory is available for running the four applications. Application A requires 400 KB, application B requires 100 KB, application C requires 400 KB, and application D requires 200 KB. Also assume that half of the application space is dedicated to code and that the other half is required for data.

Because the combined memory requirement of the four applications exceeds 1 MB, they cannot all be in memory simultaneously. After A, B, and C are loaded, not enough room remains for all of task D. (See Figure 3-12 on the following page.) The operating system loads the code portion of task D but not the data segment. It does, however, create descriptors for both the code and the data segments of task D, marking the data segment descriptor as not present.

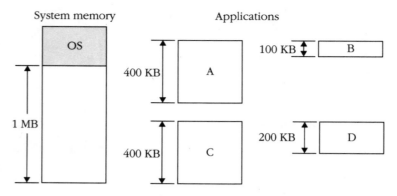

**Figure 3-11.** *Initial state of a multitasking system.*

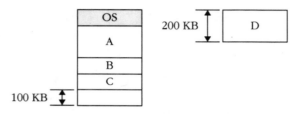

**Figure 3-12.** *Initial tasks loaded into memory.*

This is a multitasking system, so the starting address (CS:EIP) of each task is passed to the scheduler portion of the operating system, and execution begins. Task A starts and is allowed to execute for a few milliseconds. The scheduler then takes control and allows task B to run for a few milliseconds. However, part way through its allotted time slice, task B reads the keyboard for input from the operator. Because no keys have yet been pressed, the operating system takes control and marks task B as *suspended.*

The scheduler then gives control to task C, which runs through its allotted execution time. Control now passes to task D. It begins to execute, but as soon as it tries to refer to the data segment, the processor generates the not-present interrupt.

The operating system determines which task was executing when the interrupt occurred and what caused the interrupt. It determines that task D needs access to its data segment, so it evaluates the status of the other tasks. Task B is suspended, so the operating system decides to temporarily remove it from memory to make room for the data segment of task D.

The memory image of B is written to disk, and the descriptors for B are marked as not present. Task B is said to have been swapped out, and operating systems that implement virtual memory in a similar manner are implementing swapping.

The data segment for D is copied into memory at the physical location just vacated by B, and the descriptor for D is updated to reflect the new base address and to show that the segment is now present in memory. Figure 3-13 reflects the new state of the system.

Descriptor table

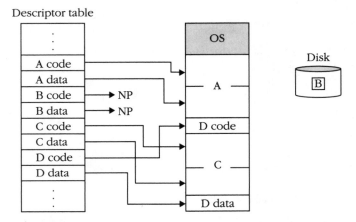

**Figure 3-13.** *Swapping tasks B and D.*

The scheduler now rotates execution time among tasks A, C, and D. At some point the computer operator sees the prompt for input from task B and in response presses a key on the keyboard. This action causes a hardware interrupt, and the operating system realizes that it must now schedule task B. However, because none of the other tasks are suspended, the system might choose to suspend task A temporarily.

Because task B is small, it displaces only part of task A. The code segment of task A is marked as not-present, task B is swapped in, and the descriptors for tasks A and B are updated as shown in Figure 3-14 on the following page. Notice that task B is now running at a different physical address than when it began. This is invisible to the application, however, because the selectors loaded into the segment registers do not change and because the memory offsets used by the instructions in the code segment are relative to the starting point of the segment, regardless of the physical origin of the segment.

The system will continue to operate as previously described, with occasional swapping and shifting of segments. If no external condition exists that causes a segment to swap, the operating system might swap segments, based either on which tasks have run the longest or on another system of priority.

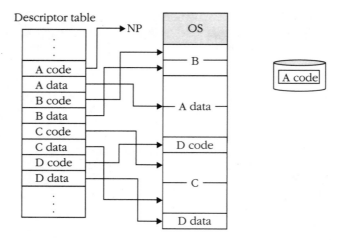

**Figure 3-14.** *Swapping tasks A and B.*

## Performance considerations

As the previous example shows, virtual memory doesn't create RAM out of thin air; it uses *secondary* storage, usually disk, to supplement the *primary* (RAM) storage and give the appearance of more primary storage than exists in the system. The cost of keeping up appearances is the amount of time it takes to move data between primary and secondary storage. The more time the system has to spend swapping, the less time it can spend executing the applications. In extreme cases, a system can be so overextended that it spends all its time swapping segments in and out. This pathological situation is called *thrashing*.

An operating system designer can improve the performance of a virtual memory system. For example, in the Intel protection mechanism, code segments are immutable. Because the contents of a code segment do not change, it doesn't have to be written to disk when swapped out. You can re-create the contents from the original executable image of the program. Only swapping in requires access to secondary memory. The operating system, therefore, can swap code segments twice as fast as it can swap data segments. Actually, if you recall the contents of a descriptor, you will remember that certain kinds of data segments can be marked as read-only. As with code segments, read-only data segments do not have to be written to secondary storage when swapped out.

Another trick that designers can use also relies on knowledge about code segments. The technique of *segment sharing* lets two or more tasks share the same code. This is primarily effective in multiuser systems. In the previous example, assume that tasks A, B, C, and D represent users running applications. Suppose that users A and C are running the same application, perhaps a spreadsheet. Now users A and C are operating on different data and require separate data segments. They are, however, executing the same code. Figure 3-15 shows how all four applications can fit in physical memory in this situation. The users maintain separate descriptors for their code and data, but the base addresses for the code segments of A and C point to the same location.

Descriptor table

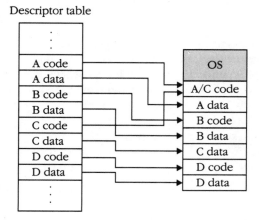

**Figure 3-15.** *Tasks A, B, C, and D in physical memory.*

Finally, a segment-oriented virtual memory system can provide a way to compact memory. Compacting memory helps solve a problem called *fragmentation*. Fragmentation occurs when memory that is not contiguous is available to run additional applications. To put it another way, the pieces of available memory are small and scattered throughout physical memory, and to be useful they need to be next to one another. Figure 3-16 illustrates this problem. Because applications deal with virtual addresses, they are not affected by a change in location. The process does take up CPU time, however.

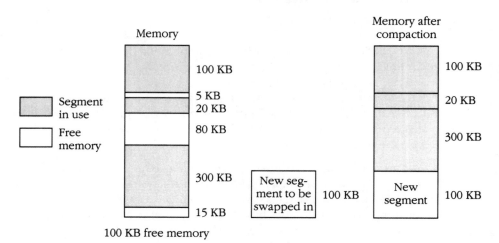

**Figure 3-16.** *Memory fragmentation.*

## Why bother?

Because virtual memory is plagued with potential performance problems and adds to the complexity of operating systems by forcing them to deal with fragmentation and with identifying shareable segments, you might be tempted to ask, "Is it worth the effort?" In most cases, the answer is "Yes."

One clear advantage of virtual memory is that a user doesn't have to spend money for extra memory simply to get an application to run. Any application will run in existing memory; it will simply run more slowly if it has to be swapped out. Let's say that I have a system with 2 MB of physical memory and that 90 percent of my applications fit into physical memory. However, 10 percent of the time I run an application that requires 5 MB of memory. Without virtual memory, I can't run the large application unless I spend the extra money to buy 3 MB of memory that will remain unused 90 percent of the time. With virtual memory, I can at least run the application and decide whether I want to spend money to improve its performance.

Virtual memory also makes life easier for the application designer. What if you are writing a program that manipulates a large array? If virtual memory is not available, you have to worry about how much memory your typical user will have and how to make your program fit into a system of that size. As a designer, you can no longer worry about simply solving the problem at hand (the array manipulation). You must also be concerned about breaking your program into pieces that will fit on the typical system. The complexity of your application increases, and the application is thus more likely to contain bugs.

This situation might be likened to giving a speech simultaneously in two different languages. By letting someone else handle the translation, you can concentrate on your job—presenting your information.

## The dark side of the force

So far, only the advantages of segmentation have been discussed. Let's take another look at segments and see if we can uncover some problem areas. One advantage of segmentation is virtual addressing. The application deals with selectors, whereas the linear memory address for the segment is in the descriptor. Thus, every time a selector is loaded into a segment register, the contents of the descriptor must be fetched as well. Every instruction that causes a segment register to be loaded also causes the 8-byte descriptor for the segment to load. In addition, the descriptor is marked as accessed when it is loaded, so a memory write is required to set the bit in the descriptor.

At a minimum, therefore, a segment register load has an overhead of two memory read cycles and one memory write cycle in addition to any memory cycles required to fetch the operand of the load instruction. Because of this and the protection checking that the CPU does based on the type of segment, size of descriptor table, and privilege level, loading a segment register can take as long as 22 clocks as opposed to the typical 2 clocks that it takes to load a general-purpose register.

Another advantage of segmentation is the limit checking that the processor performs. If a data object such as an array is placed in its own segment, the CPU monitors all references to the object and triggers an interrupt if any instruction refers to a point beyond the bounds of the object. Limit checking is an excellent tool for helping programmers discover flaws in their programs. Unfortunately, using this tool means having many data segments. Having many data segments implies many segment register load operations, which slow down the program. You must also deal with 48-bit pointers—16 bits of selector and 32 bits of offset.

The 80386 and 80486 do not provide many instructions for handling these irregularly sized items, nor do many programming languages. Consequently, they are awkward to manipulate, and they cause more work for the programmer.

Finally, you must deal with the problem of fragmentation. Because segments come in odd sizes, the operating system must work harder to arrange physical memory space in which to load applications.

# Summary

As you have seen, segmentation is a mixed blessing. On the one hand, it provides a method for implementing virtual memory and a mechanism for implementing a secure operating system via privilege levels, and the segment limits assist programmers in tracking bugs that arise from invalid pointers or array boundary errors. On the other hand, segmentation gives rise to unwieldy 48-bit pointers, extracts a performance penalty, and can cause fragmentation when used to implement virtual memory.

The flexibility of the 80386 family offers system designers three choices. You can ignore segmentation completely by creating only one code segment and one data segment that encompass the entire address space. You can use a limited form of segmentation in which only two segments, code and data, exist for every user or task on the system. In this instance, the application sees a uniform address space, and only the operating system needs to deal with segments. Or you can implement a fully segmented system in which each large data object and each module of code is in a separate segment.

Each implementation has advantages. The first method gives you an architecture similar to the M68000 or VAX. Although it might seem that you lose the capability to implement virtual memory with this method, you can implement a form of virtual memory other than the one described here by using paging, which is discussed in Chapter 6. A system of this design, however, loses the privilege-level protection features provided by segmentation.

The second method strikes a balance between the other two. Protection is provided on a task-by-task basis, and virtual memory can be implemented through segmentation, paging, or both.

The third method is the most similar to that provided by OS/2 on the 80286 and to programming in the large memory model. This type of system can provide a very secure environment, but the system will run somewhat slower.

One beauty of the 80386 family is that it supports these divergent environments and allows designers to build systems that meet their needs, whether those needs be for high security or for high performance.

# 4

# THE BASIC
# INSTRUCTION
# SET

The 80386 family of processors are classic *stored program,* or *von Neumann,* processors—that is, the memory attached to the CPU stores not only data to be operated on but the instructions that specify the operations. The term von Neumann is used in honor of the mathematician John von Neumann, who wrote a series of papers in the mid-1940s outlining the design of stored program computers. Almost all commercially available computers have designs based on the von Neumann model, and those using the 80386 and the 80486 microprocessors are no exception.

Built into every stored program computer is a set of commands that cause the CPU to read from a location in memory, interpret the contents as an instruction (that is, as a command to perform some function), execute the function, and start the cycle over again. Because this sequence is often implemented in microcode, it is commonly referred to as the *microcycle.*

In one of the earliest stored program computers, the EDVAC, each machine instruction was broken down into five fields: A bit pattern in one field designated the operation to be performed, two fields designated input operands, one field specified where the result was to be stored, and the final field specified the location of the next instruction. Computer designers soon learned that if they placed one instruction after another, they could eliminate the field that specified the address of the next instruction. A register called the program counter or instruction pointer was used to point to the next instruction and was incremented to point to the next one as soon as each instruction was fetched.

This method has never been modified, and the typical microcycle can now be expressed algorithmically like this:

top:

    fetch the instruction at EIP

    increment EIP by the size (in bytes) of the instruction

    execute the instruction

    goto top

This is, of course, a simple view of the microcycle. In actuality, it is much more complex because of the parallelism built into the 80386 family (see Chapter 1) and because of the necessity of saving the state of the processor if an instruction faults and has to be restarted. However, the basic algorithm is all that is necessary to understand the process.

# Instruction Format

Instructions are stored in memory in the same way that characters, floating-point numbers, integers, or any other type of data is stored in memory. The value 0F5H, for example, is the encoding for the CMC (complement carry flag) instruction. An instruction can range from 1 byte to 16 bytes in length.

In general, the format of an 80386 or 80486 instruction looks like this:

| opcode | mod r/m | s-i-b | displ | data |
|--------|---------|-------|-------|------|

The opcode is 1 or 2 bytes. The mod r/m and s-i-b bytes specify the operands and memory addressing modes. The displ (displacement) field is part of the memory address and can be 1, 2, or 4 bytes. The data field specifies an immediate operand value and can also be 1, 2, or 4 bytes. As many as four prefix-bytes can precede the opcode field.

Not all fields are present in all instructions. The CMC instruction, as shown previously, consists of only a single opcode byte. The instruction:

```
XCHG EAX, EBX
```

consists of only the opcode and mod r/m fields. All fields are present in the instruction:

```
ADD [EBP+8][ESI*4], 17
```

Appendix D specifies the bit patterns used to encode instructions, and Appendix E contains a table that lets you decode bit patterns into the original assembly language mnemonics.

# Instruction Operands

The instructions stored in memory command the CPU to manipulate one or more *operands*. Instruction operands can be specified in one of five ways: They can be *implicit, register, immediate, I/O,* or *memory reference* operands.

## Implicit operands

An operand is implicit if the instruction itself specifies it. The CLI instruction, for example, operates on the IF bit in the EFLAGS register. The programmer does not have to specify anything beyond the instruction. The stack is an implicit operand in a number of instructions—for example, PUSH, POP, CALL, and IRET. However, because the stack resides in memory, I will discuss stack operands in the section on memory reference operands. The following are examples of instructions that have implicit operands.

| *Instruction* | *Explanation* |
|---|---|
| AAA | Adjust register AL after ASCII add |
| CMC | Complement the value of the carry flag |
| CLD | Clear direction flag to 0 |

## Register operands

An instruction with a register operand performs an action on the value that is stored in one of the internal registers (shown in Figure 4-1 on the following page). Specify register operands by using the name of the register in the operand field of the instruction. Notice that not all registers are legal operands for all instructions. The general registers (EAX, CL, and so on) are most commonly used in data manipulation instructions. You cannot, for example, increment the contents of a segment register or use a control or debug register to store a memory address.

The following examples illustrate typical instructions using register operands.

| *Instruction* | *Explanation* |
|---|---|
| INC   ESI | Add 1 to contents of ESI |
| SUB   ECX, ECX | Subtract ECX from itself, leaving 0 |
| MOV  AL, DL | Copy contents of DL into AL |
| MOV  EAX, CR0 | Copy CR0 contents into EAX |
| CALL EDI | Invoke subroutine whose address is in EDI |

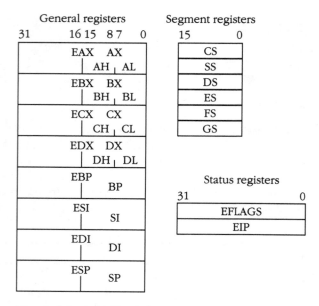

**Figure 4-1.** *80386/80486 register set.*

## Immediate operands

An immediate operand is specified when a value is part of the instruction itself. Consider the instruction ADD EAX, 3. In addition to the register operand EAX, the numeric value 3 is coded in the instruction and is stored in the code segment with the bit pattern that represents ADD. Other examples of instructions that use immediate operands include:

| Instruction | Explanation |
| --- | --- |
| MOV EAX, 7 | Store the value 7 in register EAX |
| AND CL, 0F0H | Mask off the low-order bits of CL |
| BT EDI, 3 | Copy bit 3 of EDI to carry flag |
| JC 3C1H | Branch to offset 3C1H if CF is set |

## I/O operands

External devices that transfer data from the computer to another environment are called I/O (input/output) devices. Typically, a processor communicates with these devices via a special address. The most straightforward way is for the device to have its own address (or set of addresses) called *I/O ports*. I/O addressing is similar to memory addressing, but different hardware control lines are activated. In addition, the processor sensibly refrains from attempting to cache values read from or written to I/O ports. The 80386 and 80486 each support a total of 65,536 separate I/O addresses.

I/O communication is done in 8-bit, 16-bit, or 32-bit quantities. I/O addresses must be aligned on even boundaries for word I/O and *mod 4* boundaries for doubleword I/O. The accumulator is always the source or the destination for the I/O instruction, and the I/O port is specified with an immediate operand or by the contents of the DX register. Notice that I/O ports expressed as immediate operands cannot exceed 8 bits, or a value of 0FFH. Examples of instructions that use I/O operands include:

| *Instruction* | *Explanation* |
| --- | --- |
| IN    AL, 04H | Input a byte from port 04H |
| OUT  1CH, AX | Output a word to port 1CH |
| IN    AX, DX | Input a word from port specified by DX |
| IN    EAX, DX | Input a doubleword from port specified by DX |

## Memory reference operands

To operate on the contents of memory, you must specify the address of the data value you want to use. The 80386 family provides a number of *addressing modes*. There is rarely a performance penalty for using a complex addressing mode, so use the addressing mode that is most appropriate to your program's needs.

When you specify a memory address, you specify the offset from the beginning of the appropriate segment. Address 0 is the first byte of the memory segment, address 1 is the second byte, and so on, regardless of the segment's physical starting address. Chapter 3 contains a detailed description of how segmentation is used to generate memory addresses.

By default, the segment used in most instructions is the one pointed to by the DS register. Forcing an instruction to operate on values in other segments is possible, however, by programming a segment prefix opcode immediately before the instruction. Normally, the instruction MOV AL, [0] reads the first byte of the data segment into register AL. By applying a segment prefix, you can force the data to be fetched from another segment. The instructions:

```
SS:
MOV    AL, [0]
```

load the AL register with the first byte of the stack segment. Although the segment prefix byte comes before the instruction in the code stream, for readability the prefix is usually written as part of the memory operand. The previous example is normally written:

```
MOV    AL, SS:[0]
```

### Direct addressing

The simplest form of memory reference is called *direct addressing,* where the instruction itself includes the location of the operand. The location is specified as a 16-bit or 32-bit offset in the current segment. This offset is also known as the *displacement*. The table below shows three examples of direct addressing. The brackets differentiate data values (no brackets) and memory addresses (brackets).

| Instruction | Explanation |
|---|---|
| INC   DWORD PTR [17H] | Add 1 to the 32-bit value at offset 17 |
| MOV  AL, [1A33D4H] | Copy the memory byte to register AL |
| SHL   BYTE PTR [1FFH], 3 | Shift the memory byte left 3 bits |

In the examples in this chapter, I generally use numeric memory addresses to illustrate where the address values are used in an instruction. You might never need to use numeric memory addresses. Your programming environment will provide assemblers and compilers that name locations in memory, and you will use these names in your program. This technique is called *symbolic addressing*.

Symbolic addressing has a number of advantages over absolute numeric addressing. You are much less likely to make a mistake if you can refer to a variable by a mnemonic name, such as *queue_top*, rather than by a number, such as 32081A3H. Also, if you use symbolic names, the assembler keeps track of the type of the data item. For example, the opcode for the increment instruction is INC, but the same opcode can apply to 8-bit, 16-bit, or 32-bit operands. If you define a symbolic variable, the correct instruction encoding is chosen for you. Without symbolic addressing, you must specify both the size and the location of the operand. For example, notice the difference between these two operations:

```
        INC     DWORD PTR [15F2H] ; 32-bit operand
```

and

```
COUNT   DD      ?                   ; allocate 32 bits with name COUNT
        INC     COUNT               ; increment variable
```

Here are some additional examples of instructions that use symbolic addressing.

| Instruction | Explanation |
|---|---|
| COUNT DD   10 | Reserve 32-bit value, initial value 10 |
| FLAG    DW   ? | Reserve a single word |
| NAME   DB   20 DUP (?) | Reserve 20 consecutive bytes |
| DEC  COUNT | Subtract 1 from the value at COUNT |
| MOV  AL, NAME | Copy first byte of NAME |
| MOV  AL, NAME[1] | Copy second byte of NAME to AL |
| OR    FLAG, 4000H | Set one bit in the specified word |

## Based addressing

In based addressing, a register holds the address of an operand. The register containing the memory address is called the base register, and you can use any of the seven general registers as a base register. When you use ESP or EBP as a base register, the address is assumed to be an offset from the stack segment (SS) rather than from the data segment (DS). You specify based addressing by placing the register name in brackets, as the following examples illustrate.

```
MOV     AL, [ECX]           ; copy byte of memory at ECX into AL
DEC     WORD PTR [ESI]      ; decrement 16-bit word at ESI
XCHG    EBX, [EBX]          ; swap contents of EBX with dword at EBX
CALL    [EAX]               ; EAX holds pointer to
                            ; address of subroutine
```

## Base plus displacement addressing

Base plus displacement addressing is a variant of based addressing that uses a base register to specify a nearby location. An integer offset then modifies the base address to form the final destination. Base plus displacement addressing is commonly used in addressing components of data structures and in stack-relative addressing. For example, if ESI points to a record of type *point,* where *point* is a structure whose first element is the $x$ coordinate and whose second element is the $y$ coordinate, then you could use the instruction MOV EAX, [ESI+4] to fetch the $y$ coordinate.

Similarly, because the base pointer EBP commonly points to the current stack frame, any values pushed onto the stack can be addressed by an offset from EBP. Offsets can be positive or negative and are interpreted as signed 32-bit integers. The assembler provides a construct called a *struc* that makes keeping track of offsets within data structures simple. Here is the above "point" data type example redone symbolically:

```
POINT   struc                   ; define record layout
    X       DD      ?
    Y       DD      ?
POINT   ends
CORNER  POINT<>                 ; reserve memory
        LEA     ESI, CORNER     ; get address of variable
        MOV     EAX, [ESI].X    ; fetch the x component
        INC     [ESI].Y         ; increment the y component
```

## Index plus displacement addressing

Indexing is implemented by using the contents of a register as a component of an address. Any of the seven general registers (except ESP) is a legal index register. Index plus displacement addressing is most useful in dealing with arrays. A direct address points to the starting address of the array, and the index specifies the element of the array. Here are three examples of index plus displacement addressing:

```
MOV     AL, 7ACH[ESI]       ; get byte of array based at 7AC w/index
IMUL    VECTOR[ECX]         ; multiply EAX by element indexed by ECX
SUB     ARRAY[EAX], 2       ; subtract 2 from element of array
```

It might appear that index plus displacement is the same as base plus displacement. However, indexing offers a capability that based addressing does not have.

The C language code fragment in the following example computes the sum of the squares of an array.

```
int V[V_MAX];
        register int i;

        sum = 0;
        for (i = 0; i < V_MAX; i++)
        sum += v[i] * v[i];
```

Assuming that the size of an integer is 32 bits, two separate values are required to progress through the array: the index variable $i$ and the offset in memory of V[$i$]. For example, when $i$ is 3, the address of V[3] is the address of V plus 12 ($4 \times 3$) bytes. Every time $i$ is used as an index into the array, it must be multiplied by the size of the array element. The assembly code to execute the above loop might look like this:

```
        XOR     ECX, ECX        ; clear ECX (counter) to 0
        MOV     SUM, ECX        ; copy 0 to SUM
L1:     CMP     ECX, V_MAX      ; is counter > or = V_MAX?
        JGE     DONE            ;   yes - go on
        MOV     EAX, ECX        ; copy counter to EAX
        SHL     EAX, 2          ; shift EAX 2 bits (multiply by 4)
        MOV     EAX, V[EAX]     ; load contents of array into EAX
        IMUL    EAX             ; square the array element
        ADD     SUM, EAX        ; compute the sum
        INC     ECX             ; bump the counter
        JMP     L1              ; loop back to the top
DONE:
```

The highlighted code shows the conversion from array index to memory offset and the addressing of the selected item.

The 80386 and the 80486 provide a special optimization for arrays whose elements are 1, 2, 4, or 8 bytes. The processor adjusts the index to produce a memory offset. This adjustment is called *scaling* and is indicated in assembly language by placing a multiply operation in the brackets that enclose the index register. The above example becomes:

```
        XOR     ECX, ECX        ; clear ECX (counter) to 0
        MOV     SUM, ECX        ; copy 0 to SUM
L1:     CMP     ECX, V_MAX      ; is counter > or = V_MAX?
        JGE     DONE            ;   yes - go on
        MOV     EAX, V[ECX*4]   ; load contents of array into EAX
        IMUL    EAX             ; square the array element
        ADD     SUM, EAX        ; compute the sum
        INC     ECX             ; bump the counter
        JMP     L1              ; loop back to the top
DONE:
```

The second version of the program does not require the index value to be copied and multiplied, so the program runs faster. Also, the instruction:

```
MOV       EAX, V[ECX*4]
```

takes no longer to execute than the instruction:

```
MOV       EAX, V[EAX]
```

When EBP is used as a scaled index register, it does not force the memory reference relative to the stack segment as it does when used as a base register. When an instruction specifies both a base register and an index register and one of them is EBP, EBP is assumed to be the base register unless a scale factor is present. If a scale factor exists, EBP is assumed to be the index register. The following table shows four examples:

| *Instruction* | *Explanation* |
|---|---|
| ADD  [ECX][EBP], 7 | EBP is base, SS segment used |
| MOV  AX, ARRAY[EBP] | EBP is base, SS segment used |
| MOV  EAX, [ECX][EBP*4] | ECX is base, DS segment used |
| INC  BYTE PTR [ECX*8][EBP].X | EBP is base, SS segment used |

Unlike the 8086 and the 8088, which require anywhere from 5 through 17 clocks to compute the operand address (depending on the complexity of the operands), the 80386 requires no additional time to compute the effective address unless both a base register *and* an index register are used to select the operand. When both registers select the operand, execution time increases by only one clock cycle. In the 80486, an additional clock might or might not be required, depending on how the instructions have been pipelined. However, in the 80486, 1 clock must be added to the execution times of instructions that use based addressing if the base register was loaded by the instruction immediately preceding the instruction that uses it.

## Base plus displacement plus index addressing

Base plus displacement plus index addressing is the most complex addressing mode. This addressing form is used to address data structures stored on the stack or to address arrays whose base address is contained in a register. When these arrays are being addressed, the displacement value is 0 and the programmer need not specify it, although the assembler encodes a 0 displacement into the instruction. The index register can contain a scale value, as it does in index plus displacement addressing mode. Following are examples of base plus displacement plus index addressing:

| Instruction | Explanation |
|---|---|
| MOV EAX, [EBP+8][ESI] | Array is on stack beginning at EBP + 8 |
| INC WORD PTR [EBX+EAX*2] | 16-bit vector based at EBX, with index |
| MOV EDX, PT[EAX*8][ESI].Y | Array of "point" data structures |

The final example above appears to contain two displacement values: the initial displacement that specifies the start of the array, and the displacement of structure element Y in the indexed array element. The assembler simply offers these values for clarity. In the machine instruction, the displacement field contains the sum of the two values, as calculated by the assembler.

## Stack-based addressing

A stack is a data structure in which the value most recently stored is the first value retrieved. The acronym LIFO (last in, first out) describes the action of a stack and contrasts with the FIFO (first in, first out) structure. Figure 4-2 illustrates the LIFO and FIFO structures.

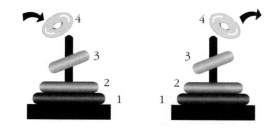

Stack — last in, first out (LIFO)

Queue — first in, first out (FIFO)

**Figure 4-2.** *LIFO, FIFO.*

Stack instructions typically refer to only a single operand. The other operand, the stack, is implicit in the instruction. The processor assumes that all memory in the stack segment (that is, the segment pointed to by the SS register) belongs to the stack, but this is not always true. Often, DS and SS point to the same segment; part of the segment contains program data, and part is reserved for the stack. In this situation, the programmer might need to write code to check for stack overflow, which occurs if too many items are pushed onto the stack and it runs over into the data area.

When a value is stored on the stack, or pushed, the ESP register is tested to see whether it is greater than or equal to 4. If it is not, a stack fault (interrupt 12) is generated; otherwise, ESP is decremented by 4, and the operand is stored at SS:[ESP]. The most recently pushed value, to which register ESP always points, is called the top-of-stack.

The POP operation retrieves the most recently pushed value from the stack. First, ESP is compared with the limit of the stack segment. If the memory reference is outside the limit, a stack fault is generated; otherwise, the value at SS:[ESP] is read, and ESP is incremented by 4.

The PUSH and POP instructions cause immediate values, register values, or the contents of a memory location to be stored to and retrieved from the stack. Also, some instructions that cause a transfer of control (change the EIP register) push the old execution address onto the stack. This allows the subroutine to return to the previous point of execution.

The most commonly used instruction that changes the EIP register is CALL. The CALL instruction has one operand, the address of a routine to be executed. The value of EIP (which points to the instruction immediately following the CALL) is pushed onto the stack, and EIP is set to the address specified by the CALL operand. The RET (or return) instruction pops the current top-of-stack into the EIP register, returning control to the instruction after the initial CALL.

A routine passes information to another routine by storing values on the stack before executing a CALL instruction. The standard way this information is structured is called the *frame* of the called routine or the call stack. Figure 4-3 on the following page illustrates a subroutine call and shows how the stack frame is structured.

Programs can push and pop 16-bit values by specifying registers AX, BX, SI, and so on or by specifying 16-bit memory references. It is more efficient, however, to push the contents of the 32-bit register (for example, EAX for AX) and to disregard the high-order bits. Use the MOVSX or MOVZX instruction to copy memory operands to a register and extend them to 32 bits before they are pushed onto the stack. The reason for doing this relates to how the 80386 and the 80486 interface with memory. If the physical memory address is a multiple of 4 (that is, if the address is on a dword boundary), then a single memory reference cycle can fetch as many as 4 bytes. If the physical memory address is offset from the dword boundary, then at least two additional clock cycles are required to read or to write a 32-bit value.

Therefore, after executing a 16-bit push, all subsequent 32-bit stack references degrade in performance by at least 30 percent. In addition, if a 32-bit program with 16-bit pushes is ever run on the 80486 with alignment checking enabled, the program will generate an alignment fault. In protected mode, 80386 and 80486 generate 32-bit references when the 16-bit segment registers (CS, SS, DS, ES, FS, and GS) are pushed or popped, so performance degradation is not an issue in this case.

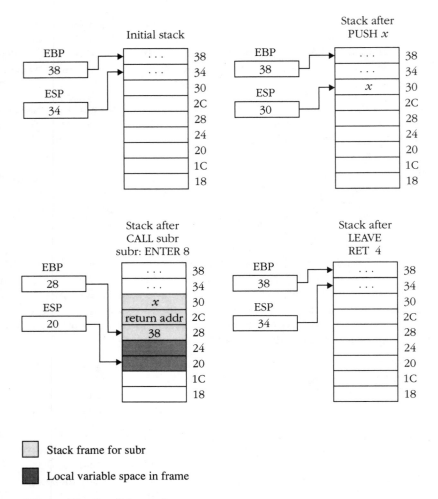

**Figure 4-3.** *Use of the stack.*

# Instruction Categories

The operations that can be performed vary widely, reflecting both the wide range of the CPU's capabilities and its compatibility with previous processors. In this section, I divide the instruction set into a number of related categories and identify the most important instructions of each category.

## Arithmetic

Arithmetic instructions perform signed and unsigned integer operations on operands of 8, 16, and 32 bits. With few exceptions, these instructions have the form:

```
OPCODE   dest, src
```

Generally, arithmetic instructions operate on source and destination operands and store the result in the location specified by the destination operand. The destination operand can be a memory reference or a register, and the source operand can be memory, a register, or an immediate data value. Both the source and the destination operands cannot be memory references, however. The instructions that fit this format are:

| Instruction | Explanation |
|---|---|
| ADD | Integer addition |
| ADC | Add with carry |
| SUB | Subtract |
| SBB | Subtract with borrow |
| CMP | Compare integers |

These instructions affect the AF, CF, OF, PF, SF, and ZF bits of the EFLAGS register, depending on the results of the operation.

In addition to the double-operand (or *dyadic*) instructions, there are single-operand (or *monadic*) instructions:

| Instruction | Explanation |
|---|---|
| INC | Increment by 1 |
| DEC | Decrement by 1 |

Each of these instructions takes a single operand, either a register or a memory reference. These instructions also affect the same EFLAG bits, except that they do not modify the carry flag (CF).

Finally, there are the irregular integer arithmetic instructions:

| Instruction | Explanation |
|---|---|
| DIV | Unsigned divide |
| IDIV | Signed divide |
| MUL | Unsigned multiply |
| IMUL | Signed multiply |

The DIV, IDIV, and MUL instructions take a single source operand. The destination operand is implicitly the accumulator and depends on the size of the operands. Destination operands are defined as follows:

| Operand Size | Register |
|---|---|
| 8 bits | AL |
| 16 bits | AX |
| 32 bits | EAX |
| 64 bits | EDX,EAX |

Because of its usefulness in computing array and structure element offsets, the IMUL instruction has three different forms:

| Instruction | Explanation |
|---|---|
| IMUL src | accum = accum × src |
| IMUL dest, src | dest = dest × src |
| IMUL dest, src, data | dest = src × data |

The DIV and IDIV instructions leave the status flags in undefined states. The MUL and IMUL instructions modify CF and OF, leaving SF, ZF, AF, and PF undefined.

## Decimal arithmetic

Six instructions help implement decimal math routines. The standard integer instructions perform computations, and the following instructions adjust the result because the operands are not integers but BCD encodings. The following instructions have either the AL or the AX accumulator as an implicit operand:

| Instruction | Explanation |
|---|---|
| AAA | ASCII adjust after addition |
| AAD | ASCII adjust before division |
| AAM | ASCII adjust after multiply |
| AAS | ASCII adjust after subtraction |
| DAA | Decimal adjust after addition |
| DAS | Decimal adjust after subtraction |

## Logical

The following instructions are called *logical* because they make no semantic assumptions about their operands—that is, they do not regard the operands as integers, BCD digits, character strings, or so on. The instructions are strictly Boolean, or bit-by-bit, operations. First is a set of dyadic functions similar to the arithmetic instructions:

| Instruction | Explanation |
|---|---|
| AND | Boolean AND |
| OR | Boolean OR |
| XOR | Exclusive OR |
| TEST | Performs an AND but modifies only the EFLAGS register |

A single monadic instruction, NOT, performs a logical complement of the operand. With the exception of NOT, the logical instructions modify each of the OF, SF, ZF, PF, and CF flags according to the outcome of the operation. The AF flag is left undefined.

A series of instructions operates on bit strings. These instructions have the form:

```
OPCODE  dest, index
```

where *dest* selects a bit string, either in memory or in a register, and *index* identifies the particular bit in the bit string that is the subject of the operation. The *index* value is either contained in a register or specified as an immediate value. If *dest* is a memory location, *index* is treated as a signed integer and can take on any value from $-2^{31}$ through $+2^{31}$. Instructions that operate on bit strings are BT, BTC, BTR, and BTS.

| Instruction | Explanation |
|---|---|
| BT | Bit test (save the value of the selected bit in CF) |
| BTC | Bit test and complement (save bit, then complement *dest* bit) |
| BTR | Bit test and reset (save bit, then clear *dest* bit to 0) |
| BTS | Bit test and set (save bit, then set *dest* bit to 1) |

Figure 4-4 shows bit indexing in these instructions.

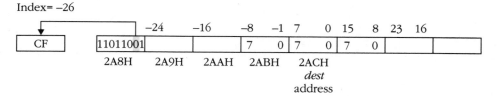

**Figure 4-4.** *Bit indexing in BT instructions.*

Two instructions search bit strings. These instructions have the form:

| *Instruction* | | *Explanation* |
|---|---|---|
| BSF | *dest, src* | Bit scan forward |
| BSR | *dest, src* | Bit scan reverse |

where *src* indicates the location of a bit string. The *dest* operand must be a register that receives the index of the first nonzero bit. The *dest* operand can be only a 16-bit or 32-bit register and indicates whether the *src* operand is a 16-bit or 32-bit quantity. Figure 4-5 shows how these instructions work.

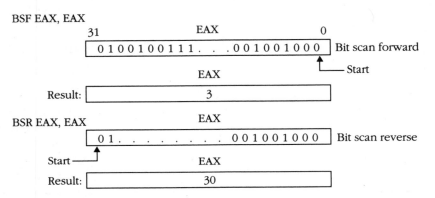

**Figure 4-5.** *Bit scanning.*

The final logical instructions are shift and rotate instructions. Figure 4-6 illustrates what shift and rotate instructions do.

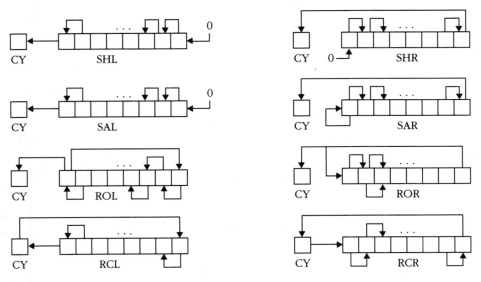

**Figure 4-6.** *Shift and rotate instructions.*

Most of these instructions have the form:

```
OPCODE   dest, COUNT
```

The destination is either a memory reference or a register. The COUNT is either an immediate value or the CL register. The following instructions fit this format:

| Instruction | Explanation |
|---|---|
| SHL | Shift left logical |
| SHR | Shift right logical |
| SAL | Shift arithmetic left |
| SAR | Shift arithmetic right |
| ROL | Rotate left |
| ROR | Rotate right |
| RCL | Rotate through carry left |
| RCR | Rotate through carry right |

The following double shift instructions are also provided:

| Instruction | Explanation |
|---|---|
| SHLD   *dest*, *src*, COUNT | Shift left double |
| SHRD   *dest*, *src*, COUNT | Shift right double |

In the above instructions, the source and the destination are concatenated and shifted, and the result is truncated and stored in the destination operand. Figure 4-7 illustrates double shift instructions.

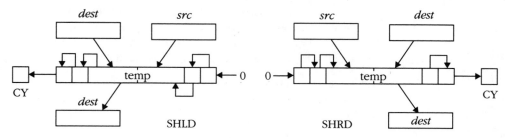

**Figure 4-7.** *Double shifts.*

## Data transfer

Probably the most frequently used instructions are in the data transfer category. To the assembly programmer, a single instruction appears to do almost all the work. Actually, the MOV mnemonic is encoded into one of several opcodes, depending on the operands involved. The general form of the MOV instruction is:

```
MOV     dest, src
```

Either the *dest* or the *src* operand can be a memory reference, but not both. Both operands can be registers, and the *src* operand can be an immediate value for most choices of *dest*. This instruction is not restricted to operating on the general registers. The MOV instruction is the only instruction you can use to read or modify the control registers (CR0–CR3) and the debug and test registers (DR0–DR7, TR6–TR7). You can also use the MOV instruction to load and store the segment registers DS, SS, ES, FS, and GS.

Not all possible combinations of *src* and *dest* are legal instructions. The restrictions are covered in Chapter 8.

Here are five additional data transfer instructions:

| *Instruction* | | *Explanation* |
|---|---|---|
| XCHG | *dest, src* | Exchange the contents of the two operands |
| BSWAP | *reg* | Convert to other-endian (80486 only) |
| MOVSX | *dest, src* | Move *src* into *dest* sign-extending *src* |
| MOVZX | *dest, src* | Move *src* into *dest* zero-extending *src* |
| SET*cc* | *dest* | Set *dest* to 0 or 1 depending on condition codes |

The XCHG instruction takes two operands and swaps their contents. One operand must be a register; the other can be a register or a memory reference. Because this instruction is frequently used to implement semaphores, the hardware bus LOCK signal is asserted whenever one of the operands is a memory reference.

The BSWAP instruction operates on a 32-bit register and swaps byte 0 with byte 3 and byte 2 with byte 1. This will convert a "big-endian" number to "little-endian" format, and vice versa.

The MOVSX and MOVZX instructions are similar to MOV, but they take a *src* operand of a single byte and either sign-extend it (MOVSX) or zero-extend it (MOVZX) into a 16-bit or 32-bit integer at the *dest* location. If *src* is a word, it is extended appropriately to a doubleword.

SET*cc* instructions move a 0 or a 1 into the destination, depending on the value of the condition codes in the EFLAGS register. The conditions supported are:

| *Instruction* | | *Explanation* |
|---|---|---|
| SETA | *dest* | Set to 1 if above (unsigned x > y) / CF = 0 & ZF = 0 |
| SETAE | *dest* | Set to 1 if above or equal / CF = 0 |
| SETB | *dest* | Set to 1 if below (unsigned x < y) / CF = 1 |
| SETBE | *dest* | Set to 1 if below or equal / CF = 1 │ ZF = 1 |
| SETC | *dest* | Set to 1 if carry / CF = 1 |
| SETE | *dest* | Set to 1 if equal / ZF = 1 |
| SETG | *dest* | Set to 1 if greater (signed x > y) / SF = OF & ZF = 0 |
| SETGE | *dest* | Set to 1 if greater or equal / SF = OF |
| SETL | *dest* | Set to 1 if less (signed x < y) / SF != OF |
| SETLE | *dest* | Set to 1 if less or equal / SF != OF or ZF = 1 |
| SETNA | *dest* | Set to 1 if not above (SETBE) |
| SETNAE | *dest* | Set to 1 if not above or equal (SETB) |
| SETNB | *dest* | Set to 1 if not below (SETAE) |
| SETNBE | *dest* | Set to 1 if not below or equal (SETA) |
| SETNC | *dest* | Set to 1 if no carry / CF = 0 |
| SETNE | *dest* | Set to 1 if not equal / ZF = 0 |
| SETNG | *dest* | Set to 1 if not greater (SETLE) |
| SETNGE | *dest* | Set to 1 if not greater or equal (SETL) |
| SETNL | *dest* | Set to 1 if not less (SETGE) |
| SETNLE | *dest* | Set to 1 if not less or equal / SF = OF & ZF = 0 (Set G) |
| SETNO | *dest* | Set to 1 if no overflow / OF = 0 |
| SETNP | *dest* | Set to 1 if no parity / PF = 0 |
| SETNS | *dest* | Set to 1 if no sign / SF = 0 |
| SETNZ | *dest* | Set to 1 if not 0 / ZF = 0 |
| SETO | *dest* | Set to 1 if overflow / OF = 1 |
| SETP | *dest* | Set to 1 if parity / PF = 1 |
| SETPE | *dest* | Set to 1 if parity even / PF = 1 |
| SETPO | *dest* | Set to 1 if parity odd / PF = 0 |
| SETS | *dest* | Set to 1 if sign / SF = 1 |
| SETZ | *dest* | Set to 1 if 0 / ZF = 1 |

## Stack

The stack instructions store and retrieve data from the stack. The PUSH instruction writes its operand to the stack, and the POP instruction removes the top-of-stack element and stores it in the location specified by its operand.

The PUSHAD and POPAD instructions require no operands and save or restore all the general registers to the stack. Figure 4-8 on the following page shows the stack after a PUSHAD has been executed. Although PUSHAD stores the value of the ESP register, POPAD does not reload ESP from the saved image. The new ESP value is always the old ESP value plus the number of bytes required to store the general register context.

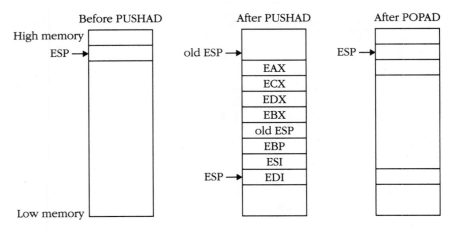

**Figure 4-8.** *PUSHAD context.*

## Control transfer

Control transfer instructions affect the flow of execution. Normally, an instruction is fetched from the address held in the EIP register, and then EIP is incremented by the size of the instruction so that it points to the next instruction. The new opcode is fetched, and the cycle continues.

The 80386 supports branch instructions, which alter EIP, and subroutine call instructions, which save the old EIP and then modify the EIP register. The software interrupt instruction is similar to the subroutine call except that an interrupt number is specified rather than an address. The address of the destination routine is then determined by a gate in the IDT. Figure 4-9 shows how JMP and CALL instructions affect the flow of execution.

Branch instructions exist in both conditional and unconditional forms. Unconditional jumps occur immediately when the appropriate instruction is encountered. All calls and software interrupts are unconditional.

Conditional branches test certain bits in the EFLAGS register to determine whether to branch or not. These bits are usually set as the result of a compare instruction (CMP) or as the result of an arithmetic or a logical operation. These branches are to relative addresses; the offset is a ± displacement from the current EIP. The following list shows the conditions that can be tested for and the mnemonic for each instruction.

Flow of instructions

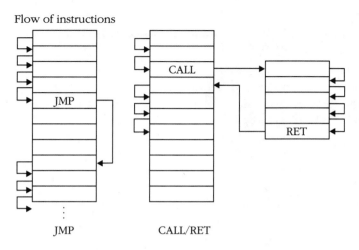

JMP                     CALL/RET

**Figure 4-9.** *JMP and CALL instructions.*

| Instruction | | Explanation |
|---|---|---|
| JA | *offset* | Jump above (unsigned x > y) / CF = 0 & ZF = 0 |
| JAE | *offset* | Jump above or equal / CF = 0 |
| JB | *offset* | Jump below (unsigned x < y) / CF = 1 |
| JBE | *offset* | Jump below or equal / CF = 1 │ ZF = 1 |
| JC | *offset* | Jump if carry / CF = 1 |
| JCXZ | *offset* | Jump if CX = 0 |
| JECXZ | *offset* | Jump if ECX = 0 |
| JE | *offset* | Jump equal / ZF = 1 |
| JG | *offset* | Jump greater (signed x > y) / SF = OF & ZF = 0 |
| JGE | *offset* | Jump greater or equal / SF = OF |
| JL | *offset* | Jump less (signed x < y) / SF != OF |
| JLE | *offset* | Jump less or equal / SF != OF or ZF = 1 |
| JNA | *offset* | Jump not above (JBE) |
| JNAE | *offset* | Jump not above or equal (JB) |
| JNB | *offset* | Jump not below (JAE) |
| JNBE | *offset* | Jump not below or equal (JA) |
| JNC | *offset* | Jump no carry / CF = 0 |
| JNE | *offset* | Jump not equal / ZF = 0 |
| JNG | *offset* | Jump not greater SF != OF or ZF = 1 |
| JNGE | *offset* | Jump not greater or equal (JL) |

*(continued)*

**87**

*continued*

| Instruction | | Explanation |
|---|---|---|
| JNL | *offset* | Jump not less (JGE) |
| JNLE | *offset* | Jump not less or equal (JG) |
| JNO | *offset* | Jump no overflow / OF = 0 |
| JNP | *offset* | Jump no parity / PF = 0 |
| JNS | *offset* | Jump no sign / SF = 0 |
| JNZ | *offset* | Jump not 0 / ZF = 0 |
| JO | *offset* | Jump if overflow / OF = 1 |
| JP | *offset* | Jump if parity / PF = 1 |
| JPE | *offset* | Jump parity even / PF = 1 |
| JPO | *offset* | Jump parity odd / PF = 0 |
| JS | *offset* | Jump if sign / SF = 1 |
| JZ | *offset* | Jump if 0 / ZF = 1 |

Three other conditional branch instructions are the loop instructions. Loop instructions decrement the ECX register and branch if the conditions outlined in the following list are met.

| Instruction | | Explanation |
|---|---|---|
| LOOP | *offset* | Decrement, branch if ECX != 0 |
| LOOPZ | *offset* | Decrement, branch if ECX != 0 and ZF = 1 |
| LOOPNZ | *offset* | Decrement, branch if ECX != 0 and ZF = 0 |

LOOPE and LOOPNE are synonyms for LOOPZ and LOOPNZ.

## String

String instructions handle large blocks of memory with ease. A string instruction can move a block from one location in memory to another, compare one block with another, or search a string for a specific value. String instructions use specific registers for storing operands. DS and ESI always point to the source memory block. ES and EDI point to the destination. These pointers are incremented (or decremented) by the size of the operand (1, 2, or 4 bytes) every time the string instruction executes.

The direction flag (DF) determines whether the source and the destination pointers are incremented or decremented. When the direction flag is 0, the addresses are incremented. When the flag is 1, addresses are decremented. The string instructions provide the following capabilities:

| Instruction | Explanation |
|---|---|
| MOVS | Move string—copy string at DS:ESI to ES:EDI |
| CMPS | Compare string—compare DS:ESI to ES:EDI |
| STOS | Store the accumulator at ES:EDI |
| LODS | Load the accumulator with DS:ESI |
| SCAS | Scan string, compare ES:EDI with accumulator |

You can execute any of these instructions repeatedly by placing a count value in the ECX register and preceding the string instruction with the REP prefix. The compare and scan instructions, which modify the flag bits, can also be prefixed by the REPE (repeat while equal) and REPNE (repeat while not equal) instructions, allowing fast compare and search operations.

## Pointer manipulation

Pointer manipulation instructions load a 48-bit pointer into any pair of the segment and general registers. The format of these instructions is:

```
Lxx     reg, mem
```

where xx stands for the segment register (SS, DS, ES, FS, or GS), reg is any general register, and mem is a memory operand.

The LEA (load effective address) instruction computes 32-bit addresses. LEA loads a 32-bit register with the address defined by the memory operand, which is unusual because other instructions operate on the value stored at the memory operand location. The following example shows how to use the LEA instruction to compute a pointer:

```
VECTOR  DD      20 DUP (?)          ; array of 20 elements
        MOV     EAX, 9              ; array index
        LEA     EAX, VECTOR[EAX*4]  ; get pointer to 9th array element
        PUSH    EAX                 ; push pointer on stack
        CALL    MYSUBR              ; invoke subroutine
```

Because the LEA instruction essentially performs only additions and shifts on the values of the displacement and the base and index registers, it can perform simple multiplications faster than the hardware multiply instructions can. For a value stored in a general register (such as EAX in the sample operations), the following operations can be performed:

| Instruction | Explanation |
|---|---|
| LEA  EAX, [EAX*2] | Multiply by 2 (index) |
| LEA  EAX, [EAX+EAX*2] | Multiply by 3 (base + index) |
| LEA  EAX, [EAX*4] | Multiply by 4 (index) |
| LEA  EAX, [EAX+EAX*4] | Multiply by 5 (base + index) |
| LEA  EAX, [EAX*8] | Multiply by 8 (index) |
| LEA  EAX, [EAX+EAX*8] | Multiply by 9 (base + index) |

Using the LEA instruction in this way does not affect the flags. You cannot tell when arithmetic overflow has occurred, when the result is 0, and so on. Use LEA only to compute addresses such as array or structure indexes where overflow is not likely to occur. You can also view the LEA instruction as an addition instruction with four operands instead of two. The content of the index register is added to the base register and the displacement. By treating the displacement simply as a constant, the following formula expresses the action of LEA:

*dest reg <– index reg + base reg + const*

For example, the result of the LEA ECX, [EAX][ESI][3] instruction is equivalent to the following operations:

```
MOV     ECX, EAX
ADD     ECX, ESI
ADD     ECX, 3
```

## Input/Output

Because I/O ports are usually connected to system devices, it is important to protect against indiscriminate access to them. Secure system routines that run with I/O privilege (CPL≤IOPL) can execute any I/O instruction. A less privileged task can execute an I/O instruction; however, a general protection fault (interrupt 13) will occur unless the operating system has granted the task permission to access the specific port(s). The operating system grants permission by setting the appropriate bits in the I/O permission bitmap of the task's TSS (task state segment).

Both the input and output instructions have three forms. The simplest form is:

```
IN      acc, port
OUT     port, acc
```

where *acc* is one of the accumulator registers (AL, AX, or EAX) and *port* is a value from 0 to 0FFH. These instructions can be used to address only the first 256 I/O addresses, and the 80386 supports as many as 65,536 I/O ports. To access the entire range, use the following form of the instructions:

```
IN      acc, DX
OUT     DX, acc
```

In the above instructions, the I/O address is contained in the DX register.

String instructions are the third type of I/O instructions. INS (input string) takes input from the port specified by DX and stores the result at ES:EDI, adjusting EDI according to the direction flag bit. OUTS (output string) reads the value at DS:ESI and writes it to the port specified by DX. INS and OUTS can be prefixed by the REP instruction, which causes the I/O instruction to repeat until ECX is decremented to 0.

## Prefix

Prefix instructions precede other 80386 instructions. Prefixes modify the action of the instructions they precede. You can apply more than one prefix to an instruction.

The most commonly used prefixes are the repeat prefixes, discussed previously with the string instructions. If a repeat prefix is applied to any instruction other than a string instruction, an undefined opcode fault (interrupt 6) occurs. The following table lists the repeat prefix instructions:

| *Instruction* | *Explanation* |
| --- | --- |
| REP | Repeat until ECX = 0 |
| REPE / REPZ | Repeat until ECX = 0 or ZF = 0 |
| REPNE / REPNZ | Repeat until ECX = 0 or ZF = 1 |

You can apply a segment override prefix to almost any memory reference instruction. Each of the six segment registers has a prefix instruction. The override forces the memory reference of the modified instruction to the segment specified by the prefix rather than to the default segment. The following table lists segment override prefixes:

| *Prefix* | *Explanation* |
| --- | --- |
| CS: | Refer to the code segment |
| SS: | Refer to the stack segment |
| DS: | Refer to the data segment |
| ES: | Refer to the segment pointed to by ES |
| FS: | Refer to the segment pointed to by FS |
| GS: | Refer to the segment pointed to by GS |

For example, the instruction MOV EAX, [42H] copies the dword at offset 42H of the data segment into EAX. When the instruction is prefixed with SS:, the dword is read from the stack segment. Most assemblers let you specify the prefix before the instruction or as part of the instruction. For example:

```
SS:
MOV     EAX, [42H]
```

or

```
MOV     EAX, SS:[42H]
```

The only memory reference instructions that cannot be prefixed by a segment over-ride are SCAS, STOS, and INS. These are string instructions that operate on memory at ES:[EDI]. When a prefix instruction is applied to any other string instruction, it overrides the DS:[ESI] pointer only. The MOVS and CMPS string instructions have both a source (ESI) and a destination (EDI) pointer and are allowed a single prefix instruction that overrides the DS:[ESI] pointer.

You can apply the LOCK prefix to any of the following instructions when reading or modifying a memory location:

```
ADC, ADD, AND, BT, BTC, BTR, BTS, DEC, INC, NEG, NOT, OR,
SBB, SUB, XCHG, XOR
```

Notice that the XADD instruction is available only on the 80486. The LOCK prefix asserts the hardware signal LOCK\, which ensures exclusive access to a memory location in a multiprocessor environment. The assembler usually inserts two addi-tional prefix instructions, but Intel does not give them mnemonics. I call them OP-SIZ (operand size prefix) and ADRSIZ (address size prefix). OPSIZ toggles the operand word size of the processor for the next instruction. Normally, the machine word size is 32 bits. Prefixing a 32-bit instruction with OPSIZ converts it to a 16-bit instruction. Similarly, when code is run in 8086-compatible or 80286-compatible mode, the default machine word size is 16 bits; applying the OPSIZ prefix converts a 16-bit instruction to a 32-bit instruction.

In real mode, virtual 8086 mode, and 80286-compatible mode, the byte 40H is inter-preted as INC AX, but in native (32-bit) mode, it is interpreted as INC EAX. To incre-ment the AX register in native mode, you must prefix the instruction byte with the OPSIZ instruction. The assembler does all the work, however. If you enter the in-struction INC AX in a native-mode code segment, the assembler generates the bytes 66H and 40H. The following table illustrates the bytes that the assembler generates.

### Opcode Generation in Different Modes

| Native Mode | Real, Virtual, or 80286-Compatible Mode |
| --- | --- |
| INC AX → 66H, 40H | INC AX → 40H |
| INC EAX → 40H | INC EAX → 66H, 40H |

Similarly, the ADRSIZ prefix toggles between 16-bit addressing and 32-bit address-ing. This prefix is useful for programmers writing 80386 code that will run under a 16-bit operating system. In 16-bit mode (real, virtual, or 80286-compatible), memory offsets are limited to 16 bits, and more rules restrict which registers you can use as base and index values in generating addresses. These restrictions are listed in Ap-pendix D. The ADRSIZ toggle allows you to use the full addressing capabilities of the 80386 and 80486.

If you use 32-bit addressing under a 16-bit operating system, be consistent about register usage. For example, a programmer who wants to use the scaled index feature in a program that runs under MS-DOS might code the following instruction sequence:

```
        ; Increment each member of an array of 16-bit integers
        MOV     CX, count       ; get size of array
L1:     INC     array-2[ECX*2]  ; increment array element
        LOOP    L1              ; decrement index, branch if not 0
```

These instructions would probably not work because the scaled address feature requires the full 32-bit ECX register and the programmer has loaded only the 16-bit CX register. The value of the high-order 16 bits in ECX is unknown. The correct approach is:

```
        ; increment each member of an array of 16-bit integers
        MOVZX   ECX, count      ; get array size, zero-extend into ECX
L1:     INC     array-2[ECX*2]  ; increment array element
        LOOP    L1              ; decrement index, branch if not 0
```

## System

Application programs do not execute system instructions. In some cases, system instructions cannot be executed unless the process has a high privilege level. The following table lists system instructions. More detailed information about these instructions is given in Chapter 8.

| Instruction | | Explanation |
|---|---|---|
| LGDT | *mem* | Load GDT base address and limit |
| SGDT | *mem* | Store GDT base and limit |
| LIDT | *mem* | Load IDT base address and limit |
| SIDT | *mem* | Store IDT base and limit |
| LTR | *src* | Load a selector into the task register |
| STR | *dest* | Store the TR selector |
| LLDT | *src* | Load a selector into the LDT register |
| SLDT | *dest* | Store the LDT selector |
| VERR | *dest* | Verify read access for *dest* selector |
| VERW | *dest* | Verify write access for *dest* selector |
| LAR | reg, *dest* | Load access rights for *dest* selector |
| LSL | reg, *dest* | Load limit for *dest* segment |
| ARPL | *dest, src* | Adjust privilege level for *dest* |
| HLT | | Halt the CPU until reset or interrupt |
| INVD | | Invalidate internal cache (80486 only) |
| WBINVD | | Write back and invalidate internal cache (80486 only) |
| INVLPG | *mem* | Invalidate the TLB (translation lookaside buffer) entry, which maps *mem* (80486 only) |

## Miscellaneous

A few instructions don't fit into any category. For example, the NOP instruction performs no operation.

On the 80386, the WAIT instruction tests the hardware pin READY\. If the READY\ pin is not active, the CPU waits until it becomes active. If the 80386 is waiting, it continues to respond to hardware interrupts; however, it returns to the WAIT after the interrupt completes. The 80287 and 80387 coprocessors hold READY\ inactive while they perform floating-point operations. If your program might execute on the 80386 or 80386SX, you should execute a WAIT instruction before you use the result of a floating-point computation to ensure that the coprocessor has finished execution. The 80486 has no READY\ pin, and a WAIT is essentially a NOP. The WAIT does, however, cause the floating-point unit to check for unmasked exceptions that can result in a math interrupt.

# Floating-Point Extensions

As discussed in Chapter 2, the 80387 NDP extends the instruction set of the 80386 by providing hardware support for floating-point operations. In the 80486, the floating-point execution unit is contained on the same chip as the basic execution unit. The floating-point programming model is a stack-oriented model rather than the two-operand register/memory model of the basic execution unit. Most arithmetic instructions can be specified in three ways: with no operands, with a single operand, or with two operands. Following are some examples that illustrate the floating-point addition instructions.

| *Instruction* | *Explanation* |
| --- | --- |
| FADD | No operands |
| FADD   ST(3) | Single-stack operand |
| FADD   [EBP+6] | Single-memory operand |
| FADD   ST(2), ST | Two operands |

When no operands are specified, the operands are implicit. The following pseudocode illustrates what happens when no operand is specified:

```
temp <- pop()
ST <- ST <function> temp
```

When a single operand is specified, the top-of-stack is implicitly the first operand, so the instruction becomes:

```
ST <- ST <function> op
```

When two operands are specified, both operands must be floating-point registers, and one must be the top-of-stack. You can store the result of the operation in either register, which you designate by making it the first operand.

```
op1 <- op1 <function> op2
```

Several instructions have a form that discards the current top-of-stack after the function is performed. A suffix of P (for pop) is added to the instruction mnemonic. For example, the instruction:

```
FMULP    ST(3), ST
```

causes the top-of-stack and ST(3) to be multiplied and stores the result in ST(3). Then the top-of-stack is discarded, leaving the newly created value at ST(2).

## Load and store

The load instructions push a new value onto the top of the floating-point stack, but the store instructions do not pop a value off unless explicitly indicated. Following are the relevant instructions:

| Instruction | | Explanation |
|---|---|---|
| FBLD | *mem* | Push an 80-bit BCD integer |
| FILD | *mem* | Push a 16-, 32-, or 64-bit integer |
| FLD | ST(n) | Push a copy of a value already loaded |
| FLD | *mem* | Push a 32-, 64-, or 80-bit real |
| FLD1 | | Push 1.0 |
| FLDL2E | | Push $\log_2 e$ |
| FLDL2T | | Push $\log_2 10$ |
| FLDLG2 | | Push $\log_{10} 2$ |
| FLDLN2 | | Push $\log_e 2$ |
| FLDPI | | Push *pi* |
| FLDZ | | Push 0.0 |
| FBSTP | *mem* | Store ST in an 80-bit packed BCD integer and pop (discard from stack) |
| FIST | *mem* | Store ST in a 16- or 32-bit integer |
| FISTP | *mem* | Store ST in a 16-, 32-, or 64-bit integer and pop |
| FST | ST(n) | Store a copy of ST in ST(n) |
| FST | *mem* | Store ST in a 32- or 64-bit real |
| FSTP | *mem* | Store ST in a 32-, 64-, or 80-bit real and pop |

Because the floating-point execution unit operates in parallel with the basic execution unit (via coprocessing on the 80386/80387 and internally in the 80486) and because integer instructions generally execute more rapidly than floating-point operations, issue a WAIT (or FWAIT) instruction before using the result of a floating-point store operation. This ensures that the value has been written to memory and that the 80386 code can access the value.

## Arithmetic

The following table lists the arithmetic operations that the FPU performs. See Chapter 8 for a description of the types of operands that each instruction supports.

| Instruction | | Explanation |
|---|---|---|
| F2XM1 | | Compute $2^{ST}-1$ where $-1 \le ST \le 1$ |
| FABS | | Take absolute value of ST |
| FADD | [op(s)] | Add two floating-point numbers |
| FADDP | op1, op2 | Add op1 and op2, pop stack |
| FIADD | mem | Add 16- or 32-bit integer to ST |
| FCHS | | Change the sign of ST |
| FCOM | op | Compare ST with op (register or memory) |
| FCOMP | op | Compare ST with op and pop |
| FCOMPP | | Compare ST with ST(1), pop both |
| FICOM | mem | Compare ST with 16- or 32-bit integer |
| FICOMP | mem | Compare with integer and pop |
| FUCOM | op | Compare allowing quiet NaNs |
| FUCOMP | op | Like FCOMP |
| FUCOMPP | op | Like FCOMPP |
| FCOS | | Cosine of ST |
| FDIV | [op(s)] | Floating-point divide |
| FDIVP | op1, op2 | Divide op1 by op2, pop |
| FIDIV | mem | Divide ST by 16- or 32-bit integer |
| FDIVR | [op(s)] | Reverse divide (op2 by op1) |
| FDIVRP | op1, op2 | Reverse divide (op2 by op1) and pop |
| FIDIVR | mem | Divide integer by ST |
| FMUL | [op(s)] | Floating-point multiply |
| FMULP | op1, op2 | Multiply op1 by op2 and pop stack |
| FIMUL | mem | Multiply ST by 16- or 32-bit integer |
| FPATAN | | Arctangent of ST(1)/ST, pop |
| FPREM | | Partial remainder of ST/ST(1) |
| FPREM1 | | Compute partial remainder to IEEE spec |
| FPTAN | | Compute tangent of ST, push(1.0) |
| FRNDINT | | Round ST to integer |
| FSCALE | | Multiply ST by $2^{ST(1)}$ |
| FSIN | | Compute sine of ST |
| FSINCOS | | temp = ST, ST = sin(temp), push(cos(temp)) |

*(continued)*

*continued*

| Instruction | | Explanation |
|---|---|---|
| FSQRT | | Take the square root of ST |
| FSUB | *[op(s)]* | Floating-point subtraction |
| FSUBP | *op1, op2* | Subtract *op2* from *op1* and pop |
| FISUB | *mem* | Subtract 16- or 32-bit integer from ST |
| FSUBR | *[op(s)]* | Reverse subtraction |
| FSUBRP | *op1, op2* | Subtract *op1* from *op2* and pop stack |
| FISUBR | *mem* | Subtract ST from 16- or 32-bit integer |
| FTST | | Compare ST with 0.0 |
| FXAM | | Examine ST and set condition codes |
| FXTRACT | | Decompose ST to exponent and significand, ST = exponent, push significand |
| FYL2X | | ST(1) = ST(1) × login2ST, pop stack |
| FYL2XP1 | | ST(1) = ST(1) × login2(ST + 1), pop stack |

## Control

Control instructions save or alter the state of the NDP. Some have a special "no wait" form, indicated by the letter N as the second character of the mnemonic. The "no wait" instructions execute without the implicit WAIT that occurs between two floating-point instructions.

Normally a WAIT instruction is implied before every coprocessor operation. The following two instruction streams are equivalent.

```
FADD    ST(3), ST      WAIT
FMUL    ST(1)          FADD    ST(3), ST
                       WAIT
                       FMUL    ST(1)
```

WAIT causes the CPU to check whether unmasked exceptions have occurred. In the 80387, this is done via the ERROR\ signal. In the 80486, the error state is maintained internal to the CPU. If a coprocessor error is signaled, a floating-point exception (interrupt 16) occurs. "No wait" instructions allow you to save the NDP state without worrying about processing any floating-point exceptions.

The processor state of the FPU is held in the registers discussed in Chapter 3. Some of these registers are addressable individually, but others, such as the tag word and error pointer registers, are not. The combination of the control word, status word, and error pointers is called the *environment.* The environment layout is shown in Figure 4-10 on the following page.

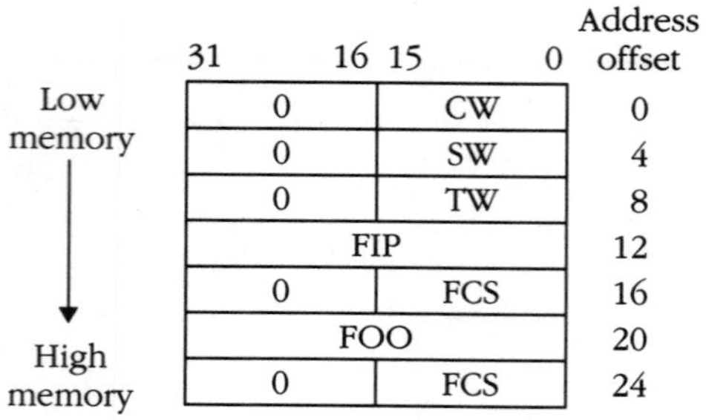

|  | 31 | 16 | 15 | 0 | Address offset |
|---|---|---|---|---|---|
| Low memory | 0 | | CW | | 0 |
| | 0 | | SW | | 4 |
| | 0 | | TW | | 8 |
| | FIP | | | | 12 |
| | 0 | | FCS | | 16 |
| | FOO | | | | 20 |
| High memory | 0 | | FCS | | 24 |

**Figure 4-10.** *Environment layout.*

The following table lists the floating-point control instructions and their functions.

| *Instruction* | | *Explanation* |
|---|---|---|
| F[N]CLEX | | Clear all exception flags |
| FDECSTP | | Decrement the TOP field in the CW |
| FFREE | ST(n) | Mark ST(n) as unused |
| FINCSTP | | Increment the control word TOP field |
| F[N]INIT | | Initialize the NDP |
| FLDCW | *mem* | Load the control word register |
| FLDENV | *mem* | Load the floating-point environment |
| FNOP | | No operation |
| FRSTOR | *mem* | Reload the entire FPU machine state |
| F[N]SAVE | *mem* | Store the entire FPU state in memory |
| F[N]STCW | *mem* | Store the control word in memory |
| F[N]STENV | *mem* | Store the floating-point environment |
| F[N]STSW | *mem* | Store the status word |
| F[N]STSW AX | | Copy the status word to register AX |

The entire state, including all registers, tags, and pointers, must be saved and restored when multitasking between two or more programs that rely on the FPU. The FSAVE and FRSTOR instructions load and save the memory image shown in Figure 4-11.

The memory images described in Figure 4-11 are slightly different in a 80386 system using the 80287. See Appendix F for information pertaining to the 80287.

|  | 31 | 0 | Address offset |
|---|---|---|---|
|  | 0 | CW | 0 |
|  | 0 | SW | 4 |
|  | 0 | TW | 8 |
|  | FIP | | 12 |
|  | 0 | FCS | 16 |
|  | FOO | | 20 |
|  | 0 | FCS | 24 |
|  | $ST(0)_{0..31}$ | | 28 |
|  | $ST(0)_{32..63}$ | | 32 |
|  | $ST(1)_{0..15}$ | $ST(0)_{64..79}$ | 36 |
|  | $ST(1)_{16..47}$ | | 40 |
|  | $ST(1)_{48..79}$ | | 44 |
|  | $ST(2)_{0..31}$ | | 48 |
|  | $ST(2)_{32..63}$ | | 52 |
|  | $ST(3)_{0..15}$ | $ST(2)_{64..79}$ | 56 |
|  | $ST(3)_{16..47}$ | | 60 |
|  | $ST(3)_{48..79}$ | | 64 |
|  | $ST(4)_{0..31}$ | | 68 |
|  | $ST(4)_{32..63}$ | | 72 |
|  | $ST(5)_{0..15}$ | $ST(4)_{64..79}$ | 76 |
|  | $ST(5)_{16..47}$ | | 80 |
|  | $ST(5)_{48..79}$ | | 84 |
|  | $ST(6)_{0..31}$ | | 88 |
|  | $ST(6)_{32..63}$ | | 92 |
|  | $ST(7)_{0..15}$ | $ST(6)_{64..79}$ | 96 |
|  | $ST(7)_{16..47}$ | | 100 |
|  | $ST(7)_{48..79}$ | | 104 |

**Figure 4-11.** *FSAVE and FRSTOR memory layout.*

# 5

# THE PROTECTION MECHANISM

The role of computers in society is becoming more and more significant. Computers process our financial transactions, count our votes at election time, control medical equipment, and more. As our dependency on computers grows, we need systems that can process multiple tasks and maintain reliability at the same time.

In support of these goals, Intel designers implemented the protected virtual address mode (commonly, protected mode) on the 80286. Protected mode allows multiple applications to run concurrently but isolates them from one another so that failures in one application do not affect any other application. Although it was possible to implement multitasking on previous Intel microprocessors, every application had access to all portions of the system. A flaw in one application could easily crash the entire system or corrupt data associated with another task.

The 80386 was the second Intel processor to support protected mode, and the 80486 is the third. However, the basic mechanism is essentially unchanged from the 80286, except that it has been extended by use of 32-bit addressing. There is no difference between the 80386 and 80486 in regard to protection. This chapter discusses how the protection mechanism works, including privilege levels, task separation, and how virtual addressing is used to support the protection model.

## Selectors

The central feature of the protection mechanism is the *selector*. Rather than directly accessing any part of the system, a program deals with a selector, which grants access to a system object. Associated with each object is information about it—for example, the object's location, size, and type, and any restrictions on its use.

This information is not stored in the selector for two reasons. The selector would be very large, and passing it from routine to routine would take a lot of computer time. More importantly, keeping the object information in a separate location prevents an unscrupulously designed or errant program from corrupting the information.

A selector is like a sealed envelope. Inside the envelope is important data that must be kept secure. Like a messenger permitted only to see envelopes and pass them to other messengers, a program can store and retrieve selectors and pass them to other routines. Only the operating system has access to the data inside the envelope, which is called a descriptor.

# Descriptors

Aptly named, *descriptors* describe a system object in detail. Memory segments, as illustrated in Chapter 3, are one kind of system object. Other system objects include tables that support the protection mechanism, special segments that store the processor state, and access control objects called gates.

Descriptors are grouped in descriptor tables. By examining a selector, the CPU determines which descriptor is associated with the selector and with the object to which the descriptor points. One item that the descriptor indicates is the privilege level of the object. This value is stored in the DPL field of the descriptor. When a program requests access to a system object with a selector, one of the following happens:

- Access is denied. If the request violates a rule of the protection mechanism (more on this later), control passes from the program to a designated routine in the operating system. The operating system usually terminates the process.

- Access is permitted but impossible to grant. For example, if the object is not currently in memory, an operating system routine is called that swaps the object into memory and returns control to the program. The program is then permitted to retry access to the object.

- Access is granted at the requested privilege level.

# Privilege

The protection mechanism supports four levels of increasing privilege, numbered 3, 2, 1, and 0. Privilege level 0 is the most privileged level.

The privilege level of the selector in the CS register identifies the precedence of the currently executing routine and is called the *current privilege level* (CPL). For reliability, only the most trustworthy and crash-resistant code in the operating system should run at the most privileged level (CPL = 0). Applications that might fail or compromise the integrity of the system should run at the least privileged level (CPL = 3).

Because the number of programs that can run at high privilege levels diminishes near level 0 and because level 0 code is likely to exist only in the core of the operating system, the classic illustration of the privilege system is one of concentric rings, as shown in Figure 5-1.

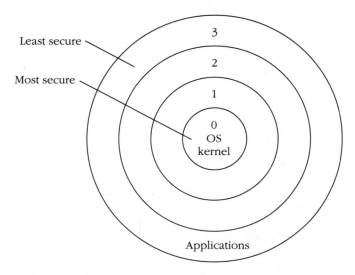

**Figure 5-1.** *Privilege rings.*

The concentric ring image is so well integrated into the understanding of privilege that programmers often speak of code that runs "in ring 0" or "in ring 3"—another way of saying that the CPL of the procedure is 0 or 3. Every system object (that is, everything referred to by a descriptor) is associated with a privilege level and "resides" in a particular ring.

The word *privilege* connotes rights or advantages not normally granted. On the 80386 family, procedures running in the innermost rings can access data objects in the outer rings (which have less privilege), but outer-ring procedures cannot access objects with greater privilege. In addition, to prevent the operating system from crashing due to bad code, procedures cannot call other procedures that might be less reliable (procedures in outer rings).

For example, a procedure running in ring 1 may access a data segment residing in ring 2 or ring 3 but is prevented from accessing a segment whose privilege level is 0. A ring 1 procedure, however, cannot invoke a subroutine residing in ring 2 or ring 3, nor can it call one in ring 0. Figure 5-2 on the following page illustrates this concept.

An operating system does not need to support all four privilege levels. UNIX systems, for example, typically implement only two levels, 0 and 3. OS/2 supports three levels: The operating system code runs in ring 0, applications run in ring 3, and special routines that need access to I/O devices run in ring 2.

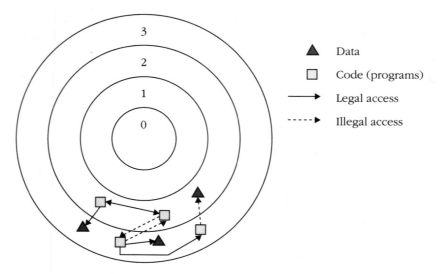

**Figure 5-2.** *Access between rings.*

## Interlevel communication

As a security measure, concentric rings of privilege work well, but the possibility exists that an application running in ring 3 might need service from the operating system. The operating system, however, omnipotent in ring 0, is not accessible to the application. The application, in effect, might say, "Oh most great and worthy of operating systems, please grant me, thy humble and obedient servant, additional RAM for my stack," but because of the access restrictions, it has no way of calling on the operating system.

Various cultures have established a priesthood whose job is to act as intermediator, but the Intel design engineers apparently despaired of fitting something that complicated into only a few hundred thousand transistors, so they resorted to something simpler. It's called a gate.

### Gates

A gate is a system object (that is, it has its own descriptor) that points to a procedure in a code segment, but the gate has a privilege level separate from that of the code segment. Figure 5-3 shows how this changes the legal subroutine call path.

A gate allows execute-only access to a routine in an inner ring from a less privileged procedure. The restriction on outward calls, however, remains in force. The protection mechanism supports four types of gates: *call, interrupt, trap,* and *task.* Call gates are invoked via the standard subroutine call instruction. Interrupt gates and trap gates are invoked by the INT instruction or by hardware interrupts. Task gates are invoked by JMP, CALL, or INT instructions or by hardware interrupts.

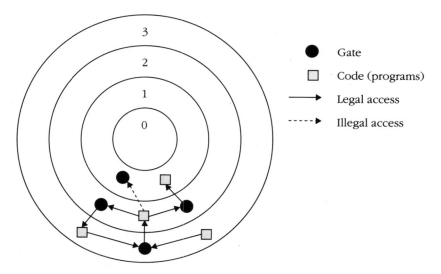

**Figure 5-3.** *Call paths through gates.*

In a standard subroutine call, the return address and any parameters are stored on the stack, and execution continues at the start of the subroutine. When invoking a subroutine through a gate, the privilege level of the executing routine changes to the level of the code segment to which the gate points. When the subroutine returns, the privilege level is set back to that of the calling procedure. For example, an application executing in ring 3 might call the operating system to allocate some memory. The operating system code runs in ring 0, and a call gate in ring 3 points to the allocation routine.

This approach solves the communication problem but introduces another one. Because the return address (and possibly some system call parameters) is on the stack and the stack is a ring 3 (application) data segment, the address and parameters are no longer secure. The application could corrupt them while the operating system is processing the request. To solve this problem, part of the stack is copied to a more privileged stack segment as it moves through the gate, as shown in Figure 5-4 on the following page. Each call gate descriptor contains a field called the dword count, which indicates the number of 32-bit stack words to copy from the outer-ring stack to the inner-ring stack.

Every application must have as many stack segments as there are privilege levels in the operating environment under which it is running. If this seems excessive, remember that you can use the virtual memory capability to your advantage. An application can have descriptors for more than one stack segment, but stack segments can be marked as not present and never take up any physical memory if they are not used.

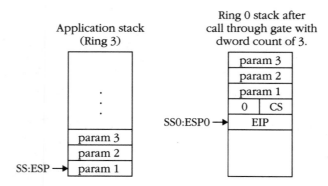

**Figure 5-4.** *Stack privilege increase.*

If the idea of four stack segments has you flipping back to the register diagram look-ing for additional registers, you won't find them. The active stack pointer is held in the SS and ESP registers. The others are stored in a system object called the *task state segment,* or TSS.

## Task state segments

A TSS is a special memory segment that the processor uses to support multitasking. Its format is outlined in Figure 5-5, and it contains a copy of all the registers that must be saved to preserve the state of a task. It also contains values that are associ-ated with the task but that are not stored in CPU registers.

The TSS contains three additional stack segment selectors (SS0, SS1, and SS2) and three stack pointers (ESP0, ESP1, and ESP2), as shown in Figure 5-5. When a call or interrupt through a gate causes a change in privilege, the new SS and ESP are loaded from the TSS. The task register (TR) contains the selector of the currently active TSS.

When a task switch occurs, all the executing task's registers are saved in the active TSS. The task register is then loaded with the selector of a new TSS, and each gen-eral register is loaded with the values from the new TSS. Other fields in the TSS and multitasking are discussed later in this chapter.

## Descriptor tables

As mentioned earlier, the descriptors for the memory segments, TSSs, gates, and other system objects are grouped into descriptor tables. The three types of descrip-tor tables are the interrupt descriptor table (IDT), the global descriptor table (GDT), and the local descriptor tables (LDTs).

The IDT contains descriptors that relate to hardware and software interrupts. A spe-cial register, IDTR, contains the linear base address and size (limit) of the IDT. The IDT is discussed in detail later in this chapter in the section "Interrupts and Exceptions."

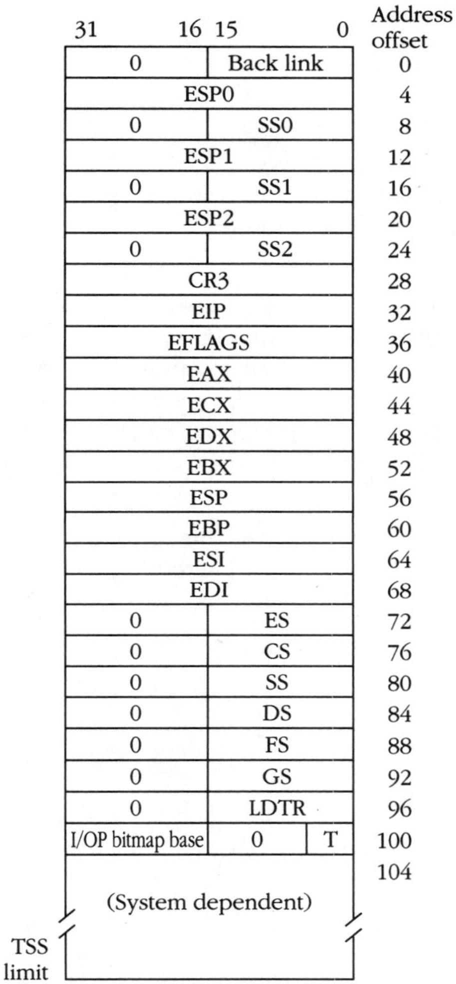

| 31 | 16 | 15 | 0 | Address offset |
|---|---|---|---|---|
| 0 | | Back link | | 0 |
| ESP0 | | | | 4 |
| 0 | | SS0 | | 8 |
| ESP1 | | | | 12 |
| 0 | | SS1 | | 16 |
| ESP2 | | | | 20 |
| 0 | | SS2 | | 24 |
| CR3 | | | | 28 |
| EIP | | | | 32 |
| EFLAGS | | | | 36 |
| EAX | | | | 40 |
| ECX | | | | 44 |
| EDX | | | | 48 |
| EBX | | | | 52 |
| ESP | | | | 56 |
| EBP | | | | 60 |
| ESI | | | | 64 |
| EDI | | | | 68 |
| 0 | | ES | | 72 |
| 0 | | CS | | 76 |
| 0 | | SS | | 80 |
| 0 | | DS | | 84 |
| 0 | | FS | | 88 |
| 0 | | GS | | 92 |
| 0 | | LDTR | | 96 |
| I/OP bitmap base | 0 | | T | 100 |
| | | | | 104 |
| (System dependent) | | | | |

TSS limit

**Figure 5-5.** *Task state segment (TSS).*

The GDT is the primary descriptor table. The GDT register (GDTR) contains the linear base address and limit of the GDT. Important descriptors that the operating system uses reside in the GDT. An operating system can be built using only the GDT and the IDT. The LDTs, however, provide an additional layer of protection and are helpful in building reliable systems.

The following illustration shows the mechanism used to identify a descriptor given a 16-bit selector. The selector is composed of three fields: the index, the table indicator (TI), and the requested privilege level (RPL).

| 15 | | 3 2 | 1 0 |
|---|---|---|---|
| Index | | T I | R P L |

The RPL can be used to request access to an object at a *less* privileged level than is normally granted. If you're a canny operating system designer, you don't necessarily want access at the most privileged level available to you. Using the RPL in this manner guards against misuse of highly privileged routines that can subvert the system.

Consider a programmer who tries to snoop in a "secure" system. This programmer knows that an application program that attempts to access the operating system's code will fail. Therefore, the programmer tries another tactic. The snooping application calls the operating system's disk write routine and passes it a pointer to the system segment to which it wants access. The operating system routine has enough privilege to gain access to the segment, so no protection violation occurs, and the clever programmer has a disk file that contains the desired segment. Figure 5-6 illustrates this scenario.

A secure operating system can foil attempts such as this by ensuring that the RPL field of any selector is set to the CPL of the calling routine. The ARPL (adjust

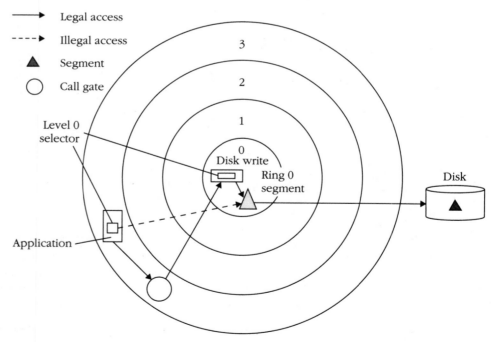

Application passes the ring 0 selector (which is illegal for it to use) to the ring 0 routine. The ring 0 routine gains access to the ring segment and writes it to disk.

**Figure 5-6.** *Access to an operating system segment.*

requested privilege level) instruction performs this function. When this is done, the system can detect that the requested privilege level (RPL) of the selector is less than (numerically higher than) the DPL of the desired segment and can refuse to complete the operation. Figure 5-7 shows the behavior of a secure operating system in this situation.

The TI bit of a selector identifies the table from which the descriptor is selected. When TI is set to 0, the selector refers to the index[th] descriptor in the GDT. A selector value of 0033H, for example, points to the GDT descriptor number 6. The first slot in the global descriptor table, GDT(0), is never used. A selector value of 0 is used as a null selector.* The null selector can be loaded into a data segment register without triggering a protection fault.

When TI is set to 1, the index refers to a descriptor in the current LDT. LDT(0) can be used to hold a valid descriptor. LDTs are usually created on a per task basis and serve two purposes. First, because a selector is 16 bits and the index field is only 13 bits, you can address a maximum of 8192 descriptors. Multiple LDTs allow you to store more descriptors. If there were only one LDT as there is only one GDT, an operating system might run out of space to store descriptors.

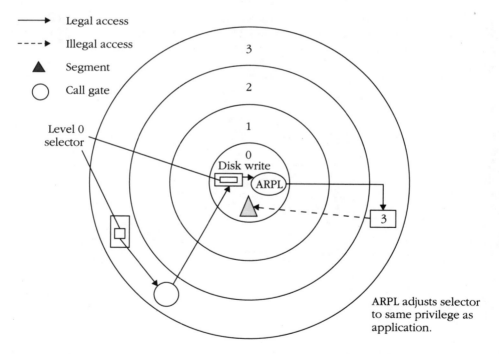

**Figure 5-7.** *Secure operating system using ARPL.*

---

* The RPL portion of the null selector is ignored, so any of the values 0, 1, 2, or 3 are valid null selectors.

Second, the LDT also gives you increased security. Figure 5-8 represents an operating system that uses only the GDT to store descriptors. The descriptors below 100 point to various operating system objects and are all ring 0 objects. GDT(100) is a ring 3 descriptor for the code segment of application A, and GDT(101) is the data segment descriptor, also in ring 3. Descriptors 102 and 103 are the descriptors for the code and the data of application B.

Any attempt by application A to access outside its code and data segments results in a protection violation. However, what if application A attempts to forge a selector? That is, what if the application tries to create an otherwise valid selector for a segment that doesn't belong to it? Creating a selector for any of the first 100 GDT slots results in a protection violation because the operating system descriptors are ring 0 objects. If application A creates a selector for GDT(103), however, it can potentially access (or destroy) data for application B. The 80386 family prevents access between rings but not inside the same ring.

Figure 5-9 shows the solution to the problem. If each application is given its own LDT, the GDT can be reserved for system use. All descriptors in the GDT point to objects in rings 0, 1, or 2. The LDT for each task contains the ring 3 (application) code and data segments. Each application has a separate LDT, so a forged selector can refer to objects only in the GDT, which are more privileged and therefore inaccessible, or to objects in its own LDT. Thus, the LDT defines a virtual address space for the application, and each task has a separate, nonoverlapping address space.

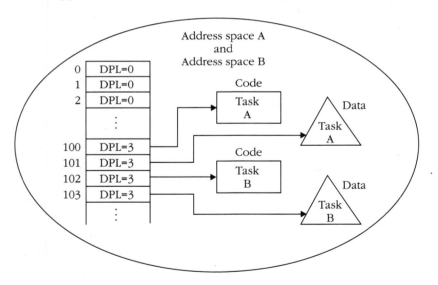

**Figure 5-8.** *Operating system using only the GDT.*

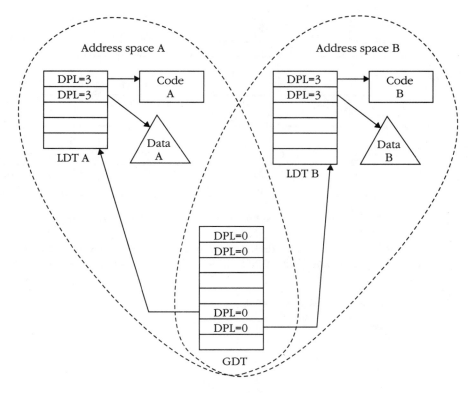

**Figure 5-9.** *Operating system using a GDT and LDTs.*

As Figure 5-9 indicates, an LDT is also a system object with its own descriptor. The next section illustrates the general format of descriptors.

# Descriptor Formats

Figure 5-10 on the following page illustrates the formats for three types of descriptors. The following are the descriptor types: program memory segments, system segments, and gates. Program memory segment descriptors were introduced in Chapter 3. System segment descriptors describe LDTs and TSSs. Like program memory segment descriptors, system segment descriptors describe regions of memory and have a base and a limit. However, you cannot load a descriptor for an LDT or a TSS into a segment register and read or write the contents as data. For an operating system to update an LDT or a TSS, it must create a memory segment descriptor with the same base address and limit, called an *alias*. Programs such as debuggers, which let you modify your program's code segments, must also create aliases because code segments are not writable under the 80386-family protection rules.

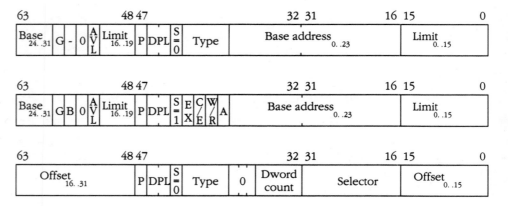

**Figure 5-10.** *General descriptor format: system, memory, and gate descriptors.*

System segments are differentiated from memory segments by a value of 0 in the S bit of the descriptor. The TYPE field of a system descriptor can hold any of the following values:

**0**—Unused (invalid descriptor)

**1**—80286 TSS

**2**—LDT

**3**—Busy 80286 TSS

**9**—80386/80486 TSS

**11**—Busy 80386/80486 TSS

A gate descriptor does not delineate a memory region and therefore has no base address or limit fields. Instead, a gate points to another descriptor via a selector. Call, interrupt, and trap gates must contain the selector for a code segment and an offset into the segment. Task gates hold a selector for a TSS, and the offset portion of the descriptor is unused.

Gate descriptors, like system segment descriptors, have the S bit set to 0 and can contain one of the following values in the TYPE field:

**4**—80286 call gate

**5**—Task gate

**6**—80286 interrupt gate

**7**—80286 trap gate

**12**—80386/80486 call gate

**14**—80386/80486 interrupt gate

**15**—80386/80486 trap gate

TYPE field values of 8, 10, and 13 are reserved for future Intel processors.

Descriptor types 1, 3, 4, 6, and 7 are used on the 80286. Operating systems designed for the 80286 (such as OS/2 V1.x) run without modification on the 80386, so these descriptor types are fully supported. A native mode system (such as OS/2 V2.x), however, or one that supports both 16-bit and 32-bit programs, uses full 32-bit descriptors. You can use 16-bit code and data descriptors in a 32-bit system, but using 16-bit system descriptors (such as task state segments) can lead to difficulties.

# Multitasking

I have previously shown how the processor uses call gates to implement interlevel subroutine calls. Interrupt and trap gates are discussed later in this chapter. The following sections show how the remaining system objects (TSSs, LDTs, and task gates) are used to implement robust multitasking operating systems.

Simply defined, a task is "a sequence of related actions leading to the accomplishment of some goal." In a computer, the resources required to accomplish the goal are usually included in the definition of a task—that is, the amount of memory, CPU time, disk space, and so on.

The term *multitasking* refers to the ability of a computer to execute more than one task simultaneously. The basic execution unit cannot execute more than one instruction stream at once, but it can execute one instruction stream, switch to another, execute it, switch to a third, execute it, switch back to the original, and so on. Because the CPU executes so rapidly, all tasks appear to execute simultaneously. *Concurrency* and *multiprogramming* are synonyms for multitasking.

An executing task is called a *process*. Thus, some people refer to multitasking as multiprocessing. Others, however, use the word *multiprocessing* to refer to systems in which multiple CPUs or processors are running simultaneously. To avoid confusion, I do not use the term multiprocessing, and I refer to computers with more than one CPU as multiprocessor systems.

Assume that each task in a computer is implemented by a single program; therefore, multiple programs must share the CPU. Various strategies exist for sharing the CPU, but to discuss and compare these strategies is beyond the scope of this book. At some level, each system must turn over control of the CPU from one task to another.

The first task might be in the middle of a computation when control is wrested from it and passed to another task; when the first task resumes, it must be able to continue processing as though nothing had happened. All the registers that the task was using must be restored to their original values when that task regains control.

The 80386/80486 hardware supports this kind of task switching via the TSS. Figure 5-11 on the following page depicts the memory layout of the TSS. Each TSS has only one descriptor, which defines its base memory address and limit. Figure 5-11 shows the TSS descriptor format immediately above the TSS. To allow access to the TSS by different privilege levels or via interrupts, you must use task gates.

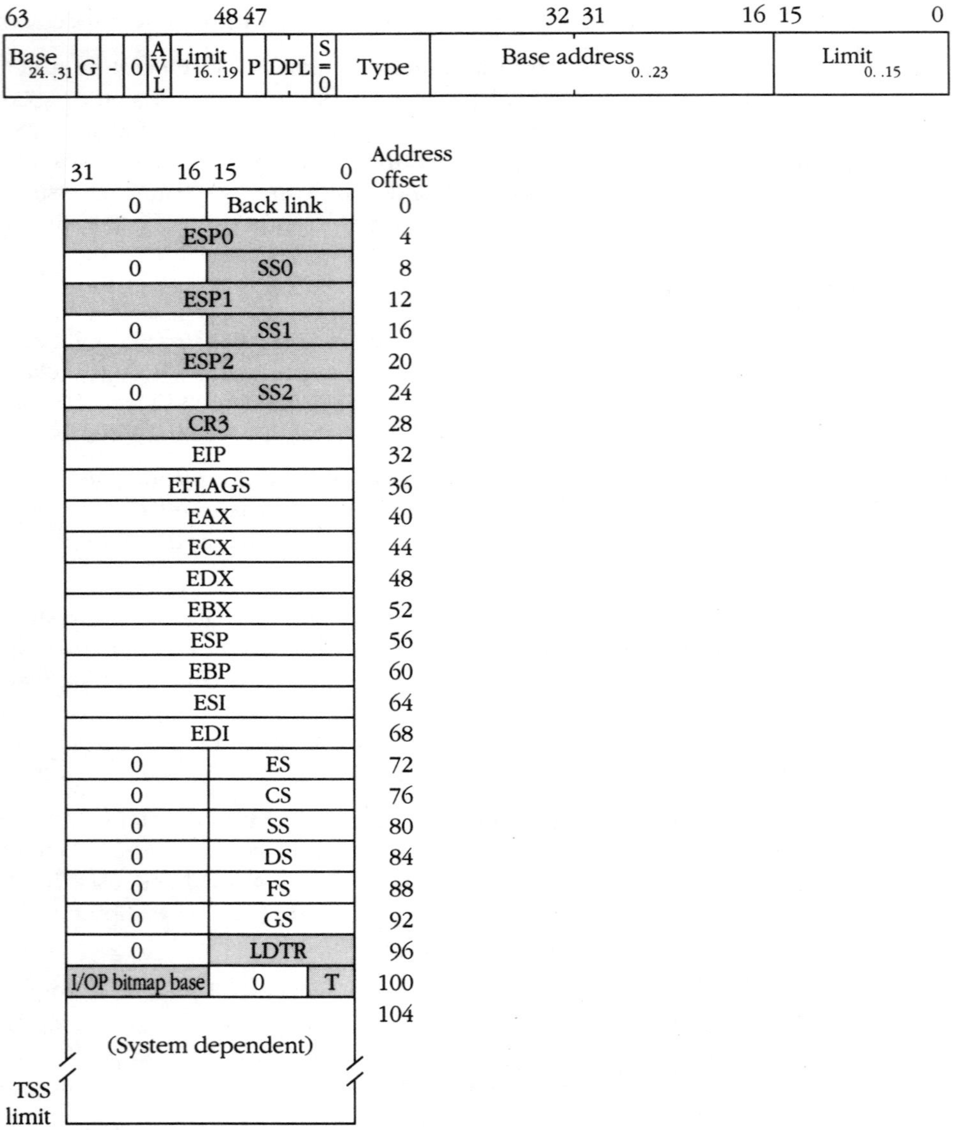

| 63 | | | | 48 | 47 | | | | | 32 | 31 | 16 | 15 | 0 |
|----|---|---|---|----|----|---|---|---|---|----|----|----|----|---|
| Base 24..31 | G | - | 0 | AVL | Limit 16..19 | P | DPL | S =0 | Type | | Base address 0..23 | | Limit 0..15 | |

| 31 | 16 | 15 | 0 | Address offset |
|----|----|----|---|---|
| 0 | | Back link | | 0 |
| ESP0 | | | | 4 |
| 0 | | SS0 | | 8 |
| ESP1 | | | | 12 |
| 0 | | SS1 | | 16 |
| ESP2 | | | | 20 |
| 0 | | SS2 | | 24 |
| CR3 | | | | 28 |
| EIP | | | | 32 |
| EFLAGS | | | | 36 |
| EAX | | | | 40 |
| ECX | | | | 44 |
| EDX | | | | 48 |
| EBX | | | | 52 |
| ESP | | | | 56 |
| EBP | | | | 60 |
| ESI | | | | 64 |
| EDI | | | | 68 |
| 0 | | ES | | 72 |
| 0 | | CS | | 76 |
| 0 | | SS | | 80 |
| 0 | | DS | | 84 |
| 0 | | FS | | 88 |
| 0 | | GS | | 92 |
| 0 | | LDTR | | 96 |
| I/OP bitmap base | | 0 | T | 100 |
| | | | | 104 |
| (System dependent) | | | | |

TSS
limit

**Figure 5-11.** *Task state segment and descriptor.*

The TSS descriptor is similar to that of a typical memory segment; however, the S bit is 0, indicating that the TSS is a system segment. The TYPE field for a TSS contains either a binary 1001B or 1011B (decimal 9 or 11). The variable bit is called the *busy bit.* This bit is set to 1 in the currently executing task and in any tasks that have called the current task, establishing a chain of nested tasks. Any attempt to invoke a task that is marked as busy triggers an exception.

The selector in the task register (TR) identifies the current task. Usually, this register is loaded once at initialization time and then is managed by the task switch operation. Loading TR does not cause a task switch; it does identify the active TSS, however.

When a task switch occurs, the state of the currently executing task is saved in its TSS, and the CPU registers are loaded from the image of the new or destination TSS. The task register contains a selector for the currently active TSS. TSS descriptors can be located only in the GDT.

Part of the TSS in Figure 5-11 is gray. The gray portion indicates values that are not stored in the outgoing TSS during a task switch, although new values are loaded from the destination TSS. If any gray value changes during execution of the task, the operating system must ensure that the TSS is kept current. The application cannot change these values; they require kernel support (privilege level 0) to be modified.

The bulk of the TSS holds copies of the general register set: EAX–EDI, the segment registers, EFLAGS, and EIP. In addition, the TSS contains these fields:

**Back link**—The selector of the TSS that was previously executing.

**SS*n*, ESP*n***—The stack pointers for ring *n* execution, as discussed in the section on call gates.

**CR3**—Control register 3, which defines the physical memory address of the page tables for the task.

**LDTR**—The selector of the LDT for the task.

**T**—The "trap on task switch" bit. A debug fault (interrupt 1) occurs when this bit is set to 1 in the incoming TSS.

**I/OP bitmap base**—A 16-bit offset into the TSS that indicates the start of the I/O permission bitmap. If this field is set to 0, no I/O permission bitmap exists.

**System dependent**—The portion of the TSS that the operating system can use to store any operating system-specific information about the task.

**I/O permission bitmap**—The field that starts at the offset indicated by the I/OP bitmap base and continues to the end of the TSS or to the base plus 8192.

## Task switching

Four events can cause a task switch:

- The current task executes a FAR CALL or JMP instruction in which the selector points to a TSS descriptor.

- The current task executes a FAR CALL or JMP instruction, and the selector points to a task gate.

■ The current task executes an IRET instruction to return to the previous task. An IRET causes a task switch only if the NT (nested task) bit of the EFLAGS register is set to 1.

■ An interrupt or exception occurs, and the IDT entry for the vector is a task gate.

For any task switch, the following events take place:

1. If the task switch is not caused by a hardware interrupt, an exception, or an IRET, the descriptor privilege rules are checked. The DPL of the descriptor (TSS or task gate) must be numerically less than the current task's CPL and the selector's RPL.

2. The present bit and limit of the descriptor for the current (outgoing) TSS is checked to ensure that the TSS is present and can hold at least 104 bytes of state information. If so, the current machine state is saved; otherwise, an exception occurs.

3. The present bit and limit of the descriptor for the new (incoming) TSS is checked. If the TSS is not present or is too small, an exception occurs; otherwise, all the register images are loaded. If the value of CR3 has changed, the TLB cache (see Chapter 7) is flushed.
   At this point, all the general and segment registers are loaded, but the shadow registers are not. CS might have a value of 217FH, but the descriptor for selector 217FH has not been loaded. The state of the outgoing task has been saved, however, and any exceptions that occur are in the context of the new state, even if the CS descriptor is not present or is invalid.

4. The linkage to the outgoing task is established. What happens next depends on what caused the task switch.

   a. If the task switch was caused by a JMP instruction, the TSS descriptor of the outgoing task is marked as not busy, and the incoming task descriptor is identified as a busy TSS.

   b. If the task switch was caused by an interrupt or a CALL instruction, the outgoing task remains busy, and the incoming task is also marked as a busy TSS. Additionally, the NT bit of the EFLAGS register is set to 1, and the back link field of the incoming TSS is set to the selector of the outgoing TSS.

   c. If the task switch was caused by an IRET instruction, the outgoing task is set to not busy.

5. The task switched (TS) bit in CR0 is set to 1, and the current privilege level for the incoming task is taken from the RPL field of the CS selector in the TSS.

6. The LDTR shadow registers are loaded if the LDTR contains a valid selector. If the LDTR value is 0 (the null selector), no action is taken. If the selector is invalid or if the new LDT is not present, an exception occurs.

7. The descriptors for CS, SS, DS, ES, FS, and GS are loaded into the shadow registers in that order. All descriptors are tested for privilege violations (CPL has already been established) and must be marked present; otherwise an exception occurs.

8. The local enable bits in DR7 are cleared to 0.

9. If the T bit of the incoming TSS is set to 1, a debug fault (interrupt 1) occurs.

10. The new task begins executing by fetching the instruction at CS:EIP.

## I/O permission bitmap

Two conditions determine whether a task is allowed to perform I/O: the I/O privilege level and the I/O permission bitmap. The IOPL bits in the EFLAGS register determine the I/O privilege level. The IOPL defines the least privileged level that can perform an I/O instruction without restriction. For example, if IOPL = 2, I/O instructions can be performed by procedures executing at levels 0, 1, or 2. An attempt to execute an instruction by a ring 3 application must be further validated by the I/O permission bitmap.

If the CPL of the current task is greater than IOPL (that is, if I/O is restricted for that task), the I/O permission bitmap is checked. This protects the I/O address space on an individual I/O port basis. The TSS stores an I/O permission bitmap for every task. The bitmap begins at the offset in the TSS specified by the 16-bit I/O map base value. The I/O map base value must be greater than or equal to 68H.

The I/O permission bitmap is a maximum of 8192 bytes, with one bit for each of the possible 65,536 I/O ports. If the bit in the bitmap corresponding to the I/O port is set to 1, then the task does not have access to the port, and a general protection fault will occur if the task attempts to execute an I/O instruction at that port.

The I/O permission bitmap is not required to be 8192 bytes. The limit field of the TSS descriptor specifies the end of the bitmap. If the I/O map base value is greater than or equal to the limit value, the TSS contains no I/O permission bitmap. All ports that do not have a bitmap position in the TSS are protected from access.

Figure 5-12 on the following page shows a sample bitmap. The task with this TSS can access ports 8, 9, 10, 11, and 12. A subroutine in this task can access byte ports 8, 9, 10, 11, and 12, word ports 8 and 10, or dword port 8.

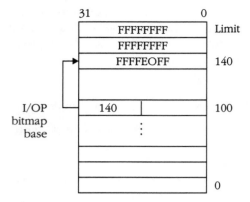

**Figure 5-12.** *I/O permission bitmap in TSS.*

# Interrupts and Exceptions

*Interrupt* is a term that refers to a variety of similar control transfers. The specific items implied by this term are true interrupts (hardware interrupts) and *exceptions,* which are further subdivided into *traps, faults,* and *aborts.*

All interrupts and exceptions share a common feature: The current execution location (CS:EIP) and flags register (EFLAGS) are saved on the stack, and control transfers to a software routine called an *interrupt handler* via a gate in the interrupt descriptor table (IDT). The processor supports a maximum of 256 descriptors in the IDT. Every interrupt or exception is associated with one of these interrupt numbers. Interrupt numbers 0 through 31 are reserved for specific purposes assigned by Intel; the operating system can assign numbers 32 through 255.

The kinds of interrupts and exceptions are:

**Interrupts**—True interrupts are caused by hardware signals that originate outside the CPU. Two pins on the 80386 or 80486, NMI and INTR, signal interrupts. Pulling the NMI pin low activates a nonmaskable interrupt. The NMI interrupt always invokes the routine associated with interrupt vector (IDT entry) 2.

An active signal on the INTR line causes a maskable interrupt. The CPU does not respond to a maskable interrupt unless the IF bit of the EFLAGS register is set to 1. When the IF bit is 0, interrupts are not recognized and are said to be *masked.* If the processor responds, it issues an interrupt-acknowledge bus cycle, and the interrupting device must respond with an interrupt number. Use only values 32–255 for maskable interrupts.

**Traps**—These are conditions that the processor regards as errors and detects after the execution of a software instruction. The saved instruction pointer (CS:EIP) on the stack points to the instruction immediately after an instruction that has trapped.

A classic example of a trap is the INTO instruction. When INTO is executed, the processor checks the value of the overflow flag (OF). If OF = 1, the CPU vectors through IDT descriptor 4.

All software interrupt (INT) instructions are handled as traps. To issue one of these instructions, however, a procedure must have access privilege to the IDT descriptor for the interrupt number. For example, if a ring 3 application executes an INT 47 instruction, the descriptor at IDT(47) must have DPL = 3; otherwise, a protection fault occurs. This mechanism prevents applications from issuing INT instructions for vectors associated with hardware interrupts because the gates for these vectors point to operating system code that runs at high privilege levels, usually ring 0.

**Faults**—When the execution unit detects an error *during* the processing of an instruction (for example, when the instruction's operand is stored in a page frame marked not present), a fault occurs. A specific interrupt number is associated with each fault condition. The instruction pointer saved on the stack after a fault occurs points to the instruction that caused the fault. Thus, the operating system can correct the condition and resume executing the instruction.

**Aborts**—When an error is so severe that some context is lost, the result is an abort. It might be impossible to determine the cause of an abort, or it might be that the instruction causing the abort is not able to be restarted.

The following table lists all of the exceptions handled by the processor:

**80386/80486 Exceptions**

| Interrupt Number | Class | Description |
| --- | --- | --- |
| 0 | Fault | Divide error |
| 1 | Fault or trap | Debugger interrupt |
| 2 | Interrupt | Nonmaskable interrupt |
| 3 | Trap | Breakpoint |
| 4 | Trap | Interrupt on overflow (INTO) |
| 5 | Fault | Array boundary violation (BOUND) |
| 6 | Fault | Invalid opcode |
| 7 | Fault | Coprocessor not available |
| 8 | Abort | Double fault |
| 9 | Abort | Coprocessor segment overrun (reserved, on 80486) |
| 10 | Fault | Invalid TSS |
| 11 | Fault | Segment not present |
| 12 | Fault | Stack exception |
| 13 | Fault | General protection violation |
| 14 | Fault | Page fault |
| 15 | Reserved | |
| 16 | Fault | Coprocessor error |
| 17 | Fault | Alignment check (80486 only) |
| 18–31 | Reserved | |
| 32–255 | Interrupt or trap | System dependent |

One class of error is more severe than an abort. If the processor is unable to continue processing an exception, it shuts down. In a protected-mode environment, the system should shut down only if a hardware failure occurs. To prevent shutdown, the vectors that handle the double fault (interrupt 8) and invalid TSS (interrupt 10) conditions should be separate tasks, and IDT entries 8 and 10 should be task gates. This approach allows the CPU to load a new machine state from which to handle the exceptions. If this is not done, the exception handler might be running in the same environment that caused the failures and might not be able to continue processing.

## Interrupt gates, trap gates, and task gates

The only types of descriptors that can reside in the IDT are interrupt gates, trap gates, and task gates. Task gates in the IDT are identical to those in the GDT and operate in the same manner.

When a task gate is invoked with an interrupt or with an exception, the machine state is saved in the existing TSS, and a new state is loaded from the TSS associated with the task gate. Thus, an interrupt can have its own address space, including its own page tables and LDT. In addition, the interrupt handler is prevented from using too much of the interrupted application's stack and from corrupting any registers. A task switch takes longer to execute than a gate transfer, however, and the advantages of invoking a task gate must be weighed against performance considerations.

The most common entries in the IDT are interrupt gates and trap gates. These descriptors have identical formats—only the type code is different. Figure 5-13 illustrates the descriptor format for interrupt gates. The only difference in behavior between the two gates is that when an interrupt gate is activated, the IF bit of the EFLAGS register is cleared to 0. Hardware interrupts are masked until the interrupt handler deems it safe to reenable them. Transferring control through a trap gate does not modify the interrupt flag.

| 63 | 48 | 47 | | | 32 | 31 | 16 | 15 | 0 |
|---|---|---|---|---|---|---|---|---|---|
| Offset$_{16..31}$ | | P | DPL | S = 0 | Type | 0 | | Selector | Offset$_{0..15}$ |

**Figure 5-13.** *Interrupt gate and trap gate descriptor format.*

The behavior of interrupt gates and trap gates is similar to that of call gates. Although interrupt gates and trap gates do not contain a word count field, they can point to code segments of specific privilege levels or to conforming segments. Figure 5-14 shows the layout of the stack when an interrupt handler is invoked.

An interrupt handler must return to the calling routine via an IRET instruction. The IRET restores the original instruction pointer, flags, and stack segment. If the NT (nested task) bit was set in the EFLAGS register, a task switch to the original TSS also occurs. The programmer should remove any error code (generated by the fault) from the stack before returning from the interrupt handler.

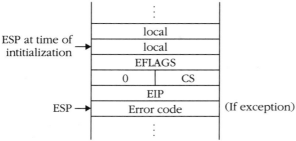

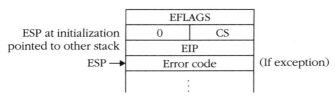

**Figure 5-14.** *Interrupt stack without and with privilege transition.*

## 80386-family processor exceptions

The following sections explain the faults, traps, and aborts that can occur during program execution. Some exceptions cause a control transfer via the IDT; others cause an error code to be pushed onto the stack as well. If an error code is pushed, it is pushed onto the stack of the interrupt handler; that is, it is pushed after any privilege level or task transition. Exceptions that cause error codes to be pushed onto the stack are indicated in the following sections with the symbol *[ec]*. The value of the error code is either 0 or as defined in the following illustration:

| 31 | 16 | 15 | | 2 | 1 | 0 |
|---|---|---|---|---|---|---|
| Undefined | | Selector index | | TI | I | EX |

The selector index and TI fields are taken from the selector of the segment associated with the exception. Instead of an RPL field, however, the error code has an I bit and an EX bit. The I bit is set to 1 when the index refers to an IDT index, and the TI bit is ignored. When I = 0, the TI bit indicates whether the selector is from the GDT (TI = 0) or from the current LDT (TI = 1). If the EX bit is set to 1, the fault was caused by an event outside the executing program.

### Interrupt 0—Divide (fault)

A divide fault occurs if division by zero is attempted or if the result of a divide operation does not fit into the destination operand. (This applies only to division by DIV or DIY, not to floating-point division.)

### Interrupt 1—Debugger (fault or trap)

This exception is triggered by one of the following conditions:

Debug register breakpoint

Single step trap

Task switch trap

The "Debugging" section later in this chapter covers the triggering and handling of debug traps in detail.

### Interrupt 2—NMI (interrupt)

IDT vector 2 is reserved for the hardware NMI condition. No exceptions trap through vector 2.

### Interrupt 3—Breakpoint (trap)

Debuggers use the breakpoint interrupt (INT 3), which is covered in the "Debugging" section later in this chapter.

### Interrupt 4—Overflow (trap)

The overflow trap occurs after an INTO instruction has executed if the OF bit is set to 1. The INTO instruction is useful in languages such as Ada that require arithmetic instructions either to produce a valid result or to raise an exception.

### Interrupt 5—Bounds check (fault)

Like interrupt 4, the bounds check trap occurs as the result of a software instruction. The BOUND instruction compares an array index with an upper bound and a lower bound. If the index is out of range, the processor traps to vector 5.

### Interrupt 6—Invalid opcode (fault)

An interrupt 6 fault occurs if:

- The processor tries to decode a bit pattern that does not correspond to any legal machine instruction.

- The processor tries to execute an instruction that contains invalid operands.

- The processor tries to execute a protected-mode instruction while running in real mode or in virtual 8086 mode.

- The processor tries to execute a LOCK prefix with an instruction that cannot be locked.

Opcodes that are illegal on the 8086 or cause an invalid opcode fault on the 80286 do not always cause an exception when the 80386/80486 executes in real mode. The opcodes might correspond to new instructions that are valid in any 80386/80486 operating mode.

### Interrupt 7—Coprocessor not available (fault)

When a computer does not contain an 80287 or 80387 coprocessor, the operating system can set the EM bit of register CR0 to indicate NDP software emulation. If the EM bit of register CR0 is set, an interrupt 7 fault occurs each time a floating-point instruction is encountered.

This fault also occurs if the MP bit of CR0 is set and the 80386 executes a WAIT or floating-point instruction after a task switch. The task switch sets the TS bit to 1. The operating system can clear TS after a task switch to prevent the fault from occurring. The 80386 uses this method to signal that the state of the math coprocessor needs to be saved so that it can be used by another task.

### Interrupt 8—Double fault (abort) [ec]

Processing an exception sometimes triggers a second exception. For example, suppose that a divide fault occurs during the processing of an application and that the trap gate for interrupt 0 points to a conforming segment so that the privilege level does not change. Now suppose that the user stack does not have room for the CS, EIP, and EFLAGS pushed by the divide fault. The condition of being unable to process the divide exception correctly would result in a double fault.

Not all exception pairs result in double faults. In some cases, most notably when getting access to the fault handler causes a page fault, the second fault is processed first, and then control transfers to the initial exception handler. The following table shows the exception pairs that trigger a double fault:

| Initial Exception | Double Fault If Followed By |
| --- | --- |
| 0 (Divide fault) | 0, 9*, 10, 11, 12, 13 |
| 9* (NDP segment overrun) | 0, 9*, 10, 11, 12, 13 |
| 10 (Invalid TSS) | 0, 9*, 10, 11, 12, 13 |
| 11 (Not present) | 0, 9*, 10, 11, 12, 13 |
| 12 (Stack fault) | 0, 9*, 10, 11, 12, 13 |
| 13 (General protection) | 0, 9*, 10, 11, 12, 13 |
| 14 (Page fault) | 0, 9*, 10, 11, 12, 13, 14 |

*Does not apply to the 80486.

A task gate can best handle the double fault vector, although a secure ring 0 segment usually works. You should use the method best suited for placing the system in a known state, because the processor shuts down if a third fault occurs while the processor is trying to start the interrupt 8 exception handler.

The shutdown state is similar to the halt state. Only a processor reset or NMI (if the NMI vector is valid) can bring the processor out of shutdown. A special shutdown signal is placed on the bus so that external hardware can detect the shutdown. An error code of 0 is pushed onto the stack when a double fault exception occurs.

### Interrupt 9—Coprocessor segment overrun (abort)

The coprocessor segment overrun exception is signaled when a floating-point instruction causes a memory access that runs beyond the end of a segment. If the starting address of a floating-point operand is outside the segment limit, a general protection fault (interrupt 13) occurs rather than an interrupt 9.

The segment overrun exception is classified as an abort because the instruction cannot be restarted. You must use the FNINIT instruction to reinitialize the 80387 coprocessor. The CS:EIP saved on the stack will point to the offending instruction. (Note: This interrupt is not generated by 80486 systems.)

### Interrupt 10—Invalid task state segment (fault) [ec]

Because the TSS contains a number of descriptors, a variety of causes can trigger an interrupt 10. The processor pushes an error code onto the stack to aid in diagnosing the error condition. The following table lists invalid TSS fault conditions and the value of the error code pushed onto the stack for each condition. The items are listed in the order in which they are checked by the CPU.

| Condition | Error Code Value |
|---|---|
| Outgoing TSS limit < 103 | TSS index : TI : EXT |
| Incoming TSS limit < 103 | TSS index : TI : EXT |
| LDT selector has TI = 1 | LDT index : TI : EXT |
| LDT descriptor has S = 1 | LDT index : TI : EXT |
| LDT descriptor TYPE != 2 | LDT index : TI : EXT |
| LDT descriptor not present | LDT index : TI : EXT |
| CS selector is null | CS index |
| CS descriptor has S = 0 | CS index |
| CS descriptor not executable | CS index |
| CS conforming, DPL > CPL | CS index |
| CS not conforming, DPL != CPL or DPL < RPL | CS index |
| SS selector is null | SS index |
| SS selector RPL != CPL | SS index |
| SS descriptor has S = 0 | SS index |
| SS descriptor not writable | SS index |
| The following checks are made for all other selectors in the order DS, ES, FS, and GS: | |
| Descriptor has S = 0 | DS, ES, FS, or GS index |
| Descriptor is execute only | DS, ES, FS, or GS index |
| Descriptor not conforming, DPL < CPL or DPL < RPL | DS, ES, FS, or GS index |

The CPL value is taken from the RPL of the incoming CS selector. If one of the memory segment descriptors is marked not present, a not present fault or stack fault occurs rather than the invalid TSS fault. The TSS load stops at the point of the fault, and the other exception handler must ensure that the remaining segment registers get loaded.

### Interrupt 11—Not present (fault) [ec]

The not present interrupt lets you implement virtual memory via the segmentation mechanism. An operating system can mark a memory segment as not present and swap its contents out to disk. The interrupt 11 fault is triggered when an application needs to access the segment.

This fault occurs when the processor tries to gain access to a descriptor that is not present (P = 0). Loading DS, ES, FS, or GS triggers the fault, as does a FAR CALL or JMP that either loads CS with a segment marked not present or accesses a gate whose descriptor is marked not present. In addition, the LLDT and LTR instructions cause descriptors to be loaded and can trigger the fault.

A segment fault that occurs when loading the SS register results in a stack fault (interrupt 12) rather than in a not present fault. Additionally, when the LDTR is loaded during a task switch rather than by the LLDT instruction, an invalid TSS exception occurs if the descriptor has P = 0.

The CS and EIP that are pushed onto the stack as a result of the exception usually point to the offending instruction. Also pushed is an error code that identifies the selector involved in the fault. The only time that CS:EIP does not point to the offending instruction is when a task switch occurs and a selector in the new task image causes the not present exception.

In this case, the CS:EIP points to the first instruction of the new task. The selectors are loaded in the order SS, DS, ES, FS, and GS, and the task switch terminates at the point of the fault. The interrupt 11 fault handler must handle the fault and validate the remaining selectors. If the interrupt 11 fault handler is invoked via a task gate, this happens on the IRET that ends interrupt 11. If a trap gate invokes the interrupt, however, the fault handler must test each selector with the LAR instruction.

### Interrupt 12—Stack (fault) [ec]

A task gate should handle this exception because the state of the stack is unknown when a stack fault occurs. You can use a level 0 trap gate, but if a stack fault occurs at ring 0, the trap to the interrupt 12 handler results in an immediate double fault.

A stack fault with an error code of 0 occurs if a normal instruction refers to memory beyond the limits of the stack segment. This includes instructions such as PUSH and POP, and instructions that use an SS: segment override or use EBP as a base register. In addition, the ENTER instruction causes the same fault if it causes ESP to be decremented beyond the lower bound of the segment. Instructions such as SUB ESP, 10 do not cause stack faults.

If the stack fault is triggered by loading SS with a not present selector or if the fault occurs during gated transition between privilege rings, an error code indicating the offending selector is pushed onto the stack. Loading SS with invalid descriptors (out of range, segment not writable, and so on) results in a general protection fault rather than a stack fault.

When the error code is 0, this usually means that a given stack segment is too small. If the operating system supports expand-down segments, it can expand the stack of the faulting application. The saved CS:EIP points to the faulting instruction, which can always be restarted; however, the same caveat that applies to task switches and not present exceptions also applies to stack faults. See the final paragraph of "Interrupt 11—Not present (fault)[ec]" for more details.

## Interrupt 13—General protection (fault) [ec]

Any condition not covered by some other exception triggers a general protection fault. This fault usually indicates that the program has been corrupted and should be "terminated with prejudice," as the old UNIX phrase goes.

The exception to this rule is that V86 mode tasks trigger general protection faults when the system needs to be "virtualized." For example, a V86 task that tries to disable interrupts or issue a software interrupt instruction triggers a general protection fault when IOPL < 3. In such a case, the interrupt handler must determine the proper behavior and return control to the faulting task.

The operating system can restart any instruction that triggers a general protection fault, although doing so is often inappropriate. An error code is always pushed onto the stack as part of the exception; in many cases, however, the value is 0. When the value is not 0, the value indicates the selector that caused the exception.

## Interrupt 14—Page (fault) [ec]

The page fault interrupt lets you implement virtual memory on a demand-paged basis. An interrupt 14 occurs whenever an access to a page directory entry or page table entry refers to an entry with the present bit set to 0. The operating system makes the page present, updates the table entry, and restarts the faulting instruction. A page fault also occurs when a paging protection rule is violated. In this case, the operating system needs to take other appropriate action.

When a page fault occurs, the CR2 register is loaded with the linear address that caused the fault, and an error code is pushed onto the stack. The page fault error code is different from that of the other exceptions and has this format:

| 31 | | 3 | 2 | 1 | 0 |
|---|---|---|---|---|---|
| Undefined | | | U/S | W/R | P |

The three low-order bits of the error code provide more information about why the address in CR2 caused the fault. The P bit is set to 1 if the fault was a page protection fault rather than a page not present fault. The W/R bit is set to 1 if the faulting instruction was attempting to write to memory. The bit is cleared to 0 if the fault occurred during a read. Finally, the U/S bit is set to 1 if the faulting instruction was executing in user mode and is cleared to 0 if the instruction was a supervisor instruction. (User mode and supervisor mode are discussed in Chapter 7.)

Because of the large number of divergent memory accesses that occur during a task switch, operating system designers should ensure that important task tables (the GDT, application TSS, and application LDT) are resident in memory before executing the task switch. The situations that arise if page faults occur during a task switch are not impossible to deal with; system design is simpler if you avoid them.

### Interrupt 15
This vector is reserved for future Intel processors.

### Interrupt 16—Coprocessor error (fault)
This interrupt occurs at the start of an ESC (coprocessor) instruction when an unmasked floating-point exception has been signaled by a previous instruction. (Because the 80386 does not have direct access to the FPU, it checks the ERROR\ pin to test this condition.)

The interrupt is also triggered by a WAIT instruction if the EM bit at CR0 is set.

Either of these conditions will automatically trigger the interrupt in the 80386. In the 80486, however, you must also set the NE bit in CR0 to enable the interrupt. If NE is 0, the processor will halt until an external hardware interrupt occurs.

Note: The NE bit is new in the 80486; this requirement does not apply to 80386 systems.

### Interrupt 17—Alignment check (fault) [ec]
This interrupt occurs only on the 80486. Interrupt 17 is reserved on the 80386. It occurs when code executing at the application level (privilege level 3) attempts to access a word operand that is not on an even-address boundary, a doubleword operand whose address is not divisible by four, or a long real or temp real whose address is not divisible by eight. Alignment checking is disabled when the processor is first powered up. It is enabled by setting the AC bit in the EFLAGS register and the AM bit in CR0.

### Interrupts 18–31
These vectors are reserved for future Intel processors.

### Interrupts 32–255
These vectors are available for use by an operating system. The system can install interrupt, trap, or task gates in any IDT slot corresponding to one of these interrupts. The interrupt handlers can be invoked by software INT $n$ instructions or by hardware that signals the CPU via the INTR pin.

## Interrupt masking and priority

The only programming mechanisms for masking interrupts are the CLI/STI instructions, which affect the hardware INTR line. However, other situations prevent certain types of interrupts, either by design or because a more important interrupt is pending. Interrupts have the following priority ranking:

1. Nondebug faults

2. Trap instructions (software interrupts INT 0, INT 3, INT *n*)

3. Debug traps for the current instruction

4. Debug faults for the pending instruction

5. Hardware NMI

6. Hardware INTR interrupt

For example, if a page fault and a debug fault are triggered on the same instruction, the page fault takes priority, and the debug fault is masked. However, when the page fault handler completes its operation and restarts the faulting instruction, the debug fault is retriggered.

Other interrupt masking conditions occur when:

- An NMI is triggered. Further NMIs are masked until the next IRET instruction occurs.

- A debug fault occurs. Debug faults cause the RF bit in the EFLAGS register to be set, masking additional debug interrupts. The processor clears RF upon successfully completing an instruction.

- The SS register is loaded. Hardware interrupts (both NMI and INTR) and debug exceptions (including single-step) are masked for the duration of one instruction after SS is loaded. Thus, the ESP register can load without risk of invoking an interrupt handler with an invalid stack pointer. The instruction that loads ESP can, however, receive a page fault, and the interrupt 14 routine will be invoked with an invalid stack pointer, possibly leading to a double fault. You can avoid this by loading both SS and ESP using a single instruction, LSS.

## Debugging

Traditionally, microprocessors have never contributed much to solving the problem of debugging. Debugging on microprocessors has been accomplished with breakpoint instructions and with the ability to single-step (execute one instruction at a time); but for difficult problems, programmers have had to turn to in-circuit emulators or hardware-assisted debuggers.

As microcomputer systems become more sophisticated, hardware's ability to determine what is going on inside the CPU diminishes. For example, assume that a programmer wants to be notified that a particular data structure has been modified.

Because of paging, the structure might not be in contiguous memory. The operating system's virtual memory capability allows it to move the program out from under the eye of the debugging hardware, and thus the program's linear and symbolic addresses bear no relation to the generated hardware addresses.

Fortunately, the chip designers at Intel recognized these problems and added features to their processors that system software can use to aid in debugging. Four mechanisms trigger debug interrupts under different conditions: trap flag, task switch trap, breakpoint registers, and software breakpoint.

### Trap flag

Setting the TF bit in the EFLAGS register causes a single-step fault (interrupt 1) to occur before the next instruction. The CPU clears the TF bit before invoking the handler pointed to by IDT(1), although the saved image of EFLAGS on the stack has the trap flag set.

When a software interrupt instruction (INT, INTO) is executed, the TF bit is cleared. A debugger should not attempt to single-step an INT instruction but should place a breakpoint either at the destination of the gate pointed to by INT or immediately after the INT instruction.

A call gate does not clear the trap flag, so a debugger should check all FAR CALLs and JMPs to see whether they cause a change in privilege level. If so, programmers should not be allowed to single-step into code more privileged than their applications.

### Task switch trap

When the T bit of a TSS is set to 1, switching to the TSS's task invokes the debugger fault (interrupt 1). The fault does not occur until after the contents of the TSS are loaded and before the first instruction of the task is executed.

### Breakpoint registers

The debug registers (DR0–DR7) implement four address breakpoints. When the debug address registers are correctly initialized, each identifies a linear address. If the processor accesses that address, then a debugger fault (interrupt 1) occurs. The debug registers are described in detail in "Programming the debug registers" in this chapter.

### Software breakpoint

The single-byte INT 3 (0CCH) instruction triggers this interrupt. By replacing the first byte of an instruction with an INT 3, a debugger can cause a breakpoint to occur when the execution stream reaches the INT 3. Because the software interrupts are classified as traps, the saved CS and EIP on the stack point to the byte immediately after INT 3. To restart the program, the debugger must replace the 0CCH value with the first byte of the original instruction, decrement EIP so that it points to the start of the instruction, and execute an IRET to return from the interrupt handler.

This method of implementing breakpoints is much clumsier than using the debug registers because it requires creating a writable alias for a code segment, saving the original instruction byte, replacing the instruction with an INT 3, and undoing the above when the breakpoint has been triggered. However, because the debug registers allow only four active breakpoints at once, a reasonable trade-off is to use debug registers for data space breakpoints and INT 3 for code space breakpoints.

## Programming the debug registers

Figure 5-15 shows the layout of the debug registers. To load a value into one of the registers, use a MOV DR*x*, reg instruction. Similarly, using MOV reg, DR*x* reads the contents of a debug register into one of the 32-bit general registers.

The first four registers (DR0–DR3) are address registers. The linear address of a desired breakpoint must be loaded into one of these registers. The debug registers are not affected by paging. Only the linear address (from the descriptors) is used to match a breakpoint address. Debug registers DR4 and DR5 are reserved for future Intel microprocessors.

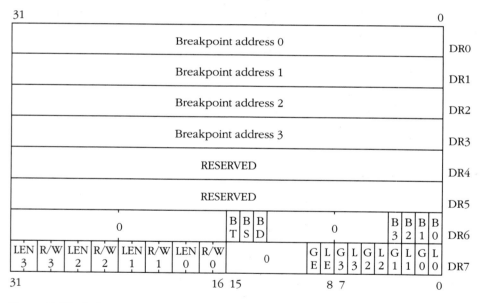

**Figure 5-15.** *Debug registers.*

Register DR6 is the status register. It indicates the conditions that lead to the interrupt. A bit is set to 1 in DR6 if the condition associated with the bit has been met. The following table identifies the bits and the reasons for the interrupt.

| Bit | Reason |
|-----|--------|
| B0 | Breakpoint register 0 triggered |
| B1 | Breakpoint register 1 triggered |
| B2 | Breakpoint register 2 triggered |
| B3 | Breakpoint register 3 triggered |
| BD | Intel ICE hardware active |
| BS | Single step (TF set to 1) |
| BT | Task with switch occurred; new task's TSS T bit set to 1 |

Bits B0–B3 are set to 1 if the breakpoint in DR0–DR3 was matched during execution, even if the breakpoint was *not* enabled and did not cause the debug fault.

When Intel ICE hardware is used, the debug registers are reserved for the in-circuit emulator. The BD bit is set to 1, and any attempt to place (MOV) a value into one of the debug registers triggers an interrupt 1.

The debug interrupt handler must clear the contents of register DR6. The CPU sets bits, but bits can be cleared only programmatically.

DR7 is the debug control register. Merely placing an address in DR0–DR3 will not enable a breakpoint. The enable bit(s) in DR7 must be set, as must the breakpoint length and condition.

The LEN$n$ fields let you specify the length of breakpoint $n$. The length values are encoded as follows:

**00**—Byte / breakpoint legal at any address

**01**—Word (2 bytes) / breakpoint must be on even address

**10**—Reserved for future use

**11**—Dword (4 bytes) / breakpoint address must be on dword boundary

The R/W$n$ field allows you to specify the type of memory access that triggers breakpoint $n$. This field is encoded as follows:

**00**—Execution breakpoint

**01**—Memory write breakpoint

**10**—Reserved for future use

**11**—Memory read or write breakpoint

When R/W is set to 00B, an execution breakpoint, the corresponding LEN field also must be set to 00B. An execution breakpoint is triggered only if the breakpoint address is set to the first byte of the instruction. If any prefix bytes are part of the instruction, the breakpoint must be set to the address at the first prefix byte.

The L$n$ and G$n$ bits allow breakpoints to be locally or globally enabled. If neither the L nor the G bit is set, the breakpoint is disabled and does not trigger an interrupt, although the corresponding bit in DR6 is set if the breakpoint condition is met.

If only the L bit is set, the breakpoint is locally enabled. A task switch clears the L bits. The system should mark the T bit in the TSS of the task using locally enabled breakpoints so that an interrupt 1 occurs when the task is reactivated. Then the L bits can be reset.

If the G bit is set, the breakpoint is globally enabled and can be disabled only by clearing G to 0. (Setting both the L and G bits equals setting the G bit.)

Register DR7 contains two other bits, LE and GE. When either bit is set, it enables the exact match condition. When exact match is enabled, the processor slows to ensure that the interrupt 1 fault reports the instruction that triggered the breakpoint. If LE and GE are 0, the execution unit might get ahead of the debug unit because of the internal parallelism in the processor, and the CS and EIP on the interrupt handler stack might point one or two instructions beyond the one that triggered the fault. The performance loss is not significant, and LE and GE should be enabled. The difference between the two bits is that LE is cleared after a task switch, as are the L$n$ bits.

## Triggering the debug interrupt

The following table shows how the address and control fields define a breakpoint condition and gives examples of instructions that do or do not trigger the breakpoint. The table assumes a base address of CS = 0003A000H and DS = 0004C000H and that G0 = 0.

| Debug Register Settings | Instruction | Break-point | Reason |
|---|---|---|---|
| **DR0: 0004C020H** | | | |
| DR7: L0 = 1, R/W0 = 00B LEN0 = 00B | MOV AL, [20] | N | Execution breakpoint |
| **DR0: 0004C020H** | | | |
| DR7: L0 = 1, R/W0 = 11B LEN0 = 00B | MOV AL, [20] | Y | Byte 4C020H read |
| **DR0: 0004C020H** | | | |
| DR7: L0 = 1, R/W0 = 01B LEN0 = 00B | MOV AL, [20] | N | Breakpoint on write access only |
| **DR0: 0004C020H** | | | |
| DR7: L0 = 1, R/W0 = 11B LEN0 = 11B | MOV AL, [23] | Y | Breakpoint covers 4 bytes |
| **DR0: 0004C020H** | | | |
| DR7: L0 = 1, R/W0 = 11B LEN0 = 11B | INC DWORD PTR [01E] | Y | Dword extends into breakpoint area |

*(continued)*

*continued*

| Debug Register Settings | Instruction | Break-point | Reason |
|---|---|---|---|
| **DR0: 0004C020H** | | | |
| DR7: L0 = 0, R/W0 = 11B LEN0 = 11B | INC DWORD PTR [01E] | N | Breakpoint not enabled |
| **DR0: 0003A000H** | | | |
| DR7: L0 = 1, R/W0 = 00B LEN0 = 00B | CS:0000 MOV AL, 37H | Y | Execution breakpoint |
| **DR0: 0003A001H** | | | |
| DR7: L0 = 1, R/W0 = 00B LEN0 = 00B | CS:0000 MOV AL, 37H | N | Execution breakpoint not at first byte of instruction |

# MEMORY ARCHITECTURE: PAGING AND CACHE MANAGEMENT

This chapter covers the paging mechanism, which is nearly identical in both the 80386 and 80486, and the internal cache, which is present only in the 80486. Many computer systems built with 80386s have caches, but the cache is implemented in external hardware. In some 80486 machines, there will be two caches: the 8-KB internal cache and a system cache similar to those in advanced 80386 systems. This chapter's descriptions refer only to the 80486 internal cache, but 80386 users may still be interested in it, as the general concepts apply to any caching system.

## Paging

Paging is used to implement virtual memory based on fixed-size blocks called *pages*. Paging is probably the most widely used virtual memory technique on today's minicomputers and mainframes.

Like segmentation, paging translates virtual addresses into physical addresses. Addresses are translated by mapping fixed-size blocks of memory into physical memory locations called *page frames*. Consider a physical memory system composed of page frames 0, 1, 2, and 3, each having 10 bytes of memory. A virtual address consists of a frame name and an offset, so assume that the frames have the names A, B, C, and D. The memory system also contains a page table for converting the virtual address into a physical address. Figure 6-1 shows how virtual address C7 is mapped into physical address 17. The arrows indicate the page mapping.

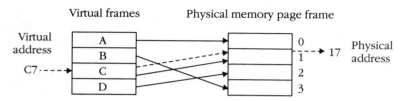

**Figure 6-1.** *Translating a virtual address to a physical address.*

Segmentation and paging are similar: A name and an offset are translated to an address. This mapping is the essence of virtual memory. However, segmentation and mapping are also different. Assume that any virtual address from the previous example consists of a two-digit number and that the digit in the 10's place is the frame name, rather than a letter, as in Figure 6-1. A virtual memory translation would resemble Figure 6-2. In this example, virtual address 27 is translated to physical address 17.

Because pages have a fixed size, a virtual address can be easily separated into a name and an offset. A page table lookup converts every virtual address into a physical address.

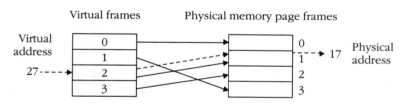

**Figure 6-2.** *Virtual address translation of fixed-size elements.*

## Advantages and disadvantages

A fixed page size is the key to the advantages of paging over segmentation. Because a disk is usually the secondary storage for a virtual memory system, you can choose page sizes that map well into the sector size of the disk. Paging also avoids the fragmentation problem of segmentation. Every time a page is swapped out, another page fits exactly into the freed page frame.

Another advantage of paging is that allocation for a large object (for example, a memory segment) does not have to be contiguous. An object that was contained in virtual pages 1 and 2 in Figure 6-2 would not be stored in consecutive physical memory locations.

Finally, paging is invisible to the programmer. Unlike segmentation, which requires you to know the virtual name (segment) and offset of an object in memory, paging requires you to know only one address. The virtual address is broken down into its components by the virtual memory mechanism in the hardware.

Paging isn't perfect. Using paging means losing the protection rings implemented with segmentation. Paging is also subject to a different kind of fragmentation, called *internal fragmentation,* which occurs when you store objects that do not fit into a page or a sequence of pages. For example, if the page size is 10 bytes, an 11-byte object requires two pages, which wastes memory.

Additionally, paging incurs more overhead than does segmentation. In a segmented system, the table lookups that are needed to convert a virtual address to a physical one occur only when a new segment is loaded. In a paged system, a virtual-to-physical translation must be performed for every memory access. This would not be an issue if the entire page table could be stored in the CPU, but processors with gigabyte address spaces require very large page tables.

These problems are not insurmountable, however. You can implement a simple protection scheme with paging alone; you can also use segmentation and paging together. Internal fragmentation is not usually as serious as segment fragmentation, and the CPU's internal parallelism and a special cache called the translation look-aside buffer (TLB) are used to help alleviate the page translation overhead. The TLB is a special-purpose cache used only by the paging unit. It exists in all members of the 80386 family and is not to be confused with the internal cache of the 80486.

## The Intel paging implementation

The size of a page frame on the 80386 family is 4096, or $2^{12}$, bytes. Paging is enabled when the PG bit of CR0 is set to 1. (Once paging is enabled, usually by operating system software, it will probably not be disabled.) Translation treats the linear address generated by the segmentation unit as a virtual address and performs page mapping on it. Thus, memory references on the 80386 family go through the following stages:

Segment:offset → linear address → physical address

A linear address is a 32-bit value. To interpret it as a virtual address, take the high-order 20 bits as a frame name, and use the low-order 12 bits as an offset into the 4096-byte page. To generate a 32-bit physical address, each entry in the page table must translate the frame name to a frame address. Frame address 0 corresponds to physical addresses 0–4095, frame address 1 identifies physical addresses 4096–8191, and so on. A page table entry must also provide additional page status bits for a protection model and for swapping. Thus, a page table entry has this format:

| 31                   12 | 11 | | | | | P C D* | P W T* | U / S | R / W | P |
|---|---|---|---|---|---|---|---|---|---|---|
| Page frame address 31. . .12 | Avail | 0 | 0 | D | A | | | | | |

\* 80486 only

The bits marked 0 are reserved for use by future Intel processors. The field marked *Avail* can be used by system programmers to mark pages that are shared among tasks, to hold usage information, or to store other paging data. The page frame address becomes the high-order bits of the physical address. The CPU sets the D (dirty) bit to 1 when a write operation occurs within the specified page. The CPU sets the A (accessed) bit to 1 when any memory access (read, write, or fetch) occurs within the page.

The PCD (page cache disable) and PWT (page write-through) bits are the page-level equivalent of the CD and WT bits in control register 0. PCD is used to disable caching or cache write-through on a page-by-page basis. PWT is a "policy" bit only for external cache hardware; it has no effect on the processor. Setting PWT = 1 defines a "write through" cache policy: PWT = 0 stands for "write back." Because the 80386 has no internal cache, these bits should always be set to 0 in 80386 software.

The U/S and R/W bits are part of paging's protection mechanism. They are discussed in this chapter's "Page Protection" section.

When the P (present) bit is set to 1, the page is present in memory. If P = 0, the page is assumed to be swapped to disk, and any attempt to access the page results in a page fault (interrupt 14). When P = 0, all other bits in the page table (31–1) are irrelevant and can be used by the system programmer. Frequently, a swapped page's location on disk is stored in those bits when the page is not present.

## Page tables and page directories

Each page is $2^{12}$ bytes, and physical address space is $2^{32}$ bytes, so $2^{20}$ (more than 1 million) page table entries are required to implement a virtual-to-physical translation table. Because each entry takes up 4 bytes, a page table requires 4 MB of memory. If a frame address alone indicated the page table entry, the page table would require 4 MB of contiguous memory. In a multitasking system that provides a separate virtual address space for each task, each task requires a 4-MB block of memory in addition to its code and data.

The solution to this space problem, swapping out the page table, cannot be implemented with a simple, one-level page table. For example, if a program tries to access address $x$, the page table entry (PTE) for $x$ must be brought into memory. Because the page table is itself paged, the PTE for PTE($x$) must be brought into memory first. Swapping continues until the initial page of the page table is swapped in.

A better solution, the one implemented by the 80386 family, is a two-level page table. In this scheme, the virtual name component of the virtual address (the high-order 20 bits) is split into two parts. The high-order 10 bits are used as an index into a *page directory*. A page directory entry (PDE) points to a scaled-down page table that contains 1024 entries. The 10 bits left over in the virtual address select the page table entries from the page table. Figure 6-3 illustrates the two-level page structure.

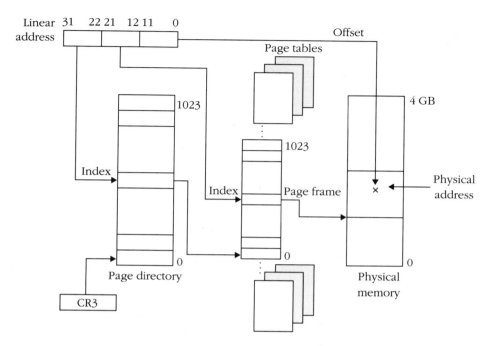

**Figure 6-3.** *Page table/directory structure.*

This structure solves the problem of swapping out the page table because the initial lookup goes through the page directory. The page directory, with 1024 32-bit entries, takes up only 4 KB and is permanently stored in memory. Each page table also takes up 4 KB (fits right into a page!) and has 1024 page table entries.

Register CR3 contains the physical address of the page directory for a task. CR3 is the only register that contains a physical (as distinct from virtual) memory address. A page directory entry has the same format as a page table entry except that the D bit is unused and the A bit is set to 1 whenever one of the page tables pointed to by the page directory is used.

## A detailed example

Figure 6-4 on the following page shows a linear address that is translated to a physical address via paging. Assume that an instruction refers to the linear address 13A49F01H. The frame name (13A49H) is split into a directory index (04EH) and a page table index (249H). The page directory is at the address specified by register CR3, location 1C000H. The page directory element number 04EH is selected. It contains the value 3A7A2*xxx*H, where *xxx* represents the page status bits. If the present bit is set, the page table begins at location 3A7A2000H, and page table entry number 249H is selected. In the example, this entry contains the value 2C115*xxx*H, where *xxx* represents the contents of the status bits. The offset of the linear address is appended to the page frame to yield a physical address of 2C115F01H.

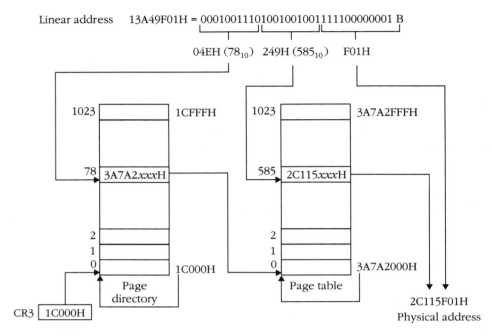

**Figure 6-4.** *Page translation process.*

As the example shows, referring to a single memory location when paging is enabled requires three references: a memory read of the page directory, a read of the page table, and the target memory access.

## The translation lookaside buffer

To eliminate the extra bus cycles that paging imposes on memory references, the paging unit contains the TLB, a content-addressable cache memory. The TLB stores the 32 most frequently used page table entries and page directory entries on the processor chip. Whenever a page table request occurs, the TLB is checked first. If the table entry is found (a "cache hit"), the processor translates the address with no additional memory overhead. More than 98 percent of all references result in a cache hit, leaving less than 2 percent of all memory references degraded by additional cycles.

The TLB is flushed whenever register CR3 is loaded with a new base address. Because the table entries are cached on chip, maintaining page table consistency in multiprocessor environments is important. When one processor modifies a page table (that may be in another processor's cache) or a page directory, the processor must signal the other processors and force them to flush their TLBs. The other processors must then load the modified tables. The LOCK prefix should precede any accesses to the page tables to eliminate simultaneous access.

The references to the page tables and page directories are no different from standard memory read cycles; as such, they will go through the 8-KB internal cache of the 80486. Because page table hits are relatively infrequent (around 2 percent of references), you may wish to keep page table information out of the internal cache, saving cache space for application code and data. To do this, set the CD bit to 1 in CR0 and the PCD bit to 1 in the page directory entries (but not in the page table entries). The page tables themselves will not be cached; however, the data in each page can be.

## Page faults

If a page descriptor is marked not present (P = 0), a page fault (interrupt 14) occurs. When this happens, register CR2 stores the linear address that caused the fault, and an error code is pushed onto the stack. Page faults can also be caused by violations of the page protection rules, described in the next section. Chapter 5 contains additional information about page faults in the "Interrupts and Exceptions" section.

### Page protection

The format of a page directory entry and of a page table entry includes bits marked U/S and R/W. The U/S bit specifies whether a page is a user page (U/S = 1) or a supervisor page (U/S = 0). A supervisor page cannot be used by any procedure running with a CPL of 3. However, a procedure with a CPL of 0, 1, or 2 can access a supervisor page. User pages are accessible regardless of the CPL. If a page directory entry is marked with U/S = 0, only a supervisor procedure can access pages in the page table pointed to by that directory entry, regardless of the U/S setting in the individual page table entries.

You can control the type of memory accesses allowed by setting the R/W bit. The effect of the R/W bit is modified by the WP (write protect) bit in the CR0. The 80386 does not have the WP bit, so its operation is equivalent to an 80486 operating with WP = 0. In this mode, a user level program (CPL = 3) can read or execute from any page where U/S = 0 and can write to any page with U/S = 0 and R/W = 1. A supervisor level program (CPL <= 2) can read from, write to, or execute from all pages.

In the 80486, when the WP bit is set to 1, access to pages by user level programs is identical to the operation described above. Supervisor level programs, however, are restricted to writing only to those pages with the R/W bit set to 1, regardless of the U/S bit setting. The rules are summarized by the following formulas:

*User programs (CPL = 3)*

read_access(addr) = PDE(U/S) = 1 & PTE(U/S) = 1

write_access(addr) = read_access(addr) & PDE(R/W) = 1 & PTE(R/W) = 1

*Supervisor programs (CPL <= 2)*

read_access(addr) = TRUE

write_access(addr) = (WP = 0)| PDE(R/W) = 1 & PTE(R/W) = 1

When a user level process loads a selector, issues a software interrupt, or generates an access to the GDT, LDT, TSS, or IDT to load a descriptor, system table reads and writes are treated as supervisor level accesses. Pushing values onto an inner-ring stack segment is also treated as a supervisor level access. If the system tables had to be stored in user level pages, they would be less secure than if stored in supervisor level pages.

## Combined paging and segmentation

Although simulating a pure flat address space is possible in the 80386 family, most operating systems will probably use some segmentation. No special restrictions apply when combining segmentation and paging, although observing certain rules can make life easier for the operating system designer.

For example, segments do not need to fit into a single page or into a multiple of $n$ pages; a page can contain portions of more than one segment, or vice versa. However, memory management is easier if all segments are multiples of 4096 bytes. You can mark all segment limits as page granular (G = 1 in the segment descriptor), and each segment limit field will contain the number of pages required to hold the segment, less one.

To support page protection, an operating system should implement at least level 0 and level 3 segment protection rings. This is not a problem, even in systems simulating a flat memory architecture. All user level programs can share the same level 3 code segment and level 3 data segment, and the operating system can use two level 0 segments. Both sets of segments can map into the same linear address space, so the use of different selectors will be invisible except for the privilege level.

## Multitasking

Operating system designers can choose to support either a single memory map (one for each task) or multiple memory maps (one for the system and one for each application). A single virtual memory space is the simplest approach; however, any system that supports multiple virtual 8086-mode tasks needs a different set of page tables for each V86 task. In V86 mode, each task accesses linear addresses 0 to 1 MB. A separate physical address space must exist for each linear address space. Figure 6-5 shows how V86 tasks can be mapped to physical memory.

The CPU architecture supports different page tables for each task by saving and restoring the CR3 register in the task state segment. To save itself from having one 4-MB page table per task, an operating system can limit the linear address space of an application to a subset of paging's 32-bit, 4-GB virtual memory size.

For example, if an operating system limits each application to 8 MB of linear address space, it needs to manage only two page tables and the page directory. Each unused page directory entry is marked not present (P = 0). Trying to access an illegal memory address results in a page fault, and the operating system can tell whether the fault represents a swapped-out page or an illegal memory reference. Figure 6-6 illustrates such a system.

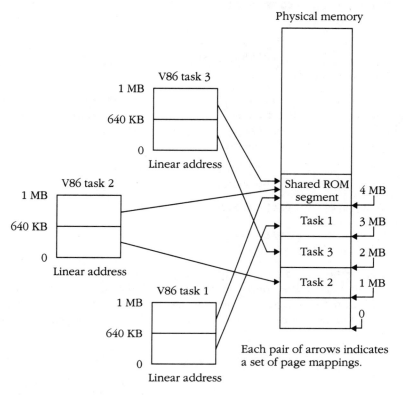

**Figure 6-5.** *Mapping V86 tasks to physical memory.*

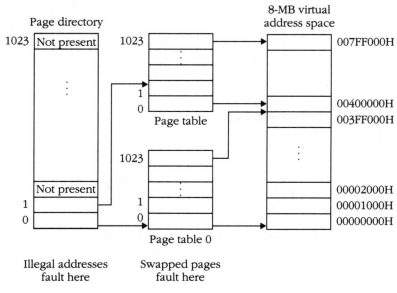

**Figure 6-6.** *Page tables required to support 8 MB of memory.*

Application designers should understand address space restrictions. Some operating systems might have a way to request a larger virtual address space with a system call, but others might not.

Performance is another concern for application designers in a demand-paged system. A key to system performance is the size of the application's *working set*. The working set is the number of application pages that the operating system tries to keep in physical memory at one time.

For example, assume that an application is computing the sum of two arrays into a third array, as represented by the following program fragment:

```
int a[1024], b[1024], c[1024];
    ⋮
for (i = 0; i < 1024; i++)
    a[i] = b[i] + c[i];
```

The code for the program resides in one page, and each array (a, b, and c) resides in a separate page. If the operating system provided a working set of three pages per application, this program would run slowly because two pages would have to be swapped to disk for every *for* loop iteration. Figure 6-7 illustrates the swap.

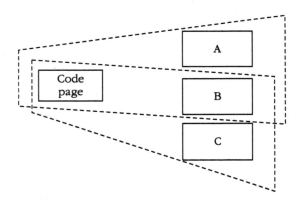

Working set allows only 3 pages in memory simultaneously. *A* must be swapped out and *C* swapped in, then *C* swapped out and *A* swapped back in. This cycle will repeat 1024 times.

**Figure 6-7.** *Swapping a working set.*

Most operating systems provide working sets much larger than three pages per application, but applications with large memory requirements might see similar results. If you write an application that requires a large amount of memory, you might improve its performance by changing the program's *locality of reference*.

The previous program fragment needs access to many pages for every cycle through the loop. If this program were running under the operating system described previously, you could increase its performance by changing the data structure so that a[i], b[i], and c[i] reside in the same page.

```
struct {
    int a, b, c;
    } block[1024];
:
for (i = 0; i < 1024; i++)
    block[i].a = block[i].b + block[i].c;
```

The program now runs with only two page swaps, as shown in Figure 6-8.

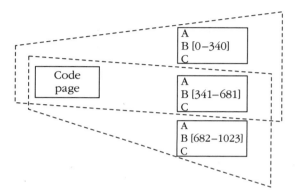

Initial working set allows 67% of the loop to execute without any swapping; then first block is swapped out and last block is swapped in to complete the loop.

**Figure 6-8.** *Reducing swapping via locality of reference.*

Application designers should consider how paging affects their programs. Although many designers will see no impact on their programs, others might need to modify code. A classic example is a program such as a LISP interpreter, which manipulates a large number of linked-list data structures. Unless a mechanism forces locality of reference on the lists, a user could end up with lists that have pointers to cells scattered throughout the address space, resulting in excessive swapping overhead.

# The Internal Cache

The 80486 introduced an 8-KB internal cache to the processor architecture. While the cache can be looked at strictly as a performance aid (as distinct from a true architectural change), it is the cache that allows the 80486 to achieve RISC-like speeds. A number of instructions execute in a single clock cycle when assisted by the cache.

## The purpose of the cache

The memory requirements of computers have always outweighed the processing requirements. The ratio of storage locations to processor is several million to one, even in multiprocessor systems. This means that storage costs must be kept low, or the price of a complete system would be forbiddingly high. To keep memory cheap, it is usually implemented on devices that are much slower than the main processor.

Disk storage is a typical example. Unfortunately, using only such slow devices negates the value of having a fast processor, because the CPU spends all its time waiting for data to be read from or written to memory.

One solution to this problem is to provide more than one kind of memory: A very fast memory for the most important stuff, and a slower memory for the stuff that's not currently in use. We are all familiar with this setup. The familiar CPU/RAM/disk triad exemplifies this model. Current RAM technology, however, still lags CPU performance, at least at reasonable data densities. The cache is simply another variant of this model; the initial accesses are to the fastest memory and the cache; then system RAM is used, and then disk storage.

To make effective use of very fast memory in the cache, it is necessary to reduce the problem of data density; the 80486 cache is only 8 KB. Because we can't have a lot of cache memory, we'll make that memory smarter.

## An intelligent RAM

In a standard memory system, the CPU presents an address, and the memory system returns the data stored at that address. Because a cache is small (and can't store all the data we'd like it to), its behavior is a little different. The cache can be looked upon as storing a set of ordered pairs, in the form *(address, value)*. The CPU presents the cache with a memory address. The cache looks through all its ordered pairs. If it finds an address match, it returns the associated value; otherwise, it passes the address to the standard memory system on the bus. When the value comes back from memory, the cache will store it in case the processor requests the value again. This process is illustrated in Figure 6-9. Finding a match in the cache is called a cache "hit," and it eliminates the need to access the slower system RAM.

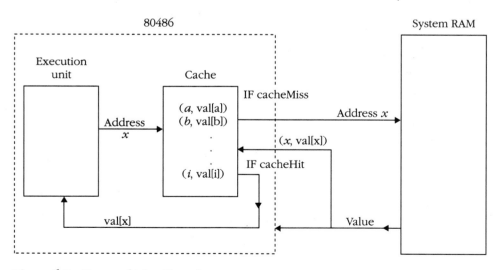

**Figure 6-9.** *Memory fetch with cache.*

Memory writes are handled in a somewhat different manner. Writes always go to system RAM because system memory must contain the correct values if the cache is ever disabled. First, however, the cache is checked for an address match. If a match occurs, then the cache value is updated. If no match occurs, the cache remains unchanged and only system RAM is updated.

When new data is brought into the cache by a read or fetch cycle, it usually means that some other data must be disposed of. The cache checks to see which addresses have been accessed least frequently and replaces the least recently used ordered pair with the address and data just read from system RAM. This assures that tight program loops and frequently referenced variables will be accessed as quickly as possible.

## Cache lines and associativity

Because of the way that a cache works (using a lookup-by-association technique), caches are sometimes referred to as *associative memories*. The amount of memory required to store the address portion of an ordered pair is not taken into account when determining the size of the cache. Thus, the 8-KB cache of the 80486 means that there is room for 8 KB of data values.

In fact, to speed operation of the cache, reduce the amount of memory required for the address portion; and to decrease chip complexity, the full 32 bits of the memory address is not stored. Instead, the cache is organized into *sets* and *lines*.

A cache line in the 80486 is simply 16 bytes of data. Whenever a cache miss occurs, the cache loads the entire 16 bytes, beginning at *address AND FFFFFFF0H*, from system memory. The 80486 bus supports a special "burst mode" expressly for this purpose. This means that the cache need not store the low-order four bits of memory addresses, because the entire 16 bytes is present in the cache. Loading an entire line also has the advantage of "prefilling" the cache, on the assumption that memory addresses are frequently localized and often sequential.

Notice that the 80486 will always fill an entire line. If, for instance, you accessed the byte at location 3A75H, and there was a cache miss, the processor would start a burst read at 3A70H and cache the 16 bytes through 3A7FH.

## Cache control

A number of factors influence whether or not a line of data will be cached. Initially, there is simply the question "Is the cache enabled?" to contend with. Bits 29 and 30 of control register 0 control the cache on a global basis. After the cache has been enabled by setting bits 29 and 30 to 0, it can be flushed by a hardware signal, disabled on a page-by-page basis in software, or disabled on a line-by-line basis in hardware.

The hardware signal FLUSH\ is asserted when external hardware wants the 80486 to invalidate all current cache lines. Caching remains enabled, but all current data is marked invalid. This is useful in multiprocessor systems with shared memory.

When one processor writes to shared memory, it can force the other processor to flush their caches, ensuring that they read the fresh data.

The page table entries contain mask bits for the CD and NW bits in CR0. By masking these values, individual memory pages can be marked as never cacheable. In IBM PC-compatible systems, for example, the video memory locations are almost never read, and it is more efficient to prevent them from being cached altogether.

Finally, external hardware can detect that certain addresses should not be cached. Addresses of memory-mapped I/O devices, for example, should not be cached. External hardware can use the KEN\ line to enable caching or to ensure that data at a particular address is not cached.

# 7

# THREE IN ONE

In earlier chapters I alluded to the capability of Intel microprocessors to run software written for previous processor generations. This chapter explores this capability in the 80386 and the 80486 and discusses how to make the most of it.

The 80386 and the 80486 provide an almost ideal upgrade path from the 8086 and 80286 families of Intel processors. In real mode, the new 32-bit machines can run 8086-family programs. They can switch into protected mode and execute 80286 software. The native mode of the 80386 and the 80486 expands the protected-mode capabilities with 32-bit operations and eliminates the 64-KB segment restrictions of the 80286. Virtual 8086 mode lets you run real-mode programs in protected mode; this is advantageous because many more real-mode applications are currently available than protected-mode applications. With the release of Windows 3.0 and OS/2 V2.0, however, this situation is almost certain to change in the 1990s.

## Real Mode

When the 80386 or the 80486 is powered up or reinitialized via the hardware RESET\ line, the CPU is in real (real-address) mode. In real mode, all of the CPU's protection features are disabled, paging is not supported, and program addresses correspond to physical memory addresses. The address space is limited to 1 MB of physical memory. Real mode is compatible with the 8086, the 8088, the 80186, the 80188, and real mode of the 80286. Minor differences in real mode among the various processors are listed in Appendix F.

When the processor is reset, the registers are initialized to the values shown in the table on the following page:

| Register | Value | Explanation |
|----------|-------|-------------|
| 1 | 3 or 4 | 3 for 80386, 4 for 80486 |
| DL | <id> | Identifies revision number of CPU |
| EFLAGS | 2 | |
| IDTR (see "Interrupt Processing," below) | 0 (base), 3FFH (limit) | |
| CS | F000H | Descriptor base set to FFFF0000H |
| IP | FFF0H | First instruction at FFFFFFF0H |
| SS | 0 | Base address 0 |
| ESP | ? | Undefined, load SS:ESP before using stack |
| DS | 0 | Base address 0 |
| ES | 0 | Base address 0 |
| FS | 0 | Base address 0 |
| GS | 0 | Base address 0 |
| CR0(80486) | 60000000H | Cache disabled |
| CR0(80386) | 000000x0H | Bit 4 = 1 if 80387 present, 0 otherwise. Bits 5–31 are undefined |

## Memory addressing

Shadow registers (segment descriptor caches) provide a key to understanding real-mode memory addressing. Each segment register that holds a selector has an invisible component called a shadow register. In protected mode, every time a selector is loaded into a segment register, the contents of the descriptor indicated by the selector are loaded into the shadow portion. In real mode, the shadow register is loaded with a computed value rather than with a value extracted from a descriptor. Figure 7-1 illustrates the shadow registers.

When the processor is reset, the shadow registers for segments other than CS are loaded with a base address value of 0 and a limit of 0FFFFH, with attributes set to 16-bit addressing; 16-bit instruction set; read, write, and execute ability; and privilege level 0. The CS shadow registers are set with the same limit and access bits as

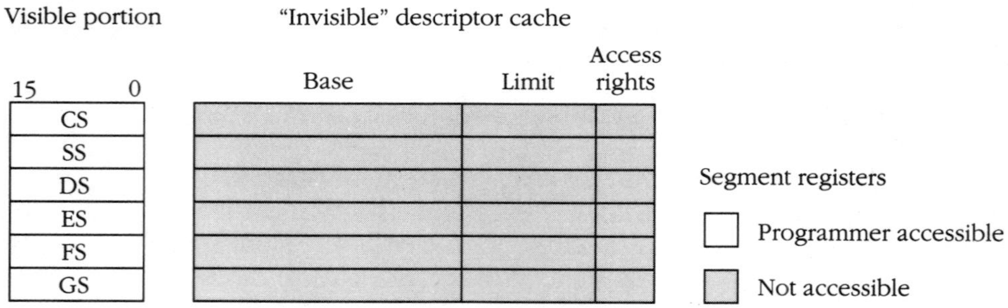

**Figure 7-1.** *Shadow registers.*

the other shadow registers but have a base address of FFFF0000H. Except for the registers listed in the above table, 80386-family registers are undefined. There is one exception to this in the 80486. If the chip's built-in self test (BIST) has been enabled at reset time (by activating pin AHOLD during the falling edge of the RESET signal), register EAX will be set to zero if the BIST completed successfully.

At reset, the limit portions of the shadow registers are set to 0FFFFH, which indicates a 64-KB segment. The access rights portion is set to a value indicating that the segment is readable, writable, and executable and that 16-bit addressing and operand modes are enabled. These values remain constant while the processor is in real mode, and only the base address value is altered. Each time a segment register is loaded, the base address portion of the shadow register is set to 16 times the value of the selector. For example, loading DS with the value of 001AH sets the base address of the DS segment to 01A0H. Because all the segments in real mode are 64 KB, the segment addressable via DS extends from 01A0H to 1019FH. Figure 7-2 illustrates physical address generation in real mode.

The highest segment base address that can be generated in real mode is 0FFFF0H, 16 bytes short of 1 MB. Because that segment extends for 64 KB, memory beyond 1 MB can be addressed. Thus, 32-bit real-mode addressing is somewhat incompatible with that of the 8086, which hardware address lines limit to 1 MB. Generally, this limitation can be ignored because 8086 programs do not use it. If needed, external hardware can be added to limit system address space in 80386 systems to 20 bits while the system is operating in real mode; in 80486 systems, activating pin A20M\ forces address-space wraparound of 1MB.

The reset state of the CS shadow register does not follow the "selector times 16" rule. Because the initial base address for the code segment is set to FFFF0000H, ROMs that handle processor reset can be placed at the end of the address space. The first CALL or JMP instruction that loads CS after reset forces the base address into the first megabyte of address space.

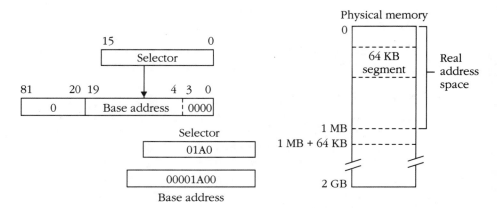

**Figure 7-2.** *Real-mode addressing.*

## 16-bit instruction set

The predefined shadow register values cause another side effect. The D bit in the access rights field is always set to 0 in real mode. Thus, an 80386 or an 80486 is forced to operate in 16-bit mode unless it encounters an OPSIZ or ADRSIZ prefix.

To understand how the D bit works, examine the 8086 instruction set. Most 8086 instructions execute with either a byte operand or a word operand. The byte/word indicator is encoded in one bit in the instruction. For example, the opcode for negating a byte operand is 11110110B, and the opcode for negating a word operand is 11110111B.

Rather than invent new opcodes for 32-bit (dword) operands, Intel's designers changed the meaning of the opcode bit that signifies a word operand. When executing in a native-mode (32-bit) segment, where the D bit in the segment descriptor is set to 1, executing opcode 11110110B means negate *byte* and 11110111B means negate *dword*. The instructions refer to bytes and dwords rather than to bytes and words. When the D bit of a descriptor is set to 0, however, the opcodes retain their original meanings.

The D bit also affects address computation for memory operands and the stack. When D = 0, corresponding to the 8086, the 16-bit registers are used in calculating segment offsets, as in MOV AL, [SI+8]. When D = 1, corresponding to the 32-bit native mode, the same opcode bits cause the memory address to be calculated using the 32-bit registers, and the instruction becomes MOV AL, [ESI+8]. When D = 0 in stack segment descriptors, PUSH and POP instructions access 16-bit operands. When D = 1, 32-bit pushes and pops are executed.

The OPSIZ and ADRSIZ prefixes can override the current D-bit setting for an instruction. Thus, 32-bit native-mode instructions can be prefixed to use 16-bit operands, and 16-bit code can be prefixed to access 32-bit operands and 32-bit addressing modes. The extended addressing features (such as indexing) are not available in segments that have the D bit set to 0 unless the ADRSIZ prefix is used. Note: You need not explicitly specify the prefix instructions; use extended-addressing mode, and the assembler will insert the prefix.

When using extended addressing in real mode, observe the 64-KB segment size limitation. In real mode, address offsets greater than 65535 return an interrupt 13.

## Interrupt processing

Interrupt handling is different in real mode than in protected mode. As in protected mode, the IDTR contains the base address and limit of the interrupt table. For 8086 compatibility, the base is initialized to physical address 0 with a limit of 3FFH. In real mode, however, the interrupt table does not hold descriptors; each interrupt has a 32-bit selector:offset address that points to the routine to be invoked when an interrupt occurs. Thus, each entry is 4 bytes rather than 8 bytes. Figure 7-3 illustrates the real-mode interrupt vector table.

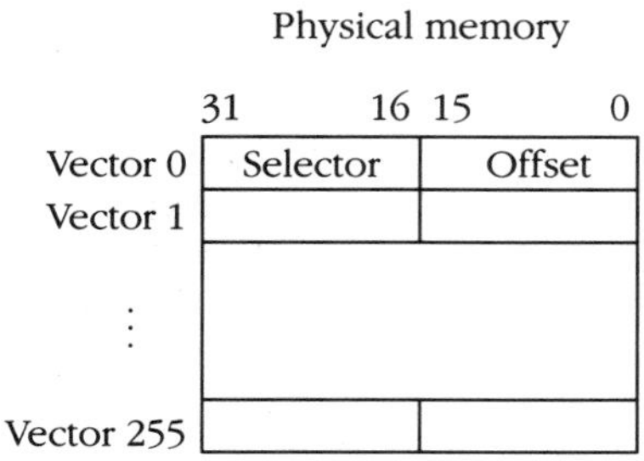

Physical memory

**Figure 7-3.** *Real-mode interrupt vector table.*

The processing of an interrupt in real mode is similar to that in protected mode except for the use of vectors instead of descriptors. A software or hardware interrupt causes the 16-bit FLAGS register to be pushed onto the stack, followed by the current CS and IP. The IF and TF flags are cleared to 0, disabling interrupts and single-stepping.

The pointer from the interrupt table is loaded into CS and IP, and processing continues at the new location. Automatic task switching and interrupt gates are not present because no descriptor tables exist in real mode. The vector in the interrupt table specifies a new execution address only.

## Real-mode restrictions

You can use all the instructions added to the architecture since the introduction of the 8086, with the exception of:

| | | |
|---|---|---|
| INVD* | LSL | VERR |
| INVLPG* | LTR | VERW |
| LAR | SLDT | WBINVD* |
| LLDT | STR | |

*80486 only

Real mode does not support the ways that these instructions access protected-mode selectors, descriptors, or tables. Executing one of these instructions causes an undefined opcode fault (interrupt 6).

You can execute all other 16-bit and 32-bit instructions. Real-mode programs can access any register, including the control, debug, and test registers.

Real mode does not support paging. Setting the PG bit in register CR0 to enable paging causes a protection fault.

Appendix F outlines the differences among the operations of the 8086, the 80286 in real mode, the 80386, and the 80486.

# Protected Mode

Setting the low-order bit of CR0 to 1 switches the processor into protected mode. The processor will run in protected mode even if no setup is done—that is, it will run until the first interrupt, FAR program transfer, or segment register load. At this point, the processor needs to access a descriptor table. Because the protection mechanism depends on descriptor tables, the system will shut down if the descriptor tables have not been initialized.

Protected-mode initialization requires you to set up a global descriptor table and interrupt descriptor tables and to create a task state segment for the first process. The initial descriptor tables can be stored in ROM, but they must be copied to RAM before you set the GDTR and IDTR to point to them because the CPU needs to write to the descriptors as well as read from them.

Figure 7-4 shows a simple initial GDT. This GDT would be sufficient to run additional startup code. You could also build the operating system image in real mode and then switch into protected mode. An advantage of switching into protected mode as soon as possible after reset is that the hardware can help trap startup bugs early in the code development cycle.

In Figure 7-4, GDT(0) is unused because a selector value of 0 is treated as a special case, a NULL pointer. Thus, any descriptor at GDT(0) will never be used. GDT(1) points to the GDT as a writable data segment, allowing the operating system to add, delete, and change descriptors as needed. GDT(2) points to the IDT as a writable

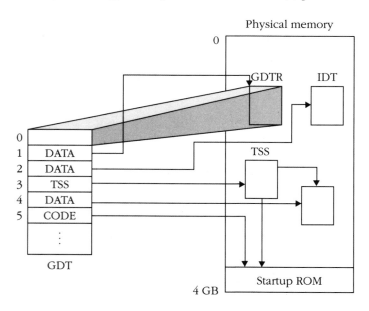

**Figure 7-4.** *A simple GDT.*

data segment for the same reason. GDT(3) defines the TSS for the startup task, GDT(4) defines the task's data segment, and GDT(5) defines the task's code segments, which are in ROM.

Before you enable protected mode by setting the PE bit, the GDTR must be loaded with the address and limit of the GDT. The IDT should contain gates that point to code and that trap any faults that occur during startup. The IDTR is initialized to point to the IDT, and TR is loaded with the selector of GDT(3). The PE bit is then set in the CR0 register to enable protected mode. Next, a FAR jump instruction loads the CS register with a valid protected-mode descriptor. Finally, the stack segment, stack pointer, and data segment registers are loaded. The initialization will build the rest of the operating system, enable paging, and start application programs.

## 80286 compatibility

Protected-mode 80286 code executes on the 80386 or the 80486 if the fourth word of each descriptor is initialized to 0. Descriptors are 64 bits on all three processors, but the high-order 16 bits are unused on the 80286. On the 80386 and the 80486, the extra bits specify the high order of the base address and the limit fields and contain the G and D control bits. These new fields should be set to 0, restricting segment limits to 64 KB and activating the 16-bit instruction set (which is compatible with the 80286).

The 80286, the 80386, and the 80486 operate similarly; the few differences in operation concern performance and newly implemented features and instructions. The 80386 and the 80486 allow the LOCK prefix to precede the following instructions only when they modify memory:

| | | | |
|---|---|---|---|
| ADC | BTC | INC | SBB |
| ADD | BTR | NEG | SUB |
| AND | BTS | NOT | XCHG |
| BT | DEC | OR | XOR |

Illegal use of the LOCK prefix results in a protection fault on the 80386 or the 80486. Additionally, the 80286 locks all of physical memory during the instruction; on the 80386 and the 80486, the locked area is the memory region with the same starting address and length as the operand of the locked instruction.

The machine status word (MSW) is the low-order 16 bits of register CR0. The MSW is initialized to 0FFF0H on the 80286, but it is initialized to 0 on the 80386 and the 80486. Registers that are specified as undefined at reset might have different values than they do on the 80286.

At reset, the base address of the CS register is different on the 80386 and the 80486 than on the 80286. The CS register is set to the same logical location—that is, to the last 16 bytes of the address space—but the 80286 supports only 24-bit addresses, whereas the 80386 and the 80486 support 32-bit addresses.

## Returning to real mode

In general, an operating system should not switch to real mode after running in protected mode. Returning to real mode compromises operating system security because real mode is more vulnerable to crashes. To run real-mode programs while in protected mode, create special tasks that run in virtual 8086 (V86) mode. The next section discusses this process.

If you must return to real mode, follow this procedure: If paging is enabled, turn it off by branching to a routine whose linear and physical addresses are the same, clearing the PG bit in CR0, and moving 0 into CR3 to clear the PDBR (page directory base register), which will also flush the TLB.

The attribute bits in each segment descriptor must be set to values compatible with real-mode operation—that is, they must be byte granular segments with a limit of 0FFFFH, and the B and D bits must be 0. CS must be marked "executable," and SS, DS, ES, FS, and GS should be writable segments. (Change the CS selector by issuing a FAR jump or call instruction.)

Disable interrupts, and load the IDTR with a base address of 0 and a limit of 3FFH. Clear the PE bit of the CR0 register to return to real mode, and execute a FAR jump to flush the instruction queue and initialize CS to a valid real-mode base address.

After you load the stack pointer (SS:SP) and the other segment registers, programs can continue processing in real mode.

# Virtual 8086 Mode

Just as virtual memory allows the processor to create the impression of memory that isn't really there, virtual 8086 mode allows the 80386 and the 80486 to create the illusion of multiple 8086 processors. This illusion is so nearly complete that multiple 8086-based operating systems can run under a supervisory protected-mode operating system. For example, assume that the native-mode operating system for an 80386 computer is UNIX and that support for V86 mode is built in. In addition to running multiple UNIX tasks, the user can run a copy of MS-DOS and a word processor in a V86 window. The user can also invoke another virtual 8086 session running a spreadsheet under Windows. Each V86 task believes that it is running on a separate 8086 machine but actually runs concurrently with host operating system tasks.

V86 mode was designed in response to the negative reaction to 80286 protected mode. Application designers developed a large software base for the 8086 family under MS-DOS. The 8086 and 8088 processors support only real-mode programming, and MS-DOS is sensitive to the mapping between selector values and physical addresses. When Intel introduced the 80286, developers found that MS-DOS programs had problems running in protected mode.

If MS-DOS were less sensitive to physical addressing, most applications could be easily ported to 80286 protected mode. Operating systems such as Concurrent CP/M and Microsoft Windows created environments that relied less on the idiosyncrasies of real mode, but because of DOS's wide popularity the marketplace demanded support of real mode.

V86 mode was Intel's response. V86 mode is available in the 80386, the 80386SX, and the 80486. The paging and multitasking capabilities of these processors enabled designers to implement V86 mode, which overcomes the 1-MB nonprotected limitations of real mode. Because a TSS contains an image of all the general registers, it is the basis of a register image for a virtual machine (in this case, an 8086). Additionally, the TSS contains the extra information needed for protected mode: the inner-ring stack pointers and the page directory base register (CR3). The operating system creates a V86 task by setting the VM bit in the EFLAGS image of the task's TSS.

When a task is invoked and the EFLAGS register is loaded (setting the processor's VM bit), the task's code portion behaves as if it were running in real mode. The task does not use descriptors; base addresses are generated by multiplying the selector value by 16. The difference between real mode and V86 mode is that real-mode addresses are *physical addresses* and V86 mode addresses are *linear addresses* that can be mapped via paging hardware.

Thus, the executing program makes the same assumptions about selectors and addresses that a real-mode program does, but the paging hardware, under control of the native-mode supervisor, controls which physical addresses are used by the V86 task. The entire 4-GB address space is available for remapping the V86 task's addresses. The other issue that Intel's designers had to face was the integration of real-mode programs into a secure, protected-mode environment.

Memory references were not a problem. The paging hardware can isolate the V86-mode program address space from protected-mode programs, preventing data corruption. Besides memory, the only external interfaces to the CPU are I/O ports and interrupts.

## I/O in V86 mode

In protected mode, the I/O privilege level (IOPL) determines whether a procedure can perform I/O instructions. In V86 mode, IOPL protects the interrupt flag (IF), and I/O port protection is performed through the I/O permission bits in the TSS. V86 mode programs run in ring 3; thus, they cannot alter the value of IOPL.

The CPL of a V86 mode task is always 3. If the system IOPL is less than 3, the instructions below return a general protection fault (interrupt 13) with an error code of 0. I/O instructions are not IOPL sensitive in V86 mode.

| | |
|------|------|
| CLI | POPF |
| INT | PUSHF |
| IRET | STI |
| LOCK | |

If the system runs with an IOPL of 3, the V86 mode task will execute the instructions above without triggering the general protection fault. This creates a problem because these instructions modify the interrupt flag. Although performance might be higher when IOPL = 3, this operating mode is not recommended. Allowing a V86-mode task to disable interrupts could result in data loss or a system shutdown. For example, the following two-line assembly program locks the system and requires a complete power cycle to bring the system back on line:

```
        cli
11:     jmp     11
```

Designing a reliable system that runs V86-mode tasks with IOPL = 3 requires hardware support and cannot be implemented with software alone. For example, a watchdog timer can be connected to the NMI interrupt, forcing control back to the operating system if an application appears to have crashed the system.

The I/O permission bitmap of the V86 task state segment determines whether the I/O instruction executes or causes an exception. Figure 7-5 illustrates a typical I/O permission bitmap in a V86 task state segment.

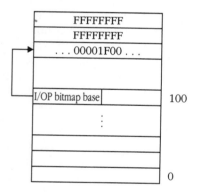

**Figure 7-5.** *I/O permission bitmap.*

A trade-off exists between performance and protection. If you allow all tasks to issue I/O instructions, more than one task might access a device simultaneously. However, if you trap all I/O instructions, programs might run slowly. A compromise is to mark I/O address space as inaccessible until the first fault occurs. By trapping the first I/O instruction to a given port, the operating system can determine whether another task is using the device. If not, the permission bits for the faulting task can be modified to grant access to the specific device, and the task can resume processing at full speed. If some other task is accessing the device, the faulting task can be suspended or terminated.

Memory-mapped devices must be controlled through paging hardware. Pages that correspond to device addresses can be marked "not present" to cause a fault, or they can be mapped to other devices or memory locations for subsequent processing. (The latter is effective for display devices.)

## Interrupt handling in V86 mode

Because V86 mode is part of the protected-mode environment, interrupts are handled through the standard protected-mode IDT. The interrupt causes the processor to switch to an inner-ring stack segment. The stack segment's selector is taken from the TSS and is a standard protected-mode selector, as opposed to the value of SS that the V86 mode task is using. Hardware interrupts are fielded by the routines or tasks designated by the gates in the IDT. Software interrupt instructions in the V86 task usually refer to routines in the virtual machine operating system; they are unlikely to correspond to the vectors implemented by the supervisory operating system. Therefore, any operating system that supports V86 tasks must be aware of two possible outcomes of a software INT instruction executed by a V86 mode program.

The more likely outcome is a general protection fault (interrupt 13). Because V86 tasks execute at privilege level 3, accessing a more privileged ring's descriptor causes a general protection fault. The interrupt 13 fault handler must detect when it has been invoked due to a software interrupt instruction from a V86 task.

The error code on the stack indicates the vector that caused the general protection fault. The handler can fetch the contents of the V86 interrupt vector from the V86 task image and branch back to the V86 routine.

A less likely outcome occurs only when IOPL = 3 and when the gate in the IDT has a level 3 descriptor. In this case, the software interrupt causes a branch to the routine pointed to by the gate. This routine must be in ring 0 to prevent a general protection fault. Any interrupt routine that can be invoked by a level 3 gate in the IDT must examine the VM bit in the EFLAGS image on the stack to determine whether the interrupt handler was invoked by a standard protected-mode routine or by a V86 task.

Whenever an interrupt occurs while the processor is executing a V86 mode task, control moves to a ring 0 code segment. Control may transfer directly to ring 0, or it may transfer to the general protection fault handler (which must be in ring 0). The ring 0 stack is slightly different when control comes from a V86 task than when it comes from a protected-mode procedure. All segment registers are pushed onto the ring 0 stack when an interrupt or a trap occurs in a V86 task. Figure 7-6 on the following page illustrates the differences in the stacks. Notice that an error code will also be pushed for certain exception interrupts.

In addition to the extra values pushed onto the stack, all segment registers are reloaded during the transition through the gate. DS, ES, FS, and GS are loaded with a null selector (0), SS is loaded from the ring 0 stack selector in the TSS for the V86 task, and CS is loaded with the descriptor from the interrupt or task gate.

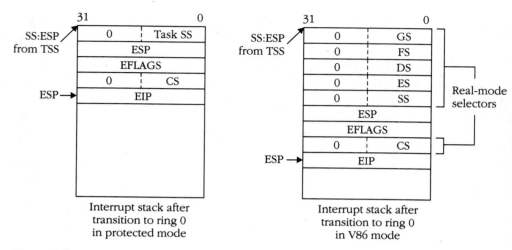

**Figure 7-6.** *Ring 0 interrupt stacks: protected mode vs. V86 mode.*

The segment registers must be loaded with new values if the executing task is a V86 task. Before an interrupt, the segment registers contain real-mode style segment addresses, which are not valid selectors for the protected-mode interrupt handler. When the interrupt handler returns via the IRET instruction, the CPU checks the saved EFLAGS image in the level 0 stack. If the saved VM bit is set, the CPU recognizes that it is returning to a V86 mode task and reloads the segment registers with the saved values on the stack.

# REFERENCE
# SECTION

This chapter of *Microsoft's 80386/80486 Programming Guide* provides a reference for the instruction sets. The instructions are in alphabetic order, with floating-point instructions following the basic instructions.

The experienced user can find information with a quick glance at the first part of an instruction; a less experienced user can refer to the detailed descriptions and examples.

## Operators

The following reference pages use these operators:

| Operator | Meaning | Operator | Meaning |
|----------|-------------|----------|-------------------------|
| +        | Addition    | &        | Boolean AND             |
| −        | Subtraction | >        | Greater than            |
| *        | Multiplication | <     | Less than               |
| ÷        | Division    | >>       | Shift right             |
| ~        | Not         | <<       | Shift left              |
| =        | Equal to    | ≤        | Less than or equal to   |
| !=       | Not equal to | ≥       | Greater than or equal to |
| \|       | Or          | ←        | Assignment              |
| ^        | Exclusive OR |         |                         |

**MNEMONIC.**
*Used by the assembler to represent the instruction.*

**NAME.**
*Name of instruction*

**PROCESSOR TYPE.**
*Processors that support the instruction. Note that earlier processors supported only 8-bit or 16-bit forms.*

**OPERAND SIZES.**
*When many different operands may be used, this field indicates legal sizes. If the instruction requires more than one operand, they are assumed to be the same size. Unless otherwise stated, 8 = 8-bit operands; 16 = 16-bit operands; 32 = 32-bit operands; 16p = The instruction accepts 16-bit operands by using the 32-bit form and the OPSIZ instruction prefix.*

**SYNTAX.**
*Generic instruction format.*

**OPERATION.**
*Pseudocode operation description.*

**DESCRIPTION.**
*Description of the instruction.*

**FAULTS.**
*Faults that may be triggered by the instruction. The abbreviations used include:*
*#UD (undefined opcode)*
*#NP (not present)*
*#TS (task switch)*
*#GP (general protection)*
*#SS (stack fault)*
*#PF (page fault)*
*#AC (alignment check); 80486 only*
*A value in parentheses indicates that an error code is pushed onto the stack.*

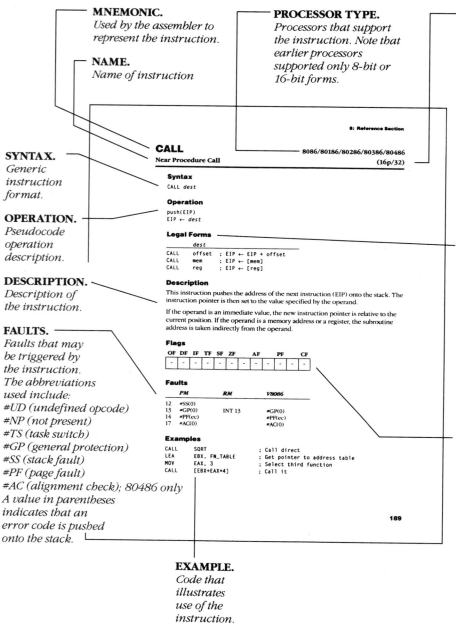

**8: Reference Section**

## CALL
Near Procedure Call

8086/80186/80286/80386/80486
(16p/32)

**Syntax**
CALL dest

**Operation**
push(EIP)
EIP ← dest

**Legal Forms**

|  | dest |  |
|---|---|---|
| CALL | offset | : EIP ← EIP + offset |
| CALL | mem | : EIP ← [mem] |
| CALL | reg | : EIP ← [reg] |

**Description**
This instruction pushes the address of the next instruction (EIP) onto the stack. The instruction pointer is then set to the value specified by the operand.

If the operand is an immediate value, the new instruction pointer is relative to the current position. If the operand is a memory address or a register, the subroutine address is taken indirectly from the operand.

**Flags**

| OF | DF | IF | TF | SF | ZF | AF | PF | CF |
|---|---|---|---|---|---|---|---|---|
| - | - | - | - | - | - | - | - | - |

**Faults**

| PM | RM | V8086 |
|---|---|---|
| 12 #SS(0) | | |
| 13 #GP(0) | INT 13 | #GP(0) |
| 14 #PF(ec) | | #PF(ec) |
| 17 #AC(0) | | #AC(0) |

**Examples**

```
CALL    SQRT            : Call direct
LEA     EBX, FN_TABLE   : Get pointer to address table
MOV     EAX, 3          : Select third function
CALL    [EBX+EAX*4]     : Call it
```

189

**LEGAL FORMS.**
*Legal forms of the instruction. reg = one of the general registers EAX, ESI, BX, DL, BP, DX, etc. mem = a memory operand [021AH], [EBP + EAX * 3], [ECX+ 7], etc. idata = an immediate data value (32, 17A3H, etc.) sreg = a segment register. offset = an offset from the current CS:IP.*

**FLAGS.**
*OF = Overflow flag.*
*DF = Direction flag.*
*IF = Interrupt enable flag.*
*TF = Trap flag.*
*SF = Sign flag.*
*ZF = Zero flag.*
*AF = Auxiliary flag.*
*PF = Parity flag.*
*CF = Carry flag.*
*An "x" in a box indicates that the specified bit is modified by the instruction. An "-" in a box means that the specified bit value remains unchanged. A "?" means that the instruction sets the flag to an unknown value. If a "0" or "1" is in a box, the instruction sets the specified bit to that value.*

**EXAMPLE.**
*Code that illustrates use of the instruction.*

# AAA

**ASCII Adjust After Addition**

8086/80186/80286/80386/80486

(8)

## Syntax

AAA

## Operation

```
if (AF | ((AL & 0FH) > 9)) then
    AL ← (AL + 6) & 0FH
    AH ← AH + 1
    CF, AF ← 1
else
    CF, AF ← 0
endif
```

## Legal Form

AAA

## Description

This instruction ensures that an ASCII or BCD addition results in a valid BCD digit. After executing an ADD or ADC instruction that leaves a single BCD or ASCII digit in register AL, execute AAA to produce a valid BCD result.

If the value in AL produces a decimal overflow, the BCD digit is forced into the legal range (0–9), and AH is incremented. The high-order nibble is zeroed so that AL contains only the resulting single BCD digit, and the AF and CF flags are set to 1.

If no overflow occurs, the AF and CF flags are reset to 0.

## Flags

| OF | DF | IF | TF | SF | ZF | AF | PF | CF |
|----|----|----|----|----|----|----|----|----|
| ? | – | – | – | ? | ? | x | ? | x |

## Faults

None.

## Example

```
MOV     AL, '5'         ; Binary 35H
ADD     AL, '7'         ; Add binary 37H yielding 6CH
AAA                     ; AL ← 02H, AH ← AH + 1, decimal carry set
OR      AL, 30H         ; Convert resulting digit to ASCII '2'
```

# AAD

ASCII Adjust Before Division

## Syntax

```
AAD
```

## Operation

```
AL ← AH * 10 + AL
AH ← 0
```

## Legal Form

```
AAD
```

## Description

This instruction supports BCD division. Before execution, the AL register should contain a single, unpacked BCD digit. The AH register should hold the next higher-order BCD digit. After executing the AAD instruction, AX contains the binary equivalent of the two BCD digits. You can then issue the divide instruction, which leaves a binary result.

## Flags

| OF | DF | IF | TF | SF | ZF | | AF | | PF | | CF |
|----|----|----|----|----|----|----|----|----|----|----|----|
| ? | - | - | - | x | x | - | ? | - | x | - | ? |

## Faults

None.

## Example

```
MOV     AH, '4'         ; High-order digit
MOV     AL, '2'         ; Low-order digit (AX = ASCII 42)
AND     AX, 0F0FH       ; Convert to unpacked BCD
AAD                     ; AX ← 2AH (42 decimal)
MOV     BL, 6           ; Divisor for 42/6
DIV     BL              ; AL ← 7(quotient), AH ← 0(remainder)
OR      AL, 30H         ; Convert result to ASCII '7'
```

# AAM
## ASCII Adjust After Multiplication

8086/80186/80286/80386/80486

(8)

### Syntax

AAM

### Operation

AH ← AL div 10
AL ← AL mod 10

### Legal Form

AAM

### Description

The AAM instruction converts the result of a single-digit BCD multiplication (a value 0–81) in the AX register to two unpacked BCD digits, the high-order digit in AH and the low-order digit in AL.

### Flags

| OF | DF | IF | TF | SF | ZF | | AF | | PF | | CF |
|----|----|----|----|----|----|----|----|----|----|----|----|
| ? | - | - | - | x | x | - | ? | - | x | - | ? |

### Faults

None.

### Example

```
MOV     AL, 4           ; Multipland
MOV     AH, 8           ; Multiplier
MUL     AH              ; AX ← 20H, 32 decimal
AAM                     ; AH ← 3, AL ← 2
OR      AX, 3030H       ; Convert to ASCII '32'
```

# AAS
## ASCII Adjust After Subtraction

### Syntax

AAS

### Operation

```
if (AF | (AL & OFH) > 9) then
    AL ← (AL - 6) & OFH
    AH ← AH - 1
    CF, AF ← 1
else
    CF, AF ← 0
endif
```

### Legal Form

AAS

### Description

This instruction ensures that an ASCII or BCD subtraction results in a valid BCD digit. After executing a SUB or SBB instruction that leaves a single BCD or ASCII digit in register AL, execute AAS to produce a valid BCD result.

If the value in AL produces a decimal borrow, the BCD digit is forced into the legal range (0–9) and AH is decremented. The high-order nibble is zeroed so that AL contains only the resulting single BCD digit, and the AF and CF flags are set to 1.

If no borrow occurs, the AF and CF flags are reset to 0.

### Flags

| OF | DF | IF | TF | SF | ZF | | AF | | PF | | CF |
|----|----|----|----|----|----|----|----|----|----|----|----|
| ? | - | - | - | ? | ? | - | x | - | ? | - | x |

### Faults

None.

### Example

```
MOV    AL, '5'        ; 35H
SUB    AL, '7'        ; Subtract 37H yielding OFEH
AAS                   ; AL ← 08H, carry set indicating "borrow"
OR     AL, 30H        ; Convert result back to ASCII '8'
```

# ADC

**Add with Carry**

**8086/80186/80286/80386/80486**

**(8/16p/32)**

## Syntax

ADC *dest, src*

## Operation

*dest* ← *dest* + *src* + CF

## Legal Forms

|     | dest | src   |
| --- | ---- | ----- |
| ADC | reg, | idata |
| ADC | mem, | idata |
| ADC | reg, | reg   |
| ADC | reg, | mem   |
| ADC | mem, | reg   |

## Description

This instruction adds the contents of the *dest* and *src* operands, increments the result by 1 if the carry flag is set, and stores the result in the location specified by *dest*. The operands must be of the same size. If the operands are signed integers, the OF flag indicates an invalid result. If the operands are unsigned, the CF flag indicates a carry out of the destination.

## Flags

| OF | DF | IF | TF | SF | ZF |   | AF |   | PF |   | CF |
| -- | -- | -- | -- | -- | -- | - | -- | - | -- | - | -- |
| X  | -  | -  | -  | X  | X  | - | X  | - | X  | - | X  |

## Faults

|    | **PM**   | **RM** | **V8086** |
| -- | -------- | ------ | --------- |
| 12 | #SS(0)   |        |           |
| 13 | #GP(0)   | INT 13 | #GP(0)    |
| 14 | #PF(ec)  |        | #PF(ec)   |
| 17 | #AC(0)   |        | #AC(0)    |

## Example

```
; Subroutine to add two 64-bit integers
ENTER   0, 0                ; Create stack frame
MOV     EAX, [EBP+8]        ; Get low-order of first value
MOV     EDX, [EBP+12]       ; Get high-order of first value
ADD     EAX, [EBP+16]       ; Add low-order bits, generating carry
ADC     EDX, [EBP+20]       ; Add high-order bits with previous carry
LEAVE                       ; Undo stack frame
RET                         ; Return with value in EDX:EAX
```

# ADD

8086/80186/80286/80386/80486

**Integer Addition**

(8/16p/32)

## Syntax

ADD *dest, src*

## Operation

*dest ← dest + src*

## Legal Forms

|     | *dest* | *src*  |
|-----|--------|--------|
| ADD | reg,   | idata  |
| ADD | mem,   | idata  |
| ADD | reg,   | reg    |
| ADD | reg,   | mem    |
| ADD | mem,   | reg    |

## Description

This instruction adds the contents of the *dest* and *src* operands and stores the result in the location specified by *dest*. The operands must be of the same size. If the operands are signed integers, the OF flag indicates an invalid result. If the operands are unsigned, the CF flag indicates a carry out of the destination. If the operands are unpacked BCD digits, the AF flag indicates a decimal carry.

## Flags

| OF | DF | IF | TF | SF | ZF |   | AF |   | PF |   | CF |
|----|----|----|----|----|----|---|----|---|----|---|----|
| X  | -  | -  | -  | X  | X  | - | X  | - | X  | - | X  |

## Faults

|    | *PM*    | *RM*   | *V8086* |
|----|---------|--------|---------|
| 12 | #SS(0)  |        |         |
| 13 | #GP(0)  | INT 13 | #GP(0)  |
| 14 | #PF(ec) |        | #PF(ec) |
| 17 | #AC(0)  |        | #AC(0)  |

## Examples

```
ADD     AL, [4211A]     ; 8-bit addition
ADD     AX, 34          ; 16-bit immediate value addition
ADD     ESI, [EBP+8]    ; 32-bit memory addition to register
```

# AND

**Boolean AND**

8086/80186/80286/80386/80486

(8/16p/32)

## Syntax

AND *dest, src*

## Operation

*dest* ← *dest* & *src*
CF ← 0
OF ← 0

## Legal Forms

|     | dest | src |
|-----|------|------|
| AND | reg, | idata |
| AND | mem, | idata |
| AND | reg, | reg |
| AND | reg, | mem |
| AND | mem, | reg |

## Description

This instruction performs a bit-by-bit AND operation on the *dest* and *src* operands and stores the result in the *dest* operand. The AND operation is defined as follows:

0 & 0 = 0

0 & 1 = 0

1 & 0 = 0

1 & 1 = 1

## Flags

| OF | DF | IF | TF | SF | ZF |   | AF |   | PF |   | CF |
|----|----|----|----|----|----|---|----|---|----|---|----|
| 0  | -  | -  | -  | x  | x  | - | ?  | - | x  | - | 0  |

## Faults

|    | *PM* | *RM* | *V8086* |
|----|--------|--------|---------|
| 12 | #SS(0) |        |         |
| 13 | #GP(0) | INT 13 | #GP(0)  |
| 14 | #PF(ec) |       | #PF(ec) |
| 17 | #AC(0) |        | #AC(0)  |

## Examples

```
AND     AL, 0FH              ; Zero high-order nibble of AL
AND     EBX, ECX             ; Compute EBX ← EBX & ECX
AND     BYTE PTR[EBP+6], 7FH ; Mask off high-order bit of memory operand
```

# ARPL

**Adjust RPL Field of Selector**

80286/80386/80486

(16)

## Syntax

ARPL *dest, src*

## Operation

```
if (dest.RPL < src.RPL) then
    dest.RPL ← src.RPL
    ZF ← 1
else
    ZF ← 0
endif
```

## Legal Forms

|      | dest  | src |
|------|-------|-----|
| ARPL | reg,  | reg |
| ARPL | mem,  | reg |

## Description

System software uses this instruction to modify a selector's requested privilege level (RPL) field. Both the *dest* and *src* operands must be valid selectors.

If the RPL of the *dest* operand is numerically less than the RPL of the *src*, that is, if the *dest* selector is more privileged, the *dest* selector's RPL is changed to match that of the *src*, and the ZF flag is set to 1. If the *dest* selector is less privileged (numerically higher) than the *src*, the ZF flag is cleared to 0, and the *dest* operand is not modified.

Operating system routines that are passed selectors from applications should use ARPL to ensure that the calling routine has not passed a selector with a higher privilege than the application is allowed. Use the calling routine's CS register as the *src* operand.

## Flags

| OF | DF | IF | TF | SF | ZF | | AF | PF | | CF |
|----|----|----|----|----|----|----|----|----|----|----|
| -  | -  | -  | -  | -  | X  | -  | -  | -  | -  | -  |

## Faults

| | *PM* | *RM* | *V8086* |
|---|---|---|---|
| 6 | | INT 6 | #UD() |
| 12 | #SS(0) | | |
| 13 | #GP(0) | | |
| 14 | #PF(ec) | | |
| 17 | #AC(0) | | #AC(0) |

## Example

```
MOV     AX, [EBP+12]     ; Get parameter off the stack
ARPL    AX, [EBP+2]      ; Adjust to caller's RPL (previous CPL) by
                         ; using CS of return address on stack
JNZ     bad_param        ; Branch if caller passed a bad selector
```

# BOUND

80186/80286/80386/80486

## Check Array Boundaries

(16p/32)

### Syntax

BOUND *dest*, *src*

### Operation

```
if ((dest < src[0]) | (dest > src[1])) then
    INT 5
endif
```

### Legal Forms

| | dest | src |
|---|---|---|
| BOUND | reg, | mem |

### Description

This instruction compares the *dest* operand, which must be a register containing a signed integer, with two values, a lower bound stored at the address specified by *src*, and an upper bound stored in the following location. The bounds can be 16-bit or 32-bit values.

If the *dest* value is less than the lower bound or greater than the upper bound, an interrupt 5 occurs. The return address pushed onto the stack by the exception is the starting address of the BOUND instruction that caused the interrupt.

### Flags

| OF | DF | IF | TF | SF | ZF | | AF | | PF | | CF |
|----|----|----|----|----|----|---|----|---|----|---|----|
| -  | -  | -  | -  | -  | -  | - | -  | - | -  | - | -  |

### Faults

| | PM | RM | V8086 |
|---|---|---|---|
| 5 | INT 5 | INT 5 | INT 5 |
| 6* | #UD( ) | INT 6 | #UD( ) |
| 12 | #SS(0) | | |
| 13 | #GP(0) | INT 13 | #GP(0) |
| 14 | #PF(ec) | | #PF(ec) |
| 17 | #AC(0) | | #AC(0) |

*The undefined opcode fault occurs only if the instruction encoding of the BOUND instruction specifies an *src* operand that is a register.

## Example

```
VC_LIMITS:
    DD   1, 20                  ; Bounds for 20-element array
VC  DD   20 DUP (?)             ; Array storage area
    .
    .
    MOV  EAX, [EBP-6]           ; Get array index
    BOUND EAX, VC_LIMITS        ; Check against limits
```

# BSF

**Bit Scan Forward**

## Syntax

```
BSF dest, src
```

## Operation

```
if (src = 0) then
    ZF ← 1
    dest ← ???
else
    ZF ← 0
    temp ← 0
    while (bit(src, temp) = 0)
        temp ← temp + 1
    dest ← temp
endif
```

## Legal Forms

|     | dest | src |
| --- | ---- | --- |
| BSF | reg, | reg |
| BSF | reg, | mem |

## Description

This instruction scans the *src* operand and writes the bit position of the first 1-bit in *src* to the *dest* register. If the *src* operand is 0, the ZF flag is set to 1, and the instruction ends with the *dest* register in an undefined state.

If the *src* operand is not 0, each bit is examined, beginning with bit 0, until a 1-bit is found. The bit position of the first 1-bit (index) is stored in the *dest* register.

## Flags

| OF | DF | IF | TF | SF | ZF | | AF | | PF | | CF |
| -- | -- | -- | -- | -- | -- | -- | -- | -- | -- | -- | -- |
| ? | – | – | – | ? | x | – | ? | – | ? | – | ? |

## Faults

|    | *PM*    | *RM*   | *V8086* |
| -- | ------- | ------ | ------- |
| 12 | #SS(0)  |        |         |
| 13 | #GP(0)  | INT 13 | #GP(0)  |
| 14 | #PF(ec) |        | #PF(ec) |
| 17 | #AC(0)  |        | #AC(0)  |

**174**

## Example

```
        XOR     ECX, ECX             ; Index into sector map
L1:     BSF     EAX, SECTORS[ECX*4]  ; Scan a dword
        JNZ     GOT_ONE              ; Branch if any bits set
        INC     ECX                  ; Go on to next dword
        CMP     ECX, TABLE_SIZE      ; Done searching?
        JL      L1                   ; No, scan next table entry
        JMP     NO_SECTORS           ; No bits set in entire table
GOT_ONE:
```

# BSR

**Bit Scan Reverse**

## Syntax

BSR *dest, src*

## Operation

```
if (dest in [AX, BX, CX, DX, SI, DI, BP, SP]) then
    startbit ← 15
else
    startbit ← 31
endif
if (src - 0) then
    ZF ← 1
    dest ← ???
else
    ZF ← 0
    temp ← startbit
    while (bit(src, temp) - 0)
        temp ← temp - 1
    dest ← temp
endif
```

## Legal Forms

|       | dest  | src  |
|-------|-------|------|
| BSR   | reg,  | reg  |
| BSR   | reg,  | mem  |

## Description

This instruction scans the *src* operand in reverse, searching for a 1-bit beginning at the high order of the *src* operand. If the *src* operand is 0, the ZF flag is set to 1, and the instruction ends with the *dest* register in an undefined state.

If the *src* operand is not 0, each bit is examined, beginning with the high-order bit (either 15 for word operands or 31 for doubleword operands), until a 1-bit is found. The bit position (index) of the first 1-bit is stored in the *dest* register.

## Flags

| OF | DF | IF | TF | SF | ZF |   | AF |   | PF |   | CF |
|----|----|----|----|----|----|---|----|---|----|---|----|
| ?  | -  | -  | -  | ?  | x  | - | ?  | - | ?  | - | ?  |

## Faults

| | PM | RM | V8086 |
|---|------|--------|---------|
| 12 | #SS(0) | | |
| 13 | #GP(0) | INT 13 | #GP(0) |
| 14 | #PF(ec) | | #PF(ec) |
| 17 | #AC(0) | | #AC(0) |

## Example

```
          MOV      ECX, SEM_MAX-1          ; Index of last entry in
                                           ; semaphore table
L1:       BSR      EAX, SEMAPHORE[ECX*4]   ; Scan for non-zero bits
          JNZ      found_it                ; Branch if valid index
          LOOP     L1                      ; Decrement CX, loop back
                                           ; if not zero
none_found:                                ; Get here
                                           ; if entire table is zero
```

# BSWAP

**Byte Swap**

80486

(32)

## Syntax

```
BSWAP reg
```

## Operation

```
temp ← dest
dest[0..7]   ← temp[24..31]
dest[8..15]  ← temp[16..23]
dest[16..23] ← temp[8..15]
dest[24..31] ← temp[0..7]
```

## Legal Form

| dest |
| --- |
| BSWAP    reg32 |

## Description

The order of the four bytes in the 32-bit register operand are swapped. This converts between "big-endian" and "little-endian" storage formats. This instruction is useful when exchanging data between processors with different architectures.

## Flags

None.

## Faults

None.

## Example

```
CALL  getdata   ; Read 32 bits from the network into EAX
BSWAP EAX       ; Convert to local format
STOSD           ; Write to buffer
LOOP  getmore
```

# BT

**Bit Test**

**80386/80486**

**(16p/32)**

## Syntax

BT *dest, index*

## Operation

CF ← BIT(*dest, index*)

## Legal Forms

|    | *dest* | *index* |
|----|--------|---------|
| BT | reg,   | idata   |
| BT | mem,   | idata   |
| BT | reg,   | reg     |
| BT | mem,   | reg     |

## Description

This instruction tests the bit specified by the operands and places the value of the bit into the carry flag.

The *index* operand holds a bit index into the bit string specified by *dest*, which can be a 16-bit or 32-bit register or a memory location. The state of the bit is copied into the carry flag.

If the *index* operand is an immediate data value, it can range from 0 through 31. If the *index* is held in a register, it can take on any integral value. Some assemblers might let you specify immediate *index* values greater than 31. If so, they modify the effective address by an appropriate value so that the *index* can be scaled back to between 0 and 31.

BT does not accept byte operands, so do not use it with memory-mapped I/O devices because the instruction causes either the 16-bit word or the 32-bit word containing the selected bit to be read. This could affect more than one I/O device register. You should use a single-byte MOV instruction to read the I/O register and then test the contents of the register.

## Flags

| OF | DF | IF | TF | SF | ZF |   | AF |   | PF |   | CF |
|----|----|----|----|----|----|---|----|---|----|---|----|
| ?  | -  | -  | -  | ?  | ?  | - | ?  | - | ?  | - | x  |

## Faults

| | *PM* | *RM* | *V8086* |
|---|---|---|---|
| 12 | #SS(0) | | |
| 13 | #GP(0) | INT 13 | #GP(0) |
| 14 | #PF(ec) | | #PF(ec) |
| 17 | #AC(0) | | #AC(0) |

## Example

```
MOV    EAX, 192          ; Bit index
BT     SEMAPHORES, EAX   ; Test semaphore number 192
JC     sem_set           ; Branch if the bit was set
```

# BTC/80486

**Bit Test and Complement**

## Syntax

BTC *dest, index*

## Operation

CF ← BIT(*dest, index*)
BIT(*dest, index*) ← ~BIT(*dest, index*)

## Legal Forms

|     | dest  | index |
| --- | ----- | ----- |
| BTC | reg,  | idata |
| BTC | mem,  | idata |
| BTC | reg,  | reg   |
| BTC | mem,  | reg   |

## Description

This instruction copies the bit specified by the operands into CF, then complements the original value of the bit in the *dest* operand.

The *index* operand holds a bit index into the bit string specified by *dest*, which can be a 16-bit or 32-bit register or a memory location. The state of the bit is copied into the carry flag, and the bit of the *dest* operand is complemented.

If the *index* operand is an immediate data value, it can range from 0 through 31. If the *index* is held in a register, it can take on any integral value. Some assemblers might let you specify immediate *index* values greater than 31. If so, they modify the effective address by an appropriate value so that the *index* can be scaled back to between 0 and 31.

BTC does not accept byte operands, so do not use it with memory-mapped I/O devices because the instruction causes either the 16-bit word or the 32-bit word containing the selected bit to be read. This could affect more than one I/O device register. You should use a single-byte MOV instruction to read the I/O register and then test the contents of the register.

## Flags

| OF | DF | IF | TF | SF | ZF |   | AF |   | PF |   | CF |
| -- | -- | -- | -- | -- | -- | - | -- | - | -- | - | -- |
| ?  | –  | –  | –  | ?  | ?  | – | ?  | – | ?  | – | x  |

## Faults

|    | *PM*    | *RM*   | *V8086* |
|----|---------|--------|---------|
| 12 | #SS(0)  |        |         |
| 13 | #GP(0)  | INT 13 | #GP(0)  |
| 14 | #PF(ec) |        | #PF(ec) |
| 17 | #AC(0)  |        | #AC(0)  |

## Example

```
MOVZX   EAX, BYTE PTR [04A2H] ; Read memory byte into 32-bit register
BTC     EAX, 2                ; Test and complement bit number 2
MOV     [04A2H], AL           ; Write modified byte back to memory
JC      bitset                ; Branch if the bit was set
```

# BTR

**80386/80486**

**Bit Test and Reset**

**(16p/32)**

## Syntax

BTR *dest, index*

## Operation

CF ← BIT(*dest, index*)
BIT(*dest, index*) ← 0

## Legal Forms

|     | *dest* | *index* |
| --- | ------ | ------- |
| BTR | reg,   | idata   |
| BTR | mem,   | idata   |
| BTR | reg,   | reg     |
| BTR | mem,   | reg     |

## Description

This instruction copies the bit specified by the operands into CF, then clears the original bit in *dest* to 0.

The *index* operand holds a bit index into the bit string specified by *dest*, which can be a 16-bit or 32-bit register or a memory location. The state of the bit is copied into the carry flag, and the bit of the *dest* operand is cleared to 0.

If the *index* operand is an immediate data value, it can range from 0 through 31. If the *index* is held in a register, it can be any integer. Some assemblers might let you specify immediate *index* values greater than 31. If so, they modify the effective address by an appropriate value so that the *index* can be scaled back to between 0 and 31.

BTR does not accept byte operands, so do not use it with memory-mapped I/O devices because the instruction causes either the 16-bit word or the 32-bit word containing the selected bit to be read. This could affect more than one I/O device register. You should use a single-byte MOV instruction to read the I/O register and then test the contents of the register.

When using a BTR instruction to implement a signaling function in a multiprocessor environment, the LOCK instruction prefix should immediately precede any BTR instruction that modifies shared memory.

## Flags

| OF | DF | IF | TF | SF | ZF |   | AF |   | PF |   | CF |
| -- | -- | -- | -- | -- | -- | - | -- | - | -- | - | -- |
| ?  | -  | -  | -  | ?  | ?  | - | ?  | - | ?  | - | x  |

## Faults

| | *PM* | *RM* | *V8086* |
|----|--------|--------|---------|
| 12 | #SS(0) | | |
| 13 | #GP(0) | INT 13 | #GP(0) |
| 14 | #PF(ec) | | #PF(ec) |
| 17 | #AC(0) | | #AC(0) |

## Example

```
BTR     MY_FLAG, 7          ; Zero the high-order bit of byte MY_FLAG
JNC     NOT_SET             ; Bit was already reset
```

# BTS

**Bit Test and Set**

## Syntax

BTS *dest*, *index*

## Operation

CF ← BIT(*dest*, *index*)
BIT(*dest*, *index*) ← 1

## Legal Forms

|     | dest | index |
| --- | --- | --- |
| BTS | reg, | idata |
| BTS | mem, | idata |
| BTS | reg, | reg |
| BTS | mem, | reg |

## Description

This instruction copies the specified bit into CF, then sets the original bit in *dest* to 1.

The *index* operand holds a bit index into the bit string specified by *dest*, which can be a 16-bit or 32-bit register or a memory location. The state of the bit is copied into the carry flag, and the bit of the *dest* operand is set to 1.

If the *index* operand is an immediate data value, it can range from 0 through 31. If the *index* is held in a register, it can be any integer. Some assemblers might let you specify immediate *index* values greater than 31. If so, they modify the effective address by an appropriate value so that the *index* can be scaled back to between 0 and 31.

BTS does not accept byte operands, so do not use it with memory-mapped I/O devices because the instruction causes either the 16-bit word or the 32-bit word containing the selected bit to be read. This could affect more than one I/O device register. You should use a single-byte MOV instruction to read the I/O register and then test the contents of the register.

When using a BTS instruction to implement a semaphore function in a multiprocessor environment, the LOCK instruction prefix should immediately precede any BTS instruction that modifies shared memory.

## Flags

| OF | DF | IF | TF | SF | ZF |   | AF |   | PF |   | CF |
| --- | --- | --- | --- | --- | --- | --- | --- | --- | --- | --- | --- |
| ? | - | - | - | ? | ? | - | ? | - | ? | - | x |

## Faults

| | PM | RM | V8086 |
|---|---|---|---|
| 12 | #SS(0) | | |
| 13 | #GP(0) | INT 13 | #GP(0) |
| 14 | #PF(ec) | | #PF(ec) |
| 17 | #AC(0) | | #AC(0) |

## Example

```
BTS     MY_FLAG, 7          ; Set the high-order bit of byte MY_FLAG
JC      WAS_SET             ; Bit was already set
```

# CALL

**8086/80186/80286/80386/80486**

**Far Procedure Call**

**(32p/48)**

## Syntax

CALL *dest*

## Operation

```
push(CS)
push(EIP)
CS:EIP ← dest
```

## Legal Forms

| | *dest* | |
|------|-------|------------------|
| CALL | idata | ; CS:EIP ← idata |
| CALL | mem   | ; CS:EIP ← [mem] |

## Description

The far procedure call saves the current code segment selector and the address of the next instruction (EIP) on the stack. Control then transfers to the destination specified by the operand. The operand can be an immediate selector:offset value or the address of a 48-bit FAR pointer in memory.

The selector can point to another code segment, a call gate, a task gate, or a task state segment. If the selector points to a gate or TSS, the offset portion of the CALL is ignored. If the selector points to a code segment, control transfers to the specified offset within that segment.

All flags are affected by a task switch.

## Flags

| OF | DF | IF | TF | SF | ZF | | AF | | PF | | CF |
|----|----|----|----|----|----|---|----|---|----|---|----|
| -  | -  | -  | -  | -  | -  | - | -  | - | -  | - | -  |

## Faults

| | *PM* | *RM* | *V8086* |
|----|---------|--------|----------|
| 10 | #TS(0)  |        |          |
| 10 | #TS(sel)|        | #TS(sel) |
| 11 | #NP(sel)|        | #NP(sel) |
| 12 | #SS(0)  |        |          |
| 12 | #SS(SS) |        |          |
| 13 | #GP(0)  | INT 13 | #GP(0)   |
|    | #GP(CS) | INT 13 | #GP(0)   |
| 14 | #PF(ec) |        | #PF(EC)  |
| 17 | #AC(0)  |        | #AC(0)   |

## Examples

```
CALL      16A3:0000          ; Direct call
CALL      FWORD PTR [005AH]   ; Indirect call
```

# CALL

**Near Procedure Call**

## Syntax

CALL *dest*

## Operation

push(EIP)
EIP ← *dest*

## Legal Forms

| | *dest* | |
|---|---|---|
| CALL | offset | ; EIP ← EIP + offset |
| CALL | mem | ; EIP ← [mem] |
| CALL | reg | ; EIP ← [reg] |

## Description

This instruction pushes the address of the next instruction (EIP) onto the stack. The instruction pointer is then set to the value specified by the operand.

If the operand is an immediate value, the new instruction pointer is relative to the current position. If the operand is a memory address or a register, the subroutine address is taken indirectly from the operand.

## Flags

| OF | DF | IF | TF | SF | ZF | | AF | | PF | | CF |
|----|----|----|----|----|----|---|----|---|----|---|----|
| - | - | - | - | - | - | - | - | - | - | - | - |

## Faults

| | *PM* | *RM* | *V8086* |
|---|---|---|---|
| 12 | #SS(0) | | |
| 13 | #GP(0) | INT 13 | #GP(0) |
| 14 | #PF(ec) | | #PF(ec) |
| 17 | #AC(0) | | #AC(0) |

## Examples

```
CALL    SQRT            ; Call direct
LEA     EBX, FN_TABLE   ; Get pointer to address table
MOV     EAX, 3          ; Select third function
CALL    [EBX+EAX*4]     ; Call it
```

# CBW

8086/80186/80286/80386/80486

**Convert Byte to Word**

(8)

## Syntax

```
CBW
```

## Operation

```
if BIT(AL, 7) then
    AH ← 0FFH
else
    AH ← 0
endif
```

## Legal Form

```
CBW
```

## Description

This instruction sign-extends the byte in AL to AX.

## Flags

| OF | DF | IF | TF | SF | ZF | | AF | | PF | | CF |
|----|----|----|----|----|----|----|----|----|----|----|----|
| -  | -  | -  | -  | -  | -  | -  | -  | -  | -  | -  | -  |

## Faults

None.

## Example

```
MOV     AL, TINY        ; Read a byte into AL
CBW                     ; Convert to 16-bit signed integer
ADD     BX, AX
```

# CDQ

**Convert Doubleword to Quadword**

## Syntax

```
CDQ
```

## Operation

```
if (BIT(EAX, 31) = 1) then
    EDX ← 0FFFFFFFFH
else
    EDX ← 0
endif
```

## Legal Form

```
CDQ
```

## Description

This instruction sign-extends the 32-bit EAX register to a 64-bit dword. It is most frequently used before the integer divide instruction, which operates on a 64-bit dividend.

## Flags

| OF | DF | IF | TF | SF | ZF | | AF | | PF | | CF |
|----|----|----|----|----|----|---|----|---|----|---|----|
| -  | -  | -  | -  | -  | -  | - | -  | - | -  | - | -  |

## Faults

None.

## Example

```
MOV     EAX, [400H]        ; Copy dividend to EAX
CDQ                        ; Extend to 64 bits
IDIV    DWORD PTR [20H]    ; Divide
```

# CLC

8086/80186/80286/80386/80486

**Clear Carry Flag**

( )

## Syntax

CLC

## Operation

CF ← 0

## Legal Form

CLC

## Description

This instruction clears the carry flag in the EFLAGS register to 0.

## Flags

| OF | DF | IF | TF | SF | ZF | | AF | | PF | | CF |
|----|----|----|----|----|----|----|----|----|----|----|----|
| -  | -  | -  | -  | -  | -  | -  | -  | -  | -  | -  | 0  |

## Faults

None.

## Example

```
NO_ERROR:
        CLC                    ; Clear carry
        RET                    ; Return from subroutine with success
                               ; indicated by CF
```

# CLD

**Clear Direction Flag**

8086/80186/80286/80386/80486

( )

## Syntax

CLD

## Operation

DF ← 0

## Legal Form

CLD

## Description

This instruction clears the direction flag in the EFLAGS register to 0. When DF is 0, any string instructions increment the index registers (ESI or EDI).

## Flags

| OF | DF | IF | TF | SF | ZF | | AF | | PF | | CF |
|----|----|----|----|----|----|----|----|----|----|----|----|
| -  | 0  | -  | -  | -  | -  | -  | -  | -  | -  | -  | -  |

## Faults

None.

## Example

```
MOV ECX, STR_LEN        ; String move count
CLD                     ; Clear direction flag
REP MOVSB               ; Copy the string
```

# CLI

## Clear Interrupt Flag

8086/80186/80286/80386/80486

( )

## Syntax

```
CLI
```

## Operation

```
IF ← 0
```

## Legal Form

```
CLI
```

## Description

This instruction clears the interrupt bit in the EFLAGS register to 0, disabling hardware interrupts (except NMI). The procedure executing the CLI instruction must be of equal or higher privilege than the current IOPL, that is, CPL ≤ IOPL, or a general protection fault occurs.

## Flags

| OF | DF | IF | TF | SF | ZF |   | AF |   | PF |   | CF |
|----|----|----|----|----|----|---|----|---|----|---|----|
| -  | -  | 0  | -  | -  | -  | - | -  | - | -  | - | -  |

## Faults

| PM | | RM | V8086 |
|----|----|----|----|
| 13 | #GP(0) | | #GP(0) |

## Example

```
CLI                      ; Disable interrupts
MOV AL, SEMAPHORE        ; Get memory value
DEC AL                   ; Decrement counter
JZ done                  ; Skip if value was 0
MOV SEMAPHORE, AL        ; Update
DONE:
STI                      ; Enable interrupt
```

# CLTS

**Clear Task Switched Bit**

## Syntax

CLTS

## Operation

BIT(CR0, 3) ← 0

## Legal Form

CLTS

## Description

This instruction clears the task switched (TS) bit in the CR0 register to 0. The TS bit allows the 80386 to efficiently manage the floating-point unit. Whenever a task switch occurs, the CPU sets the TS bit to 1. If the TS bit is 1 when a coprocessor escape (ESC) executes, a coprocessor not available fault (int 7) occurs. A WAIT instruction will also trigger INT 7 if both the TS and MP bits on CR0 are 1.

The fault handler can clear the TS bit, save the NDP state, load the NDP state for the current task, and return to the instruction that faulted. Switching between tasks that do not use floating point will not cause the fault, and you avoid the overhead of saving and restoring the NDP state.

Only procedures running at a CPL of 0 can execute CLTS without causing a general protection fault.

CLTS is valid in real mode to allow initialization for protected mode.

## Flags

| OF | DF | IF | TF | SF | ZF | | AF | | PF | | CF |
|----|----|----|----|----|----|---|----|---|----|---|----|
| -  | -  | -  | -  | -  | -  | - | -  | - | -  | - | -  |

## Faults

| PM | | RM | V8086 |
|-----|--------|----|--------|
| 13  | #GP(0) |    | #GP(0) |

## Example

```
CLTS                    ; Clear task switched bit
CALL SWAP_NDP_STATE     ; Save/restore math coprocessor state
```

# CMC

8086/80186/80286/80386/80486

**Complement the Carry Flag**

( )

## Syntax

CMC

## Operation

CF ← ~CF

## Legal Form

CMC

## Description

The carry bit of the EFLAGS register is complemented; that is, if the initial value of the carry bit is 0, it is set to 1. If the initial value is 1, the flag is cleared to 0 as a result of the instruction.

## Flags

| OF | DF | IF | TF | SF | ZF | | AF | | PF | | CF |
|----|----|----|----|----|----|----|----|----|----|----|----|
| -  | -  | -  | -  | -  | -  | -  | -  | -  | -  | -  | x  |

## Faults

None.

## Example

```
        BT      EAX, 1          ; Test a bit, save in CF
        JC      EXIT            ; Bit was set--we're done
        JMP     TRY_AGAIN       ; Not ready yet
EXIT:
        CMC                     ; Return, CF clear
        RET
```

# CMP

**Compare Integers**

## Syntax

CMP *op1, op2*

## Operation

NULL ← *op1 - op2*

## Legal Forms

|     | *op1* | *op2* |
| --- | --- | --- |
| CMP | reg, | idata |
| CMP | mem, | idata |
| CMP | reg, | reg |
| CMP | reg, | mem |
| CMP | mem, | reg |

## Description

This instruction subtracts the contents of *op2* from *op1* and discards the result. Only the EFLAGS register is affected. The following table illustrates how the flags are set based on the operand values.

| *Condition* | *Signed Compare* | *Unsigned Compare* |
| --- | --- | --- |
| *op1 > op2* | ZF = 0 and SF = OF | CF = 0 and ZF = 0 |
| *op1 ≥ op2* | SF = OF | CF = 0 |
| *op1 = op2* | ZF = 1 | ZF = 1 |
| *op1 ≤ op2* | ZF = 1 and SF != OF | CF = 1 or ZF = 1 |
| *op1 < op2* | SF != OF | CF = 1 |

If *op1* is a 16-bit or 32-bit operand and *op2* is an 8-bit immediate value, *op2* is sign-extended to match the size of *op1*.

## Flags

| OF | DF | IF | TF | SF | ZF | | AF | | PF | | CF |
| --- | --- | --- | --- | --- | --- | --- | --- | --- | --- | --- | --- |
| X | - | - | - | X | X | - | X | - | X | - | X |

## Faults

|     | *PM* | *RM* | *V8086* |
| --- | --- | --- | --- |
| 12 | #SS(0) | | |
| 13 | #GP(0) | INT 13 | #GP(0) |
| 14 | #PF(ec) | | #PF(ec) |

## Examples

```
CMP     AL, [4211A]          ; 8-bit compare
CMP     AX, [BX+3]           ; 16-bit real/virtual mode
CMP     CX, [EBP+8][EAX*2]   ; 16-bit protected mode
CMP     ESI, 7               ; 32-bit compare with sign-extended
                                  op2 operand
```

# CMPS

Compare String

8086/80186/80286/80386/80486

(8/16p/32)

## Syntax

CMPS

## Operation

```
when opcode is (CMPSB, CMPSW, CMPSD) set opsize ← (1, 2, 4)
NULL ← DS:[ESI] - ES:[EDI]
if (DF = 0) then
    ESI ← ESI + opsize
    EDI ← EDI + opsize
else
    ESI-opsize
    EDI-opsize
endif
```

## Legal Forms

```
CMPSB                    ; Compare string byte
CMPSW                    ; Compare string word
CMPSD                    ; Compare string doubleword
```

## Description

This instruction subtracts the memory operand pointed to by DS:ESI from the operand at ES:EDI and discards the result, as in the CMP instruction. The size of the operand is either a byte, word, or doubleword, depending on the opcode used. The flags are set as the comparison dictates, and the contents of ESI and EDI are modified, either incremented by the size of the operand, or decremented, depending on the setting of the DF bit in the EFLAGS register. ESI and EDI are incremented when DF = 0.

You can precede the CMPS instruction with either the REPE or REPNE prefix to repeatedly compare operands while the ZF bit remains 1 (REPE) or 0 (REPNE). Register ECX holds the maximum compare count.

You can also apply a segment override prefix to the CMPS instruction to override the DS segment of the DS:[ESI] operand. You cannot override the ES segment assumption for the EDI operand.

## Flags

| OF | DF | IF | TF | SF | ZF | AF | PF | CF |
|----|----|----|----|----|----|----|----|----|
| x  | -  | -  | -  | x  | x  | -  | x  | - | x | - | x |

## Faults

| | PM | RM | V8086 |
|---|---|---|---|
| 12 | #SS(0) | | |
| 13 | #GP(0) | INT 13 | #GP(0) |
| 14 | #PF(ec) | | #PF(ec) |
| 17 | #AC(0) | | #AC(0) |

## Example

```
LEA       ESI, standard        ; DS:ESI points to default
LES       EDI, [EBP+12]        ; ES:EDI loaded from stack frame
MOV       ECX, 31              ; Count is a constant
CLD                            ; Ensure direction flag set correctly
REPE CMPSB                     ; Compare byte string
JNE       not_eq               ; Branch if strings not equal
```

# CMPXCHG

**Compare and Exchange**

80486
**(8/16p/32)**

## Syntax

CMPXCHG *dest, src*

## Operation

```
if acc = dest then
     ZF ← 1
     dest ← src
else
     ZF ← 0
     acc ← dest
```

## Legal Forms

|          | dest  | src  |
|----------|-------|------|
| CMPXCHG  | reg,  | reg  |
| CMPXCHG  | mem,  | reg  |

## Description

The value of *dest* is read and compared with the accumulator (AL, AX, or EAX). If the values are equal, the value of *src* is written to location *dest*; otherwise, the accumulator value is replaced by *dest*. The flags are set as if a CMP *acc,dest* instruction had been executed.

When preceded by the LOCK prefix, this instruction is very useful for multiprocessor semaphore operations.

Notice that this instruction always generates both a read and a write cycle. If the compare succeeds, *src* is written to location *dest*; otherwise, the original value of *dest* is written back.

## Flags

| OF | DF | IF | TF | SF | ZF |   | AF |   | PF |   | CF |
|----|----|----|----|----|----|---|----|---|----|---|----|
| X  | -  | -  | -  | X  | X  | - | X  | - | X  | - | X  |

## Faults

| | PM | RM | V86 |
|---|---|---|---|
| 12 | #SS(0) | | |
| 13 | #GP(0) | INT 13 | #GP(0) |
| 14 | #PF(ec) | | #PF(ec) |
| 17 | #AC(0) | | #AC(0) |

## Example

```
XOR      AL,CL     ; AL ← 0, semaphore available value
MOV      BL,1      ; Semaphore hold value
CMPXCHG  sema,BL   ; Compare
JNE      failed    ; Semaphore already held
```

# CWD
## Convert Word to Doubleword

### Syntax

```
CWD
```

### Operation

```
if (BIT(AX, 15 = 1)) then
    DX ← 0FFFFH
else
    DX ← 0
endif
```

### Legal Form

```
CWD
```

### Description

This instruction sign-extends the word in AX to the DX:AX register pair. The preferred 16-bit to 32-bit conversion instruction is CWDE. CWD is used by the 8086 and 80286, which do not have 32-bit registers.

### Flags

| OF | DF | IF | TF | SF | ZF | | AF | | PF | | CF |
|----|----|----|----|----|----|----|----|----|----|----|----|
| -  | -  | -  | -  | -  | -  | -  | -  | -  | -  | -  | -  |

### Faults

None.

### Example

```
MOV     AX, divisor      ; Get 16-bit divisor
CWD                      ; Extend to DX:AX
DIV     CX               ; 16-bit division
```

# CWDE

80386/80486

## Convert Word to Doubleword Extended

(16)

### Syntax

```
CWDE
```

### Operation

```
if (BIT(EAX, 15) = 1) then
    EAX ← EAX | FFFF0000H
else
    EAX ← EAX & 0000FFFFH
endif
```

### Legal Form

```
CWDE
```

### Description

This instruction sign-extends the 16-bit value in AX to a full 32 bits in the EAX register.

### Flags

| OF | DF | IF | TF | SF | ZF | | AF | | PF | | CF |
|----|----|----|----|----|----|---|----|---|----|---|----|
| -  | -  | -  | -  | -  | -  | - | -  | - | -  | - | -  |

### Faults

None.

### Example

```
MOV    AX, short_int       ; Get 16-bit signed value
NEG    AX,                 ; Convert to negative number
CWDE                       ; Return 32-bit result
```

# DAA

**8086/80186/80286/80386/80486**

**Decimal Adjust AL After Addition**

**(8)**

## Syntax

DAA

## Operation

```
if (AF | (AL & 0FH) > 9) then
    AL ← AL + 6
    AF ← 1
else
    AF ← 0
endif
if (CF | (AL > 9FH)) then
    AL ← AL + 60H
    CF ← 1
else
    CF ← 0
endif
```

## Legal Form

DAA

## Description

This instruction ensures that AL contains a valid decimal result after an addition of two packed BCD values.

## Flags

| OF | DF | IF | TF | SF | ZF | | AF | | PF | | CF |
|----|----|----|----|----|----|---|----|---|----|---|----|
| ?  | -  | -  | -  | x  | x  | - | x  | - | x  | - | x  |

## Faults

None.

## Example

```
MOV    AL, 72H            ; 72 in packed decimal
ADD    AL, 19H            ; Yields 8BH in AL
DAA                       ; Adjusts AL to 91H
```

# DAS

8086/80186/80286/80386/80486

**Decimal Adjust AL After Subtraction**

(8)

## Syntax

DAS

## Operation

```
if (AF | ((AL & 0FH)) > 9) then
    AL ← AL - 6
    AF ← 1
else
    AF ← 0
endif
if (CF | (AL > 9FH)) then
    AL ← AL - 60H
    CF ← 1
else
    CF ← 0
endif
```

## Legal Form

DAS

## Description

This instruction ensures that AL contains a valid decimal result after a subtraction of two packed BCD values.

## Flags

| OF | DF | IF | TF | SF | ZF | | AF | | PF | | CF |
|----|----|----|----|----|----|---|----|---|----|---|----|
| ? | - | - | - | x | x | - | x | - | x | - | x |

## Faults

None.

## Example

```
MOV     AL, 42H          ; 42 in packed decimal
SUB     AL, 13H          ; Yields 2FH in AL
DAS                      ; Adjusts AL to 29H
```

# DEC

8086/80186/80286/80386/80486

**Decrement**

(8/16p/32)

## Syntax

DEC *op1*

## Operation

*op1* ← *op1* - 1

## Legal Forms

|  | *op1* |
|---|---|
| DEC | reg |
| DEC | mem |

## Description

This instruction subtracts the value 1 from *op1*. DEC is frequently used to decrement indexes and therefore does not affect the carry flag (CF). In other respects, it is equivalent to the instruction:

SUB   *op1*, 1

## Flags

| OF | DF | IF | TF | SF | ZF |  | AF |  | PF |  | CF |
|---|---|---|---|---|---|---|---|---|---|---|---|
| X | - | - | - | X | X | - | X | - | X | - | - |

## Faults

|  | *PM* | *RM* | *V8086* |
|---|---|---|---|
| 12 | #SS(0) |  | #SS(0) |
| 13 | #GP(0) | INT 13 | #GP(0) |
| 14 | #PF(ec) |  | #PF(ec) |
| 17 | #AC(0) |  | #AC(0) |

## Example

DEC      ESI                    ; Decrement contents of ESI

# DIV

**Unsigned Division**

8086/80186/80286/80386/80486<br>(8/16p/32)

## Syntax

DIV    *op1*

## Operation

low(*acc*) ← *acc* / *op1*
high(*acc*) ← *acc* modulo *op1*

## Legal Forms

|     | *op1* |
| --- | --- |
| DIV | reg |
| DIV | mem |

## Description

This instruction divides the value in the accumulator register or register pair by *op1*, storing the quotient in the low-order portion of the accumulator and the remainder in the high-order portion. The following table illustrates the registers used as accumulators, depending on the size of *op1*.

| *Size of* op1 | *Dividend* | *Quotient* | *Remainder* |
| --- | --- | --- | --- |
| Byte | AX | AL | AH |
| Word | DX,AX | AX | DX |
| Dword | EDX,EAX | EAX | EDX |

If the dividend is 0 or if the quotient is too large to fit in the result accumulator, a divide error fault (interrupt 0) occurs.

## Flags

| OF | DF | IF | TF | SF | ZF |  | AF |  | PF |  | CF |
| --- | --- | --- | --- | --- | --- | --- | --- | --- | --- | --- | --- |
| ? | - | - | - | ? | ? | - | ? | - | ? | - | ? |

## Faults

|    | *PM* | *RM* | *V8086* |
| --- | --- | --- | --- |
| 0  | INT 0 | INT 0 | INT 0 |
| 12 | #SS(0) |       |       |
| 13 | #GP(0) | INT 13 | #GP(0) |
| 14 | #PF(ec) |      | #PF(ec) |
| 17 | #AC(0) |       | #AC(0) |

## Example

```
MOV      EAX, dividend
CWDE                        ; Convert 32-bit operand to 64 bits
DIV      EBX                ; 32-bit divide
MOV      quotient, EAX      ; Save result
MOV      remainder, EDX
```

# ENTER

Enter New Stack Frame

## Syntax

```
ENTER locals, nesting
```

## Operation

```
nesting ← max (nesting, 31)
push (EBP)
temp ← ESP
if (nesting > 0) then
    nesting ← nesting - 1
    while (nesting > 0)
        EBP ← EBP - 4
        push (SS:[EBP])
        nesting ← nesting - 1
    endwhile
    push (temp)
endif
EBP ← temp
ESP ← ESP - locals
```

## Legal Forms

| | locals | nesting |
|---|---|---|
| ENTER | idata, | idata |

## Description

This instruction sets up the stack frame used by high-level languages. The form ENTER n,0 is equivalent to the instructions:

```
PUSH EBP
MOV  EBP, ESP
SUB  ESP, n
```

This saves the previous frame pointer (EBP), sets the frame to the current stack top (ESP), and allocates space for local variables. Parameters passed to the procedure are addressed as positive offsets from EBP, and local variables are addressed as negative offsets from EBP.

When the second operand is greater than 0 (which happens only in languages that allow nesting of procedure definitions), the pointers to previous stack frames are pushed onto the stack to allow addressing of stack-resident variables whose scopes are outside the current stack frame.

Languages such as FORTRAN and C do not allow lexical procedure nesting, so they always use ENTER with a nesting operand of 0. Pascal, Modula-II, and Ada allow procedure nesting, and compilers for those languages generate the more complex form of ENTER.

## Flags

| OF | DF | IF | TF | SF | ZF | | AF | | PF | | CF |
|----|----|----|----|----|----|----|----|----|----|----|----|
| -  | -  | -  | -  | -  | -  | -  | -  | -  | -  | -  | -  |

## Faults

| | *PM* | *RM* | *V8086* |
|----|------|------|---------|
| 12 | #SS(0) | | |
| 14 | #PF(ec) | | #PF(ec) |

## Example

```
ENTER   4, 0              ; Create stack frame with
                         ; space for a dword local
```

# HLT

8086/80186/80286/80386/80486

Halt                                                                    ( )

## Syntax

HLT

## Legal Form

HLT

## Description

This instruction stops all further processing. No other instructions will execute until the processor is reset or an interrupt occurs. An NMI interrupt always brings the processor out of the halt state. The IF flag must be 1 for any other hardware interrupt to be acknowledged. After processing the interrupt, execution continues with the instruction immediately following HLT.

You must execute at a CPL of 0 to issue a HLT instruction; otherwise, a general protection fault occurs.

## Flags

| OF | DF | IF | TF | SF | ZF | | AF | | PF | | CF |
|----|----|----|----|----|----|----|----|----|----|----|----|
| -  | -  | -  | -  | -  | -  | -  | -  | -  | -  | -  | -  |

## Faults

| PM | | RM | V8086 |
|----|----|----|-------|
| 13 | #GP(0) | | #GP(0) |

## Example

```
        STI
L1:     HLT                             ; Idle, processing only interrupts
        JMP     L1
```

# IDIV

**Integer (Signed) Division**

## Syntax

```
IDIV   op1
```

## Operation

```
low(acc) ← acc / op1
high(acc) ← acc modulo op1
```

## Legal Forms

| | op1 |
|------|------|
| IDIV | reg |
| IDIV | mem |

## Description

This instruction divides the value in the accumulator register or register pair by *op1*, storing the quotient in the low-order portion of the accumulator and the remainder in the high-order portion. The following table illustrates the registers used as accumulators, depending on the size of *op1*.

| *Size of* op1 | *Dividend* | *Quotient* | *Remainder* |
|---------------|------------|------------|-------------|
| Byte | AX | AL | AH |
| Word | DX,AX | AX | DX |
| Dword | EDX,EAX | EAX | EDX |

If the dividend is 0 or if the quotient is too large to fit in the result accumulator, a divide error fault (interrupt 0) occurs.

## Flags

| OF | DF | IF | TF | SF | ZF | | AF | | PF | | CF |
|----|----|----|----|----|----|----|----|----|----|----|----|
| ? | - | - | - | ? | ? | - | ? | - | ? | - | ? |

## Faults

| | *PM* | *RM* | *V8086* |
|----|---------|--------|---------|
| 0 | INT 0 | INT 0 | INT 0 |
| 12 | #SS(0) | | |
| 13 | #GP(0) | INT 13 | #GP(0) |
| 14 | #PF(ec) | | #PF(ec) |
| 17 | #AC(0) | | #AC(0) |

## Example

```
MOV     EAX, [ESP+14]      ; Get dividend
CDQ                        ; Convert to 64 bits
IDIV    ECX
```

# IMUL

### Integer (Signed) Multiplication

8086/80186/80286/80386/80486

(8/16p/32)

## Syntax

IMUL *op1*, [*op2*, [*op3*]]

## Operation

*dest* ← multiplier * multiplicand

## Legal Forms

|      | op1  | op2   | op3   |                          |
|------|------|-------|-------|--------------------------|
| IMUL | reg  |       |       | ; acc ← acc * reg        |
| IMUL | mem  |       |       | ; acc ← acc * mem        |
| IMUL | reg, | reg   |       | ; op1 ← op1 * op2        |
| IMUL | reg, | mem   |       | ; op1 ← op1 * op2        |
| IMUL | reg, | idata |       | ; op1 ← op1 * op2        |
| IMUL | reg, | reg,  | idata | ; op1 ← op2 * op3        |
| IMUL | reg, | mem,  | idata | ; op1 ← op2 * op3        |

## Description

This instruction multiplies signed, two's complement integers. The flags are left in an unknown state except for OF and CF, which are cleared to 0 if the result of the multiplication is the same size (byte, word, or dword) as the multiplicand.

In the single operand form of the instruction, the result is placed in AX if *op1* is a byte, DX:AX if *op1* is a word, and EDX:EAX if *op1* is a dword.

In the forms of IMUL that use 2 or 3 operands, the operands must all be the same size.

## Flags

| OF | DF | IF | TF | SF | ZF |   | AF |   | PF |   | CF |
|----|----|----|----|----|----|---|----|---|----|---|----|
| x  | -  | -  | -  | ?  | ?  | - | ?  | - | ?  | - | x  |

## Faults

|    | *PM*    | *RM*   | *V8086* |
|----|---------|--------|---------|
| 12 | #SS(0)  |        |         |
| 13 | #GP(0)  | INT 13 | #GP(0)  |
| 14 | #PF(ec) |        | #PF(ec) |
| 17 | #AC(0)  |        | #AC(0)  |

## Examples

```
IMUL    ECX             ; EDX:EAX ← EAX * ECX
IMUL    AL, CH, 7       ; AL = CH * 7
```

**215**

# IN

**Input from I/O Port**

8086/80186/80286/80386/80486

(8/16p/32)

### Syntax

IN acc, port

### Operation

ACC ← (port)

### Legal Forms

|    | acc  | port  |
|----|------|-------|
| IN | acc, | idata |
| IN | acc, | DX    |

### Description

This instruction reads a byte, word, or dword into the specified accumulator from the designated I/O port. If you use an immediate data value in the instruction, you can address only the first 256 ports. If the port is specified in the DX register, you can access any of the 65536 ports.

IN is a privileged instruction. A procedure that attempts to execute an input instruction must satisfy one of two conditions to avoid a general protection fault.

If the procedure that executes an IN instruction has I/O privilege (that is, if its CPL is numerically less than or equal to the IOPL field in the EFLAGS register), the input instruction executes immediately.

If the procedure does not have I/O privilege, the I/O permission bitmap for the current task is checked. If the bit(s) corresponding to the I/O port(s) is cleared to 0, the input instruction executes. If the bit(s) is set to 1, or the port(s) is outside the range of the bitmap, a general protection fault occurs. See Chapter 5 for more details on this feature.

If the IN instruction is encountered while in V86 mode, only the I/O permission bitmap is tested. The IOPL value is not a factor in validating access to the port.

### Flags

| OF | DF | IF | TF | SF | ZF |   | AF |   | PF |   | CF |
|----|----|----|----|----|----|---|----|---|----|---|----|
| -  | -  | -  | -  | -  | -  | - | -  | - | -  | - | -  |

### Faults

| PM        | RM | V8086   |
|-----------|----|---------|
| 13  #GP(0) |    | #GP(0)  |

## Examples

```
IN      AX, 72H              ; Input a 16-bit value
                             ; from ports 72H and 73H
MOV     DX, crt_port
IN      AL, DX               ; Input a byte value
```

# INC

Increment

## Syntax

```
INC op1
```

## Operation

$op1 \leftarrow op1 + 1$

## Legal Forms

| | op1 |
|---|---|
| INC | reg |
| INC | mem |

## Description

This instruction adds the value 1 to *op1*. This instruction is often used to increment indexes and therefore does not affect the carry flag (CF). In other respects, it is equivalent to the instruction:

```
ADD   op1, 1
```

## Flags

| OF | DF | IF | TF | SF | ZF | | AF | | PF | | CF |
|---|---|---|---|---|---|---|---|---|---|---|---|
| x | - | - | - | x | x | - | x | - | x | - | - |

## Faults

| | PM | RM | V8086 |
|---|---|---|---|
| 12 | #SS(0) | | |
| 13 | #GP(0) | INT 13 | #GP(0) |
| 14 | #PF(ec) | | #PF(ec) |
| 17 | #AC(0) | | #AC(0) |

## Example

```
INC     ESI              ; Increment contents of ESI
```

# INS

## Input String from I/O Port

## Syntax

```
INS
```

## Operation

```
when opcode is (INSB, INSW, INSD), set opsize ← (1, 2, 4)
ES:[EDI] ← port(DX)
if (DF = 0) then
    EDI ← EDI + opsize
else
    EDI ← EDI - opsize
endif
```

## Legal Forms

```
INSB        ; Input string byte
INSW        ; Input string word
INSD        ; Input string doubleword
```

## Description

This instruction allows the location specified by ES:[EDI] to receive data input from the I/O port contained in the DX register. An 8-bit operation (INSB) adjusts the address in EDI by 1, a 16-bit operation (INSW) adjusts EDI by 2, and a 32-bit operation (INSD) adjusts EDI by 4. The memory offset in EDI is incremented if the DF bit is 0 or is decremented if DF is 1.

Like the IN instruction, the INS instruction is privileged. The executing procedure must have a CPL equal to or numerically less than the IOPL, or access to the port specified in DX must be granted by the I/O permission bitmap in the TSS.

You can use the REP prefix with the INS instruction. Using the prefix causes register ECX to be interpreted as an instruction count.

A segment override prefix does not affect the INS instruction. The destination segment is always ES.

## Flags

| OF | DF | IF | TF | SF | ZF | | AF | | PF | | CF |
|----|----|----|----|----|----|----|----|----|----|----|----|
| -  | -  | -  | -  | -  | -  | -  | -  | -  | -  | -  | -  |

## Faults

| | *PM* | *RM* | *V8086* |
|---|---|---|---|
| 13 | #GP(0) | INT 13 | #GP(0) |
| 14 | #PF(ec) | | #PF(ec) |
| 17 | #AC(0) | | #AC(0) |

## Examples

```
LEA      EDI, new_val        ; Set up destination pointer
MOV      DX, 370H            ; Set up port address
CLD
INSD                         ; Input 32-bit value to new_val
INSD                         ; Input value to new_val + 4
```

# INT

**Software Interrupt**

## Syntax

INT *vector*

## Operation

```
push(EFLAGS)
push(CS)
push(EIP)
TF ← 0
if (IDT(vector).TYPE = INTERRUPT_GATE) then
    IF ← 0
endif
CS:EIP ← destination(IDT(vector))
```

## Legal Form

| *vector* |
| --- |
| INT     idata |

## Description

This instruction saves the current flags and execution location on the stack, and the *vector* operand indicates the IDT entry that is selected. The gate from the IDT determines the new execution location.

If the processor encounters the INT instruction while in V86 mode, the 80386 switches to the ring 0 stack (SS0:ESP0) taken from the V86 task state segment before processing the interrupt. Because the processor is running in ring 0, the IDT entry must have a DPL of 0; otherwise, a general protection fault occurs.

The INT 3 instruction is usually encoded as a single byte (0CCH) and used as a breakpoint instruction for debuggers.

## Flags

| OF | DF | IF | TF | SF | ZF |  | AF |  | PF |  | CF |
| --- | --- | --- | --- | --- | --- | --- | --- | --- | --- | --- | --- |
| - | - | x | 0 | - | - | - | - | - | - | - | - |

## Faults

|     | *PM*     | *RM*   | *V8086*  |
| --- | -------- | ------ | -------- |
| 10  | #TS(sel) |        |          |
| 11  | #NP(sel) |        |          |
| 12  | #SS(0)   |        |          |
| 13  | #GP(0)   | INT 13 | #GP(0)   |
| 14  | #PF(ec)  |        | #PF(ec)  |

## Example

```
INT    42                    ; Make a system-dependent OS call
```

# INTO
**Interrupt on Overflow**

8086/80186/80286/80386/80486

( )

## Syntax

INTO

## Operation

```
if (OF) then
    INT 4
endif
```

## Legal Form

INTO

## Description

This instruction executes an INT 4 instruction if the overflow bit (OF) in the EFLAGS register is 1. See the INT instruction for further details.

## Flags

| OF | DF | IF | TF | SF | ZF | | AF | | PF | | CF |
|----|----|----|----|----|----|----|----|----|----|----|----|
| -  | -  | x  | 0  | -  | -  | -  | -  | -  | -  | -  | -  |

## Faults

| | *PM* | *RM* | *V8086* |
|----|------|------|---------|
| 10 | #TS(sel) | | |
| 11 | #NP(sel) | | |
| 12 | #SS(0) | | |
| 13 | #GP(0) | INT 13 | #GP(0) |
| 14 | #PF(ec) | | #PF(ec) |

## Example

```
ADD     ECX, VECTOR[EDI*4]  ; Arithmetic operation
INTO                        ; Check for overflow
```

# INVD

**Invalidate Cache**

()

## Syntax

```
INVD
```

## Operation

The internal cache is invalidated.

## Legal Form

```
INVD
```

## Description

The internal cache is invalidated. A special hardware bus cycle is also initiated, which can be used to invalidate external cache hardware.

## Flags

| OF | DF | IF | TF | SF | ZF | | AF | | PF | | CF |
|----|----|----|----|----|----|----|----|----|----|----|----|
| -  | -  | -  | -  | -  | -  | -  | -  | -  | -  | -  | -  |

## Faults

None.

## Example

```
INVD                       ; Invalidate old cache
MOV   EAX,CR0              ; Get CR0
AND   EAX,060000000h      ; Enable cache
MOV   CR0,EAX             ; Rewrite CR0
```

# INVLPG

**Invalidate TLB Entry**

80486

(32)

### Syntax

INVLPG *mem*

### Operation

if PTE(*mem*) is in TLB(i) then
  invalidate TLB(i)

### Legal Form

INVLPG mem

### Description

If the page table entry for the page containing address *mem* is in the TLB, then that TLB entry is invalidated.

### Flags

| OF | DF | IF | TF | SF | ZF | | AF | | PF | | CF |
|----|----|----|----|----|----|----|----|----|----|----|----|
| –  | –  | –  | –  | –  | –  | –  | –  | –  | –  | –  | –  |

### Fault

| *PM* | *RM* | *V8086* |
|------|------|---------|
| 6˙  #UD() | INT 6 | |

˙The undefined opcode fault occurs only when the operand is encoded as a register.

### Example

INVLPG    [ESI+4]    ; Invalidate PTE for this address

# IRET

8086/80186/80286/80386/80486

**Interrupt Return**                                                        ( )

## Syntax

```
IRET
```

## Operation

```
if (NT = 1) then
    task_return (TSS.back_link)
else
    pop (EIP)
    pop (CS)
    pop (EFLAGS)
endif
```

## Legal Form

```
IRET
```

## Description

This instruction signals a return from an interrupt or, if the NT (nested task) bit is set to 1, a task switch from the current task to the one that invoked it.

When the new value of EFLAGS is popped from the stack, the IOPL bits are modified only if the CPL is 0.

Chapter 5 discusses transitions across protection rings and task switching.

If the IRET instruction executes while the processor is in V86 mode, a general protection fault occurs. It is the responsibility of the fault handler to emulate the real-mode IRET for the V86 task.

## Flags

| OF | DF | IF | TF | SF | ZF | | AF | | PF | | CF |
|----|----|----|----|----|----|---|----|---|----|---|----|
| X  | X  | X  | X  | X  | X  | – | X  | – | X  | – | X  |

## Faults

| | PM | RM | V8086 |
|---|------|--------|---------|
| 11 | | | |
| 12 | #SS(0) | | |
| 13 | #GP(0) | INT 13 | #GP(0) |
| 14 | #PF(ec) | | #PF(ec) |

## Example

```
IRET
```

# *Jcc*
## Jump if *Condition*

()

### Syntax

*Jcc offset*

### Operation

```
if (cc) then
    EIP ← EIP + sign_extend(offset)
endif
```

### Legal Forms

```
JA      offset   ; Jump above (unsigned x > y) / CF = 0 & ZF = 0
JAE     offset   ; Jump above or equal / CF = 0
JB      offset   ; Jump below (unsigned x < y) / CF = 1
JBE     offset   ; Jump below or equal / CF = 1 | ZF = 1
JC      offset   ; Jump if carry / CF = 1
JCXZ    offset   ; Jump if CX = 0
JECXZ   offset   ; Jump if ECX = 0
JE      offset   ; Jump equal / ZF = 1
JG      offset   ; Jump greater (signed x > y) / SF = OF & ZF = 0
JGE     offset   ; Jump greater or equal / SF = OF
JL      offset   ; Jump less (signed x < y) / SF != OF & ZF = 0
JLE     offset   ; Jump less or equal / SF != OF
JNA     offset   ; Jump not above (JBE)
JNAE    offset   ; Jump not above or equal (JB)
JNB     offset   ; Jump not below (JAE)
JNBE    offset   ; Jump not below or equal (JA)
JNC     offset   ; Jump no carry / CF = 0
JNE     offset   ; Jump not equal / ZF = 0
JNG     offset   ; Jump not greater / SF != OF & ZF = 1
JNGE    offset   ; Jump not greater or equal (JL)
JNL     offset   ; Jump not less (JGE)
JNLE    offset   ; Jump not less or equal (JG)
JNO     offset   ; Jump no overflow / OF = 0
JNP     offset   ; Jump no parity / PF = 0
JNS     offset   ; Jump no sign / SF = 0
JNZ     offset   ; Jump not 0 / ZF = 0
JO      offset   ; Jump if overflow / OF = 1
JP      offset   ; Jump if parity / PF = 1
JPE     offset   ; Jump parity even / PF = 1
JPO     offset   ; Jump parity odd / PF = 0
JS      offset   ; Jump if sign / SF = 1
JZ      offset   ; Jump if 0 / ZF = 1
```

## Description

The Jcc instructions test the conditions described for each mnemonic. If the condition holds true, the processor branches to the specified location. If the condition is false, execution continues with the instruction following the jump.

More than one mnemonic exists for the same condition. This lets you write the test in a manner most appropriate for the condition. For example, after OR EAX, EAX you would use JZ, and after CMP EAX,ESI you would use JE; both mnemonics test for ZF = 1.

## Flags

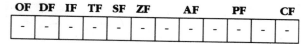

| OF | DF | IF | TF | SF | ZF | | AF | | PF | | CF |
|----|----|----|----|----|----|----|----|----|----|----|----|
| -  | -  | -  | -  | -  | -  | -  | -  | -  | -  | -  | -  |

## Fault

| PM | RM | V8086 |
|----|----|-------|
| 13   #GP(0) | | |

## Example

```
DEC     AL              ; Decrement AL
JZ      reached_zero    ; Branch if zero
```

# JMP

**Near Jump**                                                                    ( )

## Syntax

JMP *dest*

## Operation

EIP ← *dest*

## Legal Forms

|     | *dest* |                     |
| --- | ------ | ------------------- |
| JMP | *offset* | ; EIP ← EIP + offset |
| JMP | reg    | ; EIP ← reg         |
| JMP | mem    | ; EIP ← [mem]       |

## Description

This instruction loads a new value into the instruction pointer (EIP). Subsequent instructions are fetched beginning at the new location.

When you use the immediate form of the instruction, the data value is an offset from the current EIP. The other forms are indirect branches, that is, the new value of EIP is taken from the operand register or memory location.

## Flags

| OF | DF | IF | TF | SF | ZF |   | AF |   | PF |   | CF |
| -- | -- | -- | -- | -- | -- | - | -- | - | -- | - | -- |
| -  | -  | -  | -  | -  | -  | - | -  | - | -  | - | -  |

## Faults

|    | *PM*    | *RM*   | *V8086* |
| -- | ------- | ------ | ------- |
| 12 | #SS(0)  |        |         |
| 13 | #GP(0)  | INT 13 | #GP(0)  |
| 14 | #PF(ec) |        | #PF(ec) |
| 17 | #AC(0)  |        | #AC(0)  |

## Examples

```
JMP    new_label           ; Direct, relative branch
JMP    ECX                 ; Branch indirect
JMP    DWORD PTR [EBP+12]  ; Branch to routine whose
                           ; address is on stack
```

# JMP

Far Jump

( )

## Syntax

```
JMP dest
```

## Operation

```
CS:EIP ← dest
```

## Legal Forms

|      | dest  |                    |
| ---- | ----- | ------------------ |
| JMP  | idata | ; CS:EIP ← data    |
| JMP  | mem   | ; CS:EIP ← [mem]   |

## Description

A far jump instruction modifies both CS and EIP. In the immediate form of the instruction, a new 48-bit pointer is specified. In the indirect form, the *mem* operand points to a 48-bit selector:offset pointer.

The new CS selector can be a code segment selector (where the branch is to the specified offset within the code segment), or the selector can be a call gate, task gate, or task state segment. In this case, the offset portion of the JMP is ignored, and the new value of EIP is taken from the gate or the incoming TSS. If the jump causes a task switch, all flags are subject to change as EFLAGS reloads from the new task's TSS. Chapter 5 discusses the task switch operation and the use of gates.

## Flags

| OF | DF | IF | TF | SF | ZF |   | AF |   | PF |   | CF |
| -- | -- | -- | -- | -- | -- | - | -- | - | -- | - | -- |
| -  | -  | -  | -  | -  | -  | - | -  | - | -  | - | -  |

## Faults

|    | PM        | RM     | V8086   |
| -- | --------- | ------ | ------- |
| 10 | #TS(sel)  |        |         |
| 11 | #NP(sel)  |        |         |
| 12 | #SS(0)    |        |         |
| 13 | #GP(0)    | INT 13 | #GP(0)  |
| 14 | #PF(ec)   |        | #PF(ec) |
| 17 | #AC(0)    |        | #AC(0)  |

## Examples

```
JMP     21A7:000211F3H    ; Direct branch
JMP     FWORD PTR new_task ; Branch indirect
```

# LAHF

8086/80186/80286/80386/80486

**Load AH with Flags** (8)

## Syntax

LAHF

## Operation

AH ← EFLAGS & 0FFH

## Legal Form

LAHF

## Description

This instruction copies the low-order byte of the EFLAGS register into AH. After the instruction executes, the AH register has the following contents:

```
7                    0
```

| SF | ZF | ? | AF | ? | PF | ? | CF |
|----|----|---|----|---|----|---|----|

## Flags

| OF | DF | IF | TF | SF | ZF | | AF | | PF | | CF |
|----|----|----|----|----|----|---|----|---|----|---|----|
| -  | -  | -  | -  | -  | -  | - | -  | - | -  | - | -  |

## Faults

None.

## Example

```
LAHF
SHR     AH, 6
AND     AH, 1          ; AH now contains the ZF flag
```

# LAR

**Load Access Rights**

80286/80386/80486

(16p/32)

## Syntax

LAR *dest, select*

## Operation

```
if (check_access(select)) then
    ZF ← 1
    dest ← access_rights(descriptor(select)) & 00F?FF00H
else
    ZF ← 0
endif
```

## Legal Forms

|     | *dest* | *select* |
|-----|------|--------|
| LAR | reg, | reg |
| LAR | reg, | mem |

## Description

This instruction allows a program to determine whether a given selector is accessible to it without causing a protection fault.

If the *select* operand contains a valid 80386 selector that is accessible to the executing procedure and the selector type is one defined below, the zero flag (ZF) is set to 1, and the access rights field of the descriptor indicated by the selector is loaded into the destination register.

If the destination register is a 16-bit register, the high-order 8 bits of the register contain the access rights field of the descriptor.

| 15 | | | 8 7 | 0 |
|---|---|---|---|---|
| A | DPL | S | TYPE | |

If the destination is a 32-bit register, bits 8–15 contain the access rights, and bits 20–23 contain the access extension bits found in byte 6 of the descriptor.

| 31 | 23 | 20 | 16 15 | 8 7 | 0 |
|---|---|---|---|---|---|
| | G B O A | | A DPL S | TYPE | |

If the selector references a nonmemory segment with an invalid type (Type = 0, 8, 0AH, 0DH), ZF is reset and the *dest* register is not modified.

## Flags

| OF | DF | IF | TF | SF | ZF | | AF | | PF | | CF |
|----|----|----|----|----|----|----|----|----|----|----|----|
| -  | -  | -  | -  | -  | X  | -  | -  | -  | -  | -  | -  |

## Faults

| | *PM* | *RM* | *V8086* |
|---|------|------|---------|
| 6  |        | INT 6  | #UD( )   |
| 12 | #SS(0) |        |          |
| 13 | #GP(0) | INT 13 | #GP(0)   |
| 14 | #PF(ec)|        | #PF(ec)  |
| 17 | #AC(0) |        | #AC(0)   |

## Example

```
; Verify that variable X contains the selector of a call gate
; that can be legally invoked by the executing routine.
LAR     AX, X           ; Load access rights
JNZ     no_access       ; Branch if can't access
SHR     AX, 8           ; Move access rights to low order
AND     AX, 1FH         ; Save only S bit and TYPE
CMP     AX, OCH         ; Test for 386 call gate
JE      is_gate         ; Branch if accessible gate
```

# LEA

**Load Effective Address**

## Syntax

LEA *dest, src*

## Operation

*dest* ← address(*src*)

## Legal Forms

|  | *dest* | *src* |
|---|---|---|
| LEA | reg, | mem |

## Description

This instruction loads the address specified by the memory operand into the destination register. No memory access cycle takes place.

You can also use LEA to perform simple multiplication or addition as discussed in Chapter 4.

## Flags

| OF | DF | IF | TF | SF | ZF |  | AF |  | PF |  | CF |
|---|---|---|---|---|---|---|---|---|---|---|---|
| - | - | - | - | - | - | - | - | - | - | - | - |

## Faults

| PM | | RM | V8086 |
|---|---|---|---|
| 6˙ | #UD( ) | INT 6 | #UD( ) |

˙The undefined opcode fault occurs only when the *src* operand is encoded as a register.

## Examples

```
LEA     ESI, VECTOR[EBX*4]   ; Load address of array element
LEA     EDI, [EAX][ECX]      ; Add contents of EAX and ECX, store in EDI
```

# LEAVE

**Leave Current Stack Frame**

80186/80286/80386/80486

( )

## Syntax

LEAVE

## Operation

MOV ESP, EBP
POP EBP

## Legal Form

LEAVE

## Description

LEAVE is the counterpart of the ENTER instruction. ENTER is executed immediately after a procedure call to set up a new stack frame. LEAVE is executed before a RET instruction to release the returning procedure's stack frame.

## Flags

| OF | DF | IF | TF | SF | ZF | | AF | | PF | | CF |
|----|----|----|----|----|----|----|----|----|----|----|----|
| - | - | - | - | - | - | - | - | - | - | - | - |

## Faults

| PM | | RM | V8086 |
|----|----|----|-------|
| 12 | #SS(0) | | |
| 13 | | 13 | #G0(0) |

## Example

```
ENTER   4,0              ; First instruction of procedure
.
.                        ; Procedure contents
.
LEAVE                    ; Clean up stack frame
RET                      ; And return to caller
```

# LGDT

**Load GDT Register**

80286/80386/80486

( )

## Syntax

LGDT *op*

## Operation

```
GDTR.limit ← [op]
GDTR.base  ← [op + 2]
```

## Legal Form

| *op* |
| --- |
| LGDT     mem |

## Description

This instruction loads the GDTR register specifying the address and limit of the global descriptor table (GDT). The operand must point to a data structure in memory whose first 16 bits contain the limit of the global descriptor table and whose next 32 bits contain the linear base address of the GDT.

Loading the GDTR does not invalidate the currently active descriptors; however, subsequent references to selectors load descriptors from the new GDT.

A procedure must have a CPL of 0 to issue the LGDT instruction.

## Flags

| OF | DF | IF | TF | SF | ZF | | AF | | PF | | CF |
| --- | --- | --- | --- | --- | --- | --- | --- | --- | --- | --- | --- |
| - | - | - | - | - | - | - | - | - | - | - | - |

## Faults

| | *PM* | *RM* | *V8086* |
| --- | --- | --- | --- |
| 6* | #UD( ) | INT 6 | #UD( ) |
| 12 | #SS(0) | | |
| 13 | #GP(0) | INT 13 | #GP(0) |
| 14 | #PF(ec) | | #PF(ec) |
| 17 | #AC(0) | | #AC(0) |

*The undefined opcode fault only occurs when the instruction is encoded with a register value for *op*.

## Example

```
LGDT      initial_table
```

# LIDT

**Load IDT Register**

80286/80386/80486

( )

## Syntax

LIDT *op*

## Operation

IDTR.limit ← [*op*]
IDTR.base ← [*op* + 2]

## Legal Form

| *op* |
|------|
| LIDT    mem |

## Description

This instruction loads the IDTR register and specifies the address and limit of the interrupt descriptor table (IDT). The operand must point to a data structure in memory whose first 16 bits contain the limit of the interrupt descriptor table and whose next 32 bits contain the linear base address of the IDT.

After loading the IDTR, any software or hardware interrupts, faults, or traps will cause an access to the new IDT.

A procedure must have a CPL of 0 to issue the LIDT instruction.

## Flags

| OF | DF | IF | TF | SF | ZF | | AF | | PF | | CF |
|----|----|----|----|----|----|----|----|----|----|----|----|
| -  | -  | -  | -  | -  | -  | -  | -  | -  | -  | -  | -  |

## Faults

|     | *PM*     | *RM*   | *V8086*  |
|-----|----------|--------|----------|
| 6*  | #UD( )   | INT 6  | #UD( )   |
| 12  | #SS(0)   |        |          |
| 13  | #GP(0)   | INT 13 | #GP(0)   |
| 14  | #PF(ec)  |        | #PF(ec)  |
| 17  | #AC(0)   |        | #AC(0)   |

*The undefined opcode fault only occurs when the *op* operand is encoded as a register.

## Example

```
LIDT    new_int_table    ; Load IDT register
```

# LLDT

**Load LDT Register**

80286/80386/80486

(16)

## Syntax

LLDT *op*

## Operation

LDTR ← *op*

## Legal Forms

| *op* |
| --- |
| LLDT    reg |
| LLDT    mem |

## Description

This instruction loads a selector into the LDTR register and specifies a new local descriptor table (LDT). The operand to LLDT must contain a valid local descriptor table selector or the value 0.

Active descriptors that refer to the previous LDT are not invalidated; however, subsequent selector references load descriptors from the new LDT.

If the LDTR is loaded with the value 0, all LDT selector references that cause a memory reference result in a general protection fault.

The executing procedure must have a CPL of 0 to issue the LLDT instruction.

## Flags

| OF | DF | IF | TF | SF | ZF | | AF | | PF | | CF |
|----|----|----|----|----|----|----|----|----|----|----|----|
| -  | -  | -  | -  | -  | -  | -  | -  | -  | -  | -  | -  |

## Faults

| | *PM* | *RM* | *V8086* |
|---|------|------|---------|
| 6  |          | INT 6 | #UD()   |
| 11 | #NP(sel) |       |         |
| 12 | #SS(0)   |       |         |
| 13 | #GP(0)   |       |         |
| 13 | #GP(sel) |       |         |
| 14 | #PF(ec)  |       | #PF(ec) |
| 17 | #AC(0)   |       | #AC(0)  |

## Example

```
LLDT    task_B.ldtr          ; Get access to LDT for task B
```

# LMSW

**Load Machine Status Word**

## Syntax

LMSW *op*

## Operation

CR0 ← (CR0 & FFFF0000H) | *op*

## Legal Forms

| *op* |
| --- |
| LMSW     reg |
| LMSW     mem |

## Description

This instruction loads the low-order 16 bits of the CR0 register. Use it only when running 80286 operating system code. On 32-bit systems, use the instruction MOV CR0, *reg*. Note that you can use LMSW to enter protected mode but not to leave it and that you can use MOV CR0, *reg* to both enter and leave protected mode.

A procedure must be running in ring 0 to execute LMSW.

## Flags

| OF | DF | IF | TF | SF | ZF | | AF | | PF | | CF |
| --- | --- | --- | --- | --- | --- | --- | --- | --- | --- | --- | --- |
| - | - | - | - | - | - | - | - | - | - | - | - |

## Faults

| | *PM* | *RM* | *V8086* |
| --- | --- | --- | --- |
| 12 | #SS(0) | | |
| 13 | #GP(0) | INT 13 | #GP(0) |
| 14 | #PF(ec) | | #PF(ec) |
| 17 | #AC(0) | | #AC(0) |

## Example

LMSW     init_state

# LOCK

8086/80186/80286/80386/80486

**Assert Hardware LOCK\ Signal Prefix**

()

## Syntax

LOCK

## Legal Form

LOCK

## Description

The LOCK instruction prefix supports multiprocessor hardware configurations. You can use the hardware LOCK\ signal to ensure exclusive access to a particular memory byte, word, or dword. The LOCK instruction is valid only if it precedes an instruction in the list below. If you use it in combination with another instruction or in an unsupported form of one of the listed instructions, an undefined opcode fault occurs.

| Instruction | Locked Form of Instruction | Instruction | Locked Form of Instruction |
|---|---|---|---|
| BT | mem, *op* | OR | mem, *op* |
| BTS | mem, *op* | SBB | mem, *op* |
| BTR | mem, *op* | SUB | mem, *op* |
| BTC | mem, *op* | XOR | mem, *op* |
| XCHG | mem, reg | DEC | mem |
| XCHG | reg, mem | INC | mem |
| ADD | mem, *op* | NEG | mem |
| ADC | mem, *op* | NOT | mem |
| AND | mem, *op* | | |

The LOCK\ signal is asserted for the duration of the instruction, including the time required for a read-modify-write cycle. The XCHG instruction does not require the LOCK prefix because the LOCK\ signal is always asserted during a memory XCHG.

When writing software for multiprocessor systems, ensure that locked access for particular memory addresses always occurs to operands of the same size. In other words, if you use the dword at physical address 100, always get access to it as a dword and never as a byte or word. Locking is not guaranteed to operate correctly unless you observe this restriction.

## Flags

| OF | DF | IF | TF | SF | ZF | | AF | | PF | | CF |
|---|---|---|---|---|---|---|---|---|---|---|---|
| - | - | - | - | - | - | - | - | - | - | - | - |

## Faults

| | PM | RM | V8086 |
|---|---|---|---|
| 6 | #UD() | INT 6 | #UD() |

## Example

```
LOCK
BTS      semaphore, 3
```

# LODS

## Load String

## Syntax

```
LODS
```

## Operation

```
when opcode is (LODSB, LODSW, LODSD) set opsize ← (1,2,4)
acc ← DS: [ESI]
if (DF - 0) then
     ESI ← ESI + opsize
else
     ESI ← ESI - opsize
endif
```

## Legal Forms

```
LODSB        ; Load string byte
LODSW        ; Load string word
LODSD        ; Load string doubleword
```

## Description

This instruction loads the byte, word, or dword at DS:ESI into the accumulator. If the DF bit in the EFLAGS register is 0, ESI is incremented by the size of the operand (1, 2, or 4 bytes). If DF is 1, ESI is decremented.

Because LODS is one of the 80386 string instructions, you can precede it with the REP prefix; however, the resulting instruction is useless, as it continuously overwrites the contents of the accumulator.

You can precede the LODS instruction with a segment override prefix. In such a case, the operand is taken from the specified segment.

## Flags

| OF | DF | IF | TF | SF | ZF | | AF | | PF | | CF |
|----|----|----|----|----|----|----|----|----|----|----|----|
| -  | -  | -  | -  | -  | -  | -  | -  | -  | -  | -  | -  |

## Faults

| | PM | RM | V8086 |
|---|------|--------|--------|
| 12 | #SS(0) | | |
| 13 | #GP(0) | INT 13 | #GP(0) |
| 14 | #PF(ec) | | #PF(ec) |
| 17 | #AC(0) | | #AC(0) |

## Example

```
        LEA     EBX, A_to_E         ; Address of translation table
        MOV     ESI, [EBP+12]       ; Source address
        LES     EDI, [EBP+16]       ; Destination
L1:     LODSB                       ; Fetch byte from source
        OR      AL, AL              ; Test byte for zero
        JZ      DONE                ; Branch if zero
        XLATB                       ; Translate the byte
        STOSB                       ; Save translated version
        JMP     L1
DONE:
```

# LOOPcc

**Decrement ECX and Branch**

8086/80186/80286/80386/80486

()

## Syntax

```
LOOPcc offset
```

## Operation

```
ECX ← ECX - 1
if (cc & (ECX != 0)) then
    EIP ← EIP + offset
endif
```

## Legal Forms

```
LOOP     offset
LOOPZ    offset
LOOPNZ   offset
LOOPE    offset
LOOPNE   offset
```

## Description

These instructions support a decrement and branch operation. For all variants other than LOOP, the decrement and branch is combined with a test on the ZF bit. A loop counter is assumed in register ECX. The instruction decrements the register, and if the value of ECX is 0, no branch is taken. No flags are set as a result of the decrement operation.

If the value of ECX is not 0, the branch is taken unless the condition in the LOOPcc forms is not true.

## Flags

| OF | DF | IF | TF | SF | ZF | | AF | PF | | CF |
|----|----|----|----|----|----|----|----|----|----|----|
| -  | -  | -  | -  | -  | -  | -  | -  | -  | -  | -  |

## Faults

| PM | | RM | V8086 |
|----|----|----|----|
| 13 | #GP(0) | INT 13 | #GP(0) |

## Example

```
        ; Initialize array of temp reals to 1.0
        FLD1                        ; Push 1.0 onto NDP stack
        LEA     ESI, array          ; Starting address of array
        MOV     ECX, size           ; Load loop counter
11:     FLD     ST(1), ST           ; Duplicate 1.0 value on NDP stack
        FSTP    [ESI]               ; Store 1.0, pop NDP stack
        LOOP    11                  ; Continue while ECX not 0
        FSTP    ST(0), ST           ; Done--pop last 1.0 constant off
                                    ; NDP stack
```

# Lseg

**Load Segment Register**

## Syntax

Lseg dest, src

## Operation

dest ← [src]
seg ← [src + 4]

## Legal Forms

|     | dest | src |     |
| --- | ---- | --- | --- |
| LDS | reg, | mem |     |
| LES | reg, | mem |     |
| LFS | reg, | mem |     |
| LGS | reg, | mem |     |
| LSS | reg, | mem |     |

## Description

The *src* address specifies a 48-bit pointer (32-bit in real mode or V86 mode) consisting of a 32-bit offset followed by a 16-bit selector. The 32-bit offset is loaded into the *dest* register and the selector is loaded into the segment register specified by the instruction mnemonic. The 80386 protection mechanism validates the descriptor associated with the selector.

Use only the ESP register with the Lseg instruction.

## Flags

| OF | DF | IF | TF | SF | ZF |  | AF |  | PF |  | CF |
|----|----|----|----|----|----|----|----|----|----|----|----|
| -  | -  | -  | -  | -  | -  | -  | -  | -  | -  | -  | -  |

## Faults

| | PM | RM | V8086 |
|----|--------|--------|--------|
| 12 | #SS(0) |        |        |
| 13 | #GP(0) | INT 13 | #GP(0) |
| 14 | #PF(ec) |       | #PF(ec) |
| 17 | #AC(0) |        | #AC(0) |

## Example

```
LES    ESI, BIGPTR       ; Load address of array element [EBX]
LSS    ESP, OLD_STACK    ; Load a new stack pointer
```

# LSL
**Load Segment Limit**

**80286/80386/80486**

**(16p/32)**

## Syntax

LSL *dest, select*

## Operation

```
if (access_OK(select)) then
    dest ← descript(select).limit
    ZF ← 1
else
    ZF ← 0
endif
```

## Legal Forms

|     | dest  | select |
| --- | ----- | ------ |
| LSL | reg,  | reg    |
| LSL | reg,  | mem    |

## Description

If the *select* operand is accessible to the executing program as a valid selector under the protection rules, this instruction loads the *dest* register with the segment limit from the descriptor indicated by *select* and sets ZF to 1.

If the operand is not accessible or the descriptor associated with *select* does not contain a limit field, ZF is set to 0.

The value stored in the *dest* register is always the offset of the last addressable byte in the segment (page granular limits are converted to byte granular limits). Therefore, do not use a 16-bit register as the *dest* operand because the resulting value might be too large.

## Flags

| OF | DF | IF | TF | SF | ZF | | AF | | PF | | CF |
| -- | -- | -- | -- | -- | -- | - | -- | - | -- | - | -- |
| -  | -  | -  | -  | -  | x  | - | -  | - | -  | - | -  |

## Faults

| PM |         | RM    | V8086   |
| -- | ------- | ----- | ------- |
| 6  |         | INT 6 | #UD()   |
| 12 | #SS(0)  |       |         |
| 13 | #GP(0)  |       |         |
| 14 | #PF(ec) |       | #PF(ec) |
| 17 | #AC(0)  |       | #AC(0)  |

## Example

```
LSL      EAX, [BP+12]          ; Get limit of selector on stack
```

# LTR

**Load Task Register**

## Syntax

LTR *select*

## Operation

TR ← *select*

## Legal Forms

| *select* |
| --- |
| LTR    reg |
| LTR    mem |

## Description

This instruction loads the task register with the selector specified by the operand. The TSS descriptor for the selector is marked "busy." Loading the task register does not cause a task switch.

If the procedure that executes the LTR instruction is not running with a CPL of 0, a general protection fault occurs.

## Flags

| OF | DF | IF | TF | SF | ZF | | AF | | PF | | CF |
|----|----|----|----|----|----|---|----|---|----|---|----|
| -  | -  | -  | -  | -  | -  | - | -  | - | -  | - | -  |

## Faults

| | *PM* | *RM* | *V8086* |
|---|------|------|---------|
| 6  |          | INT 6 | #UD() |
| 10 | #NP(sel) |       |       |
| 12 | #SS(0)   |       |       |
| 13 | #GP(0)   |       |       |
| 13 | #GP(sel) |       |       |
| 14 | #PF(ec)  |       |       |
| 17 | #AC(0)   |       | #AC(0) |

## Example

LTR     AX         ; Load task register

# MOV

**Move Data**

## Syntax

MOV *dest, src*

## Operation

*dest ← src*

## Legal Forms

|     | dest  | src   |
| --- | ----- | ----- |
| MOV | reg,  | idata |
| MOV | mem,  | idata |
| MOV | reg,  | reg   |
| MOV | reg,  | mem   |
| MOV | mem,  | reg   |

## Description

This instruction copies the contents of the *src* operand into *dest*.

## Flags

| OF | DF | IF | TF | SF | ZF |   | AF |   | PF |   | CF |
|----|----|----|----|----|----|---|----|---|----|---|----|
| –  | –  | –  | –  | –  | –  | – | –  | – | –  | – | –  |

## Faults

| PM       | RM     | V8086   |
|----------|--------|---------|
| 12  #SS(0) |        |         |
| 13  #GP(0) | INT 13 | #GP(0)  |
| 14  #PF(ec) |       | #PF(ec) |
| 17  #AC(0) |        | #AC(0)  |

## Examples

```
MOV    AL, [ECX]      ; Get byte from memory
MOV    ESI, 182H      ; Load ESI with data value
MOV    BX, DX         ; 16-bit move
MOV    AH, 7FH        ; Load AH with 8-bit data
```

# MOV

**Move Selector**

## Syntax

MOV *dest*, *src*

## Operation

*dest* ← *src*

## Legal Forms

|     | dest   | src    |
| --- | ------ | ------ |
| MOV | sreg,  | reg    |
| MOV | sreg,  | mem    |
| MOV | reg,   | sreg   |
| MOV | mem,   | sreg   |

## Description

This instruction copies the contents of the *src* operand into the *dest* operand. If the *dest* operand is a segment register, the instruction loads the descriptor associated with the selector into the 80386/80486 shadow registers. Privilege checks and tests for descriptor legality are made unless the selector value is 0. A protection fault occurs if 0 is loaded into the SS register.

When the SS register is loaded, all hardware interrupts (including NMI) are masked until after the next instruction executes, to allow loading of the ESP register.

## Flags

| OF | DF | IF | TF | SF | ZF |   | AF |   | PF |   | CF |
|----|----|----|----|----|----|---|----|---|----|---|----|
| –  | –  | –  | –  | –  | –  | – | –  | – | –  | – | –  |

## Faults

|    | *PM*     | *RM*   | *V8086*  |
|----|----------|--------|----------|
| 10 | #NP(sel) |        |          |
| 12 | #SS(0)   |        |          |
| 13 | #GP(0)   | INT 13 | #GP(0)   |
| 14 | #PF(ec)  |        | #PF(ec)  |
| 17 | #AC(0)   |        | #AC(0)   |

## Examples

```
MOV    DS, AX           ; Load new data segment
MOV    ES, heap_seg     ; Load ES register
MOV    save_ss, SS      ; Store copy of SS register
```

# MOV

**Move Special**

## Syntax

MOV *dest, src*

## Operation

*dest* ← *src*

## Legal Forms

|     | dest | src |
| --- | --- | --- |
| MOV | reg, | reg |

## Description

This instruction copies or loads a special CPU register to or from an 80386/80486 general register. The special registers are CR0, CR2, CR3, DR0, DR1, DR2, DR3, DR6, DR7, TR6, and TR7.

A procedure must be running at a CPL of 0 to execute this instruction.

## Flags

| OF | DF | IF | TF | SF | ZF | | AF | | PF | | CF |
| --- | --- | --- | --- | --- | --- | --- | --- | --- | --- | --- | --- |
| ? | - | - | - | ? | ? | - | ? | - | ? | - | ? |

## Faults

| | *PM* | *RM* | *V8086* |
| --- | --- | --- | --- |
| 13 | #GP(0) | | #GP(0) |
| 17 | #AC(0) | | #AC(0) |

## Examples

```
MOV     EAX, CR0     ; Save CR0 in EAX
MOV     TR7, ECX     ; Load test register 7
```

# MOVS
**Move String**

## Syntax

```
MOVS
```

## Operation

```
when opcode is (MOVSB, MOVSW, MOVSD) set opsize ← (1, 2, 4)
ES:[EDI] ← DS:[ESI]
if (DF = 0) then
    ESI ← ESI + opsize
    EDI ← EDI + opsize
else
    ESI ← ESI - opsize
    ESI ← ESI - opsize
endif
```

## Legal Forms

```
MOVSB    ; Move string byte
MOVSW    ; Move string word
MOVSD    ; Move string doubleword
```

## Description

This instruction copies the memory operand pointed to by DS:ESI to the destination address specified by ES:EDI. The operand is a byte, word, or doubleword, depending on the opcode specified. The EDI and ESI registers are incremented by the size of the operand if the DF bit is 0 or decremented if the DF bit is 1.

You can apply the REP prefix to the MOVS instruction to repeat the instruction. You must place the value specifying the repeat count in the ECX register.

A segment override prefix may be applied to the MOVS instruction. It will override the DS segment of the DS:[ESI] operand. You cannot override the ES segment assumption for the EDI operand.

For dword-aligned strings, a REP MOVSD transfers data quicker than does the equivalent REP MOVSB or REP MOVSW. However, if the source and destination strings overlap, only the REP MOVSB operation works correctly.

## Flags

| OF | DF | IF | TF | SF | ZF | | AF | | PF | | CF |
|----|----|----|----|----|----|----|----|----|----|----|----|
| -  | -  | -  | -  | -  | -  | -  | -  | -  | -  | -  | -  |

## Faults

| | *PM* | *RM* | *V8086* |
|---|---|---|---|
| 12 | #SS(0) | | |
| 13 | #GP(0) | INT 13 | #GP(0) |
| 14 | #PF(ec) | | #PF(ec) |
| 17 | #AC(0) | | #AC(0) |

## Example

```
LEA     ESI, copyright_msg   ; Get source string
LES     EDI, [EBP+12]        ; ES:EDI loaded from stack frame
MOV     ECX, 31              ; Size of source string
CLD                          ; Ensure direction flag set correctly
REP MOVSB                    ; Copy byte string
```

# MOVSX

**Move with Sign Extension**

**80386/80486**

**(8/16p/32)**

## Syntax

MOVSX *dest, src*

## Operation

*dest* ← *sign_extend(src)*

## Legal Forms

|        | *dest* | *src* |
|--------|--------|-------|
| MOVSX  | reg,   | reg   |
| MOVSX  | reg,   | mem   |

## Description

This instruction copies an 8-bit operand to a 16-bit or 32-bit destination or a 16-bit operand to a 32-bit destination and sign-extends the source operand to fit. Sign extension is performed by duplicating the high-order bit of the *src* throughout the upper bits of the *dest* operand.

## Flags

| OF | DF | IF | TF | SF | ZF | AF | PF | CF |
|----|----|----|----|----|----|----|----|----|
| -  | -  | -  | -  | -  | -  | - | - | - | - | - | - |

## Faults

|    | *PM*     | *RM*    | *V8086* |
|----|----------|---------|---------|
| 12 | #SS(0)   |         |         |
| 13 | #GP(0)   | INT 13  | #GP(0)  |
| 14 | #PF(ec)  |         | #PF(ec) |
| 17 | #AC(0)   |         | #AC(0)  |

## Examples

```
MOVSX   EAX, AL             ; Extend byte to dword
MOVSX   EDI, WORD PTR [ESI] ; Extend word to dword
MOVSX   CX, DL              ; Extend byte to word
```

# MOVZX

**Move with Zero Extension**

## Syntax

MOVZX dest, src

## Operation

dest ← src

## Legal Forms

|       | dest  | src  |
|-------|-------|------|
| MOVZX | reg,  | reg  |
| MOVZX | reg,  | mem  |

## Description

This instruction copies an 8-bit operand to a 16-bit or 32-bit destination or a 16-bit operand to a 32-bit destination and zero-extends the source operand to fit. Sign extension is performed by filling the upper bits of the *dest* operand with 0.

## Flags

| OF | DF | IF | TF | SF | ZF | AF | PF | CF |
|----|----|----|----|----|----|----|----|----|
| -  | -  | -  | -  | -  | -  | -  | -  | -  |

## Faults

|    | *PM*    | *RM*   | *V8086* |
|----|---------|--------|---------|
| 12 | #SS(0)  |        |         |
| 13 | #GP(0)  | INT 13 | #GP(0)  |
| 14 | #PF(ec) |        | #PF(ec) |
| 17 | #AC(0)  |        | #AC(0)  |

## Examples

```
MOVZX   EAX, AL                 ; Extend byte to dword
MOVZX   EDI, WORD PTR [ESI]     ; Extend word to dword
MOVZX   CX, DL                  ; Extend byte to word
```

# MUL

**Unsigned Multiplication**

## Syntax

MUL *src*

## Operation

*acc ← acc * src*

## Legal Forms

| | src |
|-----|------|
| MUL | reg |
| MUL | mem |

## Description

This instruction performs unsigned integer multiplication and requires only one operand, the multiplier. The multiplicand is the accumulator, and the product is also stored in the accumulator. The size of the *src* operand determines which registers will be used, as illustrated in the following table:

| *Multiplier* (src) | *Multiplicand* | *Product* |
|--------------------|----------------|-----------|
| byte | AL | AX |
| word | AX | DX:AX |
| dword | EAX | EDX:EAX |

The flags are left in an undetermined state except for OF and CF, which are cleared to 0 if the high-order byte, word, or dword of the product is 0.

## Flags

| OF | DF | IF | TF | SF | ZF | | AF | | PF | | CF |
|----|----|----|----|----|----|---|----|---|----|---|----|
| x | – | – | – | ? | ? | – | ? | – | ? | – | x |

## Faults

| | *PM* | *RM* | *V8086* |
|----|--------|--------|---------|
| 12 | #SS(0) | | |
| 13 | #GP(0) | INT 13 | #GP(0) |
| 14 | #PF(ec) | | #PF(ec) |
| 17 | #AC(0) | | #AC(0) |

## Example

```
MOV      EAX, 3                  ; Multiplicand
MUL      DWORD PTR [ESI]         ; Multiplier
JC       res_64                  ; Branch if result requires 64 bits
MOV      res_32, EAX             ; Else store product
```

# NEG

**Negate Integer**

8086/80186/80286/80386/80486

(8/16p/32)

## Syntax

NEG *op*

## Operation

*op* ← -(*op*)

## Legal Forms

|     | *op* |
| --- | --- |
| NEG | reg |
| NEG | mem |

## Description

This instruction subtracts its operand from 0, which results in a two's complement (integer) negation of the operand.

## Flags

| OF | DF | IF | TF | SF | ZF |   | AF |   | PF |   | CF |
| --- | --- | --- | --- | --- | --- | --- | --- | --- | --- | --- | --- |
| x | - | - | - | x | x | - | x | - | x | - | x |

## Faults

|    | *PM* | *RM* | *V8086* |
| --- | --- | --- | --- |
| 12 | #SS(0) | | |
| 13 | #GP(0) | INT 13 | #GP(0) |
| 14 | #PF(ec) | | #PF(ec) |
| 17 | #AC(0) | | #AC(0) |

## Example

```
; Compute absolute value
OR    EAX, EAX          ; Test for +/-
JNS   SKIP              ; Jump if not signed (positive)
NEG   EAX               ; Negate negative number
SKIP:
```

# NOP

**No Operation**

O

## Syntax

```
NOP
```

## Legal Form

```
NOP
```

## Description

This instruction performs no function other than taking up space in the code segment.

## Flags

| OF | DF | IF | TF | SF | ZF | | AF | | PF | | CF |
|----|----|----|----|----|----|----|----|----|----|----|----|
| -  | -  | -  | -  | -  | -  | -  | -  | -  | -  | -  | -  |

## Faults

None.

## Example

```
NOP                          ; Nothing occurs
```

# NOT

**Boolean Complement**

## Syntax

NOT *op*

## Operation

*op* ← ~*op*

## Legal Forms

| | *op* |
|------|------|
| NOT | reg |
| NOT | mem |

## Description

This instruction inverts the state of each bit in the operand.

## Flags

| OF | DF | IF | TF | SF | ZF | | AF | | PF | | CF |
|----|----|----|----|----|----|---|----|---|----|---|----|
| -  | -  | -  | -  | -  | -  | - | -  | - | -  | - | -  |

## Faults

| | *PM* | *RM* | *V8086* |
|----|--------|--------|---------|
| 12 | #SS(0) | | |
| 13 | #GP(0) | INT 13 | #GP(0) |
| 14 | #PF(ec) | | #PF(ec) |
| 17 | #AC(0) | | #AC(0) |

## Example

NOT     ECX        ; Insert ECX

# OR

**Boolean OR**

## Syntax

```
OR dest, src
```

## Operation

*dest ← dest | src*

## Legal Forms

|     | dest | src   |
|-----|------|-------|
| OR  | reg, | idata |
| OR  | mem, | idata |
| OR  | reg, | reg   |
| OR  | reg, | mem   |
| OR  | mem, | reg   |

## Description

This instruction performs a Boolean OR operation between each bit of the *src* operand and the *dest* operand. The result is stored in *dest*. The truth table defining the OR operation is as follows:

$0 | 0 = 0$

$0 | 1 = 1$

$1 | 0 = 1$

$1 | 1 = 1$

## Flags

| OF | DF | IF | TF | SF | ZF |   | AF |   | PF |   | CF |
|----|----|----|----|----|----|---|----|---|----|---|----|
| 0  | -  | -  | -  | x  | x  | - | x  | - | x  | - | 0  |

## Faults

| PM     | RM     | V8086  |
|--------|--------|--------|
| 12     |        |        |
| 13 #GP(0) | INT 13 | #GP(0) |
| 14 #PF(ec) |        | #PF(ec) |
| 17 #AC(0) |        | #AC(0) |

## Example

```
OR      AL, 80H              ; Set high bit of AL
```

# OUT

**Output to Port**

8086/80186/80286/80386/80486

(8/16p/32)

## Syntax

OUT *port, acc*

## Operation

*port* ← *acc*

## Legal Forms

| | port | acc |
|------|------|-----|
| OUT | data, | acc |
| OUT | DX, | acc |

## Description

This instruction outputs the value in the accumulator to the specified data port. Placing an immediate value in the *port* operand field lets you address ports 0–255. You can address port addresses 0–65,535 by storing the port number in the DX register.

OUT is a privileged instruction. A procedure executing an output instruction must satisfy one of two conditions; otherwise, a general protection fault occurs.

If the procedure that executes an OUT instruction has I/O privilege (if its CPL is numerically less than or equal to the IOPL field in the EFLAGS register), the output instruction executes immediately.

If the procedure does not have I/O privilege, the I/O permission bitmap for the current task is checked. If the bit(s) corresponding to the I/O port(s) is cleared to 0, the output instruction executes. If the bit(s) is set to 1, or the port(s) is outside the range of the bitmap, a general protection fault occurs. See Chapter 5 for more details on this feature.

If the OUT instruction is encountered while in V86 mode, only the I/O permission bitmap is tested. The IOPL value is not a factor.

## Flags

| OF | DF | IF | TF | SF | ZF | | AF | | PF | | CF |
|----|----|----|----|----|----|----|----|----|----|----|----|
| - | - | - | - | - | - | - | - | - | - | - | - |

## Faults

| PM | RM | V8086 |
|----|----|-------|
| 13  #GP(0) | | #GP(0) |

## Example

```
MOV     DX, 378H            ; Set port address
OUT     DX, AX              ; Write to ports 378 and 379
```

# OUTS

**80186/80286/80386/80486**

Output String

**(8/16p/32)**

## Syntax

OUTS

## Operation

```
when opcode is (OUTSB, OUTSW, OUTSD) set opsize ← (1,2,4)
port (DX) ← DS:[ESI]
if (DF = 0) then
    ESI ← ESI + opsize
else
    ESI ← ESI - opsize
endif
```

## Legal Forms

```
OUTSB        ; Out string byte
OUTSW        ; Out string word
OUTSD        ; Out string doubleword
```

## Description

This instruction outputs the byte, word, or doubleword at offset ESI to the port specified in register DX. The ESI register is adjusted by the size of the memory operand—incremented if the DF bit is 0 or decremented if DF is 1.

You can precede the OUTS instruction with the REP instruction; however, register ECX must contain a count of the number of times the OUTS instruction is to be executed.

You can apply one of the segment override prefixes to the OUTS instruction, causing the operand to be taken from the specified segment rather than the segment pointed to by DS.

Output instructions are privileged instructions. The protection checks for the OUTS instructions are the same as those for the OUT instruction.

## Flags

| OF | DF | IF | TF | SF | ZF | | AF | | PF | | CF |
|----|----|----|----|----|----|----|----|----|----|----|----|
| -  | -  | -  | -  | -  | -  | -  | -  | -  | -  | -  | -  |

## Faults

| | PM | RM | V8086 |
|----|--------|--------|--------|
| 12 | #SS(0) | | #SS(0) |
| 13 | #GP(0) | INT 13 | #GP(0) |
| 14 | #PF(ec) | | #PF(ec) |
| 17 | #AC(0) | | #AC(0) |

## Example

```
LEA     ESI, IO_CHNL_CMD     ; Get pointer to string
MOV     DX, CONTROLLER       ; Get I/O port number
MOV     ECX, 8               ; Size of I/O string
REP     OUTSD                ; Output 8 doublewords
```

# POP

## Pop Segment Register

### Syntax

POP *seg*

### Operation

*seg* ← SS:[ESP]
ESP ← ESP + 4

### Legal Form

| *seg* |
| --- |
| POP     sreg |

### Description

This instruction pops a 32-bit value off the stack and stores the low-order 16 bits in the specified segment register. Register CS is not a valid destination operand, but the other segment registers (DS, ES, SS, FS, and GS) are valid.

The value stored in the segment register must be a valid selector or 0; otherwise, a protection fault occurs. (Register SS cannot be loaded with a 0.) Note also that a POP SS instruction has limited usefulness because SS and ESP are required to implement a stack. However, if you execute a POP SS, the 80386 inhibits all hardware interrupts to enable the loading of ESP and the guarding against interrupts while the stack pointer is invalid.

If the POP instruction is executed by a V86 mode task, only 16 bits are popped off the stack.

### Flags

| OF | DF | IF | TF | SF | ZF | | AF | | PF | | CF |
| --- | --- | --- | --- | --- | --- | --- | --- | --- | --- | --- | --- |
| - | - | - | - | - | - | - | - | - | - | - | - |

### Faults

| | *PM* | *RM* | *V8086* |
| --- | --- | --- | --- |
| 10 | #NP(sel) | | |
| 12 | #SS(0) | | #SS(0) |
| 13 | #GP(0) | INT 13 | #GP(0) |
| 14 | #PF(ec) | | #PF(ec) |

### Examples

POP     GS
POP     DS

# POP

**Pop Value off Stack**

## Syntax

```
POP dest
```

## Operation

```
dest ← SS:[ESP]
if (sizeof (dest) = 16) then
    ESP ← ESP + 2
else
    ESP ← ESP + 4
endif
```

## Legal Forms

|     | dest |
| --- | ---- |
| POP | reg  |
| POP | mem  |

## Description

This instruction pops the current value at the top-of-stack, stores it in the *dest* operand, and adjusts the stack pointer.

For optimum performance, keep the stack on a doubleword boundary. Pushing and popping 16-bit values might alter this alignment. For this reason, it is preferable to sign-extend or zero-extend a 16-bit operand to 32 bits before pushing or popping it.

When you execute POP in V86 mode, the stack will generally be used only for 16-bit values. This does not degrade system performance. Pushing and popping 16-bit values leads to problems only when both 32-bit and 16-bit pushes and pops are mixed in the same code.

## Flags

| OF | DF | IF | TF | SF | ZF |  | AF |  | PF |  | CF |
|----|----|----|----|----|----|----|----|----|----|----|----|
| -  | -  | -  | -  | -  | -  | -  | -  | -  | -  | -  | -  |

## Faults

| | *PM* | *RM* | *V8086* |
|---|------|------|---------|
| 12 | #SS(0) | | |
| 13 | #GP(0) | INT 13 | #GP(0) |
| 14 | #PF(ec) | | #PF(ec) |

## Example

```
POP     ECX
```

# POPA
## Pop All General Registers

### Syntax

POPA

### Operation

```
POP     DI
POP     SI
POP     BP
ADD     ESP, 2
POP     BX
POP     DX
POP     CX
POP     AX
```

### Legal Form

POPA

### Description

This instruction pops all 16-bit general registers except SP from the stack. Because the registers are stored as a 16-byte block of data, the POPA instruction does not affect doubleword alignment of the stack.

### Flags

| OF | DF | IF | TF | SF | ZF |  | AF |  | PF |  | CF |
|----|----|----|----|----|----|----|----|----|----|----|----|
| -  | -  | -  | -  | -  | -  | -  | -  | -  | -  | -  | -  |

### Faults

|    | *PM*     | *RM*   | *V8086*  |
|----|----------|--------|----------|
| 12 | #SS(0)   |        |          |
| 13 |          | INT 13 | #GP(0)   |
| 14 | #PF(ec)  |        | #PF(ec)  |

### Example

POPA

# POPAD

**Pop All General Registers**

80386/80486

(32)

## Syntax

POPAD

## Operation

```
POP    EDI
POP    ESI
POP    EBP
ADD    ESP, 4
POP    EBX
POP    EDX
POP    ECX
POP    EAX
```

## Legal Form

POPAD

## Description

This instruction pops all 32-bit general registers except ESP from the stack.

## Flags

| OF | DF | IF | TF | SF | ZF | | AF | | PF | | CF |
|----|----|----|----|----|----|----|----|----|----|----|----|
| -  | -  | -  | -  | -  | -  | -  | -  | -  | -  | -  | -  |

## Faults

| | *PM* | *RM* | *V8086* |
|----|------|------|---------|
| 12 | #SS(0) | | |
| 13 | | INT 13 | #GP(0) |
| 14 | #PF(ec) | | #PF(ec) |

## Example

POPAD

# POPF

**8086/80186/80286/80386/80486**

Pop Stack into FLAGS

**(16)**

## Syntax

POPF

## Operation

FLAGS ← SS:[ESP]
ESP ← ESP + 2

## Legal Form

POPF

## Description

This instruction pops the low-order word of the EFLAGS register from the stack. POPF provides compatibility with previous Intel microprocessors. Use the POPFD instruction in native-mode programming.

## Flags

| OF | DF | IF | TF | SF | ZF | | AF | PF | | CF |
|----|----|----|----|----|----|----|----|----|----|----|
| X | X | X | X | X | X | X | X | X | X | X | X |

## Faults

| | *PM* | *RM* | *V8086* |
|----|------|------|---------|
| 12 | #SS(0) | | |
| 13 | | INT 13 | #GP(0) |
| 14 | #PF(ec) | | #PF(ec) |

## Example

POPF

# POPFD

**Pop Stack into EFLAGS**

## Syntax

POPFD

## Operation

EFLAGS ← SS:[ESP]
ESP ← ESP + 4

## Legal Form

POPFD

## Description

This instruction pops the top-of-stack into the EFLAGS register. The VM and RF bits initially present in EFLAGS are not modified. The interrupt flag is modified only if CPL ≤ IOPL before the POPFD, that is, if the executing procedure has I/O privilege. The IOPL field is altered only if CPL = 0.

## Flags

| OF | DF | IF | TF | SF | ZF | | AF | PF | | CF |
|----|----|----|----|----|----|----|----|----|----|----|
| X | X | X | X | X | X | | X | X | | X |

## Faults

| | *PM* | *RM* | *V8086* |
|----|------|------|---------|
| 12 | #SS(0) | | |
| 13 | | INT 13 | #GP(0) |
| 14 | #PF(ec) | | #PF(ec) |

## Example

POPFD

# PUSH
## Push Value onto Stack

**8086/80186/80286/80386/80486**

**(8/16p/32)**

### Syntax

```
PUSH op
```

### Operation

```
if (sizeof(op) - 16)
    ESP ← ESP - 2
else
    ESP ← ESP - 4
endif
SS:[ESP] ← op
```

### Legal Forms

| | op |
|------|-------|
| PUSH | idata |
| PUSH | reg |
| PUSH | sreg |
| PUSH | mem |

### Description

This instruction pushes the operand onto the stack. The stack pointer is decremented before the value is pushed. If the operand is the ESP register, the value stored on the stack is the value that ESP had before the instruction was executed. (This instruction is different from the 8086 instruction, which pushes the new value.)

Note that pushing 16-bit registers and memory operands onto the stack changes the stack's memory alignment. It is more efficient to sign-extend or zero-extend the operand to 32 bits and push the dword. The 80386 uses segment registers to push an instruction value onto the stack.

When you execute the PUSH instruction in V86 mode, segment registers are pushed as 16-bit values. The stack will generally be used only for 16-bit values in V86 mode. This does not affect system performance because stack misalignment only occurs when both 16-bit and 32-bit values are pushed onto the stack.

### Flags

| OF | DF | IF | TF | SF | ZF | | AF | | PF | | CF |
|----|----|----|----|----|----|---|----|---|----|---|----|
| -  | -  | -  | -  | -  | -  | - | -  | - | -  | - | -  |

## Faults

| | *PM* | *RM* | *V8086* |
|---|---|---|---|
| 12 | #SS(0) | | |
| 13 | #GP(0) | | |
| 14 | #PF(ec) | | #PF(ec) |

## Examples

```
PUSH     7                ; Push data value
MOVSX    EAX, AX          ; Sign extend AX
PUSH     EAX              ; Then push
PUSH     array[ESI*4]     ; Push memory value
```

# PUSHA
## Push 16-Bit General Registers

80186/80286/80386/80486

(16)

### Syntax

PUSHA

### Operation

```
temp ← SP
PUSH    AX
PUSH    CX
PUSH    DX
PUSH    BX
PUSH    temp
PUSH    BP
PUSH    SI
PUSH    DI
```

### Legal Form

PUSHA

### Description

This instruction stores a copy of all eight 16-bit registers on the stack. This instruction provides compatibility with 80186 and 80286 software. Use the PUSHAD instruction in native-mode environments.

### Flags

| OF | DF | IF | TF | SF | ZF | | AF | | PF | | CF |
|----|----|----|----|----|----|----|----|----|----|----|----|
| -  | -  | -  | -  | -  | -  | -  | -  | -  | -  | -  | -  |

### Faults

| | *PM* | *RM* | *V8086* |
|----|------|------|---------|
| 12 | #SS(0) | | |
| 13 | | INT 13 | #GP(0) |
| 14 | #PF(ec) | | #PF(ec) |

### Example

PUSHA

# PUSHAD

80386/80486

**Push 32-Bit General Registers**

(32)

## Syntax

PUSHAD

## Operation

```
temp ← ESP
PUSH    EAX
PUSH    ECX
PUSH    EDX
PUSH    EBX
PUSH    temp
PUSH    EBP
PUSH    ESI
PUSH    EDI
```

## Legal Form

PUSHAD

## Description

This instruction stores a copy of all eight general registers on the stack. The value of ESP that is saved to the stack is the ESP value before execution of the PUSHAD instruction.

## Flags

| OF | DF | IF | TF | SF | ZF | | AF | | PF | | CF |
|----|----|----|----|----|----|----|----|----|----|----|----|
| - | - | - | - | - | - | - | - | - | - | - | - |

## Faults

| | *PM* | *RM* | *V8086* |
|----|------|------|---------|
| 12 | #SS(0) | | #GP(0) |
| 13 | | INT 13 | |
| 14 | #PF(ec) | | #PF(ec) |

## Example

PUSHAD

# PUSHF

## Push 16-Bit EFLAGS Register

8086/80186/80286/80386/80486

(16)

### Syntax

PUSHF

### Operation

```
ESP = ESP - 2
SS:[ESP] ← FLAGS
```

### Legal Form

PUSHF

### Description

This instruction pushes the low-order 16 bits of the EFLAGS register onto the stack. PUSHF provides compatibility with 16-bit processors and causes misalignment of the stack if used in native mode. Only 32-bit programs should use PUSHFD.

PUSHF causes a general protection fault in V86 mode if the executing procedure's IOPL is numerically less than 3.

### Flags

| OF | DF | IF | TF | SF | ZF | | AF | | PF | | CF |
|----|----|----|----|----|----|----|----|----|----|----|----|
| -  | -  | -  | -  | -  | -  | -  | -  | -  | -  | -  | -  |

### Faults

|    | *PM*    | *RM* | *V8086* |
|----|---------|------|---------|
| 12 | #SS(0)  |      |         |
| 13 |         |      | #GP(0)  |
| 14 | #PF(ec) |      | #PF(ec) |

### Example

PUSHF

# PUSHFD

**Push EFLAGS Register**

## Syntax

PUSHFD

## Operation

```
ESP = ESP - 4
SS:[ESP] ← EFLAGS
```

## Legal Form

PUSHFD

## Description

This instruction pushes the contents of the EFLAGS register onto the stack. PUSHF will cause a general protection fault in V86 mode if IOPL is less than 3.

## Flags

| OF | DF | IF | TF | SF | ZF | | AF | | PF | | CF |
|----|----|----|----|----|----|---|----|---|----|---|----|
| -  | -  | -  | -  | -  | -  | - | -  | - | -  | - | -  |

## Faults

| | *PM* | *RM* | *V8086* |
|----|------|------|---------|
| 12 | #SS(0) | | |
| 13 | | | #GP(0) |
| 14 | #PF(ec) | | #PF(ec) |

## Example

PUSHFD

# RCL

**Rotate Through Carry Left**

8086/80186/80286/80386/80486

(8/16p/32)

## Syntax

RCL *dest, count*

## Operation

```
temp ← max (count, 31)
if (temp = 1) then
    OF ← (highbit(dest) != CF)
else
    OF ← ?
endif
value ← concatenate (CF, dest)
while (temp != 0)
    x ← highbit (value)
    value ← (value << 1) + x
    temp ← temp - 1
    endwhile
CF ← highbit (value)
dest ← value
```

## Legal Forms

|     | dest | count |
| --- | --- | --- |
| RCL | reg, | idata |
| RCL | mem, | idata |
| RCL | reg, | CL |
| RCL | mem, | CL |

## Description

This instruction concatenates the carry flag (CF) with the *dest* operand and rotates the value the specified number of times. A rotation is implemented by shifting the value once and transferring the bit shifted off the high end to the low-order position of the value.

The OF bit is defined only if the rotate count is 1. The 80386 and 80486 never rotate a pattern more than 31 times. Counts greater than 31 are masked by the bit pattern 0000001FH.

## Flags

| OF | DF | IF | TF | SF | ZF |   | AF |   | PF |   | CF |
| --- | --- | --- | --- | --- | --- | --- | --- | --- | --- | --- | --- |
| x | - | - | - | - | - | - | - | - | - | - | x |

## Faults

| | *PM* | *RM* | *V8086* |
|---|---|---|---|
| 12 | #SS(0) | | |
| 13 | #GP(0) | INT 13 | #GP(0) |
| 14 | #PF(ec) | | #PF(ec) |
| 17 | #AC(0) | | #AC(0) |

## Example

```
RCL     EAX, 3          ; Rotate EAX 3 bits left
```

# RCR

**Rotate Through Carry Right**

8086/80186/80286/80386/80486

(8/16p/32)

## Syntax

RCR *dest*, *count*

## Operation

```
temp ← max (count, 31)
if (temp = 1) then
    OF ← (highbit(dest) != highbit(dest << 1))
else
    OF ← ?
endif
value ← concatenate (dest, CF)
while (temp != 0)
    x ← value & 1
    value ← (value >> 1)
    highbit (value) ← x
    temp ← temp - 1
    endwhile
CF ← highbit (value)
dest ← value
```

## Legal Forms

|     | *dest* | *count* |
| --- | --- | --- |
| RCR | reg, | idata |
| RCR | mem, | idata |
| RCR | reg, | CL |
| RCR | mem, | CL |

## Description

This instruction concatenates the carry flag (CF) with the *dest* operand and rotates the value the specified number of times. A rotation is implemented by shifting the value once and transferring the bit shifted off the low end to the high-order position of the value.

The OF bit is defined only if the rotate count is 1. The 80386 and 80486 never rotate a pattern more than 31 times. Counts greater than 31 are masked by the bit pattern 0000001FH.

## Flags

| OF | DF | IF | TF | SF | ZF |   | AF |   | PF |   | CF |
| --- | --- | --- | --- | --- | --- | --- | --- | --- | --- | --- | --- |
| x | - | - | - | - | - | - | - | - | - | - | x |

## Faults

| | PM | RM | V8086 |
|---|---|---|---|
| 12 | #SS(0) | | |
| 13 | #GP(0) | INT 13 | #GP(0) |
| 14 | #PF(ec) | | #PF(ec) |
| 17 | #AC(0) | | #AC(0) |

## Example

```
RCR     EAX, 3          ; Rotate EAX 3 bits right
```

# REP

**Repeat String Prefix**

## Syntax

REP

## Legal Forms

REP
REPE
REPZ
REPNE
REPNZ

## Description

The repeat prefix may be applied to any string instruction (CMPS, INS, LODS, MOVS, OUTS, SCAS, STOS). When the prefix is present, the string instruction executes repeatedly based on the *count* value in the ECX register. The ZF flag is also tested when executing CMPS or SCAS.

If ECX is 0 when a repeated string instruction is encountered, the string instruction will not be executed.

Refer to the individual string instructions in this chapter for additional information.

## Flags

| OF | DF | IF | TF | SF | ZF | | AF | | PF | | CF |
|----|----|----|----|----|----|----|----|----|----|----|----|
| –  | –  | –  | –  | –  | –  | –  | –  | –  | –  | –  | –  |

## Faults

| | *PM* | *RM* | *V8086* |
|---|------|------|---------|
| 6 | #UD() | INT 6 | #UD() |

## Example

```
MOV     EAX, 0
MOV     ECX, 1024/4
REP     STOSD              ; initialize 1 KB of memory to 0
```

# RET

**8086/80186/80286/80386/80486**

### Near Return from Subroutine

()

## Syntax

```
RET count
```

## Operation

```
EIP ← pop ();
ESP ← ESP + count
```

## Legal Forms

| | count |
|------|-------|
| RET | |
| RET | idata |

## Description

This instruction restores the instruction pointer to the value it held before the previous CALL instruction. The value of EIP that had been saved on the stack is popped. If the *count* operand is present, the *count* value is added to ESP, removing any operands that were pushed onto the stack for the subroutine call.

## Flags

| OF | DF | IF | TF | SF | ZF | | AF | | PF | | CF |
|----|----|----|----|----|----|---|----|---|----|---|----|
| -  | -  | -  | -  | -  | -  | - | -  | - | -  | - | -  |

## Faults

| | *PM* | *RM* | *V8086* |
|----|--------|--------|---------|
| 12 | #SS(0) | | |
| 13 | #GP(0) | INT 13 | #GP(0) |
| 14 | #PF(ec) | | #PF(ec) |

## Example

```
RET 4                    ; Return and pop one dword
```

# RETF

**Far Return from Subroutine**

8086/80186/80286/80386/80486

()

## Syntax

RETF *count*

## Operation

EIP ← pop()
CS ← pop()
ESP ← ESP + *count*

## Legal Forms

| *count* |
| --- |
| RETF |
| RETF     idata |

## Description

This variation of the RET instruction pops both a new CS and EIP from the stack. The instruction assumes that the CS value is stored as the low-order 16 bits of a dword on the stack.

If this instruction causes a privilege-level transition, the protection checks described in Chapter 5 take place.

## Flags

| OF | DF | IF | TF | SF | ZF | | AF | PF | | CF |
| --- | --- | --- | --- | --- | --- | --- | --- | --- | --- | --- |
| - | - | - | - | - | - | - | - | - | - | - |

## Faults

| | *PM* | *RM* | *V8086* |
| --- | --- | --- | --- |
| 10 | #NP(sel) | | |
| 12 | #SS(0) | | |
| 13 | #GP(0) | INT 13 | #GP(0) |
| 14 | #PF(ec) | | #PF(ec) |

## Example

RETF     ; Far return

# ROL
## Rotate Left

## Syntax

```
ROL dest, count
```

## Operation

```
temp ← max (count, 31)
if (temp = 1) then
    OF ← (highbit(dest) != CF)
else
    OF ← ?
endif
while (temp != 0)
    x ← highbit (dest)
    dest ← (dest << 1) + x
    temp ← temp - 1
    endwhile
CF ← highbit (dest)
```

## Legal Forms

|       | dest  | count |
|-------|-------|-------|
| ROL   | reg,  | idata |
| ROL   | mem,  | idata |
| ROL   | reg,  | CL    |
| ROL   | mem,  | CL    |

## Description

This instruction rotates the *dest* operand the specified number of times. A rotation is implemented by shifting the value once and transferring the bit shifted off the high end to the low-order position of the value.

The OF bit is defined only if the rotate count is 1. The 80386 and 80486 never rotate a pattern more than 31 times. Counts greater than 31 are masked by the bit pattern 0000001FH.

## Flags

| OF | DF | IF | TF | SF | ZF |   | AF |   | PF |   | CF |
|----|----|----|----|----|----|---|----|---|----|---|----|
| x  | -  | -  | -  | -  | -  | - | -  | - | -  | - | x  |

## Faults

| | PM | RM | V8086 |
|---|---|---|---|
| 12 | #SS(0) | | |
| 13 | #GP(0) | INT 13 | #GP(0) |
| 14 | #PF(ec) | | #PF(ec) |
| 17 | #AC(0) | | #AC(0) |

## Example

```
ROL     EAX, 3        ; Rotate EAX 3 bits left
```

# ROR

**Rotate Right**

## Syntax

```
ROR dest, count
```

## Operation

```
temp ← max (count, 31)
if (temp = 1) then
    OF ← (highbit(dest) != highbit(dest << 1))
else
    OF ← ?
endif
while (temp != 0)
    x ← value & 1
    value ← (value >> 1)
    highbit(value) ← x
    temp ← temp - 1
    endwhile
CF ← highbit (value)
dest ← value
```

## Legal Forms

|     | dest  | count |
|-----|-------|-------|
| ROR | reg,  | idata |
| ROR | mem,  | idata |
| ROR | reg,  | CL    |
| ROR | mem,  | CL    |

## Description

This instruction rotates the *dest* operand the specified number of times. A rotation is implemented by shifting the value once and transferring the bit shifted off the low end to the high-order position of the value.

The OF bit is defined only if the rotate count is 1. The 80386 never rotates a pattern more than 31 times. Counts greater than 31 are masked by the bit pattern 0000001FH.

## Flags

| OF | DF | IF | TF | SF | ZF |   | AF |   | PF |   | CF |
|----|----|----|----|----|----|---|----|---|----|---|----|
| X  | -  | -  | -  | -  | -  | - | -  | - | -  | - | X  |

## Faults

| | PM | RM | V8086 |
|---|---|---|---|
| 12 | #SS(0) | | |
| 13 | #GP(0) | INT 13 | #GP(0) |
| 14 | #PF(ec) | | #PF(ec) |
| 17 | #AC(0) | | #AC(0) |

## Example

```
ROR     EAX, 3        ; Rotate EAX 3 bits right
```

# SAHF

**Store AH in EFLAGS**

## Syntax

SAHF

## Operation

EFLAGS ← EFLAGS | (AH & 0D5H)

## Legal Form

SAHF

## Description

This instruction loads the contents of the AH register into bits 7, 6, 4, 2, and 0 of the EFLAGS register.

## Flags

| OF | DF | IF | TF | SF | ZF | | AF | | PF | | CF |
|----|----|----|----|----|----|----|----|----|----|----|----|
| - | - | - | - | x | x | - | x | - | x | - | x |

## Faults

None.

## Example

SAHF

# SAL

## Shift Left Arithmetic

8086/80186/80286/80386/80486

(8/16p/32)

### Syntax

SAL *dest*, *count*

### Operation

```
temp ← count & 001FH
while (temp != 0)
    CF ← highorder (dest)
    dest ← dest << 1
    temp ← temp - 1
    end
if count = 1 then
    OF ← highorder (dest) != CF
else
    OF ← ?
```

### Legal Forms

|     | *dest* | *count* |
|-----|------|-------|
| SAL | reg, | idata |
| SAL | mem, | idata |
| SAL | reg, | CL |
| SAL | mem, | CL |

### Description

This instruction shifts the *dest* operand *count* bits to the left. The arithmetic shift left (SAL) and logical shift left (SHL) are equivalent instructions.

The *count* operand must either be an immediate data value or be stored in register CL. The 80386 and 80486 mask the *count* operand with 1FH so that the *count* value is never greater than 31.

If the *count* operand is 1, the overflow flag is reset to 0 when the high-order bit and the carry flag have the same value after the shift. If the high-order bit and CF have different values, OF is set to 1. If *count* is greater than 1, OF is undefined.

A left shift is equivalent to multiplying the *dest* operand by $2^{count}$.

### Flags

| OF | DF | IF | TF | SF | ZF |  | AF |  | PF |  | CF |
|----|----|----|----|----|----|----|----|----|----|----|----|
| x  | -  | -  | -  | x  | x  | -  | -  | -  | x  | -  | x  |

## Faults

| | PM | RM | V8086 |
|----|--------|--------|---------|
| 12 | #SS(0) | | |
| 13 | #GP(0) | INT 13 | #GP(0) |
| 14 | #PF(ec) | | #PF(ec) |
| 17 | #AC(0) | | #AC(0) |

## Examples

```
SAL     ECX, 7
SAL     WORD PTR [EBP+8], CL
```

# SAR

**Shift Right Arithmetic**

## Syntax

SAR *dest*, *count*

## Operation

```
temp ← count & 001FH
while (temp != 0)
    save ← highorder (dest)
    CF = dest & 1
    dest ← dest >> 1
    highorder (dest) = save
    temp ← temp - 1
    end
if count = 1 then
    OF ← 0
else
    OF ← ?
```

## Legal Forms

|     | *dest* | *count* |
| --- | --- | --- |
| SAR | reg, | idata |
| SAR | mem, | idata |
| SAR | reg, | CL |
| SAR | mem, | CL |

## Description

This instruction shifts the *dest* operand *count* bits to the right. The shift is called arithmetic because it preserves the sign bit of the *dest* operand.

The *count* operand must be an immediate data value or it must be stored in register CL. The 80386 and 80486 mask the *count* operand with 1FH so that the *count* value is never greater than 31.

If *count* is 1, the overflow is reset to 0. If *count* is greater than 1, OF is undefined.

The arithmetic right shift is similar to dividing *dest* by $2^{count}$ except that negative values are rounded toward negative infinity, rather than toward 0 (that is, −3 shifted left 1 rounds to −2, whereas −3 divided by $2^1$ rounds to −1).

## Flags

| OF | DF | IF | TF | SF | ZF | AF | PF | CF |
| --- | --- | --- | --- | --- | --- | --- | --- | --- |
| x | - | - | - | x | x | - | - | - | x | - | x |

## Faults

| | *PM* | *RM* | *V8086* |
|-----|--------|--------|---------|
| 12 | #SS(0) | | |
| 13 | #GP(0) | INT 13 | #GP(0) |
| 14 | #PF(ec) | | #PF(ec) |
| 17 | #AC(0) | | #AC(0) |

## Examples

```
SAR     ECX, 7
SAR     WORD PTR [EBP+8], CL
```

# SBB

**Subtraction with Borrow**

8086/80186/80286/80386/80486
(8/16p/32)

## Syntax

SBB *dest, src*

## Operation

*dest* ← *dest* - *src* - CF

## Legal Forms

|     | *dest* | *src* |
| --- | --- | --- |
| SBB | reg, | idata |
| SBB | mem, | idata |
| SBB | reg, | reg |
| SBB | reg, | mem |
| SBB | mem, | reg |

## Description

This instruction subtracts the *src* operand from the *dest* operand and decrements the *dest* operand by 1 if the CF flag is set. The result is stored in *dest*.

## Flags

| OF | DF | IF | TF | SF | ZF |  | AF |  | PF |  | CF |
| --- | --- | --- | --- | --- | --- | --- | --- | --- | --- | --- | --- |
| x | - | - | - | x | x | - | x | - | x | - | x |

## Faults

| | *PM* | *RM* | *V8086* |
| --- | --- | --- | --- |
| 12 | #SS(0) | | |
| 13 | #GP(0) | INT 13 | #GP(0) |
| 14 | #PF(ec) | | #PF(ec) |
| 17 | #AC(0) | | #AC(0) |

## Example

```
; 64-bit subtraction operation EDX:EAX - EBX:ECX
SUB     EAX, ECX            ; Low-order bits
SBB     EDX, EBX            ; High-order bits
```

# SCAS

**Scan String**

## Syntax

```
SCAS
```

## Operation

```
when opcode is (SCASB, SCASW, SCASD) set opsize ← (1, 2, 4)
NULL ← acc - ES:[EDI]
if (DF = 0) then
    EDI ← EDI + opsize
else
    EDI ← EDI - opsize
endif
```

## Legal Forms

```
SCASB     ; Scan string byte
SCASW     ; Scan string word
SCASD     ; Scan string doubleword
```

## Description

This instruction compares the value in the accumulator (AL, AX, or EAX) with the operand at ES:[EDI]. The flags are set according to the compare operation, and the EDI register is adjusted by the size of the operand. If the direction flag (DF) is 0, EDI is incremented; otherwise, it is decremented.

You can apply the REPE or REPNE prefix to the SCAS instruction. The ECX register contains a repeat count, indicating the maximum number of times the instruction should be repeated. The instruction will repeat only while the repeat condition is true, that is, when ZF = 1 for REPE (REPZ) or ZF = 0 for REPNE (REPNZ).

You cannot use a segment override prefix with SCAS. The ES register is always the destination of the string to be scanned.

## Flags

| OF | DF | IF | TF | SF | ZF | | AF | | PF | | CF |
|----|----|----|----|----|----|----|----|----|----|----|----|
| X | - | - | - | X | X | - | X | - | X | - | X |

## Faults

| | PM | RM | V8086 |
|---|---|---|---|
| 12 | #SS(0) | | |
| 13 | #GP(0) | INT 13 | #GP(0) |
| 14 | #PF(ec) | | #PF(ec) |
| 17 | #AC(0) | | #AC(0) |

## Example

```
; Search for an asterisk in a string
LES     EDI, [EBP+12]       ; String pointer on stack
MOV     ECX, [EBP+20]       ; String size on stack
CLD
MOV     AL, '*'             ; Character to search for
REPNE   SCASB               ; Scan
JE      MATCH               ; Branch if found
```

# *seg*

## Segment Override Prefix

## Legal Forms

```
CS:
DS:
SS:
ES:
FS:
GS:
```

## Description

The instruction that follows these prefixes takes its memory operand from the specified segment rather than from the default segment.

You cannot override the following string instructions:

INS

SCAS

STOS

## Flags

| OF | DF | IF | TF | SF | ZF | | AF | | PF | | CF |
|----|----|----|----|----|----|----|----|----|----|----|----|
| -  | -  | -  | -  | -  | -  | -  | -  | -  | -  | -  | -  |

## Faults

None.

## Example

```
MOV     EAX, FS:[ESI]      ; Read from FS rather than DS
ADD     DS:[EBP], 7        ; Write to DS rather than SS
```

# SET*cc*

**Set Byte on** *Condition*

## Syntax

SET*cc* *dest*

## Operation

```
if (cc) then
    dest ← 1
else
    dest ← 0
endif
```

## Legal Forms

| | | |
|---|---|---|
| SETA | *dest* | ; Set if above (unsigned x > y) / CF = 0 & ZF = 0 |
| SETAE | *dest* | ; Set if above or equal / CF = 0 |
| SETB | *dest* | ; Set if below (unsigned x < y) / CF = 1 |
| SETBE | *dest* | ; Set if below or equal / CF = 1 \| ZF = 1 |
| SETC | *dest* | ; Set if carry / CF = 1 |
| SETE | *dest* | ; Set if equal / ZF = 1 |
| SETG | *dest* | ; Set if greater (signed x > y) / SF = OF & ZF = 0 |
| SETGE | *dest* | ; Set if greater or equal / SF = OF |
| SETL | *dest* | ; Set if less (signed x < y) / SF != OF |
| SETLE | *dest* | ; Set if less or equal / SF != OF & ZF = 1 |
| SETNA | *dest* | ; Set if not above (SETBE) |
| SETNAE | *dest* | ; Set if not above or equal (SETB) |
| SETNB | *dest* | ; Set if not below (SETAE) |
| SETNBE | *dest* | ; Set if not below or equal (SETA) |
| SETNC | *dest* | ; Set if no carry / CF = 0 |
| SETNE | *dest* | ; Set if not equal / ZF = 0 |
| SETNG | *dest* | ; Set if not greater (SETLE) |
| SETNGE | *dest* | ; Set if not greater or equal (SETL) |
| SETNL | *dest* | ; Set if not less (SETGE) |
| SETNLE | *dest* | ; Set if not less or equal / SF = OF & ZF = 0 |
| SETNO | *dest* | ; Set if no overflow / OF = 0 |
| SETNP | *dest* | ; Set if no parity / PF = 0 |
| SETNS | *dest* | ; Set if no sign / SF = 0 |
| SETNZ | *dest* | ; Set if not 0 / ZF = 0 |
| SETO | *dest* | ; Set if overflow / OF = 1 |
| SETP | *dest* | ; Set if parity / PF = 1 |
| SETPE | *dest* | ; Set if parity even / PF = 1 |
| SETPO | *dest* | ; Set if parity odd / PF = 0 |
| SETS | *dest* | ; Set if sign / SF = 1 |
| SETZ | *dest* | ; Set if 0 / ZF = 1 |

## Description

This instruction sets the *dest* byte to 1 if the condition described by the opcode is met; otherwise, the instruction clears the byte to 0.

## Flags

| OF | DF | IF | TF | SF | ZF | | AF | | PF | | CF |
|----|----|----|----|----|----|---|----|---|----|---|----|
| -  | -  | -  | -  | -  | -  | - | -  | - | -  | - | -  |

## Faults

| | *PM* | *RM* | *V8086* |
|---|------|------|---------|
| 12 | #SS(0) | | #SS(0) |
| 13 | #GP(0) | INT 13 | #GP(0) |
| 14 | #PF(ec) | | #PF(ec) |

## Example

```
SETNZ    AL
MOVZX    EAX, AL
```

# SGDT

**Store GDT Register**

## Syntax

SGDT *dest*

## Operation

*dest* ← GDTR.LIMIT
*dest* + 2 ← GDTR.BASE

## Legal Form

| | *dest* |
|---|---|
| SGDT | mem |

## Description

This instruction writes the limit portion of the GDTR to the *dest* memory address and writes the linear base address of the GDT to the dword at *dest* + 2.

## Flags

| OF | DF | IF | TF | SF | ZF | | AF | | PF | | CF |
|----|----|----|----|----|----|---|----|---|----|---|----|
| -  | -  | -  | -  | -  | -  | - | -  | - | -  | - | -  |

## Faults

| | *PM* | *RM* | *V8086* |
|---|---|---|---|
| 6* | #UD() | INT 6 | #UD() |
| 12 | #SS(0) | | |
| 13 | #GP(0) | INT 13 | #GP(0) |
| 14 | #PF(ec) | | #PF(ec) |
| 17 | #AC(0) | | #AC(0) |

* The undefined opcode fault occurs only when the *dest* operand is encoded as a register.

## Example

SGDT [300H]                          ; Save GDTR

# SHL

## Shift Left Logical

8086/80186/80286/80386/80486

(8/16p/32)

### Syntax

SHL *dest, count*

### Operation

```
temp ← count & 001FH
while (temp != 0)
    CF ← highorder (dest)
    dest ← dest << 1
    temp ← temp - 1
    end
if count = 1 then
    OF ← highorder (dest) != CF
else
    OF ← ?
```

### Legal Forms

|     | *dest* | *count* |
|-----|--------|---------|
| SHL | reg,   | idata   |
| SHL | mem,   | idata   |
| SHL | reg,   | CL      |
| SHL | mem,   | CL      |

### Description

This instruction shifts the *dest* operand *count* bits to the left. The arithmetic left shift (SAL) and logical left shift (SHL) are equivalent instructions.

The *count* operand must either be an immediate data value or be stored in register CL. The 80386 and 80486 mask the *count* operand with 1FH so that the *count* value is never greater than 31.

If the *count* operand is 1, the overflow flag is reset to 0 when the high-order bit and the carry flag have the same value after the shift. If the high-order bit and CF have different values, OF is set to 1. If *count* is greater than 1, OF is undefined.

A left shift is equivalent to multiplying the *dest* operand by $2^{count}$.

### Flags

| OF | DF | IF | TF | SF | ZF |   | AF |   | PF |   | CF |
|----|----|----|----|----|----|---|----|---|----|---|----|
| x  | -  | -  | -  | x  | x  | - | -  | - | x  | - | x  |

## Faults

| | PM | RM | V8086 |
|---|---|---|---|
| 12 | #SS(0) | | |
| 13 | #GP(0) | INT 13 | #GP(0) |
| 14 | #PF(ec) | | #PF(ec) |
| 17 | #AC(0) | | #AC(0) |

## Examples

```
SHL     ECX, 7
SHL     WORD PTR [EBP+8], CL
```

# SHLD

**Shift Left Double**

80386/80486

(16p/32)

## Syntax

SHLD *dest, src, count*

## Operation

```
temp ← max (count, 31)
value ← concatenate (dest, src)
value ← value << temp
dest ← value
```

## Legal Forms

|  | dest | src | count |
|------|------|------|------|
| SHLD | reg, | reg, | idata |
| SHLD | mem, | reg, | idata |
| SHLD | reg, | reg, | CL |
| SHLD | mem, | reg, | CL |

## Description

This instruction concatenates the *src* operand to the *dest* operand and shifts the resulting double-size value left. The low-order bits are stored in *dest*.

The *count* operand is masked with 1FH so that no shift counts greater than 31 are used.

## Flags

| OF | DF | IF | TF | SF | ZF |  | AF |  | PF |  | CF |
|----|----|----|----|----|----|----|----|----|----|----|----|
| ? | - | - | - | x | x | - | ? | - | x | - | x |

## Faults

| PM | | RM | V8086 |
|----|----|----|----|
| 12 | #SS(0) | | |
| 13 | #GP(0) | INT 13 | #GP(0) |
| 14 | #PF(ec) | | #PF(ec) |
| 17 | #AC(0) | | #AC(0) |

## Example

```
MOV     EAX, [ESI]          ; Get low-order dword
SHLD    EAX, [ESI+4], 7     ; 64-bit shift
```

# SHR

**Shift Right Logical**

### Syntax

SHR *dest, count*

### Operation

```
temp ← count & 001FH
while (temp != 9)
    CF = dest & 1
    dest ← dest >> 1
    temp ← temp - 1
    end
if count = 1 then
    OF ← highorder (dest)
else
    OF ← ?
```

### Legal Forms

|     | *dest* | *count* |
| --- | --- | --- |
| SHR | reg, | idata |
| SHR | mem, | idata |
| SHR | reg, | CL |
| SHR | mem, | CL |

### Description

This instruction shifts the *dest* operand *count* bits to the right. The high-order bits are cleared to 0 as the low-order bits are shifted.

The *count* operand must either be an immediate data value or be stored in register CL. The 80386 and 80486 mask the *count* operand with 1FH so that the *count* value is never greater than 31.

If the *count* operand is 1, the overflow flag is set to the high-order bit of the *dest* operand. If *count* is greater than 1, OF is undefined.

### Flags

| OF | DF | IF | TF | SF | ZF | | AF | | PF | | CF |
| --- | --- | --- | --- | --- | --- | --- | --- | --- | --- | --- | --- |
| x | - | - | - | x | x | - | - | - | x | - | x |

## Faults

| | PM | RM | V8086 |
|---|---|---|---|
| 12 | #SS(0) | | |
| 13 | #GP(0) | INT 13 | #GP(0) |
| 14 | #PF(ec) | | #PF(ec) |
| 17 | #AC(0) | | #AC(0) |

## Examples

```
SHR     ECX, 7
SHR     WORD PTR [EBP+8], CL
```

# SHRD

**Shift Right Double**

## Syntax

SHRD *dest, src, count*

## Operation

```
temp  ← max (count, 31)
value ← cat (src, dest)
value ← value >> temp
dest  ← value
```

## Legal Forms

|      | dest | src  | count |
|------|------|------|-------|
| SHRD | reg, | reg, | idata |
| SHRD | mem, | reg, | idata |
| SHRD | reg, | reg, | CL    |
| SHRD | mem, | reg, | CL    |

## Description

This instruction concatenates the *src* operand to the *dest* operand and shifts the resulting double-size value right. The low-order bits are stored in *dest*.

The *count* operand is masked with 1FH so that no shift counts greater than 31 are used.

## Flags

| OF | DF | IF | TF | SF | ZF |   | AF |   | PF |   | CF |
|----|----|----|----|----|----|---|----|---|----|---|----|
| ?  | -  | -  | -  | x  | x  | - | ?  | - | x  | - | x  |

## Faults

|    | PM      | RM     | V8086   |
|----|---------|--------|---------|
| 12 | #SS(0)  |        |         |
| 13 | #GP(0)  | INT 13 | #GP(0)  |
| 14 | #PF(ec) |        | #PF(ec) |
| 17 | #AC(0)  |        | #AC(0)  |

## Example

```
MOV    EAX, [002AH]    ; Get low-order dword
SHRD   EAX, [002EH]    ; 64-bit shift
```

# SIDT

80286/80386/80486

**Store IDT Register**

()

## Syntax

SIDT *dest*

## Operation

*dest* ← IDTR.LIMIT
*dest* + 2 ← IDTR.BASE

## Legal Form

| | *dest* |
|------|--------|
| SIDT | mem |

## Description

This instruction writes the limit portion of the IDTR to the *dest* memory address and the linear base address of the IDT to the dword at *dest* + 2.

## Flags

| OF | DF | IF | TF | SF | ZF | | AF | | PF | | CF |
|----|----|----|----|----|----|---|----|---|----|---|----|
| -  | -  | -  | -  | -  | -  | - | -  | - | -  | - | -  |

## Faults

| | PM | RM | V8086 |
|------|--------|--------|--------|
| 6*   | #UD()  | INT 6  | #UD()  |
| 12   | #SS(0) |        |        |
| 13   | #GP(0) | INT 13 | #GP(0) |
| 14   | #PF(ec)|        | #PF(ec)|
| 17   | #AC(0) |        | #AC(0) |

* The undefined opcode fault occurs only when the *dest* operand is encoded as a register.

## Example

```
SIDT      int_tab              ; Get address and limit of IDT
```

# SLDT

**Store LDT Register**

## Syntax

SLDT *dest*

## Operation

*dest* ← LDTR

## Legal Forms

| | *dest* |
|---|---|
| SLDT | reg |
| SLDT | mem |

## Description

This instruction stores the selector in the LDTR in the destination location.

## Flags

| OF | DF | IF | TF | SF | ZF | | AF | | PF | | CF |
|----|----|----|----|----|----|----|----|----|----|----|----|
| –  | –  | –  | –  | –  | –  | –  | –  | –  | –  | –  | –  |

## Faults

| *PM* | | *RM* | *V8086* |
|------|------|------|--------|
| 6 | | INT 6 | #UD( ) |
| 12 | #SS(0) | | |
| 13 | #GP(0) | | |
| 14 | #PF(ec) | | |
| 17 | #AC(0) | | #AC(0) |

## Example

SLDT      DX                          ; Put LDT selector into DX

# SMSW

**Store Machine Status Word**

## Syntax

SMSW *dest*

## Operation

*dest* ← MSW

## Legal Forms

| | *dest* |
|------|------|
| SMSW | reg |
| SMSW | mem |

## Description

This instruction stores the low-order 16 bits of register CR0 (the 80286 machine status word) in the *dest* operand.

This instruction is provided for compatibility only. Use the MOV CR0 instruction in native mode programming.

## Flags

| OF | DF | IF | TF | SF | ZF | | AF | | PF | | CF |
|----|----|----|----|----|----|----|----|----|----|----|----|
| -  | -  | -  | -  | -  | -  | -  | -  | -  | -  | -  | -  |

## Faults

| PM | | RM | V8086 |
|------|---------|--------|---------|
| 6    |         |        |         |
| 12   | #SS(0)  |        |         |
| 13   | #GP(0)  | INT 13 | #GP(0)  |
| 14   | #PF(ec) |        | #PF(ec) |
| 17   | #AC(0)  |        | #AC(0)  |

## Example

SMSW [DI]

# STC

**Set Carry Flag**                                                    O

___

## Syntax

STC

## Operation

CF ← 1

## Legal Form

STC

## Description

This instruction sets the carry flag (CF) in the EFLAGS register to 1.

## Flags

| OF | DF | IF | TF | SF | ZF | | AF | | PF | | CF |
|----|----|----|----|----|----|----|----|----|----|----|----|
| -  | -  | -  | -  | -  | -  | -  | -  | -  | -  | -  | 1  |

## Faults

None.

## Example

STC                         ; Carry flag set to 1

# STD

## Set Direction Flag

## Syntax

STD

## Operation

DF ← 1

## Legal Form

STD

## Description

This instruction sets the direction flag (DF) in the EFLAGS register to 1. This instruction indicates reverse direction in the string instructions to decrement the index registers when DF = 1.

## Flags

| OF | DF | IF | TF | SF | ZF | | AF | | PF | | CF |
|----|----|----|----|----|----|----|----|----|----|----|----|
| -  | -  | -  | -  | -  | -  | -  | -  | -  | -  | -  | -  |

## Faults

None.

## Example

```
STD         ; Prepare for reverse string operation
```

# STI

**Set Interrupt Flag**

## Syntax

STI

## Operation

IF ← 1

## Legal Form

STI

## Description

This instruction sets the interrupt flag (IF) in the EFLAGS register to 1, enabling hardware interrupts.

The executing program must have a high enough privilege (CPL ≤ IOPL) to issue the STI command to avoid a general protection fault.

## Flags

| OF | DF | IF | TF | SF | ZF |  | AF |  | PF |  | CF |
|----|----|----|----|----|----|----|----|----|----|----|----|
| - | - | - | - | - | - | - | - | - | - | - | - |

## Fault

| PM | RM | V8086 |
|----|----|-------|
| 13  #GP(0) | | |

## Example

```
        CLI                         ; Disable interrupts
        MOV     AL, semaphore       ; Get memory value
        DEC     AL                  ; Decrement counter
        J2      DONE                ; Skip if value was 0
        MOV     semaphore, AL       ; Update
DONE:
        STI                         ; Reenable interrupts
```

# STOS

**Store String**

## Syntax

```
STOS
```

## Operation

```
when opcode is (STOSB, STOSW, STOSD), set opsize ← (1, 2, 4)
ES:[EDI] ← accum
if (DF = 0) then
    EDI ← EDI + opsize
else
    EDI ← EDI - opsize
endif
```

## Legal Forms

```
STOSB  ; Store string byte
STOSW  ; Store string word
STOSD  ; Store string doubleword
```

## Description

This instruction writes the current contents of the accumulator (AL, AX, or EAX, depending on the opcode used) to the memory location pointed to by ES:EDI. It then increments or decrements EDI by the size of the operand, according to the DF bit in the EFLAGS register.

If you precede the STOS instruction with the REP prefix, register ECX must contain a count of the number of times STOS is to be executed. This fills memory with the value in the accumulator.

You cannot use a segment override prefix with the STOS instruction. The destination segment will always be selected by ES.

## Flags

| OF | DF | IF | TF | SF | ZF | | AF | | PF | | CF |
|----|----|----|----|----|----|----|----|----|----|----|----|
| -  | -  | -  | -  | -  | -  | -  | -  | -  | -  | -  | -  |

## Faults

| | PM | RM | V8086 |
|---|------|--------|----------|
| 12 | #SS(0) | | |
| 13 | #GP(0) | INT 13 | #GP(0) |
| 14 | #PF(ec) | | #PF(ec) |
| 17 | #AC(0) | | #AC(0) |

**314**

## Example

```
; Clear 100 bytes of memory beginning at location 0
MOV      EDI, 0             ; Base address
MOV      ECX, 100 / 4       ; Count (in dwords)
XOR      EAX, EAX           ; Clear accumulator to 0
CLD
REP      STOSD              ; Zero memory
```

# STR
## Store Task Register

### Syntax

STR *dest*

### Operation

*dest* ← TR

### Legal Forms

| | dest |
| --- | --- |
| STR | reg |
| STR | mem |

### Description

This instruction stores the task register selector in *dest*.

### Flags

| OF | DF | IF | TF | SF | ZF | | AF | | PF | | CF |
| --- | --- | --- | --- | --- | --- | --- | --- | --- | --- | --- | --- |
| - | - | - | - | - | - | - | - | - | - | - | - |

### Faults

| | *PM* | *RM* | *V8086* |
| --- | --- | --- | --- |
| 6 | | INT 6 | #UD( ) |
| 12 | #SS(0) | | |
| 13 | #GP(0) | | |
| 14 | #PF(ec) | | |
| 17 | #AC(0) | | #AC(0) |

### Example

STR      CX          ; Store current task's selector

# SUB

Subtraction

## Syntax

SUB *dest, src*

## Operation

*dest ← dest - src*

## Legal Forms

|      | *dest* | *src* |
|------|--------|-------|
| SUB  | reg,   | idata |
| SUB  | mem,   | idata |
| SUB  | reg,   | reg   |
| SUB  | reg,   | mem   |
| SUB  | mem,   | reg   |

## Description

This instruction subtracts the *src* operand from the *dest* operand and stores the result in *dest*.

## Flags

| OF | DF | IF | TF | SF | ZF |  | AF |  | PF |  | CF |
|----|----|----|----|----|----|--|----|--|----|--|----|
| x  | -  | -  | -  | x  | x  | -| x  | -| x  | -| x  |

## Faults

|    | *PM*    | *RM*    | *V8086*  |
|----|---------|---------|----------|
| 12 | #SS(0)  |         |          |
| 13 | #GP(0)  | INT 13  | #GP(0)   |
| 14 | #PF(ec) |         | #PF(ec)  |
| 17 | #AC(0)  |         | #AC(0)   |

## Example

```
; 64-bit subtraction operation EDX:EAX - EBX:ECX
SUB     EAX, ECX        ; Low-order bits
SBB     EDX, EBX        ; High-order bits with possible borrow
```

# TEST

**Test Bits**

## Syntax

TEST *dest, src*

## Operation

NULL ← *dest* & *src*

## Legal Forms

|      | dest | src   |
|------|------|-------|
| TEST | reg, | idata |
| TEST | mem, | idata |
| TEST | reg, | reg   |
| TEST | reg, | mem   |
| TEST | mem, | reg   |

## Description

This instruction performs a bit-by-bit AND operation on the *src* and *dest* operands and discards the result. The flag bits, however, are set as they would be after an AND instruction.

## Flags

| OF | DF | IF | TF | SF | ZF | AF | PF | CF |
|----|----|----|----|----|----|-----|-----|-----|
| 0 | - | - | - | x | x | - ? - | x - | 0 |

## Faults

|    | PM     | RM     | V8086  |
|----|--------|--------|--------|
| 12 | #SS(0) |        |        |
| 13 | #GP(0) | INT 13 | #GP(0) |
| 14 | #PF(ec)|        | #PF(ec)|
| 17 | #AC(0) |        | #AC(0) |

## Examples

```
TEST    AL, 0FH                      ; Check if any bits set in
                                     ; low nibble of AL
TEST    EBX, ECX                     ; Test EBX under mask in ECX
TEST    WORD PTR[EBP+6], 8000H       ; Check whether
                                     ; 16-bit integer is negative
```

# VERR

**Verify Read Access**

## Syntax

VERR *select*

## Operation

```
if (accessible(select)) & read_access(select)) then
    ZF ← 1
else
    ZF ← 0
endif
```

## Legal Forms

|      | *select* |
| ---- | -------- |
| VERR | reg      |
| VERR | mem      |

## Description

This instruction sets the ZF bit in EFLAGS to 1 if the current procedure can load the *select* operand into DS, ES, FS, or GS and can read a value from the memory segment without causing a privilege violation.

If the selector is for a descriptor that is not a memory segment, if the memory segment is not readable, or if the current procedure does not have a high enough privilege level to gain access to the segment, VERR clears ZF to 0. The VERR instruction does not generate a fault for referring to a selector that is invalid; however, a fault occurs if the instruction operand is a memory operand and the operand address is invalid.

Note that this instruction does not check the "present" bit of the descriptor, nor does it check access at the page protection level (U/S and R/W bits of page table entries).

## Flags

| OF | DF | IF | TF | SF | ZF | AF | PF | CF |
|----|----|----|----|----|----|----|----|----|
| -  | -  | -  | -  | -  | X  | -  | -  | -  | -  | -  |

## Faults

| *PM* | | *RM* | *V8086* |
|------|-----|-------|---------|
| 6    |        | INT 6 | #UD()   |
| 12   | #SS(0) |       |         |
| 13   | #GP(0) |       |         |
| 14   | #PF(ec)|       |         |
| 17   | #AC(0) |       | #AC(0)  |

## Example

```
      VERR    WORD PTR [EBP+8]    ; Check selector on stack
      JZ      CONTINUE           ; Branch if OK
      STC                        ; Set carry flag
      LEAVE                      ; And return if selector is invalid
      RETF
CONTINUE:
```

# VERW
**Verify Write Access**

## Syntax

VERW *select*

## Operation

```
if (accessible(select)) & write_access(select)) then
    ZF ← 1
else
    ZF ← 0
endif
```

## Legal Forms

|       | *select* |
| ----- | -------- |
| VERW  | reg      |
| VERW  | mem      |

## Description

This instruction sets the ZF bit in EFLAGS to 1 if the current procedure can load the *select* operand into DS, SS, ES, FS, or GS and can write a value to the memory segment without causing a privilege violation.

If the selector is for a descriptor that is not a memory segment, if the memory segment is not writable, or if the current procedure does not have a high enough privilege level to gain access to the segment, VERW clears ZF to 0. The VERW instruction does not generate a fault for referring to a selector that is invalid; however, a fault occurs if the instruction operand is a memory operand and the operand address is invalid.

Note that this instruction does not check the 'present' bit of the descriptor, nor does it check access at the page protection level (U/S and R/W bits of page table entries).

## Flags

| OF | DF | IF | TF | SF | ZF | | AF | | PF | | CF |
| -- | -- | -- | -- | -- | -- | -- | -- | -- | -- | -- | -- |
| -  | -  | -  | -  | -  | X  | -  | -  | -  | -  | -  | -  |

## Faults

| *PM* | | *RM* | *V8086* |
| --- | --- | --- | --- |
| 6  |         | INT 6 | #UD() |
| 12 | #SS(0)  |       |       |
| 13 | #GP(0)  |       |       |
| 14 | #PF(ec) |       |       |
| 17 | #AC(0)  |       | #AC(0) |

## Example

```
        VERW    WORD PTR [EBP+8]    ; Check selector on stack
        JZ      CONTINUE            ; Branch if OK
        STC                         ; Set carry flag
        LEAVE                       ; And return if selector is invalid
        RET
CONTINUE:
```

# WAIT

**Wait Until Not Busy** ()

## Syntax

WAIT

## Legal Form

WAIT

## Description

This instruction places the 80386 into an idle state until the BUSY\ pin is inactive. If the BUSY\ pin is inactive when the instruction executes, no idle occurs. The BUSY\ pin is usually connected to a numeric coprocessor. You should execute this instruction before any 80386 instruction that will access a value stored by the coprocessor.

If both the TS (task switched) bit in register CR0 and the MP (monitor coprocessor) bit are set, a coprocessor fault occurs. If the ERROR\ pin of the 80386 is active, indicating an unmasked exception on the coprocessor, a math fault occurs.

The 80486 has no BUSY\ pin because the numeric processor is integrated into the CPU. In the 80486, the WAIT instruction is used to force the floating-point unit to check for unmasked exceptions, the existence of which will cause a math fault.

## Flags

| OF | DF | IF | TF | SF | ZF | | AF | | PF | | CF |
|----|----|----|----|----|----|----|----|----|----|----|----|
| -  | -  | -  | -  | -  | -  | -  | -  | -  | -  | -  | -  |

## Faults

| | PM | | RM | V8086 |
|---|----|----|------|-------|
| 7 | #NM() | | INT 7 | #NM() |
| 16 | #MF() | | INT 16 | #MF() |

## Example

```
FST     result          ; Store floating-point result
WAIT                    ; Wait for coprocessor to finish
PUSH    result          ; Push the result onto the stack
CALL    fp_print        ; Print the value
```

# WBINVD

**80486**

O

## Write-Back and Invalidate Cache

### Syntax

```
WBINVD
```

### Operation

```
Invalidate cache
```

### Legal Form

```
WBINVD
```

### Description

Internal to the 80486, this instruction is indentical to INVD. However, it causes a special "write-back" bus cycle to be issued before the external-cache-flush bus cycle. This allows an external cache to write back its contents to main memory.

### Flags

| OF | DF | IF | TF | SF | ZF | | AF | | PF | | CF |
|----|----|----|----|----|----|----|----|----|----|----|----|
| -  | -  | -  | -  | -  | -  | -  | -  | -  | -  | -  | -  |

### Faults

None.

### Example

```
WBINVD    ; Invalidate and signal external write-back
```

# XADD

**Exchange and Add**

## Syntax

XADD *dest, src*

## Operation

temp ← *dest*
*dest* ← temp + *src*
*src* ← temp

## Legal Forms

|  | dest | src |
|---|---|---|
| XADD reg, reg |  |  |
| XADD | mem, | reg |

## Description

The sum of *dest* and *src* is computed and stored into *dest*. The original value of *dest* is stored into *src*. The flags are set according to the standard rules for an ADD instruction.

When preceded by the LOCK prefix, this instruction is very useful for multiprocessor semaphore operations.

## Flags

| OF | DF | IF | TF | SF | ZF | AF | PF | CF |
|---|---|---|---|---|---|---|---|---|
| X | – | – | – | X | X | X | X | X |

## Faults

| | PM | RM | V8086 |
|---|---|---|---|
| 12 | #SS(0) | | |
| 13 | #GP(0) | INT 13 | #GP(0) |
| 14 | #PF(ec) | | #PF(ec) |
| 17 | #AC(0) | | #AC(0) |

## Example

```
MOV    AL,1      ; Semaphore increment value
XADD   sema,AL   ; Increment
JB     failed    ; Semaphore < 0
```

# XCHG

**Exchange**

## Syntax

XCHG *op1*, *op2*

## Operation

temp ← *op1*
*op1* ← *op2*
*op2* ← temp

## Legal Forms

|      | op1  | op2 |
|------|------|-----|
| XCHG | reg, | reg |
| XCHG | reg, | mem |
| XCHG | mem, | reg |

## Description

This instruction swaps the contents of two operands. If either operand is a memory operand, the bus LOCK\ signal is held active during the read and write memory cycles.

## Flags

| OF | DF | IF | TF | SF | ZF | | AF | | PF | | CF |
|----|----|----|----|----|----|----|----|----|----|----|----|
| -  | -  | -  | -  | -  | -  | -  | -  | -  | -  | -  | -  |

## Faults

|    | PM      | RM     | V8086   |
|----|---------|--------|---------|
| 12 | #SS(0)  |        |         |
| 13 | #GP(0)  | INT 13 | #GP(0)  |
| 14 | #PF(ec) |        | #PF(ec) |
| 17 | #AC(0)  |        | #AC(0)  |

## Examples

```
XCHG    EAX, ECX            ; Swap EAX and ECX
XCHG    AL, [ESI+10]        ; Exchange AL with memory
```

# XLATB

8086/80186/80286/80386/80486

**Translate Byte**

()

## Syntax

XLATB

## Operation

AL ← DS:[EBX+AL]

## Legal Form

XLATB

## Description

This instruction uses the value of AL as a positive index into a table located at DS:EBX. It then stores the indexed table byte in AL, replacing the original value.

You can apply a segment override prefix to XLATB so that the table access location will be at EBX + AL in the specified segment.

## Flags

| OF | DF | IF | TF | SF | ZF | | AF | | PF | | CF |
|----|----|----|----|----|----|----|----|----|----|----|----|
| -  | -  | -  | -  | -  | -  | -  | -  | -  | -  | -  | -  |

## Faults

| | PM | RM | V8086 |
|----|-------|-------|--------|
| 12 | #SS(0) | | |
| 13 | #GP(0) | INT 13 | #GP(0) |
| 14 | #PF(ec) | | #PF(ec) |

## Example

```
        LEA     EBX, A2E_TAB     ; Load offset of ASCII to EBCDIC table
        LDS     ESI, SRC         ; Load source string pointer
        LES     EDI, DEST_BUFF   ; Load destination string pointer
        CLD                      ; Set DF = 0
L1:     LODSB                    ; Get byte of source string
        CS:                      ; Assume translate table resides in CS
        XLATB                    ; Translate byte
        STOSB                    ; Store resulting character
        OR      AL, AL           ; Test for NUL character
        JNZ     L1               ; Loop if not NUL
```

# XOR

**Boolean Exclusive OR**

8086/80186/80286/80386/80486

(8/16p/32)

## Syntax

XOR *dest, src*

## Operation

*dest* ← *dest* ^ *src*

## Legal Forms

|     | dest  | src   |
|-----|-------|-------|
| XOR | reg,  | idata |
| XOR | mem,  | idata |
| XOR | reg,  | reg   |
| XOR | reg,  | mem   |
| XOR | mem,  | reg   |

## Description

This instruction performs a bit-by-bit exclusive OR operation on the *src* and *dest* operands, storing the result in the *dest* operand. The XOR operation is defined as follows:

$0 \wedge 0 = 0$

$0 \wedge 1 = 1$

$1 \wedge 0 = 1$

$1 \wedge 1 = 0$

## Flags

| OF | DF | IF | TF | SF | ZF |   | AF |   | PF |   | CF |
|----|----|----|----|----|----|---|----|---|----|---|----|
| 0  | -  | -  | -  | x  | x  | - | ?  | - | x  | - | 0  |

## Faults

|    | *PM*    | *RM*   | *V8086* |
|----|---------|--------|---------|
| 12 | #SS(0)  |        |         |
| 13 | #GP(0)  | INT 13 | #GP(0)  |
| 14 | #PF(ec) |        | #PF(ec) |
| 17 | #AC(0)  |        | #AC(0)  |

## Examples

```
XOR     AL, OFFH        ; Change 0s to 1s and vice versa in AL
XOR     EBX, ECX        ; Compute EBX ← EBX ^ ECX
```

# Floating-Point Instruction Set

The floating-point instruction set adds support for arithmetic functions using real numbers. The 80386 cannot directly execute floating-point instructions. However, when coupled with the 80387 numeric coprocessor, the instruction set is extended to include the instructions that are described on the following pages. The 80486 requires no coprocessor, and it can directly execute any instruction marked for the 80387.

**PROCESSOR TYPE**
*Processors that support the instruction.*

**MNEMONIC**
*Used by the assembler to represent the instruction.*

**NAME**
*Name of instruction.*

**LEGAL FORMS**
*Legal forms of the instruction.*

**DESCRIPTION**
*Description of the instruction.* mem = *memory operand.*

**EXCEPTIONS**
*An "x" in a box indicates that the specified exception may be generated for the instruction. A "-" in a box indicates that the specified exception is not possible. SF = Stack fault. PE = Precision exception. UE = Underflow exception. OE = Overflow exception. ZE = Zero divide exception. DE = Denormal exception. IE = Invalid operation exception.*

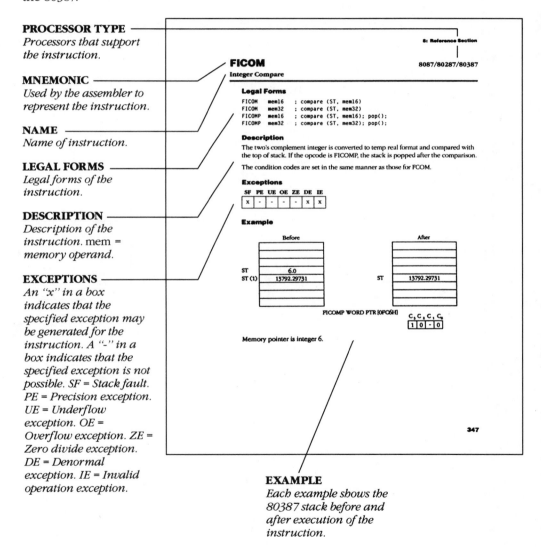

**EXAMPLE**
*Each example shows the 80387 stack before and after execution of the instruction.*

# FABS

**Absolute Value**

8087/80287/80387

## Legal Form

```
FABS        ; If (ST < 0) then ST ← ST * -1
```

## Description

This instruction replaces the original value of the element at the top of stack with its absolute value.

## Exceptions

| SF | PE | UE | OE | ZE | DE | IE |
|----|----|----|----|----|----|----|
| X  | –  | –  | –  | –  | –  | –  |

## Example

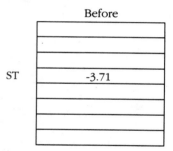

ST       -3.71                    ST       3.71

Before                           After

FABS

# FADD

**Addition**

## Legal Forms

```
FADD                    ; ST(1) ← ST + ST(1); pop();
FADD    mem32           ; ST ← ST + mem32
FADD    mem64           ; ST ← ST + mem64
FADD    ST(n)           ; ST ← ST + ST(n)
FADD    ST, ST(n)       ; ST ← ST + ST(n)
FADD    ST(n), ST       ; ST(n) ← ST(n) + ST
FADDP   ST, ST(n)       ; ST ← ST + ST(n); pop();
FADDP   ST(n), ST       ; ST(n) ← ST(n) + ST; pop();
```

## Description

This instruction adds the specified floating-point operands and optionally pops the top of stack.

If you specify a memory operand, it is converted to temp real (80-bit) format before it is added to the top of stack.

If you add a floating-point value to infinity, the result is the original infinity. If you add two infinities, they must have the same sign, and the result is the same infinity.

## Exceptions

| SF | PE | UE | OE | ZE | DE | IE |
|----|----|----|----|----|----|----|
| x  | x  | x  | x  | -  | x  | x  |

## Examples

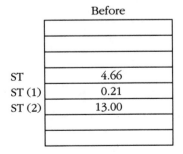

Before

| | |
|---|---|
| ST | 4.66 |
| ST (1) | 0.21 |
| ST (2) | 13.00 |

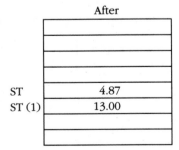

After

| | |
|---|---|
| ST | 4.87 |
| ST (1) | 13.00 |

FADD

|  | Before |
|---|---|
| ST | 4.66 |
| ST (1) | 0.21 |
| ST (2) | 13.00 |

|  | After |
|---|---|
| ST | 4.66 |
| ST (1) | 0.21 |
| ST (2) | 17.66 |

FADD ST (2), ST

# FBLD

BCD Load

## Legal Form

```
FBLD    mem80   ; push(float(mem80))
```

## Description

This instruction converts an 80-bit, 19-digit BCD integer to a temp real and pushes it onto the stack. If the memory operand is not a valid BCD integer, an undefined value is pushed onto the stack.

## Exceptions

| SF | PE | UE | OE | ZE | DE | IE |
|----|----|----|----|----|----|----|
| x  | -  | -  | -  | -  | -  | -  |

## Example

|       | Before |
|-------|--------|
|       |        |
|       |        |
|       |        |
| ST    | 102.08 |
|       |        |
|       |        |
|       |        |
|       |        |

|        | After  |
|--------|--------|
|        |        |
|        |        |
| ST     | 17.00  |
| ST (1) | 102.08 |
|        |        |
|        |        |
|        |        |
|        |        |

FBLD [ESI]

ESI points to 17 BCD.

# FBSTP

**BCD Store and Pop**

## Legal Form

```
FBSTP    mem80    ; mem80 ← BCD(ST); pop();
```

## Description

This instruction rounds the top of stack to an integer, stores in memory in BCD format, and then pops the stack.

Unlike most arithmetic operations, FBSTP signals the invalid (I) exception if either operand is a quiet NaN.

## Exceptions

| SF | PE | UE | OE | ZE | DE | IE |
|----|----|----|----|----|----|----|
| x  | -  | -  | -  | -  | -  | x  |

## Example

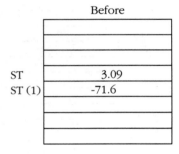

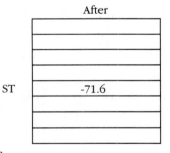

FBSTP [0A2H]

BCD 3 is stored in memory.

# FCHS

**Change Sign**

## Legal Form

FCHS                    ; ST ← ST * -1

## Description

This instruction complements the sign bit of the top of stack.

## Exceptions

| SF | PE | UE | OE | ZE | DE | IE |
|----|----|----|----|----|----|----|
| X  | -  | -  | -  | -  | -  | -  |

## Example

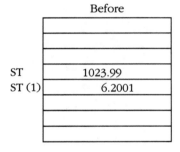
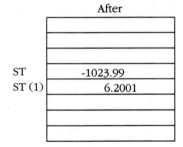

Before

| ST | 1023.99 |
| ST (1) | 6.2001 |

After

| ST | -1023.99 |
| ST (1) | 6.2001 |

FCHS

# FCLEX

**Clear Exceptions**

## Legal Forms

```
FCLEX        ; SW ← SW & 07F00H
FNCLEX       ; SW ← SW & 07F00H
```

## Description

This instruction clears the exception flags in the status word and the busy bit to 0. The FCLEX form of the instruction checks for unmasked exceptions from previous operations before clearing the status word. The FNCLEX form clears the SW bit without checking.

## Exceptions

| SF | PE | UE | OE | ZE | DE | IE |
|----|----|----|----|----|----|----|
| -  | -  | -  | -  | -  | -  | -  |

# FCOM

Compare

---

## Legal Forms

```
FCOM               ; compare ST, ST(1)
FCOM     mem32     ; compare (ST, mem32)
FCOM     mem64     ; compare (ST, mem64)
FCOM     ST(n)     ; compare (ST, ST(n))
FCOMP    mem32     ; compare (ST, mem32); pop();
FCOMP    mem64     ; compare (ST, mem64); pop();
FCOMP    ST(n)     ; compare (ST, ST(n)); pop();
FCOMPP             ; compare (ST, ST(1)); pop(); pop();
```

## Description

This instruction performs the function *compare (op1, op2)* and sets the numeric condition code according to the result of the comparison. The floating-point stack is optionally popped once or twice.

The following table shows the condition code settings that result from the compare function. FCOM considers +0.0 and −0.0 to be equal.

| Condition | C3 | C2 | C1 | C0 |
|-----------|----|----|----|----|
| *op1 > op2* | 0 | 0 | - | 0 |
| *op1 < op2* | 0 | 0 | - | 1 |
| *op1 = op2* | 1 | 0 | - | 0 |
| either *op* is a NaN | 1 | 1 | - | 1 |

The numeric condition codes are arranged in the status word so that C3, C2, and C0 map into the same bit positions as the ZF, PF, and CF bits of the EFLAGS register. Thus, issuing the following instructions sets the EFLAGS register as if the compare had been performed on the integer values.

```
FCOM     op                 ; Floating point compare
FSTSW    AX                 ; Store status word to AX
SAHF                        ; Store AH into flags
```

You can then use any conditional jump instruction (JE, JNE, JA, JAE, JB, or JBE) to branch on the result of the compare. You can use JP to test for NaN operands.

Unlike most arithmetic operations, FCOM signals the invalid (I) exception if either operand is a quiet NaN.

## Exceptions

| SF | PE | UE | OE | ZE | DE | IE |
|----|----|----|----|----|----|----|
| x | - | - | - | - | x | x |

## Examples

| Before | |
|---|---|
| | |
| | |
| | |
| ST | 21.0 |
| ST (1) | 6.0 |
| ST (2) | 0.1114 |
| | |
| | |

| After | |
|---|---|
| | |
| | |
| | |
| ST | -21.0 |
| ST (1) | 6.0 |
| ST (2) | 0.1114 |
| | |
| | |

FCOM ST (2)

| Before | |
|---|---|
| | |
| | |
| | |
| ST | -21.0 |
| ST (1) | 6.0 |
| ST (2) | 0.1114 |
| | |
| | |

| After | |
|---|---|
| | |
| | |
| | |
| | |
| | |
| ST | 0.1114 |
| | |
| | |

FCOMPP

# FCOS

Cosine

---

## Legal Form

```
FCOS            ; ST ← cos(ST)
```

## Description

This instruction computes the cosine of the value in radians at the top of stack and replaces ST with cosine.

The operand processed by FCOS must be a value between $\pm 2^{63}$ or the instruction does not execute and condition code C2 is set to 1. C2 is cleared to 0 if the instruction is executed.

## Exceptions

| SF | PE | UE | OE | ZE | DE | IE |
|----|----|----|----|----|----|----|
| x  | x  | x  | –  | –  | x  | x  |

## Example

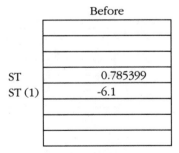

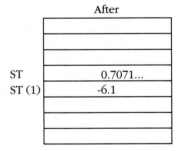

Before

| | |
|---|---|
| ST | 0.785399 |
| ST (1) | -6.1 |

After

| | |
|---|---|
| ST | 0.7071... |
| ST (1) | -6.1 |

FCOS

# FDECSTP

8087/80287/80387

**Decrement Stack Pointer**

### Legal Form

```
FDECSTP          ; TOP ← (TOP - 1) & 07H
```

### Description

This instruction allows you to manipulate the floating-point stack pointer. Issuing FDECSTP is equivalent to pushing a new value onto the stack, but no value is supplied. The tag registers are not modified.

### Exceptions

| SF | PE | UE | OE | ZE | DE | IE |
|----|----|----|----|----|----|----|
| -  | -  | -  | -  | -  | -  | -  |

### Example

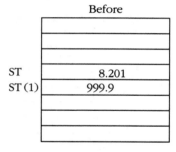

Before

|       |
|-------|
|       |
|       |
|       |
| ST    8.201 |
| ST (1)  999.9 |
|       |
|       |
|       |

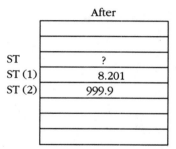

After

|       |
|-------|
|       |
|       |
| ST     ? |
| ST (1)  8.201 |
| ST (2)  999.9 |
|       |
|       |
|       |

FDECSTP

# FDIV

**Division**

## Legal Forms

| | | |
|---|---|---|
| FDIV | | ST(1) ← ST(1) / ST; pop(); |
| FDIV | mem32 | ST ← ST / mem32 |
| FDIV | mem64 | ST ← ST / mem64 |
| FDIV | ST(n) | ST ← ST / ST(n) |
| FDIV | ST, ST(n) | ST ← ST / ST(n) |
| FDIV | ST(n), ST | ST(n) ← ST(n) / ST |
| FDIVP | ST, ST(n) | ST ← ST / ST(n); pop(); |
| FDIVP | ST(n), ST | ST(n) ← ST(n) / ST; pop (); |

## Description

This instruction executes a divide operation with the above operands. If you specify a memory operand, it is converted to temp real (80-bit) format before the division is performed. A stack pop operation is performed if specified by the opcode.

Division by infinity results in 0. Infinity divided by a real number results in infinity. Infinity divided by infinity is not a valid operation.

## Exceptions

| SF | PE | UE | OE | ZE | DE | IE |
|----|----|----|----|----|----|----|
| x | x | x | x | x | x | x |

## Examples

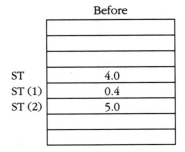

Before

| | |
|---|---|
| | |
| | |
| | |
| ST | 4.0 |
| ST (1) | 0.4 |
| ST (2) | 5.0 |
| | |
| | |

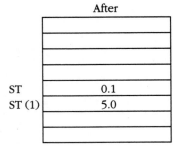

After

| | |
|---|---|
| | |
| | |
| | |
| ST | 0.1 |
| ST (1) | 5.0 |
| | |
| | |

FDIV

341

| | Before |
|---|---|
| | |
| | |
| | |
| ST | 4.0 |
| ST (1) | 0.4 |
| ST (2) | 5.0 |
| | |
| | |

| | After |
|---|---|
| | |
| | |
| | |
| ST | 4.0 |
| ST (1) | 0.4 |
| ST (2) | 1.25 |
| | |
| | |

FDIV ST(2), ST

# FDIVR

**Division Reversed**

## Legal Forms

```
FDIVR                    ST(1) ← ST / ST(1); pop();
FDIVR       mem32        ST ← mem32 / ST
FDIVR       mem64        ST ← mem64 / ST
FDIVR       ST(n)        ST ← ST(n) / ST
FDIVR       ST, ST(n)    ST ← ST(n) / ST
FDIVR       ST(n), ST    ST(n) ← ST / ST(n)
FDIVRP      ST, ST(n)    ST ← ST(n) / ST; pop();
FDIVRP      ST(n), ST    ST(n) ← ST / ST(n); pop ();
```

## Description

This instruction executes a divide operation with the above operands. This instruction is equivalent to FDIV, but the divisor and dividend operands are exchanged. If you specify a memory operand, it is converted to temp real (80-bit) format before the division is performed. A stack pop operation is performed if specified by the opcode.

Division by infinity results in 0. Infinity divided by a real number results in infinity. Infinity divided by infinity is not a valid operation.

## Exceptions

| SF | PE | UE | OE | ZE | DE | IE |
|----|----|----|----|----|----|----|
| x  | x  | x  | x  | x  | x  | x  |

## Examples

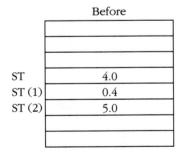

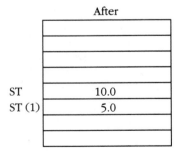

FDIVR

| Before | | |
|---|---|---|
| | | |
| | | |
| | | |
| ST | | 4.0 |
| ST (1) | | 0.4 |
| ST (2) | | 5.0 |
| | | |
| | | |

| After | | |
|---|---|---|
| | | |
| | | |
| | | |
| ST | | 4.0 |
| ST (1) | | 0.4 |
| ST (2) | | 0.8 |
| | | |
| | | |

FDIVR ST(2), ST

# FFREE

**8087/80287/80387**

**Free NDP Register**

## Legal Form

FFREE   ST(n)   ; TW(n) ← UNUSED

## Description

This instruction marks the specified stack element as unused by setting the tag word for the corresponding floating-point register. The stack pointer is not modified, nor is the actual content of the NDP register.

## Exceptions

| SF | PE | UE | OE | ZE | DE | IE |
|----|----|----|----|----|----|----|
| -  | -  | -  | -  | -  | -  | -  |

## Example

|   | Before |
|---|--------|
| ST | 190000.3 |
| ST (1) | -7.7 |
| ST (2) | 0.001 |

|   | After |
|---|-------|
| ST | 190000.3 |
| ST (1) | \<unused\> |
| ST (2) | 0.001 |

FFREE ST(1)

# FIADD

**Integer Addition**

## Legal Forms

```
FIADD    mem16    ; ST ← ST + float(mem16)
FIADD    mem32    ; ST ← ST + float(mem32)
```

## Description

This instruction converts the two's complement integer at the specified address to temp real format and adds it to the top of stack. Other than the difference in operand type, this instruction is equivalent to FADD.

## Exceptions

| SF | PE | UE | OE | ZE | DE | IE |
|----|----|----|----|----|----|----|
| X  | X  | X  | X  | -  | X  | X  |

## Example

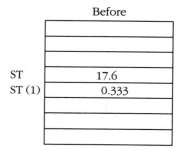
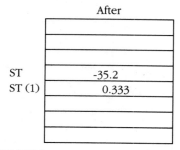

Before | After

ST 17.6 | ST -35.2
ST (1) 0.333 | ST (1) 0.333

FIADD WORD PTR [ECX]

ECX points to integer -2.

# FICOM

## Integer Compare

### Legal Forms

```
FICOM    mem16    ; compare (ST, mem16)
FICOM    mem32    ; compare (ST, mem32)
FICOMP   mem16    ; compare (ST, mem16); pop();
FICOMP   mem32    ; compare (ST, mem32); pop();
```

### Description

The two's complement integer is converted to temp real format and compared with the top of stack. If the opcode is FICOMP, the stack is popped after the comparison.

The condition codes are set in the same manner as those for FCOM.

### Exceptions

| SF | PE | UE | OE | ZE | DE | IE |
|----|----|----|----|----|----|----|
| x  | –  | –  | –  | –  | x  | x  |

### Example

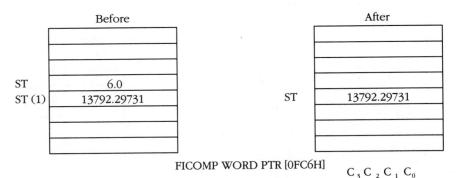

Before

| | |
|---|---|
| | |
| | |
| ST | 6.0 |
| ST (1) | 13792.29731 |
| | |
| | |

After

| | |
|---|---|
| | |
| | |
| ST | 13792.29731 |
| | |
| | |
| | |

FICOMP WORD PTR [0FC6H]

| $C_3$ | $C_2$ | $C_1$ | $C_0$ |
|----|----|----|----|
| 1  | 0  | –  | 0  |

Memory pointer is integer 6.

# FIDIV

**Integer Division**

## Legal Forms

```
FIDIV    mem16    ; ST ← ST / real(mem16)
FIDIV    mem32    ; ST ← ST / real(mem32)
```

## Description

This instruction fetches the two's complement integer from memory, converts it to temp real format, and uses it as a divisor of the top of stack. The results generated by this instruction are the same as those generated by the FDIV instruction.

## Exceptions

| SF | PE | UE | OE | ZE | DE | IE |
|----|----|----|----|----|----|----|
| X  | X  | X  | X  | X  | X  | X  |

## Example

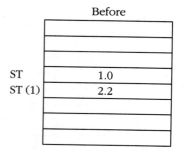

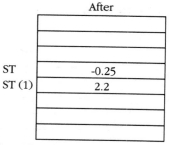

FIDIV DWORD PTR [EBP+16]

Memory pointer is integer -4.

# FIDIVR

**8087/80287/80387**

**Integer Division Reversed**

## Legal Forms

```
FIDIVR   mem16    ; ST ← real(mem16) / ST
FIDIVR   mem32    ; ST ← real(mem32) / ST
```

## Description

This instruction converts the two's complement integer at the specified memory location to temp real format and divides it by the top of stack. The results generated by this instruction are the same as those generated by the FDIVR instruction.

## Exceptions

| SF | PE | UE | OE | ZE | DE | IE |
|----|----|----|----|----|----|----|
| x | x | x | x | x | x | x |

## Example

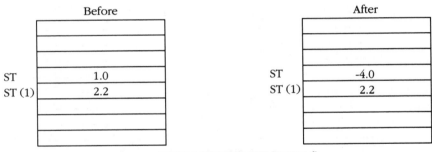

| Before | |
|--------|--|
| ST | 1.0 |
| ST (1) | 2.2 |

| After | |
|-------|--|
| ST | -4.0 |
| ST (1) | 2.2 |

FIDIVR DWORD PTR [EBP+16]

Memory pointer is integer -4.

# FILD

**Integer Load**

## Legal Forms

```
FILD    mem16    ; push (float (mem16))
FILD    mem32    ; push (float (mem32))
FILD    mem64    ; push (float (mem64))
```

## Description

This instruction converts a two's complement integer to temp real format and pushes the value onto the 80387 stack.

## Exceptions

| SF | PE | UE | OE | ZE | DE | IE |
|----|----|----|----|----|----|----|
| X  | -  | -  | -  | -  | -  | -  |

## Example

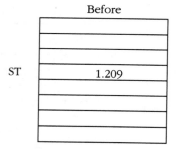
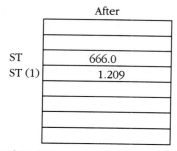

Before

ST  1.209

After

ST  666.0
ST (1)  1.209

FILD QWORD PTR [EAX]

Memory pointer is integer 666.

# FIMUL

### Integer Multiplication

## Legal Forms

```
FIMUL    mem16    ; ST ← ST * real(mem16)
FIMUL    mem32    ; ST ← ST * real(mem32)
```

## Description

This instruction converts the two's complement integer at the specified memory location to temp real format and multiplies it by the top of stack. The results of this instruction are identical to those obtained by FMUL.

## Exceptions

| SF | PE | UE | OE | ZE | DE | IE |
|----|----|----|----|----|----|----|
| x  | x  | x  | x  | -  | x  | x  |

## Example

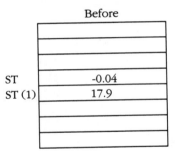
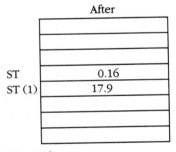

FIMUL WORD PTR [ESI+EAX]

Memory pointer is integer -4.

# FINCSTP

## Increment Stack Pointer

### Legal Forms

```
FINCSTP      ; TOP ← (TOP + 1) & 07H
```

### Description

This instruction increments the TOP field in the floating-point status word. The contents of the floating-point register previously at the top of stack and the register's associated tag word are not affected.

### Exceptions

| SF | PE | UE | OE | ZE | DE | IE |
|----|----|----|----|----|----|----|
| -  | -  | -  | -  | -  | -  | -  |

### Example

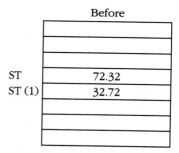

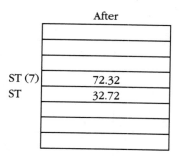

FINCSTP

# FINIT

**Initialize NDP**

## Legal Forms

```
FINIT        ; CW ← 037FH; SW ← SW & 4700H; TW ← 0FFFFH
FNINIT       ; CW ← 037FH; SW ← SW & 4700H; TW ← 0FFFFH
```

## Description

This instruction sets the FPU state to its default value. All registers are marked unused, all exceptions are masked, rounding control is set to nearest, and the operating mode is set to double-precision.

The FINIT instruction tests for any unmasked exception before clearing the NDP state, unlike FNINIT, which does not. Consequently, the first floating-point instruction of an application should be FNINIT.

## Exceptions

| SF | PE | UE | OE | ZE | DE | IE |
|----|----|----|----|----|----|----|
| -  | -  | -  | -  | -  | -  | -  |

# FIST

8087/80287/80387

**Integer Store**

## Legal Forms

```
FIST    mem16   ; mem16 ← int(ST)
FIST    mem32   ; mem32 ← int(ST)
FISTP   mem16   ; mem16 ← int(ST); pop();
FISTP   mem32   ; mem32 ← int(ST); pop();
FISTP   mem64   ; mem64 ← int(ST); pop();
```

## Description

This instruction rounds the current top of stack to an integer according to the control bits and stores the value in the specified operand. If the opcode is FISTP, the stack is popped after the store operation. Note that the sign of a floating-point 0 is lost upon conversion to the two's complement integer format.

Two differences exist between FIST and FISTP. The FISTP instruction, which pops the stack after the store operation, can store a 64-bit integer; FIST cannot. The FIST instruction generates an invalid operation exception if the top of stack is a quiet NaN; FISTP does not.

## Exceptions

| SF | PE | UE | OE | ZE | DE | IE |
|----|----|----|----|----|----|----|
| X  | X  | -  | -  | -  | -  | X  |

## Example

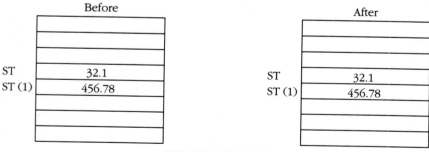

FIST DWORD PTR [EBP+42]

Integer 32 stored into memory.

# FISUB

### Integer Subtraction

## Legal Forms

```
FISUB    mem16    ; ST ← ST - real(mem16)
FISUB    mem32    ; ST ← ST - real(mem32)
```

## Description

This instruction converts the two's complement integer at the specified memory location to temp real format and subtracts it from the top of stack. The results of this instruction are identical to those obtained by FSUB.

## Exceptions

| SF | PE | UE | OE | ZE | DE | IE |
|----|----|----|----|----|----|----|
| x  | x  | x  | x  | -  | x  | x  |

## Example

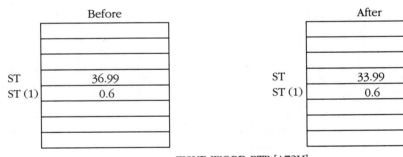

| | Before |
|---|---|
| | |
| | |
| ST | 36.99 |
| ST (1) | 0.6 |
| | |
| | |
| | |

| | After |
|---|---|
| | |
| | |
| ST | 33.99 |
| ST (1) | 0.6 |
| | |
| | |
| | |

FISUB WORD PTR [A72H]

Memory pointer is integer 3.

# FISUBR

**Integer Subtraction Reversed**

## Legal Forms

```
FISUBR   mem16    ; ST ← real(mem16) - ST
FISUBR   mem32    ; ST ← real(mem32) - ST
```

## Description

This instruction converts the two's complement integer at the specified memory location to temp real format and subtracts the top of stack from it. The results of this instruction are identical to those obtained by FSUBR.

## Exceptions

| SF | PE | UE | OE | ZE | DE | IE |
|----|----|----|----|----|----|----|
| X  | X  | X  | X  | -  | X  | X  |

## Example

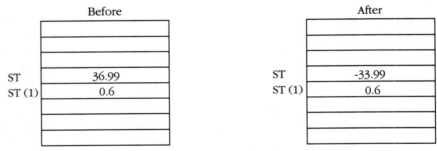

| | Before |
|---|---|
| | |
| | |
| | |
| ST | 36.99 |
| ST (1) | 0.6 |
| | |
| | |

| | After |
|---|---|
| | |
| | |
| | |
| ST | -33.99 |
| ST (1) | 0.6 |
| | |
| | |

FISUBR WORD PTR [A72H]

Memory pointer is integer 3.

# FLD

8087/80287/80387

Load Real

## Legal Forms

```
FLD     mem32    ; push(mem32)
FLD     mem64    ; push(mem64)
FLD     mem80    ; push(mem80)
FLD     ST(n)    ; push(ST(n))
```

## Description

This instruction pushes a copy of the specified operand onto the floating-point stack. If you specify a 32-bit or 64-bit floating-point memory operand, it is converted to temp real format before being stored.

If the operand is a single- or double-precision value, the FPU might generate a denormal exception. A denormal exception is not generated by a value already in temp real format.

## Exceptions

| SF | PE | UE | OE | ZE | DE | IE |
|----|----|----|----|----|----|----|
| x  | -  | -  | -  | -  | x  | x  |

## Example

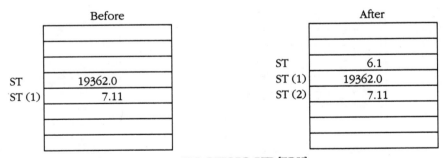

| | Before |
|----|--------|
| | |
| | |
| | |
| ST | 19362.0 |
| ST (1) | 7.11 |
| | |
| | |

| | After |
|----|--------|
| | |
| | |
| ST | 6.1 |
| ST (1) | 19362.0 |
| ST (2) | 7.11 |
| | |
| | |

FLD DWORD PTR [EDX]

Memory pointer is short real 6.1.

357

# FLDconst

## Load *Constant*

## Legal Forms

```
FLD1        ; push(1.0)
FLDL2E      ; push(log2(e))
FLDL2T      ; push(log2(10))
FLDLG2      ; push(log10(2))
FLDLN2      ; push(ln(2))
FLDPI       ; push(PI)
FLDZ        ; push(+0.0)
```

## Description

This instruction pushes the constant value specified by the opcode onto the stack. The function ln stands for log base *e*.

## Exceptions

| SF | PE | UE | OE | ZE | DE | IE |
|----|----|----|----|----|----|----|
| x  | -  | -  | -  | -  | -  | -  |

## Example

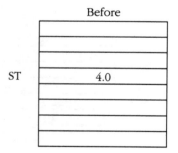

Before

ST    4.0

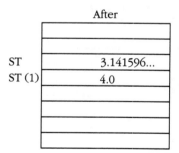

After

ST    3.141596...
ST (1)    4.0

FLDPI

# FLDCW

**8087/80287/80387**

## Load Control Word

## Legal Form

```
FLDCW    mem16    ; CW ← mem16
```

## Description

This instruction loads a new value for the control word from memory. FLDCW can unmask previously masked exceptions, triggering an unmasked exception.

## Exceptions

| SF | PE | UE | OE | ZE | DE | IE |
|----|----|----|----|----|----|----|
| x  | x  | x  | x  | x  | x  | x  |

# FLDENV

8087/80287/80387

Load Environment

## Legal Form

```
FLDENV    memp      ; NDP ← memp
```

## Description

This instruction loads the 28-byte block pointed to by *memp* into the environment registers of the FPU. The memory operand contains a new control word, status word, tag word, and error block. The memory format for the environment is shown in Figure 8-1.

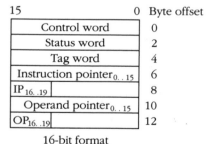

| 31 | 16 | 15 | 0 | Byte offset |
|---|---|---|---|---|
| Reserved | | Control word | | 0 |
| Reserved | | Status word | | 4 |
| Reserved | | Tag word | | 8 |
| Error offset (EIP) | | | | 12 |
| Reserved | | Error selector (CS) | | 16 |
| Data operand offset | | | | 20 |
| Reserved | | Data selector | | 24 |

32-bit format

| 15 | 0 | Byte offset |
|---|---|---|
| Control word | | 0 |
| Status word | | 2 |
| Tag word | | 4 |
| Instruction pointer$_{0..15}$ | | 6 |
| IP$_{16..19}$ | | 8 |
| Operand pointer$_{0..15}$ | | 10 |
| OP$_{16..19}$ | | 12 |

16-bit format

**Figure 8-1.** *Floating-point environment.*

Loading a new status word and control word can cause an unmasked exception.

## Exceptions

| SF | PE | UE | OE | ZE | DE | IE |
|---|---|---|---|---|---|---|
| x | x | x | x | x | x | x |

# FMUL

**Multiplication**

## Legal Forms

```
FMUL                    ; ST(1) ← ST(1) * ST; pop();
FMUL        mem32       ; ST ← ST * mem32
FMUL        mem64       ; ST ← ST * mem64
FMUL        ST(n)       ; ST ← ST * ST(n)
FMUL        ST, ST(n)   ; ST ← ST * ST(n)
FMUL        ST(n), ST   ; ST(n) ← ST(n) * ST
FMULP       ST, ST(n)   ; ST ← ST * ST(n); pop();
FMULP       ST(n), ST   ; ST(n) ← ST(n) * ST; pop();
```

## Description

This instruction multiplies the specified operands and stores them as indicated above. If you specify 32-bit or 64-bit memory operands, they are converted to temp real format before the multiplication takes place. If the opcode specifies, the stack is popped after the operation.

Multiplying any value other than 0 by infinity results in infinity. Multiplying 0 by infinity is an invalid operation.

## Exceptions

| SF | PE | UE | OE | ZE | DE | IE |
|----|----|----|----|----|----|----|
| x  | x  | x  | x  | -  | x  | x  |

## Examples

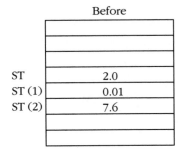

Before

| | |
|---|---|
| | |
| | |
| | |
| ST | 2.0 |
| ST (1) | 0.01 |
| ST (2) | 7.6 |
| | |
| | |

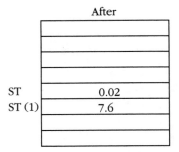

After

| | |
|---|---|
| | |
| | |
| | |
| ST | 0.02 |
| ST (1) | 7.6 |
| | |
| | |

FMUL

| Before | | After | |
|---|---|---|---|
| | | | |
| | | | |
| | | | |
| ST | 2.0 | ST | 0.02 |
| ST (1) | 0.01 | ST (1) | 0.01 |
| ST (2) | 7.6 | ST (2) | 7.6 |
| | | | |
| | | | |

FMUL ST(1)

# FNOP

**8087/80287/80387**

## No Operation

---

## Legal Form

FNOP

## Description

FNOP is an alias for the FST ST, ST instruction. It does nothing.

## Exceptions

| SF | PE | UE | OE | ZE | DE | IE |
|----|----|----|----|----|----|----|
| -  | -  | -  | -  | -  | -  | -  |

## Example

<table>
<tr><td colspan="2" align="center">Before</td></tr>
<tr><td></td><td></td></tr>
<tr><td></td><td></td></tr>
<tr><td></td><td></td></tr>
<tr><td>ST</td><td align="center">3.3</td></tr>
<tr><td>ST (1)</td><td align="center">19.6</td></tr>
<tr><td></td><td></td></tr>
<tr><td></td><td></td></tr>
<tr><td></td><td></td></tr>
</table>

<table>
<tr><td colspan="2" align="center">After</td></tr>
<tr><td></td><td></td></tr>
<tr><td></td><td></td></tr>
<tr><td></td><td></td></tr>
<tr><td>ST</td><td align="center">3.3</td></tr>
<tr><td>ST (1)</td><td align="center">19.6</td></tr>
<tr><td></td><td></td></tr>
<tr><td></td><td></td></tr>
<tr><td></td><td></td></tr>
</table>

FNOP

# FPATAN

## Partial Arctangent

### Legal Form

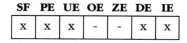

```
FPATAN              ; ST(1) ← atan(ST(1) / ST); pop();
```

### Description

This instruction computes the arctangent in radians of ST(1) ÷ ST. The mnemonic "partial arctangent" is inherited from earlier NDPs, which placed restrictions on the values of ST and ST(1). These values are not restricted on the 80387 or 80486.

### Exceptions

| SF | PE | UE | OE | ZE | DE | IE |
|----|----|----|----|----|----|----|
| x  | x  | x  | -  | -  | x  | x  |

### Example

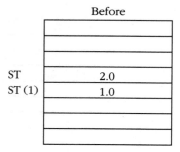

Before

| | |
|---|---|
| | |
| | |
| ST | 2.0 |
| ST (1) | 1.0 |
| | |
| | |
| | |

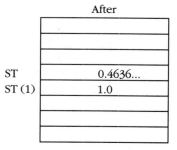

After

| | |
|---|---|
| | |
| | |
| ST | 0.4636... |
| ST (1) | 1.0 |
| | |
| | |
| | |

FPATAN

# FPREM

**Partial Remainder**

## Legal Form

```
FPREM           ; ST ← remainder (ST / ST(1))
```

## Description

This instruction uses repeated subtractions to compute the remainder of ST divided by ST(1). Because this operation could require a large number of iterations (during which time the NDP would be inaccessible), the instruction halts after producing a partial remainder. The value in ST is reduced by a factor of up to $2^{64}$ in a single iteration.

If the remainder is a partial value (that is, the operation does not complete), the C2 status bit is set to 1. If the remainder is less than the value of ST(1), the operation is complete and bit C2 is cleared to 0. By testing the value of C2, the FPREM instruction may be executed repeatedly until the remainder operation yields an exact result. Additionally, when the instruction is complete (C2 = 0), the three least significant bits of the quotient of ST ÷ ST(1) can be computed by the following formula:

$$Q = C0 \times 4 + C3 \times 2 + C1$$

where C0, C1, and C3 are the remaining status bits.

The FPREM instruction reduces operands for the transcendental functions to legal values. For example, the operand to F2XM1 must be $-1 \le ST \le 1$. FPREM produces an exact result, and the precision control and rounding control bits are ignored during execution.

The FPREM1 instruction produces the IEEE-754 standard partial remainder value, which may be different from FPREM when there are two integers equally close to ST ÷ ST(1). FPREM rounds toward 0, and FPREM1 chooses the even value.

## Exceptions

| SF | PE | UE | OE | ZE | DE | IE |
|----|----|----|----|----|----|----|
| -  | -  | -  | -  | -  | -  | -  |

## Example

|  | Before |
|---|---|
|  |  |
|  |  |
|  |  |
| ST | 6 |
| ST (1) | 4 |
|  |  |
|  |  |
|  |  |

|  | After |
|---|---|
|  |  |
|  |  |
|  |  |
| ST | 2 |
| ST (1) | 4 |
|  |  |
|  |  |
|  |  |

FPREM

C2 = 0

# FPREM1

80387

**IEEE Partial Remainder**

## Legal Form

FPREM1          ; ST ← remainder (ST ÷ ST(1))

## Description

This instruction uses repeated subtractions to compute the remainder of ST divided by ST(1). Because this operation could require a large number of iterations (during which time the NDP would be inaccessible), the instruction halts after producing a partial remainder. The value in ST is reduced by a factor of up to $2^{64}$ in a single iteration.

If the remainder is a partial value (that is, the operation is not complete), the C2 status bit is set to 1. If the remainder is less than the value of ST(1), the operation is complete and bit C2 is cleared to 0. By testing the value of C2, the FPREM1 instruction may be executed repeatedly until the remainder operations yield an exact result. Additionally, when the instruction is complete (C2 = 0), the three least significant bits of the quotient of ST ÷ ST(1) can be computed by the following formula:

$$Q = C0 \times 4 + C3 \times 2 + C1$$

where C0, C1, and C3 are the remaining status bits.

The FPREM1 instruction reduces operands for the transcendental functions of the 80387 to legal values. For example, the operand to F2XM1 must be $-1 \leq ST \leq 1$. FPREM1 always produces an exact result, and the precision control and rounding control bits are ignored during execution.

The FPREM1 instruction produces the IEEE-754 standard partial remainder value, which may be different from FPREM when there are two integers equally close to ST ÷ ST(1). FPREM always rounds toward 0, and FPREM1 always chooses the even value.

## Exceptions

| SF | PE | UE | OE | ZE | DE | IE |
|----|----|----|----|----|----|----|
| X  | -  | X  | -  | -  | X  | X  |

## Example

| | Before | | | After | |
|---|---|---|---|---|---|
| | | | | | |
| | | | | | |
| | | | | | |
| ST | 6.0 | | ST | 2.0 | |
| ST (1) | 4.0 | | ST (1) | 4.0 | |
| | | | | | |
| | | | | | |
| | | | | | |

FPREM1                     C2=0

# FPTAN

**Partial Tangent**

## Legal Form

```
FPTAN                ; ST ← tan(ST); push(1.0);
```

## Description

This instruction computes the tangent of the top of stack and arranges the NDP stack such that:

$$\frac{ST(1)}{ST} = \tan \text{ (original ST)}$$

The denominator is always 1.0 after the FPTAN instruction.

The operand value must be a positive number that is expressed in radians less than $PI \times 2^{62}$, or no operation takes place and the C2 condition code bit is set to 1. If the input operand is legal, C2 is cleared to 0.

## Exceptions

| SF | PE | UE | OE | ZE | DE | IE |
|----|----|----|----|----|----|----|
| X  | X  | X  | –  | –  | X  | X  |

## Example

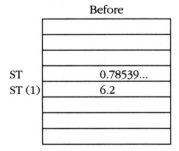

FPTAN

# FRNDINT

**Round to Integer**

## Legal Form

```
FRNDINT          ; ST ← int(ST)
```

## Description

This instruction rounds the value at the top of stack to an integer based on the settings of the round control (RC) field in the control word. See Chapter 2 for a discussion of the NDP rounding modes.

## Exceptions

| SF | PE | UE | OE | ZE | DE | IE |
|----|----|----|----|----|----|----|
| x | x | - | - | - | x | x |

## Example

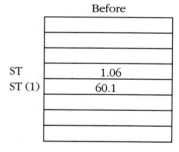

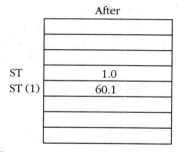

FRNDINT

# FRSTOR

8087/80287/80387

**Restore NDP State**

## Legal Form

```
FRSTOR  memp    ; NDP ← memp
```

## Description

This instruction loads the entire floating-point processor state from the 108-byte block of data beginning at *memp*. Use the FSAVE instruction to store the NDP state. Figure 8-2 shows the format of the state block.

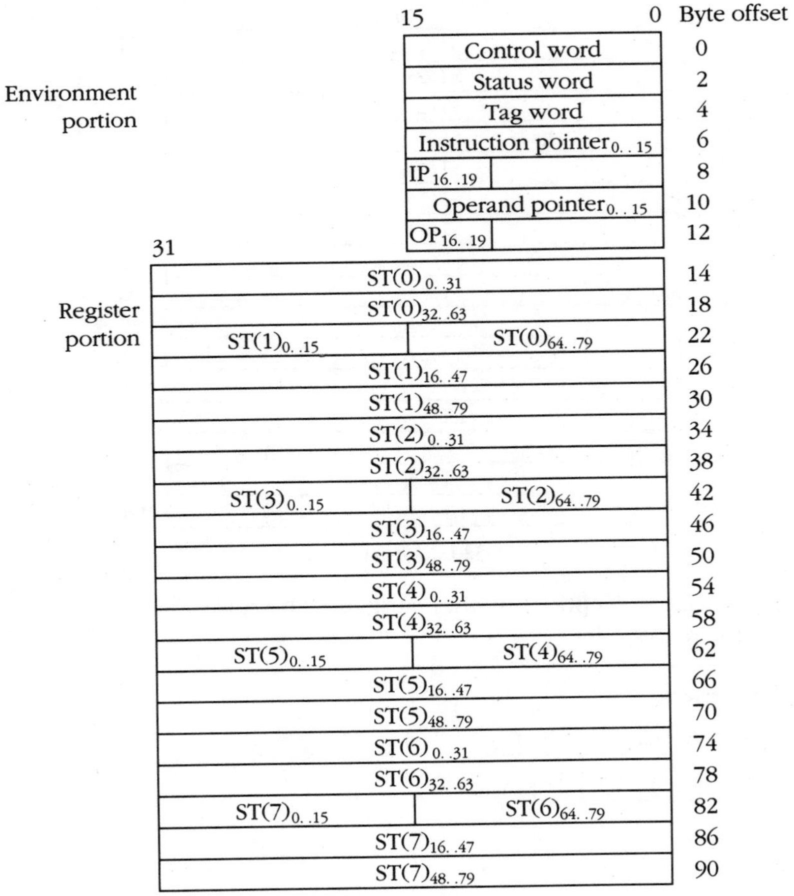

| | 15 | 0 | Byte offset |
|---|---|---|---|
| | Control word | | 0 |
| | Status word | | 2 |
| Environment portion | Tag word | | 4 |
| | Instruction pointer$_{0..15}$ | | 6 |
| | IP$_{16..19}$ | | 8 |
| | Operand pointer$_{0..15}$ | | 10 |
| | OP$_{16..19}$ | | 12 |

| 31 | | | |
|---|---|---|---|
| | ST(0)$_{0..31}$ | | 14 |
| | ST(0)$_{32..63}$ | | 18 |
| ST(1)$_{0..15}$ | | ST(0)$_{64..79}$ | 22 |
| | ST(1)$_{16..47}$ | | 26 |
| | ST(1)$_{48..79}$ | | 30 |
| | ST(2)$_{0..31}$ | | 34 |
| | ST(2)$_{32..63}$ | | 38 |
| ST(3)$_{0..15}$ | | ST(2)$_{64..79}$ | 42 |
| | ST(3)$_{16..47}$ | | 46 |
| | ST(3)$_{48..79}$ | | 50 |
| | ST(4)$_{0..31}$ | | 54 |
| | ST(4)$_{32..63}$ | | 58 |
| ST(5)$_{0..15}$ | | ST(4)$_{64..79}$ | 62 |
| | ST(5)$_{16..47}$ | | 66 |
| | ST(5)$_{48..79}$ | | 70 |
| | ST(6)$_{0..31}$ | | 74 |
| | ST(6)$_{32..63}$ | | 78 |
| ST(7)$_{0..15}$ | | ST(6)$_{64..79}$ | 82 |
| | ST(7)$_{16..47}$ | | 86 |
| | ST(7)$_{48..79}$ | | 90 |

Register portion

16-bit format (real & V86 modes)

**Figure 8-2.** *NDP state.*

(continued)

**FIGURE 8-2.** *continued*

| | 31 | 16 | 15 | 0 | Byte offset |
|---|---|---|---|---|---|
| Environment portion | Reserved | | Control word | | 0 |
| | Reserved | | Status word | | 4 |
| | Reserved | | Tag word | | 8 |
| | Error offset (EIP) | | | | 12 |
| | Reserved | | Error selector (CS) | | 16 |
| | Data operand offset | | | | 20 |
| | Reserved | | Data selector | | 24 |
| Register portion | $ST(0)_{0..31}$ | | | | 28 |
| | $ST(0)_{32..63}$ | | | | 32 |
| | $ST(1)_{0..15}$ | | $ST(0)_{64..79}$ | | 36 |
| | $ST(1)_{16..47}$ | | | | 40 |
| | $ST(1)_{48..79}$ | | | | 44 |
| | $ST(2)_{0..31}$ | | | | 48 |
| | $ST(2)_{32..63}$ | | | | 52 |
| | $ST(3)_{0..15}$ | | $ST(2)_{64..79}$ | | 56 |
| | $ST(3)_{16..47}$ | | | | 60 |
| | $ST(3)_{48..79}$ | | | | 64 |
| | $ST(4)_{0..31}$ | | | | 68 |
| | $ST(4)_{32..63}$ | | | | 72 |
| | $ST(5)_{0..15}$ | | $ST(4)_{64..79}$ | | 76 |
| | $ST(5)_{16..47}$ | | | | 80 |
| | $ST(5)_{48..79}$ | | | | 84 |
| | $ST(6)_{0..31}$ | | | | 88 |
| | $ST(6)_{32..63}$ | | | | 92 |
| | $ST(7)_{0..15}$ | | $ST(6)_{64..79}$ | | 96 |
| | $ST(7)_{16..47}$ | | | | 100 |
| | $ST(7)_{48..79}$ | | | | 104 |

32-bit format

New unmasked exceptions might be triggered because a new status word and control word are loaded.

## Exceptions

| SF | PE | UE | OE | ZE | DE | IE |
|----|----|----|----|----|----|----|
| x  | x  | x  | x  | x  | x  | x  |

# FSAVE

8087/80287/80387

**Save NDP State**

## Legal Forms

```
FSAVE    memp    ; memp ← NDP
FNSAVE   memp    ; memp ← NDP
```

## Description

This instruction stores the complete processor state of the floating-point unit in memory beginning at location *memp*. Figure 8-3 shows the format of the state block.

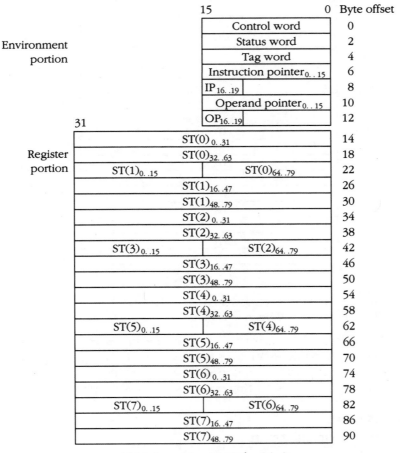

16-bit format (real & V86 modes)

**Figure 8-3.** *NDP state.*

(continued)

**Figure 8-3.** *continued*

| 31 | 16 | 15 | 0 | Byte offset |
|---|---|---|---|---|
| | Reserved | | Control word | 0 |
| | Reserved | | Status word | 4 |
| | Reserved | | Tag word | 8 |
| | Error offset (EIP) | | | 12 |
| | Reserved | | Error selector (CS) | 16 |
| | Data operand offset | | | 20 |
| | Reserved | | Data selector | 24 |
| | $ST(0)_{0..31}$ | | | 28 |
| | $ST(0)_{32..63}$ | | | 32 |
| | $ST(1)_{0..15}$ | | $ST(0)_{64..79}$ | 36 |
| | $ST(1)_{16..47}$ | | | 40 |
| | $ST(1)_{48..79}$ | | | 44 |
| | $ST(2)_{0..31}$ | | | 48 |
| | $ST(2)_{32..63}$ | | | 52 |
| | $ST(3)_{0..15}$ | | $ST(2)_{64..79}$ | 56 |
| | $ST(3)_{16..47}$ | | | 60 |
| | $ST(3)_{48..79}$ | | | 64 |
| | $ST(4)_{0..31}$ | | | 68 |
| | $ST(4)_{32..63}$ | | | 72 |
| | $ST(5)_{0..15}$ | | $ST(4)_{64..79}$ | 76 |
| | $ST(5)_{16..47}$ | | | 80 |
| | $ST(5)_{48..79}$ | | | 84 |
| | $ST(6)_{0..31}$ | | | 88 |
| | $ST(6)_{32..63}$ | | | 92 |
| | $ST(7)_{0..15}$ | | $ST(6)_{64..79}$ | 96 |
| | $ST(7)_{16..47}$ | | | 100 |
| | $ST(7)_{48..79}$ | | | 104 |

Environment portion (rows at byte offsets 0–24); Register portion (rows at byte offsets 28–104).

32-bit format

After the FSAVE is completed, the NDP state is set to the initialized state, as if an FNINIT instruction had been executed.

The FSAVE form of the instruction tests for any unmasked exceptions before executing the save, while FSAVE does not. If you use FSAVE, pending exceptions are reinstated when the state block is loaded by an FRSTOR instruction. FSAVE is not executed until previous floating-point instructions complete.

## Exceptions

| SF | PE | UE | OE | ZE | DE | IE |
|---|---|---|---|---|---|---|
| – | – | – | – | – | – | – |

# FSCALE

Scale by $2^n$

## Legal Form

FSCALE          ; ST $\leftarrow$ ST $*$ $2^{\text{int}(\text{ST}(1))}$

## Description

This instruction scales the top of stack value by the power of 2 in ST(1). If the value in ST(1) is not an integer, it is "chopped" before being used as an exponent. Chopping generates the nearest integer smaller than the original value.

The NDP does not perform a multiply operation, but it uses the identity $(x \times 2^n)$ $(1.0 \times 2^m) = x \times 2^{n+m}$ and adds the integral portion of ST(1) to the exponent of ST.

## Exceptions

| SF | PE | UE | OE | ZE | DE | IE |
|----|----|----|----|----|----|----|
| X  | X  | X  | X  | -  | X  | X  |

## Example

| | Before |
|---|---|
| | |
| | |
| | |
| ST | 1.0 |
| ST (1) | 3.01 |
| ST (2) | 92.6 |
| | |
| | |

| | After |
|---|---|
| | |
| | |
| | |
| ST | 8.0 |
| ST (1) | 3.01 |
| ST (2) | 92.6 |
| | |
| | |

FSCALE

# FSETPM

80287/80387

## Set Protected Mode

### Legal Form

FSETPM

### Description

This instruction performs no operation on the 80387 or 80486. It is required on the 80287 to signal that the CPU is entering protected mode and is supported for compatibility only.

### Exceptions

| SF | PE | UE | OE | ZE | DE | IE |
|----|----|----|----|----|----|----|
| -  | -  | -  | -  | -  | -  | -  |

# FSIN

**Sine**

## Legal Form

```
FSIN              ; ST ← sin(ST);
```

## Description

This instruction computes the sine of the top of stack and stores the result in ST. The value in ST is assumed to be in radians.

The input operand to FSIN must be a value such that $|\,ST\,| < 2^{63}$, or no operation takes place and the C2 condition code is set to 1. If the operand is a legal value, C2 is cleared to 0.

## Exceptions

| SF | PE | UE | OE | ZE | DE | IE |
|----|----|----|----|----|----|----|
| x  | x  | x  | -  | -  | x  | x  |

## Example

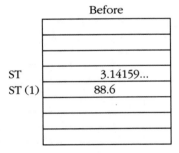

Before

| ST | 3.14159... |
|------|------------|
| ST (1) | 88.6 |

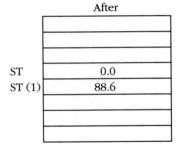

After

| ST | 0.0 |
|------|-----|
| ST (1) | 88.6 |

FSIN

# FSINCOS

**Sine and Cosine**

## Legal Form

```
FSINCOS          ; temp ← ST; ST ← sin(temp)
                 ; push(cos(temp))
```

## Description

This instruction computes both the sine and cosine of the top of stack, although the values might be less precise than those generated by FSIN and FCOS. The value in ST is assumed to be in radians.

The input operand to FSINCOS must be a value such that $|ST| < 2^{63}$ or no operation takes place and the C2 condition code is set to 1. If the operand is a legal value, C2 is cleared to 0, the top of stack is the cosine value, and ST(1) contains the sine.

## Exceptions

| SF | PE | UE | OE | ZE | DE | IE |
|----|----|----|----|----|----|----|
| x  | x  | x  | -  | -  | x  | x  |

## Example

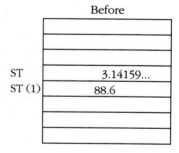

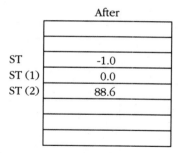

FSINCOS

# FSQRT

**Square Root**

## Legal Form

```
FSQRT           ; ST ← sqrt(ST)
```

## Description

This instruction replaces the top of stack with the square root of the original value. Taking the square root of a negative value results in an invalid operation, except that the square root of negative zero (−0.0) is defined as −0.0. The square root of infinity (positive) is defined to be infinity.

## Exceptions

| SF | PE | UE | OE | ZE | DE | IE |
|----|----|----|----|----|----|----|
| x  | x  | x  | –  | –  | x  | x  |

## Example

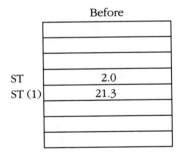

| | Before |
|---|---|
| | |
| | |
| | |
| ST | 2.0 |
| ST (1) | 21.3 |
| | |
| | |
| | |

| | After |
|---|---|
| | |
| | |
| | |
| ST | 1.4142... |
| ST (1) | 21.3 |
| | |
| | |
| | |

FSQRT

# FST

8087/80287/80387

**Store Floating Point**

## Legal Forms

```
FST     mem32    ; mem32 ← ST
FST     mem64    ; mem64 ← ST
FST     ST(n)    ; ST(n) ← ST
FSTP    mem32    ; mem32 ← ST; pop();
FSTP    mem64    ; mem64 ← ST; pop();
FSTP    mem80    ; mem80 ← ST; pop();
FSTP    ST(n)    ; ST(n) ← ST; pop();
```

## Description

This instruction stores the top of stack in the designated destination. If the opcode is FSTP, the stack top is popped (discarded) after the store operation. If the destination is a 32-bit or 64-bit real memory operand, the top of stack is rounded according to the rounding control (RC) bits of the control word.

Note that the FSTP form of this instruction can store a temp real (80-bit) value, while the FST form cannot.

## Exceptions

| SF | PE | UE | OE | ZE | DE | IE |
|----|----|----|----|----|----|----|
| X  | X  | X  | X  | -  | X  | X  |

## Example

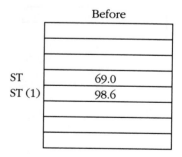

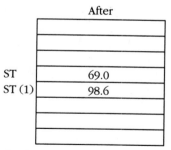

FST QWORD PTR [ESI]

Memory pointer is long real 69.0.

# FSTCW

**8087/80287/80387**

## Store Control Word

### Legal Forms

```
FSTCW    mem16    ; mem16 ← CW
FNSTCW   mem16    ; mem16 ← CW
```

### Description

This instruction stores the contents of the control word (CW) register in memory. The FSTCW form of the instruction checks for unmasked exceptions before the control word is stored, while FNSTCW does not.

### Exceptions

| SF | PE | UE | OE | ZE | DE | IE |
|----|----|----|----|----|----|----|
| -  | -  | -  | -  | -  | -  | -  |

# FSTENV

8087/80287/80387

## Store Environment

### Legal Forms

```
FSTENV   memp    memp ← env(NDP)
FNSTENV  memp    memp ← env(NDP)
```

### Description

This instruction stores the contents of the floating-point environment registers (CW, SW, TW, and error pointers) in memory beginning at *memp*. Figure 8-4 outlines the format of the 28-byte environment block.

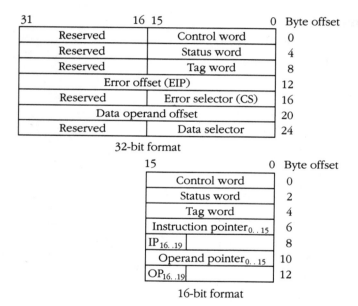

| 31 | 16 | 15 | 0 | Byte offset |
|---|---|---|---|---|
| Reserved | | Control word | | 0 |
| Reserved | | Status word | | 4 |
| Reserved | | Tag word | | 8 |
| Error offset (EIP) | | | | 12 |
| Reserved | | Error selector (CS) | | 16 |
| Data operand offset | | | | 20 |
| Reserved | | Data selector | | 24 |

32-bit format

| 15 | 0 | Byte offset |
|---|---|---|
| Control word | | 0 |
| Status word | | 2 |
| Tag word | | 4 |
| Instruction pointer$_{0..15}$ | | 6 |
| IP$_{16..19}$ | | 8 |
| Operand pointer$_{0..15}$ | | 10 |
| OP$_{16..19}$ | | 12 |

16-bit format

**Figure 8-4.** *NDP environment.*

The FSTENV form of the instruction checks for unmasked exceptions before the environment is stored, while FNSTENV does not. If unmasked exceptions are pending before FNSTENV is executed, they are reactivated if the environment block is loaded with FLDENV.

### Exceptions

| SF | PE | UE | OE | ZE | DE | IE |
|---|---|---|---|---|---|---|
| - | - | - | - | - | - | - |

# FSTSW

**8087/80287/80387**

**Store Status Word**

## Legal Forms

```
FSTSW    AX        AX ← SW
FSTSW    mem16     mem16 ← SW
FNSTSW   AX        AX ← SW
FNSTSW   mem16     mem16 ← SW
```

## Description

This instruction stores the contents of the NDP status word in memory or in the AX register. The FSTSW form of the instruction checks for unmasked exceptions before the control word is stored, while FNSTSW does not.

## Exceptions

| SF | PE | UE | OE | ZE | DE | IE |
|----|----|----|----|----|----|----|
| -  | -  | -  | -  | -  | -  | -  |

# FSUB

## Subtraction

### Legal Forms

```
FSUB                       ; ST(1) ← ST - ST(1); pop();
FSUB         mem32         ; ST ← ST - mem32
FSUB         mem64         ; ST ← ST - mem64
FSUB         ST(n)         ; ST ← ST - ST(n)
FSUB         ST, ST(n)     ; ST ← ST - ST(n)
FSUB         ST(n), ST     ; ST(n) ← ST(n) - ST
FSUBP        ST, ST(n)     ; ST ← ST - ST(n); pop();
FSUBP        ST(n), ST     ; ST(n) ← ST(n) - ST; pop();
```

### Description

This instruction subtracts the specified operands and stores the result on the stack as shown above. Optionally, the top-of-stack is also popped.

If you specify a 32-bit or 64-bit real memory operand, it is converted to temp real format before it is subtracted from ST.

If any real value is subtracted from infinity or infinity is subtracted from any real value, the result is infinity. Subtracting two infinities of the same sign is an invalid operation.

### Exceptions

| SF | PE | UE | OE | ZE | DE | IE |
|----|----|----|----|----|----|----|
| X  | X  | X  | X  | -  | X  | X  |

### Examples

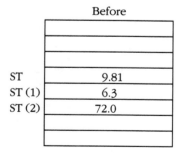

Before

| ST    | 9.81 |
| ST (1) | 6.3 |
| ST (2) | 72.0 |

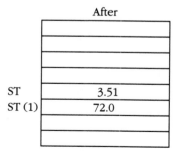

After

| ST    | 3.51 |
| ST (1) | 72.0 |

FSUB

| Before | | After | |
|---|---|---|---|
| | | | |
| | | | |
| | | | |
| ST | 9.81 | ST | 7.61 |
| ST (1) | 6.3 | ST (1) | 6.3 |
| ST (2) | 72.0 | ST (2) | 72.0 |
| | | | |
| | | | |

FSUB DWORD PTR [ESI+4]

Memory pointer is short real 2.2.

# FSUBR

**Subtraction Reversed**

## Legal Forms

```
FSUBR                       ; ST(1) ← ST(1) - ST; pop();
FSUBR       mem32           ; ST ← mem32 - ST
FSUBR       mem64           ; ST ← mem64 - ST
FSUBR       ST(n)           ; ST ← ST(n) - ST
FSUBR       ST, ST(n)       ; ST ← ST(n) - ST
FSUBR       ST(n), ST       ; ST(n) ← ST - ST(n)
FSUBRP      ST, ST(n)       ; ST ← ST(n) - ST; pop();
FSUBRP      ST(n), ST       ; ST(n) ← ST - ST(n); pop();
```

## Description

This instruction subtracts the specified operands and stores the result on the stack as shown above. This instruction is equivalent to FSUB except that the subtrahend and minuend are exchanged. Optionally, the top of stack is also popped.

If you specify a 32-bit or 64-bit real memory operand, it is converted to temp real format before it is subtracted from ST.

If any real value is subtracted from infinity or infinity is subtracted from any real value, the result is infinity. Subtracting two infinities of the same sign is an invalid operation.

## Exceptions

| SF | PE | UE | OE | ZE | DE | IE |
|----|----|----|----|----|----|----|
| X  | X  | X  | X  | -  | X  | X  |

## Examples

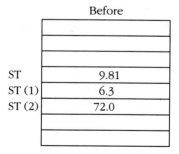

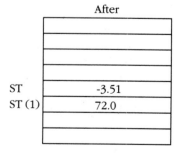

FSUBR

| | Before |
|---|---|
| | |
| | |
| | |
| ST | 9.81 |
| ST (1) | 6.3 |
| ST (2) | 72.0 |
| | |
| | |

| | After |
|---|---|
| | |
| | |
| | |
| ST | -7.61 |
| ST (1) | 6.3 |
| ST (2) | 72.0 |
| | |
| | |

FSUBR DWORD PTR [ESI+4]

Memory pointer is short real 2.2.

# FTST

**Test for Zero**

## Legal Form

```
FTST                    ; compare (ST, 0.0)
```

## Description

This instruction compares the top of stack with 0.0 and sets the floating-point condition codes according to the results of the comparison.

The following table shows the condition code settings that result from the comparison function. FTST considers +0.0 and −0.0 to be equal.

| Condition | C3 | C2 | C1 | C0 |
|-----------|----|----|----|----|
| ST > 0.0 | 0 | 0 | – | 0 |
| ST < 0.0 | 0 | 0 | – | 1 |
| ST = 0.0 | 1 | 0 | – | 0 |
| ST is a NaN | 1 | 1 | – | 1 |

The condition codes are arranged in the status word so that C3, C2, and C0 map into the same bit positions as the ZF, PF, and CF bits of the EFLAGS register. Thus, issuing the following instructions sets the EFLAGS register as if the comparison had been performed on integer values:

```
FTST                    ; Floating-point compare
FSTSW    AX             ; Store status word to AX
SAHF                    ; Store AH into flags
```

You can then use any conditional jump instruction (JE, JNE, JA, JAE, JB, or JBE) to branch on the result of the comparison. Use JP to test whether ST is a NaN.

Unlike most arithmetic operations, FTST will signal the Invalid (IE) exception if ST is a quiet NaN.

## Exceptions

| SF | PE | UE | OE | ZE | DE | IE |
|----|----|----|----|----|----|----|
| X | - | - | - | - | X | X |

## Example

| Before | | After | |
|---|---|---|---|
| | Before | | After |

| | Before |
|---|---|
| | |
| | |
| | |
| ST | -37.37 |
| ST (1) | 1.0 |
| | |
| | |
| | |

| | After |
|---|---|
| | |
| | |
| | |
| ST | -37.37 |
| ST (1) | 1.0 |
| | |
| | |
| | |

FTST

| $C_3$ | $C_2$ | $C_1$ | $C_0$ |
|---|---|---|---|
| 0 | 0 | - | 1 |

# FUCOM

80387

**Unordered Compare**

## Legal Forms

```
FUCOM               ; compare (ST, ST(1))
FUCOM     mem32     ; compare (ST, mem32)
FUCOM     mem64     ; compare (ST, mem64)
FUCOM     ST(n)     ; compare (ST, ST(n))
FUCOMP              ; compare (ST, ST(1)); pop()
FUCOMP    mem32     ; compare (ST, mem32); pop();
FUCOMP    mem64     ; compare (ST, mem64); pop();
FUCOMP    ST(n)     ; compare (ST, ST(n)); pop();
FUCOMPP             ; compare (ST, ST(1)); pop(); pop();
```

## Description

This instruction is identical to FCOM except that no exceptions are signaled if either operand in the compare function is a quiet NaN, (the comparison is unordered). FUCOM executes the function *compare* (*op1*, *op2*) and sets the floating-point condition code according to the results of the comparison. The stack is optionally popped once or twice.

The following table shows the condition code settings that result from the compare function. FUCOM considers +0.0 and −0.0 to be equal.

| Condition | C3 | C2 | C1 | C0 |
|-----------|----|----|----|----|
| *op1* > *op2* | 0 | 0 | − | 0 |
| *op1* < *op2* | 0 | 0 | − | 1 |
| *op1* = *op2* | 1 | 0 | − | 0 |
| unordered<br>(NaN compared) | 1 | 1 | − | 1 |

The condition codes are arranged in the status word so that C3, C2, and C0 map into the same bit positions as the ZF, PF, and CF bits of the EFLAGS register. Thus, the following instructions set the EFLAGS register flags as if the comparison had been performed on integer values:

```
FUCOM     op        ; Floating-point compare
FSTSW     AX        ; Store status word to AX
SAHF                ; Store AH into flags
```

You can then use any conditional jump instruction (JE, JNE, JA, JAE, JB, or JBE) to branch on the result of the comparison. Use JP to test for unordered comparison.

## Exceptions

| SF | PE | UE | OE | ZE | DE | IE |
|----|----|----|----|----|----|----|
| x  | -  | -  | -  | -  | x  | x  |

## Example

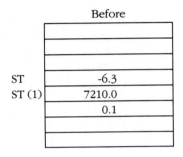

| Before | |
|--------|--|
|  |  |
|  |  |
|  |  |
| ST | -6.3 |
| ST (1) | 7210.0 |
|  | 0.1 |
|  |  |
|  |  |

| After | |
|-------|--|
|  |  |
|  |  |
|  |  |
|  |  |
| ST | 7210.0 |
| ST (1) | 0.1 |
|  |  |
|  |  |

FUCOMP ST(2)

| $C_3$ | $C_2$ | $C_1$ | $C_0$ |
|-------|-------|-------|-------|
| 0 | 0 | - | 1 |

# FWAIT

**Wait Until Not Busy**

8087/80287/80387

## Legal Form

FWAIT

## Description

This is an alternative mnemonic for the WAIT instruction, but many assemblers allow you to encode it as FWAIT because it relates to the NDP. (See "WAIT" earlier in this chapter.)

## Exceptions

| SF | PE | UE | OE | ZE | DE | IE |
|----|----|----|----|----|----|----|
| -  | -  | -  | -  | -  | -  | -  |

# FXAM

**8087/80287/80387**

### Examine Top of Stack

## Legal Form

```
FXAM              ; CC ← examine (ST)
```

## Description

This instruction sets the condition code bits in the floating-point status word (SW) according to the value of the top of stack. The following table indicates the settings that can arise based on different values of ST.

| *ST* | *C3* | *C2* | *C1* | *C0* |
|------|------|------|------|------|
| Unsupported* | 0 | 0 | s | 0 |
| NaN | 0 | 0 | s | 1 |
| Valid (normal) | 0 | 1 | s | 0 |
| Infinity | 0 | 1 | s | 1 |
| Zero | 1 | 0 | s | 0 |
| Unused (TW = empty) | 1 | 0 | s | 1 |
| Denormal | 1 | 1 | s | 0 |
| Unused (TW = empty) | 1 | 1 | s | 1 |

*Unsupported values are special bit patterns that were valid for the 8087 or 80287 but are no longer supported. These include pseudo-NaN, pseudo-zero, pseudo-infinity, and unnormals.

The s bit in C1 is set to the sign of the value of ST, with 0 indicating a positive value and 1 indicating a negative.

## Exceptions

| SF | PE | UE | OE | ZE | DE | IE |
|----|----|----|----|----|----|----|
| -  | -  | -  | -  | -  | -  | -  |

## Example

Before

| | |
|---|---|
| | |
| | |
| ST | – ∞ |
| ST (1) | 46.0 |
| | |
| | |
| | |

After

| | |
|---|---|
| | |
| | |
| ST | – ∞ |
| ST (1) | 46.0 |
| | |
| | |
| | |

FXAM

| $C_3$ | $C_2$ | $C_1$ | $C_0$ |
|---|---|---|---|
| 0 | 0 | – | 1 |

# FXCH

**Exchange Stack Elements**

## Legal Forms

```
FXCH              ; temp ← ST; ST ← ST(1); ST(1) ← temp
FXCH     ST(n)    ; temp ← ST; ST ← ST(n); ST(n) ← temp
```

## Description

This instruction swaps the contents of the specified stack registers. This allows values to move to the top of stack, which is the standard operand location for many floating-point instructions.

## Exceptions

| SF | PE | UE | OE | ZE | DE | IE |
|----|----|----|----|----|----|----|
| x  | -  | -  | -  | -  | -  | -  |

## Example

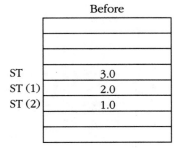

Before

| ST     | 3.0 |
| ST (1) | 2.0 |
| ST (2) | 1.0 |

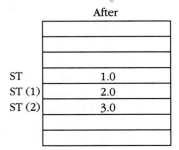

After

| ST     | 1.0 |
| ST (1) | 2.0 |
| ST (2) | 3.0 |

FXCH

# FXTRACT

8087/80287/80387

## Extract Floating-Point Components

### Legal Form

```
FXTRACT              ; temp ← ST; ST ← exponent(temp)
                     ; push(fraction(temp))
```

### Description

This instruction breaks the top of stack into its constituent parts, the significand and the exponent. The exponent is stored as a true, unbiased value, not as just the bit pattern in the exponent field of the floating-point representation. This operation leaves the fraction or significand on the top of stack and the exponent at ST(1). The original value is destroyed.

If the original top of stack is 0, the exponent portion is set to negative infinity.

### Exceptions

| SF | PE | UE | OE | ZE | DE | IE |
|----|----|----|----|----|----|----|
| x  | 0  | –  | –  | x  | x  | x  |

### Example

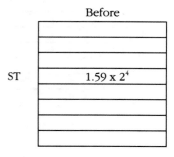

Before

| |
|---|
| |
| |
| |
| ST  1.59 x $2^4$ |
| |
| |
| |
| |

After

| |
|---|
| |
| |
| ST  1.59 |
| ST (1)  4.0 |
| |
| |
| |
| |

FXTRACT

# FYL2X

Compute $Y \times \log_2 X$

## Legal Form

```
FYL2X              ; temp ← log₂(ST); pop(); ST ← ST * temp
```

## Description

This instruction pops the top of stack, takes the base 2 logarithm, and multiplies the result by the new top of stack. Another way of expressing the function is:

$$ST(1) \times \log_2 ST$$

The initial top of stack must be a positive value, 0 through infinity. If it is not, the results of the operation are undefined.

You can also use this instruction to compute logarithms with a base other than 2, relying on the identity:

$$\log_n x = (\log_2 x) / (\log_2 n)$$

The following code fragment illustrates this computation.

```
FLD1                       ; 1.0
FLD       n                ; n, 1.0
FYL2X                      ; log₂ n
FLD1                       ; 1.0, log₂ n
FDIVP     ST(1), ST        ; 1/log₂ n
FLD       x                ; x, 1/log₂ n
FYL2X                      ; log₂ x * 1/log₂ n
```

## Exceptions

| SF | PE | UE | OE | ZE | DE | IE |
|----|----|----|----|----|----|----|
| X  | X  | X  | X  | X  | X  | X  |

## Example

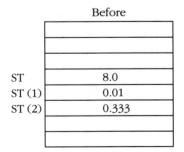

Before

| ST | 8.0 |
| ST (1) | 0.01 |
| ST (2) | 0.333 |

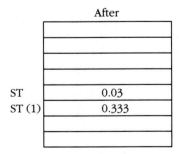

After

| ST | 0.03 |
| ST (1) | 0.333 |

FYL2X

**397**

# FYL2XP1

8087/80287/80387

## Compute $Y \times \log_2 (X + 1)$

---

### Legal Form

```
FYL2XP1              ; temp ← log₂(ST+1.0); pop(); ST ← ST * temp
```

### Description

This instruction pops the top of stack, adds 1.0 to the value, takes the base 2
logarithm, and multiplies the result by the new top of stack. Another way of expressing the instruction is:

$$ST(1) \times \log_2 (ST + 1.0)$$

The initial top of stack must be within the range $-1 + \sqrt{2}/2 \le X \le 1 - \sqrt{2}/2$, or the
result of the instruction is undefined.

This instruction is provided so that adding 1.0 to the top of stack and executing
FYL2X does not result in a precision loss. Because the FYL2XP1 function is computed differently from the FYL2X instruction, a special range restriction exists.
FYL2XP1 is also useful in computing the arcsinh, arccosh, and arctanh inverse
hyperbolic trigonometric functions.

### Exceptions

| SF | PE | UE | OE | ZE | DE | IE |
|----|----|----|----|----|----|----|
| x  | x  | x  | -  | -  | x  | x  |

### Example

| | Before | | | After |
|---|---|---|---|---|
| | | | | |
| | | | | |
| ST | 15.0 | | | |
| ST (1) | 10.0 | | ST | 40.0 |
| ST (2) | 7.7 | | ST (1) | 7.7 |
| | | | | |
| | | | | |

FYL2XP1

# F2XM1

**Compute $2^x - 1$**

## Legal Form

F2XM1                    ; ST ← $2^{ST}$ - 1

## Description

This instruction replaces the current top of stack (ST) with the value of the function $2^{ST} - 1$. However, the initial operand value must be within the range $-0.5 \le x \le +0.5$ or the result of the operation is undefined.

The function $2^x - 1$, rather than the simpler $2^x$, is provided to ensure precision when x is near 0 (for example, when computing hyperbolic trigonometric functions).

Because the range of the F2XM1 instruction is narrow, subroutines to compute $2^n$ must use FRNDINT and FSCALE to bring the instruction into a legal range and scale the result to a proper value.

You can compute the general function $x^y$ by using the identity:

$$x^y = 2^y \times \log_2 x$$

and using the FYL2X and F2XM1 instructions.

## Exceptions

| SF | PE | UE | OE | ZE | DE | IE |
|----|----|----|----|----|----|----|
| x  | x  | x  | -  | -  | x  | x  |

## Example

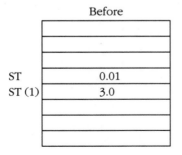

|       | Before |
|-------|--------|
| ST    | 0.01   |
| ST (1)| 3.0    |

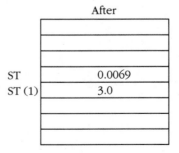

|       | After  |
|-------|--------|
| ST    | 0.0069 |
| ST (1)| 3.0    |

F2XM1

# Appendix A

# POWERS OF TWO

| Exponent | Decimal Value | Hex Value |
|---|---|---|
| 0 | 1 | 1 |
| 1 | 2 | 2 |
| 2 | 4 | 4 |
| 3 | 8 | 8 |
| 4 | 16 | 10 |
| 5 | 32 | 20 |
| 6 | 64 | 40 |
| 7 | 128 | 80 |
| 8 | 256 | 100 |
| 9 | 512 | 200 |
| 10 | 1024 | 400 |
| 11 | 2048 | 800 |
| 12 | 4096 | 1000 |
| 13 | 8192 | 2000 |
| 14 | 16384 | 4000 |
| 15 | 32768 | 8000 |
| 16 | 65536 | 10000 |
| . | . | . |
| . | . | . |
| . | . | . |
| 20 | 1048576 | 100000 |
| . | . | . |
| . | . | . |
| 31 | 2147483648 | 80000000 |
| 32 | 4294967296 | 100000000 |

# Appendix B

# ASCII CHARACTER SET

| Low-Order Bits | High-Order Bits | | | | | | | |
|---|---|---|---|---|---|---|---|---|
| | *0000* | *0001* | *0010* | *0011* | *0100* | *0101* | *0110* | *0111* |
| **0000** | NUL | DLE | space | 0 | @ | P | ` | p |
| **0001** | SOH | DC1 | ! | 1 | A | Q | a | q |
| **0010** | STX | DC2 | " | 2 | B | R | b | r |
| **0011** | ETX | DC3 | # | 3 | C | S | c | s |
| **0100** | EOT | DC4 | $ | 4 | D | T | d | t |
| **0101** | ENQ | NAK | % | 5 | E | U | e | u |
| **0110** | ACK | SYN | & | 6 | F | V | f | v |
| **0111** | BEL | ETB | ' | 7 | G | W | g | w |
| **1000** | BS | CAN | ( | 8 | H | X | h | x |
| **1001** | HT | EM | ) | 9 | I | Y | i | y |
| **1010** | LF | SUB | * | : | J | Z | j | z |
| **1011** | VT | ESC | + | ; | K | [ | k | { |
| **1100** | FF | FS | , | < | L | \ | l | \| |
| **1101** | CR | GS | – | = | M | ] | m | } |
| **1110** | SO | RS | . | > | N | ^ | n | ~ |
| **1111** | SI | US | / | ? | O | _ | o | DEL |

# OPCODE TABLES*

The following opcode tables aid in interpreting 80386/80486 object code. Use the high-order 4 bits of the opcode as an index to a row of the opcode table; use the low-order 4 bits as an index to a column of the table. If the opcode is 0FH, refer to the 2-byte opcode table, and use the second byte of the opcode to index the rows and columns of that table.

## Key to Abbreviations

Operands are identified by a two-character code of the form Zz. The first character, an uppercase letter, specifies the addressing method; the second character, a lowercase letter, specifies the type of operand.

## Codes for Addressing Method

*A* Direct address. The instruction has no mod r/m byte; the address of the operand is encoded in the instruction; no base register, index register, or scaling factor can be applied—for example, far JMP (EA).

*C* The reg field of the mod r/m byte selects a control register—for example, MOV (0FH 20H, 0FH 22H).

*D* The reg field of the mod r/m byte selects a debug register—for example, MOV (0FH 21H, 0FH 23H).

*E* A mod r/m byte follows the opcode and specifies the operand. The operand is either a general register or a memory address. If it is a memory address, the address is computed from a segment register and any of the following values: a base register, an index register, a scaling factor, or a displacement.

---

* Adapted and reprinted by permission of Intel Corporation, copyright © 1986.

*F*  Flags register.

*G*  The reg field of the mod r/m byte selects a general register—for example, ADD (00H).

*I*  Immediate data. The value of the operand is encoded in subsequent bytes of the instruction.

*J*  The instruction contains a relative offset to be added to the instruction pointer register—for example, JMP short, LOOP.

*M*  The mode r/m byte may refer only to memory—for example, BOUND, LES, LDS, LSS, LFS, LGS.

*O*  The instruction has no mod r/m byte; the offset of the operand is coded as a word or doubleword (depending on address size attribute) in the instruction. No base register, index register, or scaling factor can be applied—for example, MOV (A0H–A3H).

*R*  The mod field of the mod r/m byte may refer only to a general register—for example, MOV (0FH 20H, 0FH 26H).

*S*  The reg field of the mod r/m byte selects a segment register—for example, MOV (8CH, 8EH).

*T*  The reg field of the mod r/m byte selects a test register—for example, MOV (0FH 24H).

*X*  Memory addressed by DS:SI—for example, MOVS, COMPS, OUTS, LODS, SCAS.

*Y*  Memory addressed by ES:DI—for example, MOVS, CMPS, INS, STOS.

# Codes for Operand Type

*a*  Two single-word operands in memory or two double-word operands in memory, depending on operand size attribute (used only by BOUND).

*b*  Byte (regardless of operand size attribute).

*c*  Byte or word, depending on operand size attribute.

*d*  Doubleword (regardless of operand size attribute).

*p*  32-bit or 48-bit pointer, depending on operand size attribute.

*s*  6-byte pseudodescriptor.

*v*  Word or doubleword, depending on operand size attribute.

*w*  Word (regardless of operand size attribute).

# Register Codes

When an operand is a register encoded in the opcode, the register is identified by its name, for example, AX, CL, or ESI. The name of the register indicates whether the register is 32 bits, 16 bits, or 8 bits. A register identifier of the form eXX is used when the width of the register depends on the operand size attribute. For example, eAX indicates that the AX register is used when the operand size attribute is 16 and that the EAX register is used when the operand size attribute is 32.

# One-Byte Opcode Table

|   | 0 | 1 | 2 | 3 | 4 | 5 | 6 | 7 |
|---|---|---|---|---|---|---|---|---|
| 0 | ADD Eb,Gb | ADD Ev,Gv | ADD Gb,Eb | ADD Gv,Ev | ADD AL,Ib | ADD eAX,Iv | PUSH ES | POP ES |
| 1 | ADC Eb,Gb | ADC Ev,Gv | ADC Gb,Eb | ADC Gv,Ev | ADC AL,Ib | ADC eAX,Iv | PUSH SS | POP SS |
| 2 | AND Eb,Gb | AND Ev,Gv | AND Gb,Eb | AND Gv,Ev | AND AL,Ib | AND eAX,Iv | ES: | DAA |
| 3 | XOR Eb,Gb | XOR Ev,Gv | XOR Gb,Eb | XOR Gv,Ev | XOR AL,Ib | XOR eAX,Iv | SS: | AAA |
| 4 | INC eAX | INC eCX | INC eDX | INC eBX | INC eSP | INC eBP | INC eSI | INC eDI |
| 5 | PUSH eAX | PUSH eCX | PUSH eDX | PUSH eBX | PUSH eSP | PUSH eBP | PUSH eSI | PUSH eDI |
| 6 | PUSHAD | POPAD | BOUND Gv,Ma | ARPL Ew,Rw | FS: | GS: | OPSIZE: | ADRSIZE: |
| 7 | JO Jb | JNO Jb | JB Jb | JNB Jb | JZ Jb | JNZ Jb | JBE Jb | JNBE Jb |
| 8 | Group 1 Eb,Ib | Group 1 Ev,Iv |  | Group 1 Ev,Ib | TEST Eb,Gb | TEST Ev,Gv | XCHG Eb,Gb | XCHG Ev,Gv |
| 9 | NOP | XCHG eCX,eAX | XCHG eDX,eAX | XCHG eBX,eAX | XCHG eSP,eAX | XCHG eBP,eAX | XCHG eSI,eAX | XCHG eDI,eAX |
| A | MOV AL,Ob | MOV eAX,Ov | MOV Ob,AL | MOV Ov,eAX | MOVSB | MOVSW/D | CMPSB | CMPSW/D |
| B | MOV AL,Ib | MOV CL,Ib | MOV DL,Ib | MOV BL,Ib | MOV AH,Ib | MOV CH,Ib | MOV DH,Ib | MOV BH,Ib |
| C | Group 2 Eb,Ib | Group 2 Ev,Ib | RET(near) Iw | RET(near) | LES Gv,Mp | LDS Gv,Mp | MOV Eb,Ib | MOV Ev,Iv |
| D | Group 2 Eb,1 | Group 2 Ev,1 | Group 2 Eb,CL | Group 2 Ev,CL | AAM | AAD |  | XLAT |
| E | LOOPNE Jb | LOOPE Jb | LOOP Jb | JCXZ Jb | IN AL,Ib | IN eAX,Ib | OUT Ib,AL | OUT Ib,eAX |
| F | LOCK |  | REPNE | REP REPE | HLT | CMC | Group 3 Eb | Group 3 Ev |

NOTE: All numbers are in hex.

*(continued)*

## One-Byte Opcode Table. *continued*

|   | 8 | 9 | A | B | C | D | E | F |
|---|---|---|---|---|---|---|---|---|
| 0 | OR Eb,Gb | OR Ev,Gv | OR Gb,Eb | OR Gv,Ev | OR AL,Ib | OR eAX,Iv | PUSH CS | 2-byte escape |
| 1 | SBB Eb,Gb | SBB Ev,Gv | SBB Gb,Eb | SBB Gv,Ev | SBB AL,Ib | SBB eAX,Iv | PUSH DS | POP DS |
| 2 | SUB Eb,Gb | SUB Ev,Gv | SUB Gb,Eb | SUB Gv,Ev | SUB AL,Ib | SUB eAX,Iv | CS: | DAS |
| 3 | CMP Eb,Gb | CMP Ev,Gv | CMP Gb,Eb | CMP Gv,Ev | CMP AL,Ib | CMP eAX,Iv | DS: | AAS |
| 4 | DEC eAX | DEC eCX | DEC eDX | DEC eBX | DEC eSP | DEC eBP | DEC eSI | DEC eDI |
| 5 | POP eAX | POP eCX | POP eDX | POP eBX | POP eSP | POP eBP | POP eSI | POP eDI |
| 6 | PUSH Iv | IMUL Gv,Ev,Iv | PUSH Ib | IMUL Gv,Ev,Ib | INSB Yb,DX | INSW/D Yv,DX | OUTSB DX,Xb | OUTSW/D DX,Xv |
| 7 | JS Jb | JNS Jb | JP Jb | JNP Jb | JL Jb | JNL Jb | JLE Jb | JNLE Jb |
| 8 | MOV Eb,Gb | MOV Ev,Gv | MOV Gb,Eb | MOV Gv,Ev | MOV Ew,Sw | LEA Gv,M | MOV Sw,Ew | POP Ev |
| 9 | CBW | CWD | CALL Ap | WAIT | PUSHF Fv | POPF Fv | SAHF | LAHF |
| A | TEST AL,Ib | TEST eAX,Iv | STOSB | STOSW/D | LODSB | LODSW/D | SCASB | SCASW/D |
| B | MOV eAX,Iv | MOV eCX,Iv | MOV eDX,Iv | MOV eBX,Iv | MOV eSP,Iv | MOV eBP,Iv | MOV eSI,Iv | MOV eDI,Iv |
| C | ENTER Iw,Ib | LEAVE | RET far Iw | | INT 3 | INT Ib | INTO | IRET |
| D | ESC 0 | ESC 1 | ESC 2 | ESC 3 | ESC 4 | ESC 5 | ESC 6 | ESC 7 |
| E | CALL Av | JMP Jv | JMP Ap | JMP Jb | IN AL,DX | IN eAX,DX | OUT DX,AL | OUT DX,eAX |
| F | CLC | STC | CLI | STI | CLD | STD | Group 4 | Group 5 |

# Two-Byte Opcode Table (first byte is 0FH)

| | 0 | 1 | 2 | 3 | 4 | 5 | 6 | 7 |
|---|---|---|---|---|---|---|---|---|
| 0 | Group 6 | Group 7 | LAR Gv,Ew | LSL Gv,Ew | | | CLTS | |
| 1 | INVLPG Ea | | | | | | | |
| 2 | MOV Cd,Rd | MOV Dd,Rd | MOV Rd,Cd | MOV Rd,Dd | MOV Td,Rd | | MOV Rd,Td | |
| 3 | | | | | | | | |
| 4 | | | | | | | | |
| 5 | | | | | | | | |
| 6 | | | | | | | | |
| 7 | | | | | | | | |
| 8 | JO Jv | JNO Jv | JB Jv | JNB Jv | JZ Jv | JNZ Jv | JBE Jv | JNBE Jv |
| 9 | SETO Eb | SETNO Eb | SETB Eb | SETNB Eb | SETZ Eb | SETNZ Eb | SETBE Eb | SETNBE Eb |
| A | PUSH FS | POP FS | | BT Ev,Gv | SHLD Ev,Gv,Ib | SHLD Ev,Gv,CL | CMPXCHG Eb,Rb | CMPXCHG Ev,Rv |
| B | A6 | A7 | LSS Mp | BTR Ev,Gv | LFS Mp | LGS Mp | MOVZX Gv,Eb | MOVZX Gv,Ew |
| C | XADD Eb,Rb | XADD Ev,Rv | | | | | | |
| D | | | | | | | | |
| E | | | | | | | | |
| F | | | | | | | | |

*(continued)*

**Two-Byte Opcode Table.**  *continued*

|   | 8 | 9 | A | B | C | D | E | F |
|---|---|---|---|---|---|---|---|---|
| 0 | INVD | WBINVD | | | | | | |
| 1 | | | | | | | | |
| 2 | | | | | | | | |
| 3 | | | | | | | | |
| 4 | | | | | | | | |
| 5 | | | | | | | | |
| 6 | | | | | | | | |
| 7 | | | | | | | | |
| 8 | JS Jv | JNS Jv | JP Jv | JNP Jv | JL Jv | JNL Jv | JLE Jv | JNLE Jv |
| 9 | SETS Eb | SETNS Eb | SETP Eb | SETNP Eb | SETL Eb | SETNL Eb | SETLE Eb | SETNLE Eb |
| A | PUSH GS | POP GS | | BTS Ev,Gv | SHRD Ev,Gv,Ib | SHRD Ev,Gv,CL | | IMUL Gv,Ev |
| B | | | Group 8 Ev,Ib | BTC Ev,Gv | BSF Gv,Ev | BSR Gv,Ev | MOVSX Gv,Eb | MOVSX Gv,Ew |
| C | BSWAP EAX | BSWAP ECX | BSWAP EDX | BSWAP EBX | BSWAP ESP | BSWAP EBP | BSWAP ESI | BSWAP EDI |
| D | | | | | | | | |
| E | | | | | | | | |
| F | | | | | | | | |

# Opcodes Determined by Bits 5, 4, and 3 of mod r/m Byte: mod nnn r/m

| | | 000 | 001 | 010 | 011 | 100 | 101 | 110 | 111 |
|---|---|---|---|---|---|---|---|---|---|
| G R O U P | 1 | ADD | OR | ADC | SBB | AND | SUB | XOR | CMP |
| | 2 | ROL | ROR | RCL | RCR | SHL | SHR | | SAR |
| | 3 | TEST Ib/Iv | | NOT | NEG | MUL AL/eAX | IMUL AL/eAX | DIV AL/eAX | IDIV AL/eAX |
| | 4 | INC Eb | DEC Eb | | | | | | |
| | 5 | INC Ev | DEC Ev | CALL Ev | CALL Ep | JMP Ev | JMP Ep | PUSH Ev | |
| | 6 | SLDT Ew | STR Ew | LLDT Ew | LTR Ew | VERR Ew | VERW Ew | | |
| | 7 | SGDT Ms | SIDT Ms | LGDT Ms | LIDT Ms | SMSW Ew | | LMSW Ew | |
| | 8 | | | | | BT | BTS | BTR | BTC |

# Numeric Data Processor Extensions

The following tables show the opcode map to the 80386/80486 instruction set for the numeric data processor (NDP) extensions. The operand abbreviations for these tables are:

**Es** Effective address, short real (32-bit)

**El** Effective address, long real (64-bit)

**Et** Effective address, temp real (80-bit)

**Ew** Effective address, word (16-bit)

**Ed** Effective address, doubleword (32-bit)

**Eq** Effective address, quadword (64-bit)

**Eb** Effective address, BCD (80-bit)

**Ea** Effective address (no operand size)

**ST(i)** Stack element i

**ST** Stack top

**Format:**

| 7 6 | 5 4 3 | 2 1 0 |
|-----|-------|-------|
| mod | nnn | r/m |

## ESC 0
nnn

| | 000 | 001 | 010 | 011 | 100 | 101 | 110 | 111 |
|--|-----|-----|-----|-----|-----|-----|-----|-----|
| 00<br>mod=01<br>10 | FADD<br>Es | FMUL<br>Es | FCOM<br>Es | FCOMP<br>Es | FSUB<br>Es | FSUBR<br>Es | FDIV<br>Es | FDIVR<br>Es |
| mod=11 | FADD<br>ST,ST(i) | FMUL<br>ST,ST(i) | FCOM<br>ST,ST(i) | FCOMP<br>ST,ST(i) | FSUB<br>ST,ST(i) | FSUBR<br>ST,ST(i) | FDIV<br>ST,ST(i) | FDIVR<br>ST,ST(i) |

i=r/m

## ESC 1
nnn

| | | 000 | 001 | 010 | 011 | 100 | 101 | 110 | 111 |
|--|--|-----|-----|-----|-----|-----|-----|-----|-----|
| 00<br>mod=01<br>10 | | FLD<br>Es | | FST<br>Es | FSTP<br>Es | FLDENV<br>Ea | FLDCW<br>Ew | FSTENV<br>Ea | FSTCW<br>Ew |
| | r/m<br>000 | FLD<br>ST(0) | FXCH<br>ST(0) | FNOP | | FCHS | FLD1 | F2XM1 | FPREM |
| | 001 | FLD<br>ST(1) | FXCH<br>ST(1) | | | FABS | FLDL2T | FYL2X | FYL2XP1 |
| | 010 | FLD<br>ST(2) | FXCH<br>ST(2) | | | | FLDL2E | FPTAN | FSQRT |
| | 011 | FLD<br>ST(3) | FXCH<br>(3) | | | | FLDPI | FPATAN | FSINCOS |
| mod=11 | 100 | FLD<br>ST(4) | FXCH<br>ST(4) | | | FTST | FLDLG2 | FXTRACT | FRNDINT |
| | 101 | FLD<br>ST(5) | FXCH<br>ST(5) | | | FXAM | FLDLN2 | FPREMI | FSCALE |
| | 110 | FLD<br>ST(6) | FXCH<br>ST(6) | | | | FLDZ | FDECSTP | FSIN |
| | 111 | FLD<br>ST(7) | FXCH<br>ST(7) | | | | | FINCSTP | FCOS |

## ESC 2

nnn

| mod | 000 | 001 | 010 | 011 | 100 | 101 | 110 | 111 |
|---|---|---|---|---|---|---|---|---|
| 00 / 01 / 10 | FIADD Ew | FIMUL Ew | FICOM Ew | FICOMP Ew | FISUB Ew | FISUBR Ew | FIDIV Ew | FIDIVR Ew |
| mod=11 | | FUCOMPP* | | | | | | |

*r/m=5

## ESC 3

nnn

| mod | 000 | 001 | 010 | 011 | 100 | 101 | 110 | 111 |
|---|---|---|---|---|---|---|---|---|
| 00 / 01 / 10 | FILD Ew | | FIST Ew | FISTP Ew | FLD Et | | FSTP Et | |
| mod=11 | | | | | Group 3a | | | |

Group 3a: mod=11, nnn=100

| r/m | 000 | 001 | 010 | 011 | 100 | 101 | 110 | 111 |
|---|---|---|---|---|---|---|---|---|
| | (FENI) | (FDISI) | FCLEX | FINIT | (FSETPM) | | | |

## ESC 4

nnn

| mod | 000 | 001 | 010 | 011 | 100 | 101 | 110 | 111 |
|---|---|---|---|---|---|---|---|---|
| 00 / 01 / 10 | FADD El | FMUL El | FCOM El | FCOMP El | FSUB El | FSUBR El | FDIV El | FDIVR El |
| mod=11 | FADD ST(i),ST | FMUL ST(i),ST | FCOM ST(i),ST | FCOMP ST(i),ST | FSUB ST(i),ST | FSUBR ST(i),ST | FDIV ST(i),ST | FDIVR ST(i),ST |

i=r/m

## ESC 5

nnn

| | 000 | 001 | 010 | 011 | 100 | 101 | 110 | 111 |
|---|---|---|---|---|---|---|---|---|
| 00<br>mod=01<br>10 | FLD<br>El | | FST<br>El | FSTP<br>El | FRSTOR<br>Ea | | FSAVE<br>Ea | FSTSW<br>Ew |
| mod=11 | FFREE<br>ST(i) | | FST<br>ST(i) | FSTP<br>ST(i) | FUCOM<br>ST(i) | FUCOMP<br>ST(i) | | |

i=r/m

## ESC 6

nnn

| 000 | 001 | 010 | 011 | 100 | 101 | 110 | 111 |
|---|---|---|---|---|---|---|---|
| FIADD<br>Ed | FIMUL<br>Ed | FICOM<br>Ed | FICOMP<br>Ed | FISUB<br>Ed | FISUBR<br>Ed | FIDIV<br>Ed | FIDIVR<br>Ed |
| FADDP<br>ST(i),ST | FMULP<br>ST(i),ST | | FCOMPP*<br> | FSUBP<br>ST(i),ST | FSUBRP<br>ST(i),ST | FDIVP<br>ST(i),ST | FDIVRP<br>ST(i),ST |

*r/m=001

## ESC 7

nnn

| 000 | 001 | 010 | 011 | 100 | 101 | 110 | 111 |
|---|---|---|---|---|---|---|---|
| FILD<br>Ed | | FIST<br>Ed | FISTP<br>Ed | FBLD<br>Eb | FILD<br>Eq | FBSTP<br>Eb | FISTP<br>Eq |
| FSTSW*<br>AX | | | | | | | |

*r/m=000

# Appendix D

# INSTRUCTION FORMAT AND TIMING*

This appendix describes the 80386-family instruction set. A table lists all instructions with instruction encoding diagrams and clock counts. Details of the instruction encoding are provided in the following sections, which describe the encoding structure and the definition of fields occurring within the instructions.

## 80386/80486 Instruction Encoding and Clock Count Summary

To calculate elapsed time for an instruction, multiply the instruction clock count by the processor clock period (for example, 40 ns for a processor operating at 25 MHz).

For more information on the encodings of instructions, refer to "Instruction Encoding" (later in this appendix), which explains the structure of instruction encodings and defines the encodings of instruction fields.

### Instruction clock count assumptions

1. The instruction has been prefetched and decoded and is ready for execution.

2. Bus cycles do not require wait states.

3. There are no local bus HOLD requests delaying processor access to the bus.

4. No exceptions are detected during instruction execution.

5. If an effective address is calculated, it does not use two general-register components. One register scaling and displacement can be used within the clock

---

*Adapted and reprinted by permission of Intel Corporation, 1986.

counts shown. However, if the effective address calculation uses two general-register components, add one clock to the clock count shown on the 80386; one clock *may* be added on the 80486.

6. Accesses are aligned. Misaligned accesses require another memory read cycle.

7. On the 80486, one additional clock *may* be added under the following conditions:

   ■ The base register used as an effective address in one instruction is the destination register of the immediately preceding instruction.

   ■ Displacement mode addressing and immediate addressing are used in the same instruction.

8. A page translation hits the TLB.

9. The cache on the 80486 is enabled and the following conditions are true:

   ■ Cache fills complete before the next access to the same cache line.

   ■ JMP targets hit the cache.

   ■ No invalidate cycles occur.

   ■ Instructions that read consecutive memory words start on a 16-byte boundary.

10. In the 80386SX, add one read cycle for every 16 bits over the initial 16 bits accessed by the instruction.

## Instruction clock count notation

1. If two clock counts are given, the smaller one refers to a register operand, and the larger one refers to a memory operand.

2. *n* = number of times repeated.

3. *m* = number of components in the next instruction executed, where any displacement counts as one component, any immediate data counts as one component, and each of the other bytes of the instruction and prefix(es) counts as one component.

## Instruction notes for table

The following are instruction notes for the "General Notes" column of the table titled "80386/80486 Instruction Set Clock Summary," which begins on page 421. The instruction notes for the "Cache Notes" column are found on page 438 as table footnotes.

Notes a through c apply to real address mode only:

a. This is a protected-mode instruction. Trying to execute in real mode results in exception 6 (invalid opcode).

b. Exception 13 fault (general protection) occurs in real mode if an operand reference is made that partially or fully extends beyond the maximum CS, DS, ES, FS, or GS limit, FFFFH. Exception 12 fault (stack segment limit violation or not present) occurs in real mode if an operand reference is made that partially or fully extends beyond the maximum SS limit.

c. This instruction may be executed in real mode where it initializes the CPU for protected mode.

Notes d through g apply to real address mode and protected virtual address mode:

d. The 80386 and 80486 use an early-out multiply algorithm. The number of clocks depends on the position of the most significant bit in the operand (multiplier).

Clock counts are minimum to maximum. To calculate actual clocks, use the following formula:

$$\text{Actual Clock} = \text{if } m <> 0 \text{ then max } ([\log_2 |m|], 3) + 6 \text{ clocks}$$

$$\text{if } m = 0 \text{ then } 9 \text{ clocks (where m is the multiplier)}$$

e. An exception might occur, depending on the value of the operand.

f. LOCK is asserted, regardless of the presence or absence of the LOCK prefix.

g. LOCK is asserted during descriptor table accesses.

Notes h through r apply to protected virtual address mode only:

h. Exception 13 fault (general protection violation) occurs if the memory operand in CS, DS, ES, FS, or GS cannot be used because of a segment limit violation or because of an access rights violation. If a stack limit is violated, an exception 12 (stack segment limit violation or not present) occurs.

i. For segment load operations, the CPL, RPL, and DPL must agree with the privilege rules to avoid an exception 13 fault (general protection violation). The segment's descriptor must indicate "present" or exception 11 (CS, DS, ES, FS, or GS not present). If the SS register is loaded and a stack segment not present is detected, an exception 12 (stack segment limit violation or not present) occurs.

j. All segment descriptor accesses in the GDT or LDT made by this instruction assert LOCK to maintain descriptor integrity in multiprocessor environments.

k. JMP, CALL, INT, RET, and IRET instructions referring to another code segment cause an exception 13 (general protection violation) if an applicable privilege rule is violated.

l. An exception 13 fault occurs if CPL is greater than 0. (0 is the most privileged level.)

m. An exception 13 fault occurs if CPL is greater than IOPL.

n. The IF bit of the flag register is not updated if CPL is greater than IOPL. The IOPL and VM fields of the flag register are updated only if CPL is equal to 0.

o. The PE bit of the MSW (CR0) cannot be reset by this instruction. Use MOV into CR0 to reset the PE bit.

p. Any violation of privilege rules as applied to the selector operand does not cause a protection exception; rather, the zero flag is cleared.

q. If the coprocessor's memory operand violates a segment limit or segment access rights, an exception 13 fault (general protection exception) occurs before the ESC instruction executes. An exception 12 fault (stack segment limit violation or not present) occurs if the stack limit is violated by the operand's starting address.

r. The destination of a JMP, CALL, INT, RET, or IRET must be in the defined limit of a code segment, or an exception 13 fault (general protection violation) occurs.

# 80386/80486 Instruction Set Clock Summary

| Instruction | Format | 80486 Clocks | Cache Miss Penalty | Cache Notes | 80386 Clocks | General Notes |
|---|---|---|---|---|---|---|
| **General Data Transfer** | | | | | | |
| MOV = Move | | | | | | |
| Register to register | 1000100w  mod reg r/m | 1 | | | 2 | b,h |
| Register to register | 1000100w  mod reg r/m | 1 | | | 2 | b,h |
| Memory to register | 1000101w  mod reg r/m | 1 | 2 | | 4 | b,h |
| Immediate to register / short form | 1011w reg  immediate data | 1 | | | 2 | b,h |
| /long form | 1100011w  mod 000 r/m  immediate data | 1 | | | 2 | b,h |
| Immediate to memory | 1100011w  mod 000 r/m  immediate data | 1 | 2 | | 2 | b,h |
| Memory to accumulator | 1010000w  full displacement | 1 | | | 4 | b,h |
| Accumulator to memory | 1010001w  full displacement | 1 | | | 2 | b,h |
| Register to segment register (RM) | 10001110  mod sreg 3r/m | 3 | | | 2 | b |
| (protected mode) | | 9 | 3 | I | 18 | h,i,j |
| Memory to segment register (RM) | 10001110  mod sreg 3r/m | 3 | 2 | | 5 | b |
| (protected mode) | | 9 | 5 | I | 19 | h,i,j |
| Segment register to register/memory | 10001100  mod sreg 3r/m | 3 | | | 2 | b,h |
| MOVZX/MOVSX = Move zero/sign extension | | | | | | |
| (z = 0 MOVZX/z = 1 MOVSX) | | | | | | |
| Register to register | 00001111  1011z11w  mod reg r/m | 3 | | | 3 | b,h |
| Memory to register | 00001111  1011z11w  mod reg r/m | 3 | 2 | | 6 | b,h |
| PUSH = Push | | | | | | |
| Register / short form | 01010 reg | 1 | | | 2 | b,h |
| /long form | 11111111  mod 110 r/m | 4 | | | 5 | b,h |
| Memory | 11111111  mod 110 r/m | 4 | 1 | A | 5 | b,h |
| Segment register / short form | 000 sreg 2110 | 3 | | | 2 | b,h |
| /long form | 00001111  10 sreg 3000 | 3 | | | 2 | b,h |
| Immediate | 011010s0  immediate data | 1 | | | 2 | b,h |
| PUSHA = Push all | 01100000 | 11 | | | 18 | b,h |

*(continued)*

# 80386/80486 Instruction Set Clock Summary. *continued*

| Instruction | Format | 80486 Clocks | Cache Miss Penalty | Cache Notes | 80386 Clocks | General Notes |
|---|---|---|---|---|---|---|
| **POP = Pop** | | | | | | |
| Register / short form | `01011 reg` | 1 | 2 | | 4 | b,h |
| /long form | `10001111` `mod 000 r/m` | 4 | 1 | | 5 | b,h |
| Memory | `10001111` `mod 000 r/m` | 5 | 2 | A | 5 | b,h |
| Segment register / short (RM) | `000sreg2111` | 3 | 2 | | 7 | b |
| /long (RM) | `00001111` `10 sreg 3001` | 3 | 2 | | 7 | b |
| Protected mode / short | | 9 | 5 | I | 21 | h,i,j |
| /long | | 9 | 5 | I | 21 | h,i,j |
| **POPA = Pop all** | `01100001` | 9 | 15 | I | 24 | b,h |
| **XCHG = Exchange** | | | | | | |
| Register with register | `1000011w` `mod reg r/m` | 3 | | B | 3 | |
| Memory with register | `1000011w` `mod reg r/m` | 3 | 2 | B | 5 | b,f,h |
| Register with accumulator | `10010 reg` | 5 | | B | 3 | |
| **LEA = Load EA to register** | `10001101` `mod reg r/m` | 1 | | | 2 | |
| ***Segment Control*** | | | | | | |
| LDS = Load pointer to DS | `11000101` `mod reg r/m` | 6 | 7 | I | 7 | b |
| (protected mode) | | 12 | 10 | I | 22 | h,i,j |
| LES = Load pointer to ES | `11000100` `mod reg r/m` | 6 | 7 | I | 7 | b |
| (protected mode) | | 12 | 10 | I | 22 | h,i,j |
| LFS = Load pointer to FS | `00001111` `10110100` `mod reg r/m` | 6 | 7 | I | 7 | b |
| (protected mode) | | 12 | 10 | I | 25 | h,i,j |
| LGS = Load pointer to GS | `00001111` `10110101` `mod reg r/m` | 6 | 7 | I | 7 | b |
| (protected mode) | | 12 | 10 | I | 25 | h,i,j |
| LSS = Load pointer to SS | `00001111` `10110010` `mod reg r/m` | 6 | 7 | I | 7 | b |
| (protected mode) | | 12 | 10 | I | 25 | h,i,j |
| ***Flag control*** | | | | | | |
| CLC = Clear carry flag | `11111000` | 2 | | | 2 | |
| CLD = Clear direction flag | `11111100` | 2 | | | 2 | |

| Instruction | Format | 80486 Clocks | Cache Miss Penalty | Cache Notes | 80386 Clocks | General Notes |
|---|---|---|---|---|---|---|
| CLI = Clear interrupt enable flag | `11111010` | 5 | | | 3 | m |
| CMC = Complement carry flag | `11110101` | 2 | | | 2 | |
| LAHF = Load AH with flags | `10011111` | 3 | | | 2 | b |
| POPF = Pop flags | `10011101` | 9 | | | 5 | h,n |
| (protected mode) | | 6 | | | 5 | b |
| PUSHF = Push flags | `10011100` | 4 | | | 4 | b |
| (protected mode) | | 3 | | | 4 | h |
| SAHF = Store AH from flags | `10011110` | 2 | | | 3 | |
| STC = Set carry flag | `11111001` | 2 | | | 2 | |
| STD = Set direction flag | `11111001` | 2 | | | 2 | |
| STI = Set interrupt enable flag | `11111011` | 5 | | | 3 | m |

### Arithmetic

TTT = 0 / ADD = Add

TTT = 1 / OR = Logical OR

TTT = 2 / ADC = Add with carry

TTT = 3 / SBB = Subtract with borrow

TTT = 4 / AND = Logical AND

TTT = 5 / SUB = Subtract

TTT = 6 / XOR = Logical exclusive OR

| Instruction | Format | 80486 Clocks | Cache Miss Penalty | Cache Notes | 80386 Clocks | General Notes |
|---|---|---|---|---|---|---|
| Register to register | `00TTT0dw` `mod reg r/m` | 1 | | | 2 | |
| Memory to register | `00TTT01w` `mod reg r/m` | 2 | 2 | | 6 | b,h |
| Register to memory | `00TTT00w` `mod reg r/m` | 3 | 6 | | 7 | b,h |
| Immediate to register | `10000sw` `mod TTT r/m` immediate data | 1 | | | 2 | |
| Immediate to accumulator | `00TTT10w` immediate data | 1 | | | 2 | |
| Immediate to memory | `10000sw` `mod TTT r/m` immediate data | 3 | 6 | | 7 | b,h |
| INC = Increment | | | | | | |
| Register / short form | `01000 reg` | 1 | | | 2 | |
| / long form | `1111111w` `mod 000 r/m` | 1 | | | 2 | |

*(continued)*

| Instruction | Format | 80486 Clocks | Cache Miss Penalty | Cache Notes | 80386 Clocks | General Notes |
|---|---|---|---|---|---|---|
| Memory | 1111111w mod 000 r/m | 3 | 6 | | 6 | b,h |
| DEC = Decrement | | | | | | |
| Register / short form | 01001 reg | 1 | | | 2 | |
| / long form | 1111111w reg 001 r/m immediate data | 1 | | | 2 | |
| Memory | 1111111w mod 001 r/m immediate data | 3 | 6 | | 6 | b,h |
| NOT = Logical NOT | 1111011w mod 010 r/m | | | | | |
| Register | | 1 | | | 2 | |
| Memory | | 3 | 6 | | 6 | b,h |
| NEG = Negate | 1111011w mod 011 r/m | | | | | |
| Register | | 1 | | | 2 | |
| Memory | | 3 | 6 | | 6 | b,h |
| CMP = Compare | | | | | | |
| Register with register | 001110dw mod reg r/m | 1 | | | 2 | |
| Memory with register | 0011100w mod reg r/m | 2 | 2 | | 5 | b,h |
| Register with memory | 0011101w mod reg r/m | 2 | 2 | | 6 | b,h |
| Immediate with register | 100000sw mod 111 r/m immediate data | 1 | | | 2 | |
| Immediate with memory | 100000sw mod 111 r/m immediate data | 2 | 2 | | 5 | b,h |
| Immediate with accumulator | 0011110w immediate data | 1 | | | 2 | |
| TEST = Logical AND with no result but flags | | | | | | |
| Register with register | 1000010w mod reg r/m | 1 | | | 2 | |
| Memory with register | 1000010w mod reg r/m | 2 | 2 | | 5 | b,h |
| Immediate with register | 1111011w mod 000 r/m immediate data | 1 | | | 2 | |
| Immediate with memory | 1111011w mod 000 r/m immediate data | 2 | 2 | | 5 | b,h |
| Immediate with accumulator | 1010100w immediate data | 1 | | | 2 | |
| AAA = ASCII adjust for add | 00110111 | 3 | | | 4 | |
| AAS = ASCII adjust for subtract | 00111111 | 3 | | | 4 | |

| Instruction | Format | 80486 Clocks | Cache Miss Penalty | Cache Notes | 80386 Clocks | General Notes |
|---|---|---|---|---|---|---|
| DAA = Decimal adjust for add | `00100111` | 2 | | | 4 | |
| DAS = Decimal adjust for subtract | `00101111` | 2 | | | 4 | |
| MUL = Unsigned multiply | | | | | | |
| Accumulator with register | `1111011w` `mod 100 r/m` | | | | | |
| —byte | | 13–18 | | c | 9–14 | d |
| —word | | 13–26 | | c | 9–22 | d |
| —dword | | 13–42 | | c | 9–38 | d |
| Accumulator with memory | `1111011w` `mod 100 r/m` | | | | | |
| —byte | | 13–18 | 1 | c | 12–17 | b,d,h |
| —word | | 13–26 | 1 | c | 12–25 | b,d,h |
| —dword | | 13–42 | 1 | c | 12–41 | b,d,h |
| IMUL = Integer multiply (signed) | | | | | | |
| Accumulator with register | `1111011w` `mod 100 r/m` | | | | | |
| —byte | | 13–18 | | c | 9–14 | d |
| —word | | 13–26 | | c | 9–22 | d |
| —dword | | 13–42 | | c | 9–38 | d |
| Accumulator with memory | `1111011w` `mod 100 r/m` | | | | | |
| —byte | | 13–18 | | c | 12–17 | b,d,h |
| —word | | 13–26 | | c | 12–25 | b,d,h |
| —dword | | 13–42 | | c | 12–41 | b,d,h |
| Register with register | `00001111` `10101111` `mod reg r/m` | | | | | |
| —byte | | 13–18 | | c | 9–14 | d |
| —word | | 13–26 | | c | 9–22 | d |
| —dword | | 13–42 | | c | 9–38 | d |
| Register with memory | `00001111` `10101111` `mod reg r/m` | | | | | |
| —byte | | 13–18 | 1 | c | 12–17 | b,d,h |
| —word | | 13–26 | 1 | c | 12–25 | b,d,h |
| —dword | | 13–42 | 1 | c | 12–41 | b,d,h |

*(continued)*

## 80386/80486 Instruction Set Clock Summary. *continued*

| Instruction | Format | 80486 Clocks | Cache Miss Penalty | Cache Notes | 80386 Clocks | General Notes |
|---|---|---|---|---|---|---|
| Register with immediate to register | `0110100s1` `mod reg r/m` immediate data | | | | | |
| —byte | | 13–18 | | C | 9–14 | d |
| —word | | 13–26 | | C | 9–22 | d |
| —dword | | 13–42 | | C | 9–38 | d |
| Memory with immediate to register | `0110100s1` `mod reg r/m` immediate data | | | | | |
| —byte | | 13–18 | 2 | C | 12–17 | b,d,h |
| —word | | 13–26 | 2 | C | 12–25 | b,d,h |
| —dword | | 13–42 | 2 | C | 12–41 | b,d,h |
| DIV = Divide (unsigned) | | | | | | |
| Accumulator by register | `1111011w` `mod 110 r/m` | | | | | |
| —byte | | 16 | | | 14 | e |
| —word | | 24 | | | 22 | e |
| —dword | | 40 | | | 38 | e |
| Accumulator by memory | `1111011w` `mod 110 r/m` | | | | | |
| —byte | | 16 | | | 17 | b,e,h |
| —word | | 24 | | | 25 | b,e,h |
| —dword | | 40 | | | 41 | b,e,h |
| IDIV = Integer divide (signed) | | | | | | |
| Accumulator by register | `1111011w` `mod 111 r/m` | | | | | |
| —byte | | 19 | | | 19 | e |
| —word | | 27 | | | 27 | e |
| —dword | | 43 | | | 43 | e |
| Accumulator by memory | `1111011w` `mod 111 r/m` | | | | | |
| —byte | | 20 | | | 22 | b,e,h |
| —word | | 28 | | | 30 | b,e,h |
| —dword | | 44 | | | 46 | b,e,h |

| Instruction | Format | 80486 Clocks | Cache Miss Penalty | Cache Notes | 80386 Clocks | General Notes |
|---|---|---|---|---|---|---|
| AAD = ASCII adjust for divide | `11010101` `00001010` | 14 | | | 19 | |
| AAM = ASCII adjust for multiply | `11010100` `00001010` | 15 | | | 17 | |
| CBW = Convert byte to word | `10011000` | 3 | | | 3 | |
| CWD = Convert word to dword | `10011001` | 3 | | | 2 | |

## Logic

### Shift/Rotate

TTT = 0 / ROL = Rotate left

TTT = 1 / ROR = Rotate right

TTT = 2 / RCL = Rotate through carry left

TTT = 3 / RCR = Rotate through carry right

TTT = 4 / SHL/SAL = Shift left

TTT = 5 / SHR = Shift right

TTT = 7 / SAR = Shift arithmetic right

| Instruction | Format | 80486 Clocks | Cache Miss Penalty | Cache Notes | 80386 Clocks | General Notes |
|---|---|---|---|---|---|---|
| **Rotate through carry (RCL/RCR)** | | | | | | |
| Register by 1 | `1101000w` `mod TTT r/m` | 3 | | | 9 | b,h |
| Memory by 1 | `1101000w` `mod TTT r/m` | 4 | 6 | | 10 | b,h |
| Register by CL | `1101001w` `mod TTT r/m` | 8–30 | | D | 9 | |
| Memory by CL | `1101001w` `mod TTT r/m` | 9–31 | | E | 10 | b,h |
| Register immediate | `1100000w` `mod TTT r/m` `immed 8-bit data` | 8–30 | | D | 9 | |
| Memory immediate | `1100000w` `mod TTT r/m` `immed 8-bit data` | 9–31 | 6 | E | 10 | b,h |
| **All others (ROL/ROR/SHL/SHR/SAL/SAR)** | | | | | | |
| Register by 1 | `1101000w` `mod TTT r/m` | 3 | | | 3 | b,h |
| Memory by 1 | `1101000w` `mod TTT r/m` | 4 | 6 | | 7 | b,h |
| Register by CL | `1101001w` `mod TTT r/m` | 3 | | | 3 | |
| Memory by CL | `1101001w` `mod TTT r/m` | 4 | 6 | | 7 | b,h |
| Register immediate | `1100000w` `mod TTT r/m` `immed 8-bit data` | 2 | | | 3 | b,h |
| Memory immediate | `1100000w` `mod TTT r/m` `immed 8-bit data` | 4 | 6 | | 7 | b,h |

(continued)

# 80386/80486 Instruction Set Clock Summary. *continued*

| Instruction | Format | 80486 Clocks | Cache Miss Penalty | Cache Notes | 80386 Clocks | General Notes |
|---|---|---|---|---|---|---|
| SHRD/SHLD = Shift right/left double | | | | | | |
| r = 0 / SHLD — r = 1 / SHRD | | | | | | |
| Register by immediate | `00001111` `1010r100` `mod reg r/m` `immed 8-bit data` | 2 | | | 3 | |
| Memory by immediate | `00001111` `1010r100` `mod reg r/m` `immed 8-bit data` | 3 | 6 | | 7 | |
| Register by CL | `00001111` `1010r101` `mod reg r/m` | 3 | | | 3 | |
| Memory by CL | `00001111` `1010r101` `mod reg r/m` | 4 | 5 | | 7 | |
| BSWAP = Byte swap | `00001111` `11001 reg` | 1 | | | N/A | |
| XADD = Exchange and add | | | | | | |
| Register to register | `00001111` `1100000w` `mod reg r/m` | 3 | | | N/A | |
| Memory to register | `00001111` `1100000w` `mod reg r/m` | 4 | 6 | | N/A | |
| CMPXCHG = Compare and Exchange | | | | | | |
| Register to register | `00001111` `1011000w` `mod reg r/m` | 6 | | F | N/A | |
| Memory to register | `00001111` `1011000w` `mod reg r/m` | 7–10 | 2 | | N/A | |

### String Instructions

| Instruction | Format | 80486 Clocks | Cache Miss Penalty | Cache Notes | 80386 Clocks | General Notes |
|---|---|---|---|---|---|---|
| CMPS = Compare byte/word/dword | `1010011w` | 8 | 6 | P | 10 | b,h |
| LODS = Load byte/word/dword | `1010110w` | 5 | 2 | | 5 | b,h |
| MOVS = Move byte/word/dword | `1010010w` | 7 | 2 | P | 7 | b,h |
| SCAS = Scan byte/word/dword | `1010111w` | 6 | 2 | | 7 | b,h |
| STOS = Store byte/word/dword | `1010101w` | 5 | | | 4 | b,h |
| REPE/REPNE CMPS = Repeated compare | | | | | | |
|   ECX = 0 | | | | | | |
|   ECX > 0 | | 5 | | | 5 | b,h |
| REP LODS = Repeated load | | | | | | |
|   ECX = 0 | | 7+7c | | P,Q | 5+9c | b,h |
|   ECX > 0 | | 5 | | | 5 | b,h |
| REP MOVS = Repeated move | | | | | | |
|   ECX = 0 | | 7+4c | | P,R | 5+6c | b,h |
|   ECX = 0 | | 5 | | | 7 | b,h |

| Instruction | Format | 80486 Clocks | Cache Miss Penalty | Cache Notes | 80386 Clocks | General Notes |
|---|---|---|---|---|---|---|
| ECX = 1 | | 13 | 1 | P | 11 | b,h |
| ECX > 1 | | 12+3c | | P,S | 7+4c | b,h |
| REPE/REPNE SCAS = Repeated scan | | | | | | |
| ECX = 0 | | 5 | | | 5 | b,h |
| ECX > 0 | | 7+5c | | T | 5+8c | b,h |
| REP STOS = Repeated store | | | | | | |
| ECX = 0 | | 5 | | | 5 | b,h |
| ECX > 0 | | 7+5c | | T | 5+5c | b,h |
| XLAT = Translate byte | 11010111 | 4 | 2 | | 5 | h |
| **Bit Instructions** | | | | | | |
| BSF = Bit scan forward | | | | | | |
| Register, register | 00001111  10111100  mod reg r/m | 6-42 | | L | 10+3b | b,h |
| Memory, register | 00001111  10111100  mod reg r/m | 7-43 | 2 | M | 10+3b | b,h |
| BSR = Bit scan reverse | | | | | | |
| Register, register | 00001111  10111101  mod reg r/m | 6-103 | | N | 10+3b | b,h |
| Memory, register | 00001111  10111101  mod reg r/m | 7-104 | | O | 10+3b | b,h |
| BT = Bit test | | | | | | |
| Register, immediate | 00001111  10111010  mod 100 r/m  immed 8-bit data | 3 | | | 3 | |
| Memory, immediate | 00001111  10111010  mod 100 r/m  immed 8-bit data | 3 | 1 | | 6 | b,h |
| Register, register | 00001111  10100011  mod reg r/m | 3 | | | 3 | |
| Memory, register | 00001111  10100011  mod reg r/m | 8 | 2 | | 12 | b,h |
| Bit modify | | | | | | |
| TTT = 5 / BTS = Bit test and set | | | | | | |
| TTT = 6 / BTR = Bit test and reset | | | | | | |
| TTT = 7 / BTC = Bit test and complement | | | | | | |
| Register, immediate | 00001111  10111010  mod TTT r/m  immed 8-bit data | 6 | | | 6 | |
| Memory, immediate | 00001111  10111010  mod TTT r/m  immed 8-bit data | 8 | 2 | | 8 | b,h |

*(continued)*

## 80386/80486 Instruction Set Clock Summary. *continued*

| Instruction | Format | 80486 Clocks | Cache Miss Penalty | Cache Notes | 80386 Clocks | General Notes |
|---|---|---|---|---|---|---|
| Register, register | `00001111` `10111011` `mod TTT r/m` | 6 | | | 6 | b,h |
| Memory, register | `00001111` `10111011` `mod TTT r/m` | 13 | 3 | | 13 | |
| SETccc = Set byte on condition | `00001111` `1001cccc` `mod 000 r/m` | | | | | |
| cccc = 00 / SETO = Set if overflow | | | | | | |
| cccc = 01 / SETNO = Set if no overflow | | | | | | |
| cccc = 02 / SETB/SETNAE = Set if below/Set if not above or equal | | | | | | |
| cccc = 03 / SETNB/SETAE = Set if not below/Set if above or equal | | | | | | |
| cccc = 04 / SETE/SETZ = Set if equal/Set if zero | | | | | | |
| cccc = 05 / SETNE/SETNZ = Set if not equal/Set if not zero | | | | | | |
| cccc = 06 / SETBE/SETNA = Set if below or equal/Set if not above | | | | | | |
| cccc = 07 / SETNBE/SETA = Set if not below or equal/Set if above | | | | | | |
| cccc = 08 / SETS = Set if signed | | | | | | |
| cccc = 09 / SETNS = Set if not signed | | | | | | |
| cccc = 10 / SETP/SETPE = Set if parity/Set if parity even | | | | | | |
| cccc = 11 / SETNP/SETPO = Set if not parity/Set if parity odd | | | | | | |
| cccc = 12 / SETL/SETNGE = Set if less/Set if not greater or equal | | | | | | |
| cccc = 13 / SETNL/SETGE = Set if not less/Set if greater or equal | | | | | | |
| cccc = 14 / SETLE/SETNG = Set if less or equal/Set if not greater | | | | | | |
| cccc = 15 / SETNLE/SETG = Set if not less or equal/Set if greater | | | | | | |
| Register (condition true) | | 4 | | | 4 | h |
| Register (condition false) | | 3 | | | 4 | h |
| Memory (condition true) | | 3 | | | 5 | h |
| Memory (condition false) | | 4 | | | 5 | h |

### Conditional Branch

Jcc = Jump on condition

8-bit displacement `0111cccc` `8-bit displacement`

Full displacement `00001111` `1000cccc` `full displacement`

cccc = 00 / JO = Jump if overflow

cccc = 01 / JNO = Jump if no overflow

| Instruction | Format | 80486 Clocks | Cache Miss Penalty | Cache Notes | 80386 Clocks | General Notes |
|---|---|---|---|---|---|---|
| cccc = 02 / JB/JNAE = Jump if below/Jump if not above or equal | | | | | | |
| cccc = 03 / JNB/JAE = Jump if not below/Jump if above or equal | | | | | | |
| cccc = 04 / JE/JZ = Jump if equal/Jump if zero | | | | | | |
| cccc = 05 / JNE/JNZ = Jump if not equal/Jump if not zero | | | | | | |
| cccc = 06 / JBE/JNA = Jump if below or equal/Jump if not above | | | | | | |
| cccc = 07 / JNBE/JA = Jump if not below or equal/Jump if above | | | | | | |
| cccc = 08 / JS = Jump if signed | | | | | | |
| cccc = 09 / JNS = Jump if not signed | | | | | | |
| cccc = 10 / JP/JPE = Jump if parity/Jump if parity even | | | | | | |
| cccc = 11 / JNP/JPO = Jump if not parity/Jump if parity odd | | | | | | |
| cccc = 12 / JL/JNGE = Jump if less/Jump if not greater or equal | | | | | | |
| cccc = 13 / JNL/JGE = Jump if not less/Jump if greater or equal | | | | | | |
| cccc = 14 / JLE/JNG = Jump if less or equal/Jump if not greater | | | | | | |
| cccc = 15 / JNLE/JG = Jump if not less or equal/Jump if greater | | | | | | |
| Branch taken | | 3 | | W | 7+m | r |
| Branch not taken | | 1 | | W | 3 | |
| JCXZ/JECXZ = Jump if CX/ECX is zero | `11100011` `8-bit displacement` | | | | | |
| Branch taken | | 8 | | W | 9+m | r |
| Branch not taken | | 5 | | W | 5 | |
| LOOP = Loop ECX times | `11100010` `8-bit displacement` | | | | | |
| Branch taken | | 7 | | W | 11+m | r |
| Branch not taken | | 6 | | W | 11 | |
| LOOPE/LOOPZ = Loop if equal/Loop if zero | `11100001` `8-bit displacement` | | | | | |
| Branch taken | | 9 | | W | 11+m | r |
| Branch not taken | | 6 | | W | 11 | |
| LOOPNE/LOOPNZ = Loop if not equal/Loop if not zero | `11100000` `8-bit displacement` | | | | | |
| Branch taken | | 9 | | W | 11+m | r |
| Branch not taken | | 6 | | W | 11 | |

*(continued)*

431

# 80386/80486 Instruction Set Clock Summary. *continued*

| Instruction | Format | 80486 Clocks | Cache Miss Penalty | Cache Notes | 80386 Clocks | General Notes |
|---|---|---|---|---|---|---|
| **Control Transfer** | | | | | | |
| *JMP = Unconditional branch* | | | | | | |
| Short | `11101001` `8-bit displacement` | 3 | | | 7+m | r |
| Direct within segment | `11101001` `full displacement` | 3 | | G,W | 7+m | r |
| Register indirect within segment | `11111111` `mod 100 r/m` | 5 | | G,W | 7+m | r |
| Memory indirect within segment | `11111111` `mod 100 r/m` | 5 | 5 | G | 10+m | b,h,r |
| Direct intersegment (real mode) | `11101010` `unsigned full offset, selector` | 17 | 2 | G,V | 12+m | r |
| Direct intersegment (protected mode) | | 19 | 3 | I | 27+m | j,k,r |
| Via call gate, same privilege | | 32 | 6 | I | 45+m | h,j,k,r |
| Via task gate | | 43+task switch | 3 | I,J | 44+task switch | |
| Via TSS | | 42+task switch | 3 | I,J | 44+task switch | |
| Indirect intersegment (real mode) | `11111111` `mod 101 r/m` | 13 | 9 | G,I | 17+m | b |
| Indirect intersegment (protected mode) | | 18 | 10 | I | 31+m | h,j,k,r |
| Via call gate, same privilege | | 31 | 13 | I | 49+m | |
| Via task gate | | 41+task switch | 10 | I,J | 49+task switch | |
| Via TSS | | 42+task switch | 10 | I,J | 49+task switch | |
| *CALL = Call* | | | | | | |
| Direct within segment | `11101000` `full displacement` | 3 | | G,W | 7+m | b,r |
| Register indirect within segment | `11111111` `mod 010 r/m` | 5 | | G,W | 7+m | b,r |
| Memory indirect within segment | `11111111` `mod 010 r/m` | 5 | 5 | G | 10+m | b,h,r |
| Direct intersegment (real mode) | `10011010` `unsigned full offset, selector` | 18 | 2 | G,V | 17+m | b,h,r |
| Direct intersegment (protected mode) | | 20 | 3 | I | 34+m | b,j,k,r |
| Via call gate, same privilege | | 35 | 6 | I | 52+m | h,j,k,r |
| Via call gate, different privilege, no parameters | | 69 | 17 | I | 86+m | h,j,k,r |
| Via call gate, different privilege, x parameters | | 77+4x | 17+x | I,K | 94+4x+m | h,j,k,r |
| Via task gate | | 38+task switch | 3 | I,J | 45+task switch | |

| Instruction | Format | 80486 Clocks | Cache Miss Penalty | Cache Notes | 80386 Clocks | General Notes |
|---|---|---|---|---|---|---|
| Via TSS |  | 37+task switch | 3 | I,J | 45+task switch |  |
| Indirect intersegment (real mode) | `1111111` `mod 011 r/m` | 17 | 8 | G | 22+m | h,j,k,r |
| Indirect intersegment (protected mode) |  | 20 | 10 | I | 38+m | h,j,k,r |
| Via call gate, same privilege |  | 35 | 13 | I | 52+m | h,j,k,r |
| Via call gate, different privilege, no parameters |  | 69 | 24 | I | 86+m | h,j,k,r |
| Via call gate, different privilege, x parameters |  | 77+4x | 24+x | I,K | 94+4x+m | h,j,k,r |
| Via task gate |  | 38+task switch | 10 | I,J | 49+task switch |  |
| Via TSS |  | 37+task switch | 10 | I,J | 49+task switch |  |
| RET = Return from call |  |  |  |  |  |  |
| Within segment | `11000011` | 5 | 5 |  | 10+m | b,g,h,r |
| Within segment adjusting ESP | `11000010` `16-bit displacement` | 5 | 5 |  | 10+m | b,g,h,r |
| Intersegment (real mode) | `11001011` | 13 | 8 | G | 18+m | b |
| Intersegment adjusting ESP (real mode) | `11001010` `16-bit displacement` | 14 | 8 | G | 18+m | b |
| Intersegment (protected mode) |  | 17 | 9 | I | 32+m | g,h,j,k,r |
| Intersegment adjusting ESP (protected mode) |  | 18 | 9 | I | 32+m | g,h,j,k,r |
| Intersegment to different privilege level |  | 35 | 12 | I | 68 | h,j,k,r |
| Intersegment to different privilege level adjusting ESP |  | 36 | 12 | I | 68 | h,j,k,r |
| ENTER = Enter procedure | `11001000` `16-bit displacement, 8-bit level` |  |  |  |  |  |
| Level = 0 |  | 14 |  |  | 10 | b,h |
| Level = 1 |  | 17 |  |  | 12 | b,h |
| Level (1) > 1 |  | 17+3l |  | H | 15+4l | b,h |
| LEAVE = Leave procedure | `11001001` | 5 | 1 |  | 4 | b,h |
| **Software Interrupt** |  |  |  |  |  |  |
| INT3 = Debug interrupt | `11001100` | int |  | U | int | b |
| INTO = Interrupt on overflow | `11001110` |  |  |  |  |  |
| Interrupt taken |  | 2+int |  | U | 2+int | b,e |
| Interrupt not taken |  | 3 |  |  | 3 |  |

*(continued)*

# 80386/80486 Instruction Set Clock Summary. *continued*

| Instruction | Format | 80486 Clocks | Cache Miss Penalty | Cache Notes | 80386 Clocks | General Notes |
|---|---|---|---|---|---|---|
| INT = Interrupt n | `11001101` `type` | 4+int | | | 4+int | b,e |
| BOUND = Interrupt if out of range | `01100010` `mod reg r/m` | | | | | |
| Interrupt taken | | 24+int | 7 | U | 11+int | b,e |
| Interrupt not taken | | 7 | 7 | U | 10 | |
| IRET = Interrupt return | `11001111` | | | | | |
| Real mode/V86 mode | | 15 | 8 | | 22 | |
| Protected mode, same privilege | | 20 | 11 | I | 38 | g,h,j,k,r |
| Protected mode, different privilege | | 36 | 19 | I | 82 | g,h,j,k,r |
| Protected mode, nested task | | 32+task switch | 4 | IJ | 16+task switch | |
| Basic interrupt times (INT) | | | | | | |
| Real mode | | 26 | 2 | | 33 | |
| Protected mode via gate, same privilege | | 44 | 6 | I | 59 | |
| Protected mode via gate, different privilege | | 71 | 17 | I | 99 | |
| Protected mode via task gate | | 37+task switch | 3 | IJ | 50+task switch | |
| V86 mode via gate | | 82 | 17 | | 50+task switch | |
| V86 mode via task gate | | 37+task switch | 3 | J | 50+task switch | |
| Basic task switch time (task switch) | | | | | | |
| To 286 TSS | | 143 | 31 | | 232–237 | |
| To 386/486 TSS | | 162 | 55 | | 259–266 | |
| To V86 TSS | | 140 | 37 | | 178 | |

### *Processor Control*

| Instruction | Format | 80486 Clocks | Cache Miss Penalty | Cache Notes | 80386 Clocks | General Notes |
|---|---|---|---|---|---|---|
| HLT = Halt | `11110100` | 4 | | | 5 | 1 |
| MOV = Move to/from control or debug register | | | | | | |
| Register to CR0 | `00001111` `00100010` `11eeereg` | 17 | 2 | | 10 | 1 |
| Register to CR2-3 | `00001111` `00100010` `11eeereg` | 4 | | | 4–5 | 1 |
| CRx to register | `00001111` `00100000` `11eeereg` | 4 | | | 6 | 1 |

| Instruction | Format | 80486 Clocks | Cache Miss Penalty | Cache Notes | 80386 Clocks | General Notes |
|---|---|---|---|---|---|---|
| DR0-3 to register | `00001111` `00100001` `11eeereg` | 9 | | | 22 | 1 |
| DR6-7 to register | `00001111` `00100001` `11eeereg` | 9 | | | 16 | 1 |
| Register to DR0-3 | `00001111` `00100011` `11eeereg` | 10 | | | 22 | 1 |
| Register to DR6-7 | `00001111` `00100011` `11eeereg` | 10 | | | 14 | 1 |
| TRx to register | `00001111` `00100100` `11eeereg` | 4 | | | 12 | 1 |
| Register to TRx | `00001111` `00100110` `11eeereg` | 4 | | | 12 | 1 |
| CLTS = Clear task switched bit | `00001111` `00000110` | 7 | 2 | | 5 | c,l |
| INVD = Invalidate cache | `00001111` `00001000` | 4 | | | N/A | |
| WBINVLD = Write back and invalidate cache | `00001111` `00001001` | 5 | | | N/A | |
| INVLPG = Invalidate TLB entry | `00001111` `00000001` `mod 111 r/m` | 12 | | | N/A | |
| NOP = No operation | `10010000` | 1 | | | 3 | |

**Prefix Bytes**

| Instruction | Format | 80486 Clocks | Cache Miss Penalty | Cache Notes | 80386 Clocks | General Notes |
|---|---|---|---|---|---|---|
| ADRSIZ = Address size override | `01100111` | 1 | | | 0 | |
| OPSIZ = Operand size override | `01100110` | 1 | | | 0 | |
| LOCK = Bus lock | `11110000` | 1 | | | 0 | |
| CS = Code segment override | `00101110` | 1 | | | 0 | |
| DS = Data segment override | `00111110` | 1 | | | 0 | |
| ES = Extra segment override | `00100110` | 1 | | | 0 | |
| FS = FS segment override | `01100100` | 1 | | | 0 | |
| GS = GS segment override | `01100101` | 1 | | | 0 | |
| SS = Stack segment override | `00110110` | 1 | | | 0 | |

**Protection Control**

| Instruction | Format | 80486 Clocks | Cache Miss Penalty | Cache Notes | 80386 Clocks | General Notes |
|---|---|---|---|---|---|---|
| ARPL = Adjust requested privilege level | `01100011` `mod reg r/m` | | | | | |
| From register | | 9 | | | 20 | a |
| From memory | | 9 | | | 21 | a,h |
| LAR = Load access rights | `00001111` `00000010` `mod reg r/m` | | | | | |
| From register | | 11 | 3 | | 15 | a |
| From memory | | 11 | 5 | | 16 | a,g,h,i,p |

*(continued)*

# 80386/80486 Instruction Set Clock Summary. *continued*

| Instruction | Format | 80486 Clocks | Cache Miss Penalty | Cache Notes | 80386 Clocks | General Notes |
|---|---|---|---|---|---|---|
| LGDT = Load GDT register | 00001111 00000001 mod 010 r/m | 12 | 5 | | 11 | b,c,h,l |
| LIDT = Load IDT register | 00001111 00000001 mod 011 r/m | 12 | 5 | | 11 | b,c,h,l |
| LLDT = Load LDT register | 00001111 00000000 mod 010 r/m | | | | | |
|   From register | | 11 | 3 | | 20 | a |
|   From memory | | 11 | 6 | | 24 | a,g,h,j,l |
| LMSW = Load machine status word | 00001111 00000001 mod 110 r/m | | | | | |
|   From register | | 13 | | | 10 | b,c,h,l |
|   From memory | | 13 | 1 | | 13 | b,c,h,l |
| LSL = Load segment limit | 00001111 00000011 mod reg r/m | | | | | |
|   From register | | 10 | 3 | | 20–25 | a,g,h,j,p |
|   From memory | | 10 | 6 | | 21–26 | a,g,h,j,p |
| LTR = Load task register | 00001111 00000000 mod 001 r/m | | | | | |
|   From register | | 20 | | | 23 | a,g,h,j,l |
|   From memory | | 20 | | | 27 | a,g,h,j,l |
| SGDT = Store GDT register | 00001111 00000001 mod 000 r/m | 10 | | | 9 | b,c,h |
| SIDT = Store IDT register | 00001111 00000001 mod 001 r/m | 10 | | | 9 | b,c,h |
| SLDT = Store SDT register | 00001111 00000000 mod 000 r/m | | | | | |
|   To register | | 2 | | | 2 | a,h |
|   To memory | | 3 | | | 2 | a,h |
| SMSW = Store machine status word | 00001111 00000001 mod 100 r/m | | | | | |
|   To register | | 2 | | | 10 | b,c,h,l |
|   To memory | | 3 | | | 13 | b,c,h,l |
| STR = Store task register | 00001111 00000000 mod 001 r/m | | | | | |
|   To register | | 2 | | | 2 | a,h |
|   To memory | | 3 | | | 2 | a,h |
| VERR = Verify read access | 00001111 00000000 mod 100 r/m | | | | | |
|   Register | | 11 | 3 | | 10 | a,g,h,j,p |
|   Memory | | 11 | 7 | | 11 | a,g,h,j,p |

| Instruction | Format | Clk Count Virtual 8086 Mode | 80486 Clocks | Cache Miss Penalty | Cache Notes | 80386 Clocks | General Notes |
|---|---|---|---|---|---|---|---|
| VERW = Verify write access | 00001111 \| 0000000 \| mod 101 r/m | | | | | | |
| Register | | | 11 | 3 | | 15 | a,g,h,j,p |
| Memory | | | 11 | 7 | | 16 | a,g,h,j,p |
| **I/O Instructions** | | | | | | | |
| IN = Input from port | | | | | | | |
| Fixed port/ | 1110010w \| port number | 26 | | | | | |
| Variable port | 1110110w | 27 | | | | | |
| Real mode | | | 14 | | | 12/13 | |
| Protected mode (CPL <=IOPL) | | | 9/8 | | | 6/7 | |
| Protect mode (CPL>IOPL) | | | 29/28 | | | 26/27 | |
| V86 mode | | | 27 | | | 26/27 | |
| OUT = Output to port | | | | | | | |
| Fixed port/ | 1110011w \| port number | 24 | | | | | |
| Variable port | 1110111w | 25 | | | | | |
| Real mode | | | 16 | | | 10/11 | |
| Protected mode (CP<=IOPL) | | | 10/11 | | | 4/5 | |
| Protect mode (CPL>IOPL) | | | 31/30 | | | 24/25 | |
| V86 mode | | | 29 | | | 24/25 | |
| INS = Input string | | | | | | | |
| | 0110110w | 29 | | | | | |
| Real mode | | | 17 | | | 15 | |
| Protected mode (CPL<=IOPL) | | | 10 | | | 9 | |
| Protect mode (CPL>IOPL) | | | 32 | | | 29 | |
| V86 mode | | | 30 | | | 29 | |
| OUTS = Output string | | | | | | | |
| | 0110111w | 28 | | | | | |
| Real mode | | | 17 | | | 14 | |
| Protected mode (CPL<=IOPL) | | | 10 | | | 8 | |
| Protect mode (CPL>IOPL) | | | 32 | | | 28 | |
| V86 mode | | | 30 | | | 28 | |

*(continued)*

# 80386/80486 Instruction Set Clock Summary. *continued*

| Instruction | Format | Clk Count Virtual 8086 Mode | 80486 Clocks | Cache Miss Penalty | Cache Notes | 80386 Clocks | General Notes |
|---|---|---|---|---|---|---|---|
| REP INS = Repeated input string | 11110010  0110110w | 27+6n | | | | | |
| Real mode | | | 16+8c | | | 13+6c | |
| Protected mode (CPL<=IOPL) | | | 10+8c | | | 7+6c | |
| Protect mode (CPL>IOPL) | | | 30+8c | | | 27+6c | |
| V86 mode | | | 29+8c | | | 27+6c | |
| REP OUTS = Repeated output string | 11110010  0110111w | 26+5n | | | | | |
| Real mode | | | 17+5c | | | 12+5c | |
| Protected mode (CPL<=IOPL) | | | 11+5c | | | 6+5c | |
| Protect mode (CPL>IOPL) | | | 31+5c | | | 26+5c | |
| V86 mode | | | 30+5c | | | 26+5c | |

## Cache Notes:

A. Assuming that the operand address and stack address fall in different cache sets.

B. Always locked, no cache hit case.

C. Clocks = $10 + \max(\log_2(|m|), n)$

    m = multiplier value (min clocks for m = 0)

    n = 3/5 for ±m

D. Clocks = lquotient(count/operand length)*7+9

    = 8 if count ≤ operand length (8/16/32)

E. Clocks = lquotient(count/operand length)*7+9

    = 9 if count ≤ operand length (8/16/32)

F. Equal/not equal cases (penalty is the same regardless of lock).

G. Assuming that addresses for memory read (for indirection), stack push/pop, and branch fall in different cache sets.

H. Penalty for cache miss: add 6 clocks for every 16 bytes copied to new stack frame.

I. Add 11 clocks for every unaccessed descriptor load.

J. Refer to task switch clock counts table for value of TS.

K. Add 4 extra clocks to the cache miss penalty for each 16 bytes.

**For notes L–M:** (b = 0–3, nonzero byte number);

    (i = 0–1, nonzero nibble number);

    (n = 0–3, nonbit number in nibble);

L. Clocks = 8+4(b+1) + 3(i+1) + 3(n+1)

    = 6 if second operand = 0

M. Clocks = 9+4(b+1) + 3(i+1) + 3(n+1)

    = 7 if second operand = 0

**For notes N–O:** (n = bit position 0–31)

N. Clocks = 7 + 3(32−n)

    6 if second operand = 0

O. Clocks = 8 + 3(32−n)

    7 if second operand = 0

P. Assuming that the two string addresses fall in different cache sets.

Q. Cache miss penalty: add 6 clocks for every 16 bytes compared. Entire penalty on first compare.

R. Cache miss penalty: add 2 clocks for every 16 bytes of data. Entire penalty on first load.

S. Cache miss penalty: add 4 clocks for every 16 bytes moved. (1 clock for the first operation and 3 for the second)

T. Cache miss penalty: add 4 clocks for every 16 bytes scanned. (2 clocks each for first and second operations)

U. Refer to interrupt clock counts table for value of INT.

V. Clock count includes one clock for using both displacement and immediate.

W. Refer to assumption 6 in the case of a cache miss.

438

# Instruction Encoding

All instruction encodings are subsets of the general instruction format shown in Figure D-1. Instructions consist of one or two primary opcode bytes, possibly an address specifier consisting of the mod r/m byte and scaled index byte, a displacement if required, and an immediate data field if required.

Within the primary opcode or opcodes, smaller encoding fields can be defined. These fields vary according to the class of operation. The fields define information such as direction of the operation, size of the displacements, register encoding, and sign extension.

Almost all instructions that refer to an operand in memory have an addressing mode byte following the primary opcode byte(s). This byte, the *mod r/m* byte, specifies the address mode to be used. Certain encodings of the mod r/m byte indicate a second addressing byte, the scale-index-base byte, which fully specifies the addressing mode.

Addressing modes can include a displacement immediately following the mod r/m byte or the scaled index byte. If a displacement is present, the possible sizes are 8, 16, and 32 bits.

If the instruction specifies an immediate operand, the immediate operand follows any displacement bytes. The immediate operand is always the last field of the instruction.

Figure D-1 illustrates some of the fields that can appear in an instruction, such as the mod field and the r/m field. Several smaller fields also appear in certain instructions, sometimes within the opcode bytes. The table on the following page is a complete list of all fields appearing in the 80386-family instruction set. Detailed tables for each field appear later in this appendix.

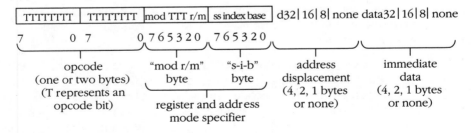

**Figure D-1.** *General instruction format.*

## Fields within 80386 Instructions

| Field Name | Description | Number of Bits |
|---|---|---|
| w | Specifies whether data is byte size or full size (full size is either 16 or 32 bits) | 1 |
| d | Specifies direction of data operation | 1 |
| s | Specifies whether an immediate data field must be sign-extended | 1 |
| reg | General register specifier | 3 |
| mod r/m | Address mode specifier (effective address can be a general register) | 2 for mod; 3 for r/m |
| ss | Scale factor for scaled index address mode | 2 |
| index | General register to be used as index register | 3 |
| base | General register to be used as base register | 3 |
| sreg2 | Segment register specifier for CS, SS, DS, ES | 2 |
| sreg3 | Segment register specifier for CS, SS, DS, ES, FS, GS | 3 |
| cccc | For conditional instructions, specifies a condition asserted or a condition negated | 4 |

NOTE: Figure D-1 shows encoding of individual instructions.

# 32-bit extensions of the instruction set

With the 80386, the 8086/80186/80286 instruction set is extended in two orthogonal directions: 32-bit forms of all 16-bit instructions support the 32-bit data types, and 32-bit addressing modes are available for all instructions referring to memory. This orthogonal instruction set extension is accomplished by having a default (D) bit in the code segment descriptor and by having two prefixes to the instruction set.

Whether the instruction defaults to operations of 16 bits or 32 bits depends on the setting of the D bit in the code segment descriptor. The D bit specifies the default length (either 16 bits or 32 bits) for both operands and effective addresses when executing that code segment. Real address mode and virtual 8086 mode use no code segment descriptors, but the 80386 internally assumes a D value of 0 when operating in those modes (for 16-bit default sizes compatible with the 8086/80186/80286).

Two prefixes, the operand size prefix and the effective address size prefix, allow overriding the default selection of operand size and effective address size. These prefixes can precede any opcode bytes and affect only the instruction they precede. If necessary, one or both prefixes can be placed before the opcode bytes. The presence of the operand size prefix and the effective address size prefix toggles the operand size or the effective address size to the value opposite that of the default setting. For example, if the default operand size is for 32-bit data operations, the presence of the operand size prefix toggles the instruction to 16-bit data operations. If the default effective address size is 16 bits, the presence of the effective address size prefix toggles the instruction to use 32-bit effective address computations.

These 32-bit extensions are available in all 80386/80486 modes, including real address mode or virtual 8086 mode. In these two modes the default is always 16 bits, so prefixes are needed to specify 32-bit operands or addresses.

Unless specified, instructions with 8-bit and 16-bit operands do not affect the contents of the high-order bits of the extended registers.

## Encoding of instruction fields

Several fields indicate register selection, addressing mode, and so on within the instruction. The encodings of these fields are defined in the following tables.

### Encoding of the operand length (w) field

For any given instruction performing a data operation, the instruction executes as a 32-bit operation or a 16-bit operation. Within the constraints of the operation size, the w field encodes the operand size as either 1 byte or the full operation size, as shown in the table below.

**Operand Length Encoding**

| w Field | Operand Size During 16-Bit Data Operations | Operand Size During 32-Bit Data Operations |
|---------|-------------------------------------------|--------------------------------------------|
| 0       | 8 bits                                    | 8 bits                                     |
| 1       | 16 bits                                   | 32 bits                                    |

### Encoding of the general register (reg) field

The general register is specified by the reg field, which can appear in the primary opcode bytes or as the reg field of the mod r/m byte, or as the r/m field of the mod r/m byte. The following tables illustrate reg field encoding.

**Encoding of reg Field When w Field Is Not Present in Instruction**

| reg Field | Register Selected During 16-Bit Data Operations | Register Selected During 32-Bit Data Operations |
|-----------|-------------------------------------------------|-------------------------------------------------|
| 000       | AX                                              | EAX                                             |
| 001       | CX                                              | ECX                                             |
| 010       | DX                                              | EDX                                             |
| 011       | BX                                              | EBX                                             |
| 100       | SP                                              | ESP                                             |
| 101       | BP                                              | EBP                                             |
| 101       | SI                                              | ESI                                             |
| 101       | DI                                              | EDI                                             |

### Encoding of reg Field When w Field Is Present in Instruction

| | Register Specified by reg Field During 16-Bit Data Operations | |
|---|---|---|
| reg Field | Function of w Field When w = 0 | Function of w Field When w = 1 |
| 000 | AL | AX |
| 001 | CL | CX |
| 010 | DL | DX |
| 011 | BL | BX |
| 100 | AH | SP |
| 101 | CH | BP |
| 110 | DH | SI |
| 111 | BH | DI |

### Encoding of reg Field When w Field Is Present in Instruction

| | Register Specified by reg Field During 32-Bit Data Operations | |
|---|---|---|
| reg Field | Function of w Field When w = 0 | Function of w Field When w = 1 |
| 000 | AL | EAX |
| 001 | CL | ECX |
| 010 | DL | EDX |
| 011 | BL | EBX |
| 100 | AH | ESP |
| 101 | CH | EBP |
| 110 | DH | ESI |
| 111 | BH | EDI |

## Encoding of the segment register (sreg) field

The sreg field in certain instructions is a 2-bit field that allows one of the four 80286 segment registers to be specified. The sreg field in other instructions is a 3-bit field that allows the FS and GS segment registers to be specified. The following two tables show the selected segment registers.

### 2-Bit sreg2 Field

| 2-Bit sreg2 Field | Segment Register Selected |
|---|---|
| 00 | ES |
| 01 | CS |
| 10 | SS |
| 11 | DS |

### 3-Bit sreg3 Field

| *3-Bit sreg3 Field* | *Segment Register Selected* |
| --- | --- |
| 000 | ES |
| 001 | CS |
| 010 | SS |
| 011 | DS |
| 100 | FS |
| 101 | GS |
| 110 | Do not use |
| 111 | Do not use |

## Encoding of address mode

Except for special instructions such as PUSH and POP, where the addressing mode is predetermined, the addressing mode for the current instruction is specified by addressing bytes following the primary opcode. The primary addressing byte is the mod r/m byte, and a second byte of addressing information, the s-i-b (scale-index-base) byte, can be specified.

The s-i-b byte is specified when using 32-bit addressing mode and the mod r/m byte has r/m = 100 and mod = 00, 01, or 10. When the s-i-b byte is present, the 32-bit addressing mode is a function of the mod, ss, index, and base fields.

The primary addressing byte, the mod r/m byte, also contains 3 bits (shown as TTT in Figure D-1) sometimes used as an extension of the primary opcode. The 3 bits, however, can also be used as a register field (reg).

When calculating an effective address, either 16-bit addressing or 32-bit addressing is used. To calculate the effective address, 16-bit addressing uses 16-bit address components, whereas 32-bit addressing uses 32-bit address components. When 16-bit addressing is used, the mod r/m byte is interpreted as a 16-bit addressing mode specifier. When 32-bit addressing is used, the mod r/m byte is interpreted as a 32-bit addressing mode specifier.

The following tables define all encodings of all 16-bit addressing modes and 32-bit addressing modes.

## Encoding of 32-Bit Address Mode with mod r/m Byte
### (no s-i-b Byte Present)

| mod r/m | Effective Address |
|---------|-------------------|
| 00 000  | DS:[EAX] |
| 00 001  | DS:[ECX] |
| 00 010  | DS:[EDX] |
| 00 011  | DS:[EBX] |
| 00 100  | s-i-b is present |
| 00 101  | DS:d32 |
| 00 110  | DS:[ESI] |
| 00 111  | DS:[EDI] |
| 01 000  | DS:[EAX+d8] |
| 01 001  | DS:[ECX+d8] |
| 01 010  | DS:[EDX+d8] |
| 01 011  | DS:[EBX+d8] |
| 01 100  | s-i-b is present |
| 01 101  | SS:[EBP+d8] |
| 01 110  | DS:[ESI+d8] |
| 01 111  | DS:[EDI+d8] |
| 10 000  | DS:[EAX+d32] |
| 10 001  | DS:[ECX+d32] |
| 10 010  | DS:[EDX+d32] |
| 10 011  | DS:[EBX+d32] |
| 10 100  | s-i-b is present |
| 10 101  | SS:[EBP+d32] |
| 10 110  | DS:[ESI+d32] |
| 10 111  | DS:[EDI+d32] |
| 11 000  | register—see below |
| 11 001  | register—see below |
| 11 010  | register—see below |
| 11 011  | register—see below |
| 11 100  | register—see below |
| 11 101  | register—see below |
| 11 110  | register—see below |
| 11 111  | register—see below |

### Register Specified by reg or r/m During 16-Bit Data Operations

| mod r/m | Function of w Field When w = 0 | Function of w Field When w = 1 |
|---------|-------------------------------|-------------------------------|
| 11 000  | AL | AX |
| 11 001  | CL | CX |
| 11 010  | DL | DX |
| 11 011  | BL | BX |
| 11 100  | AH | SP |
| 11 101  | CH | BP |
| 11 110  | DH | SI |
| 11 111  | BH | DI |

## Encoding of 32-Bit Address Mode with mod r/m Byte
## (no s-i-b Byte Present)

| | *Register Specified by reg or r/m During 32-Bit Data Operations* | |
|---|---|---|
| **mod r/m** | *Function of w Field* <br> *When w = 0* | *Function of w Field* <br> *When w = 1* |
| 11 000 | AL | EAX |
| 11 001 | CL | ECX |
| 11 010 | DL | EDX |
| 11 011 | BL | EBX |
| 11 100 | AH | ESP |
| 11 101 | CH | EBP |
| 11 110 | DH | ESI |
| 11 111 | BH | EDI |

## Encoding of 32-Bit Address Mode (mod r/m Byte and s-i-b Byte Present)

| **Mod Base** | **Effective Address** |
|---|---|
| 00 000 | DS:[EAX+(scaled index)] |
| 00 001 | DS:[ECX+(scaled index)] |
| 00 010 | DS:[EDX+(scaled index)] |
| 00 011 | DS:[EBX+(scaled index)] |
| 00 100 | DS:[ESP+(scaled index)] |
| 00 101 | DS:[d32+(scaled index)] |
| 00 110 | DS:[ESI+(scaled index)] |
| 00 111 | DS:[EDI+(scaled index)] |
| | |
| 01 000 | DS:[EAX+(scaled index)+d8] |
| 01 001 | DS:[ECX+(scaled index)+d8] |
| 01 010 | DS:[EDX+(scaled index)+d8] |
| 01 011 | DS:[EBX+(scaled index)+d8] |
| 01 100 | SS:[ESP+(scaled index)+d8] |
| 01 101 | SS:[EBP+(scaled index)+d8] |
| 01 110 | DS:[ESI+(scaled index)+d8] |
| 01 111 | DS:[EDI+(scaled index)+d8] |
| | |
| 10 000 | DS:[EAX+(scaled index)+d32] |
| 10 001 | DS:[ECX+(scaled index)+d32] |
| 10 010 | DS:[EDX+(scaled index)+d32] |
| 10 011 | DS:[EBX+(scaled index)+d32] |
| 10 100 | SS:[ESP+(scaled index)+d32] |
| 10 101 | SS:[EBP+(scaled index)+d32] |
| 10 110 | DS:[ESI+(scaled index)+d32] |
| 10 111 | DS:[EDI+(scaled index)+d32] |

NOTE: Mod field in mod r/m byte; ss, index, base fields in s-i-b byte.

| **ss** | **Scale Factor** |
|---|---|
| 00 | x1 |
| 01 | x2 |
| 10 | x4 |
| 11 | x8 |

| Index | Index Register |
|-------|----------------|
| 000 | EAX |
| 001 | ECX |
| 010 | EDX |
| 011 | EBX |
| 100 | no index reg* |
| 101 | EBP |
| 110 | ESI |
| 111 | EDI |

* When index field is 100, indicating no index register, ss field must equal 00. If index is 100 and ss does not equal 00, the effective address is undefined.

## Encoding of 16-Bit Address Mode with mod r/m Byte

| mod r/m | Effective Address |
|---------|-------------------|
| 00 000 | DS:[BX+SI] |
| 00 001 | DS:[BX+DI] |
| 00 010 | SS:[BP+SI] |
| 00 011 | SS:[BP+DI] |
| 00 100 | DS:[SI] |
| 00 101 | DS:[DI] |
| 00 110 | DS:[d16] |
| 00 111 | DS:[BX] |
| 01 000 | DS:[BX+SI+d8] |
| 01 001 | DS:[BX+DI+d8] |
| 01 010 | SS:[BP+SI+d8] |
| 01 011 | SS:[BP+DI+d8] |
| 01 100 | DS:[SI+d8] |
| 01 101 | DS:[DI+d8] |
| 01 110 | SS:[BP+d8] |
| 01 111 | DS:[BX+d8] |
| 10 000 | DS:[BX+SI+d16] |
| 10 001 | DS:[BX+DI+d16] |
| 10 010 | SS:[BP+SI+d16] |
| 10 011 | SS:[BP+DI+d16] |
| 10 100 | DS:[SI+d16] |
| 10 101 | DS:[DI+d16] |
| 10 110 | SS:[BP+d16] |
| 10 111 | DS:[BX+d16] |
| 11 000 | register—see page 447 |
| 11 001 | register—see page 447 |
| 11 010 | register—see page 447 |
| 11 011 | register—see page 447 |
| 11 100 | register—see page 447 |
| 11 101 | register—see page 447 |
| 11 110 | register—see page 447 |
| 11 111 | register—see page 447 |

### Encoding of 16-Bit Address Mode with mod r/m Byte

| | Register Specified by r/m During 16-Bit Data Operations | |
| | Function of w Field When w = 0 | Function of w Field When w = 1 |
| mod r/m | | |
| --- | --- | --- |
| 11 000 | AL | AX |
| 11 001 | CL | CX |
| 11 010 | DL | DX |
| 11 011 | BL | BX |
| 11 100 | AH | SP |
| 11 101 | CH | BP |
| 11 110 | DH | SI |
| 11 111 | BH | DI |

### Encoding of 16-Bit Address Mode with mod r/m Byte

| | Register Specified by r/m During 32-Bit Data Operations | |
| | Function of w Field When w = 0 | Function of w Field When w = 1 |
| mod r/m | | |
| --- | --- | --- |
| 11 000 | AL | EAX |
| 11 001 | CL | ECX |
| 11 010 | DL | EDX |
| 11 011 | BL | EBX |
| 11 100 | AH | ESP |
| 11 101 | CH | EBP |
| 11 110 | DH | ESI |
| 11 111 | BH | EDI |

## Encoding of operation direction (d) field

In many 2-operand instructions, the d field indicates which operand is the source and which is the destination, as shown in the following table.

### Operation Direction Encoding

| d | Direction of Operation |
| --- | --- |
| 0 | Register/Memory ← Register |
| | reg field indicates source operand; mod r/m or mod ss index base indicates destination operand |
| 1 | Register ← Register/Memory |
| | reg field indicates destination operand; mod r/m or mod ss index base indicates source operand |

## Encoding of sign extend (s) field

The s field occurs in instructions with immediate data fields. The s field has an effect only if the size of the immediate data is 8 bits and is being placed in a 16-bit or 32-bit destination. The table on the following page shows s field encoding.

## Sign Extend Encoding

| s | Effect on Immediate Data 8 | Effect on Immediate Data 16/32 |
|---|---|---|
| 0 | None | None |
| 1 | Sign extend data 8 to fill 16-bit or 32-bit destination | None |

## Encoding of conditional test (cccc) field

For the conditional instructions (conditional jumps and set on condition), cccc is encoded with the condition to test. The following table shows encoding of the cccc field.

### Conditional Test Encoding

| Mnemonic | Condition | cccc |
|---|---|---|
| O | Overflow | 0000 |
| NO | No overflow | 0001 |
| B/NAE | Below/not above or equal | 0010 |
| NB/AE | Not below/above or equal | 0011 |
| E/Z | Equal/zero | 0100 |
| NE/NZ | Not equal/not zero | 0101 |
| BE/NA | Below or equal/not above | 0110 |
| NBE/A | Not below or equal/above | 0111 |
| S | Sign | 1000 |
| NS | Not sign | 1001 |
| P/PE | Parity/parity even | 1010 |
| NP/PO | Not parity/parity odd | 1011 |
| L/NGE | Less than/not greater or equal | 1100 |
| NL/GE | Not less than/greater or equal | 1101 |
| LE/NG | Less than or equal/greater than | 1110 |
| NLE/G | Not less or equal/greater than | 1111 |

## Encoding of control, debug, and test registers (eee) field

The eee field loads and stores the control, debug, and test registers.

### Encoding of eee When Interpreted as Control Register Field

| eee Code | Reg Name |
|---|---|
| 000 | CR0 |
| 010 | CR2 |
| 011 | CR3 |

Do not use any other encoding.

### Encoding of eee When Interpreted as Debug Register Field

| eee Code | Reg Name |
|----------|----------|
| 000 | DR0 |
| 001 | DR1 |
| 010 | DR2 |
| 011 | DR3 |
| 110 | DR6 |
| 111 | DR7 |

Do not use any other encoding.

### Encoding of eee When Interpreted as Test Register Field

| eee Code | Reg Name |
|----------|----------|
| 011 | TR3 |
| 100 | TR4 |
| 101 | TR5 |
| 110 | TR6 |
| 111 | TR7 |

Do not use any other encoding.

# Floating-Point Extensions

The table beginning on the following page shows NDP extensions to the basic instruction set. In the 80486, these instructions are implemented on-chip. An 80387 is required to implement these instructions on 80386-based systems.

| INSTRUCTION | ENCODING | | | CLOCK COUNT RANGE | | | | | | | |
| --- | --- | --- | --- | --- | --- | --- | --- | --- | --- | --- | --- |
| | | | | 80387 | | | | 80486 | | | |
| | Byte 0 | Byte 1 | Optional Bytes 2–6 | 32-Bit Real | 32-Bit Integer | 64-Bit Real | 16-Bit Integer | 32-Bit Real | 32-Bit Integer | 64-Bit Real | 16-Bit Integer |
| **Data Transfer** | | | | | | | | | | | |
| FLD = Load[a] | | | | | | | | | | | |
| Integer/real memory to ST(0) | ESC MF 1 | MOD 000 R/M | SIB/DISP | 20 | 45–52 | 25 | 61–65 | 3(2) | 3(3) | 3(3) | 13–16(2) |
| Long integer memory to ST(0) | ESC 111 | MOD 101 R/M | SIB/DISP | | 56–67 | | | | 10–18(3) | | |
| Extended real memory to ST(0) | ESC 011 | MOD 101 R/M | SIB/DISP | | 44 | | | | 6(4) | | |
| BCD memory to ST(0) | ESC 111 | MOD 100 R/M | SIB/DISP | | 266–275 | | | | 70–103(4) | | |
| ST(i) to ST(0) | ESC 001 | 11000 ST(i) | | | 14 | | | | 4 | | |
| FST = Store | | | | | | | | | | | |
| ST(0) to integer/real memory | ESC MF 1 | MOD 010 R/M | SIB/DISP | 44 | 79–93 | 45 | 82–95 | 7 | 28–34 | 8 | 29–34 |
| ST(0) to ST(i) | ESC 101 | 11010 ST(i) | | | 11 | | | | 3 | | |
| FSTP = Store and pop | | | | | | | | | | | |
| ST(0) to integer/real memory | ESC MF 1 | MOD 011 R/M | SIB/DISP | 44 | 79–93 | 45 | 82–95 | 7 | 28–34 | 8 | 29–34 |
| ST(0) to long integer memory | ESC 111 | MOD 111 R/M | SIB/DISP | | 80–97 | | | | 29–34 | | |
| ST(0) to extended real | ESC 011 | MOD 111 R/M | SIB/DISP | | 53 | | | | 6 | | |
| ST(0) to BCD memory | ESC 111 | MOD 110 R/M | SIB/DISP | | 512–534 | | | | 172–176 | | |
| ST(0) to ST(i) | ESC 101 | 11001 ST(i) | | | 12 | | | | 3 | | |
| FXCH = Exchange | | | | | | | | | | | |
| ST(i) and ST(0) | ESC 001 | 11001 ST(i) | | | 18 | | | | 4 | | |
| **Comparison** | | | | | | | | | | | |
| FCOM = Compare | | | | | | | | | | | |
| Integer/real memory to ST(0) | ESC MF 0 | MOD 010 R/M | SIB/DISP | 26 | 56–63 | 31 | 71–75 | 4(2) | 15–17(2) | 4(3) | 16–20(2) |
| ST(i) to ST(0) | ESC 000 | 11010 ST(i) | | | 24 | | | | 4 | | |
| FCOMP = Compare and pop | | | | | | | | | | | |
| Integer/real memory to ST | ESC MF 0 | MOD 011 R/M | SIB/DISP | 26 | 56–63 | 31 | 71–75 | 4(2) | 15–17(2) | 4(3) | 16–20(2) |
| ST(i) to ST(0) | ESC 000 | 11011 ST(i) | | | 26 | | | | 4 | | |

| INSTRUCTION | Byte 0 | Byte 1 | Optional Bytes 2–6 | 80387 32-Bit Real | 80387 32-Bit Integer | 80387 64-Bit Real | 80387 16-Bit Integer | 80486 32-Bit Real | 80486 32-Bit Integer | 80486 64-Bit Real | 80486 16-Bit Integer |
|---|---|---|---|---|---|---|---|---|---|---|---|
| **FCOMPP = Compare and pop twice** | | | | | | | | | | | |
| ST(i) to ST(0) | ESC 110 | 11101001 | | | | 26 | | | | 5 | |
| FTST = Test ST(0) | ESC 001 | 11100100 | | | | 28 | | | | 4 | |
| FUCOM = Unordered compare | ESC 101 | 11100 ST(i) | | | | 24 | | | | 4 | |
| FUCOMP = Unordered compare and pop | ESC 101 | 11101 ST(i) | | | | 26 | | | | 4 | |
| FUCOMPP = Unordered compare and pop twice | ESC 010 | 11101001 | | | | 26 | | | | 5 | |
| FXAM = Examine ST(0) | ESC 001 | 11100101 | | | | 30–38 | | | | 8 | |
| **Constants** | | | | | | | | | | | |
| FLDZ = Load + 0.0 into ST(0) | ESC 001 | 11101110 | | | | 20 | | | | 4 | |
| FLD1 = Load + 1.0 into ST(0) | ESC 001 | 11101000 | | | | 24 | | | | 4 | |
| FLDPI = Load pi into ST(0) | ESC 001 | 11101011 | | | | 40 | | | | 8 | |
| FLDL2T = Load $\log_2(10)$ into ST(0) | ESC 001 | 11101001 | | | | 40 | | | | 8 | |
| FLDL2E = Load $\log_2(e)$ into ST(0) | ESC 001 | 11101010 | | | | 40 | | | | 8 | |
| FLDLG2 = Load $\log_{10}(2)$ into ST(0) | ESC 001 | 11101100 | | | | 41 | | | | 8 | |
| FLDLN2 = Load $\log_e(2)$ | ESC 001 | 11101101 | | | | 41 | | | | 8 | |
| **Arithmetic** | | | | | | | | | | | |
| **FADD = Add** | | | | | | | | | | | |
| Integer/real memory with ST(0) | ESC MF 0 | MOD 000 R/M | SIB/DISP | 24–32 | 57–72 | 29–37 | 71–85 | 8–20(2) | 19–32(2) | 8–20(3) | 20–35(2) |
| ST(i) and ST(0) | ESC d P 0 | 11000 ST (i) | | | | 23–31[b] | | | | 8–20 | |
| **FSUB = Subtract** | | | | | | | | | | | |
| Integer/real memory with ST(0) | ESC MF 0 | MOD 10 R/M | SIB/DISP | 24–32 | 57–82 | 28–36 | 71–83[c] | 8–20(2) | 18–32(2) | 8–20(3) | 20–35(2) |
| ST(i) and ST(0) | ESC d P 0 | 1110 R R/M | | | | 26–34[d] | | | | 8–20 | |

(continued)

# Instruction Encoding/Timing. *continued*

| INSTRUCTION | Byte 0 | Byte 1 | Optional Bytes 2–6 | 80387 32-Bit Real | 80387 32-Bit Integer | 80387 64-Bit Real | 80387 16-Bit Integer | 80486 32-Bit Real | 80486 32-Bit Integer | 80486 64-Bit Real | 80486 16-Bit Integer |
|---|---|---|---|---|---|---|---|---|---|---|---|
| **FMUL = Multiply** | | | | | | | | | | | |
| Integer/real memory with ST(0) | ESC MF 0 | MOD 001 R/M | SIB/DISP | 27–35 | 61–82 | 32–57 | 76–87 | 11(2) | 22–24(2) | 14(3) | 23–27(2) |
| ST(i) and ST(0) | ESC d P 0 | 11001R/M | | | 29–57[e] | | | | 16 | | |
| **FDIV = Divide** | | | | | | | | | | | |
| Integer/real memory with ST(0) | ESC MF 0 | MOD 11R R/M | SIB/DISP | 89 | 120–127[f] | 94 | 136–140[g] | 73(2) | 84–86(2) | 73(2) | 85–89(2) |
| ST(i) and ST(0) | ESC d P 0 | 1111 R R/M | | | 88[h] | | | | 73 | | |
| FSQRT = Square root | ESC 001 | 11111010 | | | 122–129 | | | | 83–87 | | |
| FSCALE = Scale ST(0) by ST(1) | ESC 001 | 11111101 | | | 67–86 | | | | 30–32 | | |
| FPREM = Partial remainder | ESC 001 | 11111000 | | | 74–155 | | | | 70–138 | | |
| FPREM1 = Partial remainder (IEEE) | ESC 001 | 11110101 | | | 95–185 | | | | 72–167 | | |
| FRNDINT = Round ST(0) to integer | ESC 001 | 11111100 | | | 66–80 | | | | 21–30 | | |
| FXTRACT = Extract components of ST(0) | ESC 001 | 11110100 | | | 70–76 | | | | 16–20 | | |
| FABS = Absolute value of ST(0) | ESC 001 | 11100001 | | | 22 | | | | 3 | | |
| FCHS = Change sign of ST(0) | ESC 001 | 11100000 | | | 24–25 | | | | 6 | | |
| **Transcendental** | | | | | | | | | | | |
| FCOS[k] = Cosine of ST(0) | ESC 001 | 11111111 | | | 123–772[l] | | | | 193–279 | | |
| FPTAN[k] = Partial tangent of ST(0) | ESC 001 | 11110010 | | | 191–497[l] | | | | 200–273 | | |
| FPATAN = Partial arctangent | ESC 001 | 11110011 | | | 314–487 | | | | 218–303 | | |
| FSIN[k] = Sine of ST(0) | ESC 001 | 11111110 | | | 122–771[l] | | | | 193–279 | | |
| FSINCOS[k] = Sine and cosine of ST(0) | ESC 001 | 11111011 | | | 194–809[l] | | | | 243–392 | | |
| F2XM1[l] = $2^{ST(0)} - 1$ | ESC 001 | 11110000 | | | 211–476 | | | | 140–279 | | |
| FYL2X[m] = $ST(1) \cdot \log_2(ST(0))$ | ESC 001 | 11110001 | | | 120–538 | | | | 196–329 | | |
| FYL2XP1[n] = $ST(1) \cdot \log_2(ST(0) + 1.0)$ | ESC 001 | 11111001 | | | 257–547 | | | | 171–326 | | |

| INSTRUCTION | ENCODING Byte 0 | ENCODING Byte 1 | ENCODING Optional Bytes 2–6 | CLOCK COUNT RANGE 80387 32-Bit Real | 80387 32-Bit Integer | 80387 64-Bit Real | 80387 16-Bit Integer | 80486 32-Bit Real | 80486 32-Bit Integer | 80486 64-Bit Real | 80486 16-Bit Integer |
|---|---|---|---|---|---|---|---|---|---|---|---|
| **Processor Control** | | | | | | | | | | | |
| FINIT = Initialize NPX | ESC 011 | 11100011 | | | 33 | | | | | 17 | |
| FSTSW AX = Store status word | ESC 111 | 11100000 | | | 13 | | | | | 3 | |
| FLDCW = Load control word | ESC 001 | MOD 101 R/M | SIB/DISP | | 19 | | | | | 4(2) | |
| FSTCW = Store control word | ESC 101 | MOD 111 R/M | SIB/DISP | | 15 | | | | | 3 | |
| FSTSW = Store status word | ESC 101 | MOD 111 R/M | SIB/DISP | | 15 | | | | | 3 | |
| FCLEX = Clear exceptions | ESC 011 | 11100010 | | | 11 | | | | | 7 | |
| FSTENV = Store environment | ESC 001 | MOD 110 R/M | SIB/DISP | | 103–104 | | | | | 56–67 | |
| FLDENV = Load environment | ESC 001 | MOD 100 R/M | SIB/DISP | | 71 | | | | | 34–44 | |
| FSAVE = Save state | ESC 101 | MOD 110 R/M | SIB/DISP | | 375–376 | | | | | 143–154 | |
| FRSTOR = Restore state | ESC 101 | MOD 100 R/M | SIB/DISP | | 308 | | | | | 120–131 (23–27) | |
| FINCSTP = Increment stack pointer | ESC 001 | 11110111 | | | 21 | | | | | 3 | |
| FDECSTP = Decrement stack pointer | ESC 001 | 11110110 | | | 22 | | | | | 3 | |
| FFREE = Free ST(i) | ESC 101 | 1100 ST(i) | | | 18 | | | | | 3 | |
| FNOP = No operation | ESC 001 | 11010000 | | | 12 | | | | | 3 | |

NOTES:

a. When loading single-precision or double-precision 0 from memory, add 5 clocks.

b. Add 3 clocks to the range when d = 1.

c. Add 1 clock to each range when R = 1.

d. Add 3 clocks to the range when d = 0.

e. Typical = 52. (When d = 0, 46–54, typical = 49.)

f. Add 1 clock to the range when R = 1.

g. 135–141 when R = 1.

h. Add 3 clocks to the range when d = 1.

i. $-0 \le ST(0) \le +\infty$.

j. These timings hold for operands in the range $|x| < \pi/4$. For operands not in this range, up to 76 additional clocks might be needed to reduce the operand.

k. $0 \le |ST(0)| < 2^{63}$.

l. $-1.0 \le ST(0) \le 1.0$.

m. $0 \le ST(0) < \infty$, $-\infty < ST(1) < +\infty$.

n. $0 \le |ST(0)| < (2 - SQRT(2))/2$, $-\infty < ST(1) < +\infty$.

# Appendix E

# INSTRUCTION DISASSEMBLY TABLE

The table in this appendix allows you to decode 80386 instructions. It presents the same information as the opcode table in Appendix C but is easier to use.

The table has the following format:

    [required byte(s)] [operand byte(s)]       [instruction]

At least one of the required bytes is an 8-bit hexadecimal value, and additional bytes may follow. The operand bytes have one of the following forms:

*ea*   The source and destination operands are encoded in the standard mod reg r/m format described in Appendix D.

*ea/N*   The destination operand is encoded in the mod r/m portion of the ea field, and the reg bits are set to /N.

*dataN*   N bytes of immediate data follow the instruction.

*—/n/reg*   The standard mod reg r/m encoding is interpreted so that the mod bits are ignored, the reg bits specify register *n* of a group (such as CR3), and the r/m bits select a general 32-bit register.

*dispN*   A signed displacement (N bits in length) from the current instruction pointer (EIP) follows the instruction.

The abbreviations Ea, Eb, Ew, and Ed stand for the effective address, byte, word, and doubleword indicated by the ea bits in the instruction.

Instructions preceded by an asterisk (•) are 32-bit instructions that operate on 16-bit quantities when preceded with the OPSIZ: instruction prefix. For real mode, V86 mode, and 286-compatible code segments, the behavior is reversed; that is, the instructions operate on 16-bit operands unless preceded with the OPSIZ: prefix.

## Instruction Disassembly Table

| Instruction Bytes | Operation | Instruction Bytes | Operation |
|---|---|---|---|
| 00 ea | ADD Eb, reg8 | *0F 88 disp32 | JS disp32 |
| *01 ea | ADD Ed, reg32 | *0F 89 disp32 | JNS disp32 |
| 02 ea | ADD reg8, Eb | *0F 8A disp32 | JP disp32 (JP/JPE) |
| *03 ea | ADD reg32, Ed | *0F 8B disp32 | JNP disp32 (JNP/JPO) |
| 04 data8 | ADD AL, data8 | *0F 8C disp32 | JL disp32 (JL/JNGE) |
| *05 data32 | ADD EAX, data32 | *0F 8D disp32 | JNL disp32 (JNL/JGE) |
| *06 | PUSH ES | *0F 8E disp32 | JLE disp32 (JLE/JNG) |
| *07 | POP ES | *0F 8F disp32 | JNLE disp32 (JNLE/JG) |
| 08 ea | OR Eb, reg8 | 0F 90 ea | SETO Eb |
| *09 ea | OR Ed, reg32 | 0F 91 ea | SETNO Eb |
| 0A ea | OR reg8, Eb | 0F 92 ea | SETB Eb (SETB/SETNAE/ SETC) |
| *0B ea | OR reg32, Ed | | |
| 0C data8 | OR AL, data8 | 0F 93 ea | SETNB Eb (SETNB/SETAE/ SETC) |
| *0D data32 | OR EAX, data32 | | |
| *0E | PUSH CS | 0F 94 ea | SETZ Eb (SETZ/SETE) |
| 0F 00 ea/0 | SLDT Ew | 0F 95 ea | SETNZ Eb (SETNZ/SETNE) |
| 0F 00 ea/1 | STR Ew | 0F 96 ea | SETBE Eb (SETBE/SETNA) |
| 0F 00 ea/2 | LLDT Ew | 0F 97 ea | SETNBE Eb (SETNBE/SETA) |
| 0F 00 ea/3 | LTR Ew | 0F 98 ea | SETS Eb |
| 0F 00 ea/4 | VERR Ew | 0F 99 ea | SETNS Eb |
| 0F 00 ea/5 | VERW Ew | 0F 9A ea | SETP Eb (SETP/SETPE) |
| 0F 01 ea/0 | SGDT Ea | 0F 9B ea | SETNP Eb (SETNP/SETPO) |
| 0F 01 ea/1 | SIDT Ea | 0F 9C ea | SETL Eb (SETL/SETNGE) |
| 0F 01 ea/2 | LGDT Ea | 0F 9D ea | SETNL Eb (SETNL/SETGE) |
| 0F 01 ea/3 | LIDT Ea | 0F 9E ea | SETLE Eb (SETLE/SETNG) |
| 0F 01 ea/4 | SMSW Ew | 0F 9F ea | SETNLE Eb (SETNLE/SETG) |
| 0F 01 ea/6 | LMSW Ew | *0F A0 | PUSH FS |
| *0F 02 ea | LAR reg32, Ew | *0F A1 | POP FS |
| *0F 03 ea | LSL reg32, Ew | *0F A3 ea | BT Ed, reg32 |
| 0F 06 | CLTS | *0F A4 ea data8 | SHLD Ed, reg32, data8 |
| 0F 08 | INVD | *0F A5 ea | SHLD Ed, reg32, CL |
| 0F 09 | WBINVD | 0F A6 | CMPXCHG Eb, reg8 |
| 0F 10 ea | INVLPG, ea | 0F A7 | CMPXCHG Ed, reg32 |
| 0F 20 —/n/reg | MOV CRn, reg32 | *0F A8 | PUSH GS |
| 0F 21 —/n/reg | MOV DRn, reg32 | *0F A9 | POP GS |
| 0F 22 —/n/reg | MOV reg32, CRn | *0F AB ea | BTS Ed, reg32 |
| 0F 23 —/n/reg | MOV reg32, DRn | *0F AC ea data8 | SHRD Ed, reg32, data8 |
| 0F 24 —/n/reg | MOV TRn, reg32 | *0F AD ea | SHRD Ed, reg32, CL |
| 0F 26 —/n/reg | MOV reg32, TRn | *0F AF ea | IMUL reg32, Ed |
| *0F 80 disp32 | JO disp32 | *0F B2 ea | LSS reg32, Ea |
| *0F 81 disp32 | JNO disp32 | *0F B3 ea | BTR Ed, reg32 |
| *0F 82 disp32 | JB disp32 (JB/JNAE) | *0F B4 ea | LFS reg32, Ea |
| *0F 83 disp32 | JNB disp32 (JNB/JAE) | *0F B5 ea | LGS reg32, Ea |
| *0F 84 disp32 | JZ disp32 (JZ/JE) | *0F B6 ea | MOVZX reg32, Eb |
| *0F 85 disp32 | JNZ disp32 (JNZ/JNE) | *0F B7 ea | MOVZX reg32, Ew |
| *0F 86 disp32 | JBE disp32 (JBE/JNA) | *0F BA ea/4 data8 | BT Ed, data8 |
| *0F 87 disp32 | JNBE disp32 (JNBE/ JA) | *0F BA ea/5 data8 | BTS Ed, data8 |
| | | *0F BA ea/6 data8 | BTR Ed, data8 |

*(continued)*

## Instruction Disassembly Table. *continued*

| Instruction Bytes | Operation | Instruction Bytes | Operation |
|---|---|---|---|
| *0F BA ea/7 data8 | BTC Ed, data8 | 30 ea | XOR Eb, reg8 |
| *0F BB ea | BTC Ed, reg32 | *31 ea | XOR Ed, reg32 |
| *0F BC ea | BSF reg32, Ed | 32 ea | XOR reg8, Eb |
| *0F BD ea | BSR reg32, Ed | *33 ea | XOR reg32, Ed |
| *0F BE ea | MOVSX reg32, Eb | 34 data8 | XOR AL, data8 |
| *0F BF ea | MOVSX reg32, Ew | *35 data32 | XOR EAX, data32 |
| 0F C0 | XADD Eb, reg8 | 36 | SS: |
| 0F C1 | XADD Eb, reg32 | 37 | AAA |
| 0F C8 | BSWAP EAX | 38 ea | CMP Eb, reg8 |
| 0F C9 | BSWAP ECX | *39 ea | CMP Ed, reg32 |
| 0F CA | BSWAP EDX | 3A ea | CMP reg8, Eb |
| 0F CB | BSWAP EBX | *3B ea | CMP reg32, Ed |
| 0F CC | BSWAP ESP | 3C data8 | CMP AL, data8 |
| 0F CD | BSWAP EBP | *3D data32 | CMP EAX, data32 |
| 0F CE | BSWAP ESI | 3E | DS: |
| 0F CF | BSWAP EDI | 3F | AAS |
| 10 ea | ADC Eb, reg8 | *40 | INC EAX |
| *11 ea | ADC Ed, reg32 | *41 | INC ECX |
| 12 ea | ADC reg8, Eb | *42 | INC EDX |
| *13 ea | ADC reg32, Ed | *43 | INC EBX |
| 14 data8 | ADC AL, data8 | *44 | INC ESP |
| *15 data32 | ADC EAX, data32 | *45 | INC EBP |
| *16 | PUSH SS | *46 | INC ESI |
| *17 | POP SS | *47 | INC EDI |
| 18 ea | SBB Eb, reg8 | *48 | DEC EAX |
| *19 ea | SBB Ed, reg32 | *49 | DEC ECX |
| 1A ea | SBB reg8, Eb | *4A | DEC EDX |
| *1B ea | SBB reg32, Ed | *4B | DEC EBX |
| 1C data8 | SBB AL, data8 | *4C | DEC ESP |
| *1D data32 | SBB EAX, data32 | *4D | DEC EBP |
| *1E | PUSH DS | *4E | DEC ESI |
| *1F | POP DS | *4F | DEC EDI |
| 20 ea | AND Eb, reg8 | *50 | PUSH EAX |
| *21 ea | AND Ed, reg32 | *51 | PUSH ECX |
| 22 ea | AND reg8, Eb | *52 | PUSH EDX |
| *23 ea | AND reg32, Ed | *53 | PUSH EBX |
| 24 data8 | AND AL, data8 | *54 | PUSH ESP |
| *25 data32 | AND EAX, data32 | *55 | PUSH EBP |
| 26 | ES: | *56 | PUSH ESI |
| 27 | DAA | *57 | PUSH EDI |
| 28 ea | SUB Eb, reg8 | *58 | POP EAX |
| *29 ea | SUB Ed, reg32 | *59 | POP ECX |
| 2A ea | SUB reg8, Eb | *5A | POP EDX |
| *2B ea | SUB reg32, Ed | *5B | POP EBX |
| 2C data8 | SUB AL, data8 | *5C | POP ESP |
| *2D data32 | SUB EAX, data32 | *5D | POP EBP |
| 2E | CS: | *5E | POP ESI |
| 2F | DAS | *5F | POP EDI |

*(continued)*

## Instruction Disassembly Table. *continued*

| Instruction Bytes | Operation | Instruction Bytes | Operation |
|---|---|---|---|
| •60 | PUSHAD | •83 ea/0 data8 | ADD Ed, data8 |
| •61 | POPAD | •83 ea/1 data8 | OR Ed, data8 |
| •62 ea | BOUND reg32, Ea | •83 ea/2 data8 | ADC Ed, data8 |
| 63 ea | ARPL Ew, reg16 | •83 ea/3 data8 | SBB Ed, data8 |
| 64 | FS: | •83 ea/4 data8 | AND Ed, data8 |
| 65 | GS: | •83 ea/5 data8 | SUB Ed, data8 |
| 66 | OPSIZ: | •83 ea/6 data8 | XOR Ed, data8 |
| 67 | ADRSIZ: | •83 ea/7 data8 | CMP Ed, data8 |
| •68 data 32 | PUSH data32 | 84 ea | TEST Eb, reg8 |
| •69 ea data32 | IMUL reg32, Ed, data32 | •85 ea | TEST Ed, reg32 |
| 6A data8 | PUSH data8 | 86 ea | XCHG Eb, reg8 |
| •6B ea data8 | IMUL reg32, Ed, data8 | •87 ea | XCHG Ed, reg32 |
| 6C | INSB | 88 ea | MOV Eb, reg8 |
| •6D | INSD | •89 ea | MOV Ed, reg32 |
| 6E | OUTSB | 8A ea | MOV reg8, Eb |
| •6F | OUTSD | •8B ea | MOV reg32, Ed |
| 70 disp8 | JO disp8 | 8C ea/s | MOV Ew, sreg |
| 71 disp8 | JNO disp8 | •8D ea | LEA reg32, Ea |
| 72 disp8 | JB disp8 ( JB/JNAE) | 8E ea/s | MOV sreg, Ew |
| 73 disp8 | JNB disp8 ( JNB/JAE) | •8F ea | POP Ed |
| 74 disp8 | JZ disp8 ( JZ/JE) | 90 | NOP |
| 75 disp8 | JNZ disp8 ( JNZ/JNE) | •91 | XCHG EAX, ECX |
| 76 disp8 | JBE disp8 ( JBE/JNA) | •92 | XCHG EAX, EDX |
| 77 disp8 | JNBE disp8 ( JNBE/JA) | •93 | XCHG EAX, EBX |
| 78 disp8 | JS disp8 | •94 | XCHG EAX, ESP |
| 79 disp8 | JNS disp8 | •95 | XCHG EAX, EBP |
| 7A disp8 | JP disp8 ( JP/JPE) | •96 | XCHG EAX, ESI |
| 7B disp8 | JNP disp8 ( JNP/JPO) | •97 | XCHG EAX, EDI |
| 7C disp8 | JL disp8 ( JL/JNGE) | •98 | CBW / CWDE |
| 7D disp8 | JNL disp8 ( JNL/JGE) | 99 | CWD |
| 7E disp8 | JLE disp8 ( JLE/JNG) | 9A offset32 | CALL offset32 |
| 7F disp8 | JNLE disp8 ( JNLE/JG) | 9B | WAIT |
| 80 ea/0 data8 | ADD Eb, data8 | •9C | PUSHFD |
| 80 ea/1 data8 | OR Eb, data8 | •9D | POPFD |
| 80 ea/2 data8 | ADC Eb, data8 | 9E | SAHF |
| 80 ea/3 data8 | SBB Eb, data8 | 9F | LAHF |
| 80 ea/4 data8 | AND Eb, data8 | A0 disp | MOV AL, [disp] |
| 80 ea/5 data8 | SUB Eb, data8 | •A1 disp | MOV EAX, [disp] |
| 80 ea/6 data8 | XOR Eb, data8 | A2 disp | MOV [disp], AL |
| 80 ea/7 data8 | CMP Eb, data8 | •A3 disp | MOV [disp], EAX |
| •81 ea/0 data32 | ADD Ed, data32 | A4 | MOVSB |
| •81 ea/1 data32 | OR Ed, data32 | •A5 | MOVSD |
| •81 ea/2 data32 | ADC Ed, data32 | A6 | CMPSB |
| •81 ea/3 data32 | SBB Ed, data32 | •A7 | CMPSD |
| •81 ea/4 data32 | AND Ed, data32 | A8 data8 | TEST AL, data8 |
| •81 ea/5 data32 | SUB Ed, data32 | •A9 data32 | TEST EAX, data32 |
| •81 ea/6 data32 | XOR Ed, data32 | AA | STOSB |
| •81 ea/7 data32 | CMP Ed, data32 | •AB | STOSD |

*(continued)*

## Instruction Disassembly Table. *continued*

| Instruction Bytes | Operation | Instruction Bytes | Operation |
|---|---|---|---|
| AC | LODSB | D0 ea/0 | ROL Eb, 1 |
| *AD | LODSD | D0 ea/1 | ROR Eb, 1 |
| AE | SCASB | D0 ea/2 | RCL Eb, 1 |
| *AF | SCASD | D0 ea/3 | RCR Eb, 1 |
| B0 data8 | MOV AL, data8 | D0 ea/4 | SHL Eb, 1 |
| B1 data8 | MOV CL, data8 | D0 ea/5 | SHR Eb, 1 |
| B2 data8 | MOV DL, data8 | D0 ea/7 | SAR Eb, 1 |
| B3 data8 | MOV BL, data8 | *D1 ea/0 | ROL Ed, 1 |
| B4 data8 | MOV AH, data8 | *D1 ea/1 | ROR Ed, 1 |
| B5 data8 | MOV CH, data8 | *D1 ea/2 | RCL Ed, 1 |
| B6 data8 | MOV DH, data8 | *D1 ea/3 | RCR Ed, 1 |
| B7 data8 | MOV BH, data8 | *D1 ea/4 | SHL Ed, 1 |
| *B8 data32 | MOV EAX, data32 | *D1 ea/5 | SHR Ed, 1 |
| *B9 data32 | MOV ECX, data32 | *D1 ea/7 | SAR Ed, 1 |
| *BA data32 | MOV EDX, data32 | D2 ea/0 | ROL Eb, CL |
| *BB data32 | MOV EBX, data32 | D2 ea/1 | ROR Eb, CL |
| *BC data32 | MOV ESP, data32 | D2 ea/2 | RCL Eb, CL |
| *BD data32 | MOV EBP, data32 | D2 ea/3 | RCR Eb, CL |
| *BE data32 | MOV ESI, data32 | D2 ea/4 | SHL Eb, CL |
| *BF data32 | MOV EDI, data32 | D2 ea/5 | SHR Eb, CL |
| C0 ea/0 data8 | ROL Eb, data8 | D2 ea/7 | SAR Eb, CL |
| C0 ea/1 data8 | ROR Eb, data8 | *D3 ea/0 | ROL Ed, CL |
| C0 ea/2 data8 | RCL Eb, data8 | *D3 ea/1 | ROR Ed, CL |
| C0 ea/3 data8 | RCR Eb, data8 | *D3 ea/2 | RCL Ed, CL |
| C0 ea/4 data8 | SHL Eb, data8 | *D3 ea/3 | RCR Ed, CL |
| C0 ea/5 data8 | SHR Eb, data8 | *D3 ea/4 | SHL Ed, CL |
| C0 ea/7 data8 | SAR Eb, data8 | *D3 ea/5 | SHR Ed, CL |
| *C1 ea/0 data8 | ROL Ed, data8 | *D3 ea/7 | SAR Ed, CL |
| *C1 ea/1 data8 | ROR Ed, data8 | D4 | AAM |
| *C1 ea/2 data8 | RCL Ed, data8 | D5 | AAD |
| *C1 ea/3 data8 | RCR Ed, data8 | D7 | XLAT |
| *C1 ea/4 data8 | SHL Ed, data8 | D8 | ESC 0 (NDP) |
| *C1 ea/5 data8 | SHR Ed, data8 | D9 | ESC 1 (NDP) |
| *C1 ea/7 data8 | SAR Ed, data8 | DA | ESC 2 (NDP) |
| C2 data16 | RET data16 | DB | ESC 3 (NDP) |
| C3 | RET | DC | ESC 4 (NDP) |
| *C4 ea | LES reg32, Ed | DD | ESC 5 (NDP) |
| *C5 ea | LDS reg32, Ed | DE | ESC 6 (NDP) |
| C6 ea data8 | MOV reg8, data8 | DF | ESC 7 (NDP) |
| *C7 ea data32 | MOV reg32, data32 | E0 disp8 | LOOPNE disp8 (LOOPNE/LOOPNZ) |
| C8 data16 data8 | ENTER data16, data8 | | |
| C9 | LEAVE | E1 disp8 | LOOPE disp8 (LOOPE/LOOPZ) |
| CA data16 | RETF data16 | | |
| CB | RETF | E2 disp8 | LOOP disp8 |
| CC | INT 3 | E3 disp8 | JCXZ disp8 |
| CD data8 | INT data8 | E4 data8 | IN AL, data8 |
| CE | INTO | *E5 data8 | IN EAX, data8 |
| CF | IRET | E6 data8 | OUT data8, AL |

*(continued)*

## Instruction Disassembly Table. *continued*

| Instruction Bytes | Operation | Instruction Bytes | Operation |
|---|---|---|---|
| •E7 data8 | OUT data8, EAX | •F7 ea/2 | NOT Ed |
| •E8 ea32 | CALL ea32 | •F7 ea/3 | NEG Ed |
| E9 disp32 | JMP disp32 | •F7 ea/4 | MUL EAX, Ed |
| •EA ea48 | JMP FAR ea48 | •F7 ea/5 | IMUL EAX, Ed |
| EB disp8 | JMP disp8 | •F7 ea/6 | DIV EAX, Ed |
| EC | IN AL, DX | •F7 ea/7 | IDIV EAX, Ed |
| •ED | IN EAX, DX | F8 | CLC |
| EE | OUT DX, AL | F9 | STC |
| •EF | OUT DX, EAX | FA | CLI |
| F0 | LOCK | FB | STI |
| F2 | REPNE/REPNZ | FC | CLD |
| F3 | REP/REPE/REPZ | FD | STD |
| F4 | HLT | FE ea/0 | INC Eb |
| F5 | CMC | FE ea/1 | DEC Eb |
| F6 ea/0 data8 | TEST Eb, data8 | •FF ea/0 | INC Ed |
| F6 ea/2 | NOT Eb | •FF ea/1 | DEC Ed |
| F6 ea/3 | NEG Eb | •FF ea/2 | CALL Ed |
| F6 ea/4 | MUL AL, Eb | •FF ea/3 | CALL FAR ea |
| F6 ea/5 | IMUL AL, Eb | FF ea/4 | JMP Ed |
| F6 ea/6 | DIV AL, Eb | •FF ea/5 | JMP FAR ea |
| F6 ea/7 | IDIV AL, Eb | •FF ea/6 | PUSH Ed |
| •F7 ea/0 data32 | TEST Ed, data32 | | |

## 80387/80486-NDP Extensions (NDP Escapes)

| Instruction Bytes | Operation | Instruction Bytes | Operation |
|---|---|---|---|
| D8 ea/0 | FADD Real32 | D9 ea/4 | FLDENV Ea |
| D8 ea/1 | FMUL Real32 | D9 ea/5 | FLDCW Ew |
| D8 ea/2 | FCOM Real32 | D9 ea/6 | FSTENV Ea |
| D8 ea/3 | FCOMP Real32 | D9 ea/7 | FSTCW Ew |
| D8 ea/4 | FSUB Real32 | D9 C0+i | FLD ST(i) |
| D8 ea/5 | FSUBR Real32 | D9 C8+i | FXCH ST(i) |
| D8 ea/6 | FDIV Real32 | D9 D0 | FNOP |
| D8 ea/7 | FDIVR Real32 | D9 E0 | FCHS |
| D8 C0+i | FADD ST, ST(i) | D9 E1 | FABS |
| D8 C8+i | FMUL ST, ST(i) | D9 E4 | FTST |
| D8 D0+i | FCOM, ST(i) | D9 E5 | FXAM |
| D8 D8+i | FCOMP, ST(i) | D9 E8 | FLD1 |
| D8 E0+i | FSUB ST, ST(i) | D9 E9 | FLDL2T |
| D8 E8+i | FSUBR ST, ST(i) | D9 EA | FLDL2E |
| D8 F0+i | FDIV ST, ST(i) | D9 EB | FLDPI |
| D8 F8+i | FDIVR ST, ST(i) | D9 EC | FLDLG2 |
| D9 ea/0 | FLD Real32 | D9 ED | FLDLN2 |
| D9 ea/2 | FST Real32 | D9 EE | FLDZ |
| D9 ea/3 | FSTP Real32 | D9 F0 | F2XM1 |

*(continued)*

## 80387/80486-NDP Extensions (NDP Escapes). *continued*

| Instruction Bytes | Operation | Instruction Bytes | Operation |
|---|---|---|---|
| D9 F1 | FYL2X | DC C8+i | FMUL ST(i), ST |
| D9 F2 | FPTAN | DC E0+i | FSUBR ST(i), ST |
| D9 F3 | FPATAN | DC E8+i | FSUB ST(i), ST |
| D9 F4 | FXTRACT | DC F0+i | FDIVR ST(i), ST |
| D9 F5 | FPREM1 | DC F8+i | FDIV ST(i), ST |
| D9 F6 | FDECSTP | DD ea/0 | FLD Real64 |
| D9 F7 | FINCSTP | DD ea/2 | FST Real64 |
| D9 F8 | FPREM | DD ea/3 | FSTP Real64 |
| D9 F9 | FYL2XP1 | DD ea/4 | FRSTOR Ea |
| D9 FA | FSQRT | DD ea/6 | FSAVE Ea |
| D9 FB | FSINCOS | DD ea/7 | FSTSW Ew |
| D9 FC | FRNDINT | DD C0+i | FFREE ST(i) |
| D9 FD | FSCALE | DD D0+i | FST ST(i) |
| D9 FE | FSIN | DD D8+i | FSTP ST(i) |
| D9 FF | FCOS | DD E0+i | FUCOM ST(i) |
| DA ea/0 | FIADD Int32 | DD E8+i | FUCOMP ST(i) |
| DA ea/1 | FIMUL Int32 | DE ea/0 | FIADD Int16 |
| DA ea/2 | FICOM Int32 | DE ea/1 | FIMUL Int16 |
| DA ea/3 | FICOMP Int32 | DE ea/2 | FICOM Int16 |
| DA ea/4 | FISUB Int32 | DE ea/3 | FICOMP Int16 |
| DA ea/5 | FISUBR Int32 | DE ea/4 | FISUB Int16 |
| DA ea/6 | FIDIV Int32 | DE ea/5 | FISUBR Int16 |
| DA ea/7 | FIDIVR Int32 | DE ea/6 | FIDIV Int16 |
| DA E9 | FUCOMPP | DE ea/7 | FIDIVR Int16 |
| DB ea/0 | FILD Int32 | DE C0+i | FADDP ST(i), ST |
| DB ea/2 | FIST Int32 | DE C8+i | FMULP ST(i), ST |
| DB ea/3 | FISTP Int32 | DE D9 | FCOMPP |
| DB ea/5 | FLD Real80 | DE E0+i | FSUBRP ST(i), ST |
| DB ea/7 | FSTP Real80 | DE E8+i | FSUBP ST(i), ST |
| DB E2 | FCLEX | DE F0+i | FDIVRP ST(i), ST |
| DB E3 | FINIT | DE F8+i | FDIVP ST(i), ST |
| DC ea/0 | FADD Real64 | DF ea/0 | FILD Int16 |
| DC ea/1 | FMUL Real64 | DF ea/2 | FIST Int16 |
| DC ea/2 | FCOM Real64 | DF ea/3 | FISTP Int16 |
| DC ea/3 | FCOMP Real64 | DF ea/4 | FBLD Bcd80 |
| DC ea/4 | FSUB Real64 | DF ea/5 | FILD Int64 |
| DC ea/5 | FSUBR Real64 | DF ea/6 | FBSTP Bcd80 |
| DC ea/6 | FDIV Real64 | DF ea/7 | FISTP Int64 |
| DC ea/7 | FDIVR Real64 | DF E0 | FSTSW AX |
| DC C0+i | FADD ST(i), ST | | |

# Appendix F

# 8086-FAMILY PROCESSOR DIFFERENCES

Although the 8086, 80286, 80386, and 80486 are object-code compatible, minor differences among them have arisen during the evolution of this microprocessor family. This appendix describes these differences.

## Real-Mode Differences Between the 8086 and the 80386/80486

The 8086 processor does not generate exceptions 6, 8–13, 16, or the 80486-unique exception 17.

Instructions execute more rapidly.

On the 80386/80486, the divide fault (INT 0) leaves the saved CS:EIP pointing to the faulting instruction. On the 8086, the value of CS:IP on the stack points to the instruction after the one that caused the fault.

Opcodes that were not explicitly defined on the 8086 are interpreted as new instructions or cause the undefined opcode fault (INT 6) when executed on the 80386 or 80486.

When the PUSH SP instruction is executed, the value on the stack of the 80386 or 80486 is the predecremented value, where the value pushed on the 8086 is the postdecremented value of SP. If it is necessary to re-create the same stack value, use the following sequence of instructions in place of PUSH SP:

```
PUSH    BP
MOV     BP, SP
XCHG    BP, [BP]
```

The count value for shift and rotate instructions is taken modulo 32 in the 80386 and 80486. The full value (up to 255) is used on the 8086, which can result in long instruction execution times.

An instruction (including prefixes) cannot exceed 15 bytes. If it does, a general protection fault occurs. This does not occur under normal circumstances but might occur if you use multiple redundant prefixes. The 8086 has no such restrictions.

Operands cannot extend across the segment bounds. If, for example, an instruction refers to a 16-bit operand at offset 65535, a general protection fault occurs. If the stack pointer is set to low memory (offset 2) and a 32-bit value is pushed, a stack fault occurs. In the 8086, addresses wrap around the segment boundary and are continuous from 65535 to 0. Instruction execution behaves like an operand fetch.

You can use the LOCK instruction only with certain instructions; otherwise, an undefined opcode fault occurs. (See Chapter 8 for a list of the legal instructions.) The 8086 has no such restrictions.

Sometimes the 8086 hangs while single-stepping. Later processors do not hang because the interrupt priorities are slightly different. This prevents a single-step trap from occurring until the handler returns if a hardware interrupt is invoked.

The 8086 generates a divide fault if the quotient of an IDIV instruction is the largest possible negative number. The 80386 and 80486 generate the correct result. See the earlier discussion of the divide fault in this appendix.

When the content of the FLAGS register is pushed onto the stack, bits 12–15 are always 1's on the 8086. These bits represent new flags on later processors.

The NMI interrupt masks all subsequent NMIs until an IRET is executed. NMIs are not masked on the 8086.

The 80386 uses INT 16 as the coprocessor error vector. On the 8086, the system hardware must be programmed to generate an interrupt vector, and it can be any vector. On the 80486, you can select either mode of operation.

When an NDP exception occurs on an 80386 or an 80486, the saved CS:EIP points to the faulting instruction, including any prefixes that might be part of the instruction. On the 8086, the saved CS:IP points only to the ESC portion of the faulting NDP instruction.

Additional interrupts can occur if a program contains undetected bugs, such as the use of unimplemented opcodes or addressing beyond segment boundaries.

The 8086 is limited to 1 MB of address space by having 20 physical hardware address lines. Using selectors such as FFFFH can result in linear addresses beyond 1 MB, but because there are only 20 address lines, the addresses wrap around to 0.

Because there are 32 address lines on the 80386 and 80486, addresses greater than 1 MB can be generated in real mode (up to 10FFEFH). If system software depends on the ability to wrap around to 0 after 1 MB, hardware must be added to an 80386 system to force address line 21 to 0 in real mode. The 80486 has this hardware on the processor chip.

# Differences Between Virtual 8086 Mode and the 8086

All previously listed differences also apply to V86 mode in comparison to real mode on the 8086. Following are some additional differences.

I/O instructions in V86 mode are allowed only if the I/O permission bitmap for the V86 mode task is set up.

All exceptions (hardware and software interrupts) vector to the protected-mode IDT entries rather than through the real-mode interrupt mechanism. The protected-mode handlers must simulate the real-mode vector process when appropriate.

# Differences Between the 80286 and the 80386/80486

As implemented on the 80286, the LOCK prefix causes all memory to be locked during the prefixed instruction. On the 80386 and 80486, only the memory accessed by the prefixed instruction is locked.

On RESET, any of the registers that contained undefined values on the 80286 can contain different values on later processors.

# Differences Between the 80386 and the 80486

The 80486 will optionally generate an alignment fault on any memory reference instruction of more than a single byte.

New bits have been defined in the control registers, page table entries, and flags.

# Differences Between the 8087 and the 80387/80486-NDP

Errors are signaled via a dedicated hardware pin on the 80387/80486-NDP instead of the standard CPU interrupt mechanism. The 80386 responds to coprocessor errors via interrupts 7, 9, and 16 instead of an external hardware interrupt. The 80486 generates interrupts 7 and 16—but not interrupt 9.

The format of the error information in the 80387/80486-NDP environment varies depending on whether the processor is in real mode or in protected mode. The 8087 supports only real-mode information.

The instructions FENI/FDISI are no-ops on the 80387/80486-NDP.

The 8087 does not perform automatic normalization of denormalized reals. Instead, it signals a denormal exception and relies on the application to perform this operation. The 80387/80486-NDP will normalize these values and might execute faster if the denormal exception is masked when running 8087 programs.

The 8087 requires explicit WAIT instructions before each floating-point instruction to synchronize with the 8086. The 80386 and the 80387 perform automatic synchronization, as does the 80486 and its NDP. The WAIT instructions are unnecessary, but they will not cause the program to operate incorrectly.

# Differences Between the 80287 and the 80387/80486-NDP

The FSETPM instruction is a no-op on the 80387.

The 80287 supports both affine and projective closure. Only affine closure is supported on the 80387/80486-NDP. Programs that rely on projective closure may generate different results on the 80387/80486-NDP than on the 80287.

# Differences Between the 80387 and the 80486

Interrupt 9 will not be generated on the 80486. Interrupt 13 will be generated instead.

The 80486 supports redirected error reporting of floating-point errors via the NE bit in CR0 and the FERR\ and IGNNE\ hardware pins.

# Index

## ROSS P. NELSON

Ross Nelson has several years of programming experience, all with Intel microprocessors. After earning his B.S. in computer science from Montana State University, he joined Intel Corporation in 1979. He worked there during the development of the 80286 and in the early stages of the 80386 chip's development. He is currently the manager of software engineering at Answer Software, which produces software development tools for the PC and a database line for the Macintosh.

Nelson has written for *Byte* and *Dr. Dobb's Journal*. His article on programming the 80386 was chosen as the lead feature for *Dr. Dobb's Journal* in 1986.

The manuscript for this book was prepared and submitted to Microsoft Press in electronic form. Text files were processed and formatted using Microsoft Word.

Principal word processors: Debbie Kem, Judith Bloch
Principal proofreader: Shawn Peck
Principal typographer: Lisa Iversen
Interior text designer: Darcie S. Furlan
Illustrators: Becky Geisler, Kim Eggleston, Connie Little
Cover designer: Thomas A. Draper
Cover color separator: Rainier Color Corporation

Text composition by Microsoft Press in Garamond Light, with display in Helvetica Black, using the Magna composition system and the Linotronic 300 laser imagesetter.

*Printed on recycled paper stock.*

# Great Programming Resources from Microsoft Press

# Other Titles From Microsoft Press

## MICROSOFT® MOUSE PROGRAMMER'S REFERENCE, 2nd ed.
*Microsoft Press and the Hardware Division of Microsoft Corporation*

This is the official documentation for programming the Microsoft Mouse. It provides all the software and how-to information you need to incorporate a sophisticated mouse interface for MS-DOS operating system-based programs. Fully updated to cover Microsoft BallPoint mouse and the mouse driver version 8. The two 5 ¹/₄-inch companion disks include sample mouse menus, MOUSE.LIB and EGA.LIB, and a collection of valuable programming examples in interpreted Basic, Microsoft QuickBasic, Microsoft C, Microsoft QuickC, Microsoft Macro Assembler, FORTRAN, and Pascal. The MICROSOFT MOUSE PROGRAMMER'S REFERENCE is your complete technical resource for mouse support.
**352 pages, softcover with two 5 ¹/₄-inch disks    $34.95    Order Code MOPRR2**

## THE PROGRAMMER'S PC SOURCEBOOK, 2nd ed.
### Reference Tables for IBM® PCs, PS/2,® and Compatibles; MS-DOS® and Windows™
*Thom Hogan*

This reference book saves you the frustration of searching high and low for key pieces of technical data. Here is all the information culled from hundreds of sources and integrated into convenient, accessible charts, tables, and listings. The first place to turn for immediate, accurate information about your computer and its operating system, THE PROGRAMMER'S PC SOURCEBOOK covers MS-DOS through version 5, IBM personal computers (and compatibles), including the PS/2 series, and Windows 3. Among the subjects covered are DOS commands and utilities, interrupts, mouse information, EMS support, BIOS calls and support services, memory layout, RAM parameters, keyboards, the IBM extended character set, and more.
**750 pages, softcover    8 ¹/₂ x 11    $39.95    Order Code PRPCS2**

## POWER PROGRAMMING WITH MICROSOFT® MACRO ASSEMBLER
*Ray Duncan*

A valuable and detailed programmer-to-programmer discussion of assembly language programming and a guide to the new version 6 of the Microsoft Macro Assembler. Duncan thoroughly treats the central topics of assembly language programming, including converting numbers, sorting numbers and strings, handling multiple-precision math, using floating-point coprocessors, and optimizing code. The bound-in disk offers the routines presented in the book plus an exciting collection of additional programs that demonstrate assembly language functions in action.
**400 pages, softcover with one 5 ¹/₄-inch disk    $39.95    Order Code POPRMA**
*Available October 1991*

*Microsoft Press books are available wherever quality computer books are sold.*
*Or call **1-800-MSPRESS** for ordering information or placing credit card orders.\**
*Please refer to **BBK** when placing your order.*

---

\* In Canada, contact Macmillan of Canada, Attn: Microsoft Press Dept., 164 Commander Blvd., Agincourt, Ontario, Canada M1S 3C7, or call (416) 293-8141.
In the U.K., contact Microsoft Press, 27 Wrights Lane, London W8 5TZ.